Oxford Shakespeare Topics

GENERAL EDITORS: PETER HOLLAND AND STANLEY WELLS

SHAKESPEARE
IN THE
THEATRE

An Anthology of Criticism

Compiled and Edited by
STANLEY WELLS

OXFORD
UNIVERSITY PRESS

OXFORD
UNIVERSITY PRESS

Great Clarendon Street, Oxford OX2 6DP

Oxford University Press is a department of the University of Oxford.
It furthers the University's objective of excellence in research, scholarship,
and education by publishing worldwide in

Oxford New York

Athens Auckland Bangkok Bogotá Buenos Aires Calcutta
Cape Town Chennai Dar es Salaam Delhi Florence Hong Kong Istanbul
Karachi Kuala Lumpur Madrid Melbourne Mexico City Mumbai
Nairobi Paris São Paulo Singapore Taipei Tokyo Toronto Warsaw

and associated companies in Berlin Ibadan

Oxford is a registered trade mark of Oxford University Press
in the UK and certain other countries

Published in the United States
by Oxford University Press Inc., New York

© Oxford University Press 1997, 2000

British Library Cataloguing in Publication Data
Data available

Library of Congress Cataloging in Publication Data
Data available

ISBN 0–19–871176–X

10 9 8 7 6 5 4 3 2 1

Printed in Great Britain
on acid-free paper by
Biddles Ltd,
Guildford and King's Lynn

An Anthology of Criticism

〜〜〜〜〜〜〜〜〜〜〜〜

OXFORD SHAKESPEARE TOPICS

Published and Forthcoming Titles Include:

PREFACE

IN tracking down allusions referred to in the notes I have incurred a debt of gratitude to many students, colleagues, and friends, including Mary Allen, Julia Briggs, Philip Collins, Kelley Costigan, Lawrence Danson, Jean-Michel Déprats, Paul Edmondson, Richard Foulkes, Kenneth Garlick, Joy Leslie Gibson, Madeline Huxstep (and other members of the Charles Lamb Society, especially Claude Prance), Eric Ives, Laurence Kitchin, François Laroque, Niky Rathbone, James Shaw, Richard Simmons, Maire Steadman, Kelsey Thornton, Solitaire Townsend, Marcus Walsh, Roger Warren, Martin Wiggins, and Glen Wilson. The library staff of the Shakespeare Institute and the Shakespeare Birthplace Trust have as always been unfailingly helpful. I am especially grateful to Russell Jackson for reading the typescript and allowing me to use his as-yet unpublished translation of Theodor Fontane, and to Peter Holland, who also read the typescript and made valuable comments. I have benefited greatly from the patience and expertise of Frances Whistler, of Oxford University Press, and from the scrupulous copy-editing of Christine Buckley.

This book is to be published at the time of my retirement from the Shakespeare Institute of the University of Birmingham, where I have happily spent most of my working life. I offer it to all who have studied there, and to future students, too, in the hope that it will prove both enjoyable and useful.

STANLEY WELLS

May 1997

CONTENTS

Contents

Contents

Contents

Contents

LIST OF ILLUSTRATIONS

List of Illustrations

EDITORIAL PROCEDURES

EXTRACTS from the early period have been lightly edited in the attempt to minimize quaintness. Elsewhere I have not attempted to impose uniformity of styling. I supply headnotes aimed at providing basic information about writers and performers and briefly setting the productions in context. Anthologies such as this are often printed without notes on points of detail, but the pieces included here include many quotations, allusions, and references to people, especially performers, which may be unfamiliar to readers. Once having embarked on annotation I found myself attempting to provide a fairly comprehensive guide to such matters. This may seem superfluous in the case of, for example, performers of minor roles, and I have not succeeded in tracing all the people named—from the nineteenth century onwards we lack systematic and comprehensive works of reference, and the very recent past presents difficulties because of the regrettable demise of *Who's Who in the Theatre*. And some performers are reluctant to disclose personal information; several well-known actors, male and female, decline to give a date of birth in *Who's Who*. For this reason I do not even name recent actors in the notes unless I have anything specific to say about them. But I hope the policy of providing such information when possible may bring its rewards. I find it interesting, for example, to know that Helena Faucit was only twenty years old when she played Hermione to Macready's Leontes (pp. 67–72). Some critics, such as Hazlitt, have had a tendency to rely on memory in quoting Shakespeare, but except in special cases I have not regularized or provided references to quotations from the plays, or regularized spellings of Shakespeare's name. Each extract is introduced by the date when the review was published (or occasionally by the date specified by its author, presumably that of the actual performance seen). Where, however, the account was published some time after the event, the performance date, or the range of dates when the writer can be assumed to have seen the performance, is given instead, in square brackets; in the earlier period this information is necessarily inexact.

INTRODUCTION

SHAKESPEARE AND THE THEATRE CRITICS

THE art of theatre is notoriously ephemeral, yet anyone who believes that Shakespeare wrote primarily to be performed must also believe that we can increase our enjoyment and understanding of the texts that have come down to us both by seeing them performed and by knowing about how they have been performed in the past. Ben Jonson wrote of one of his masques 'only the envy was that it lasted not still, or, now it is past, cannot by imagination, much less description, be recovered to a part of that spirit it had in the gliding by." But this is over-pessimistic. Spectators have been using their imaginations in the attempt to recover something of the excitement generated by theatre for as long as people have been going to see plays, and although in early times these attempts may have resulted in little more than conversational criticism, along with a few informal comments in print and in letters and journals, since the middle of the eighteenth century there has accumulated an increasingly large, impressive, and enjoyable body of writing about theatre which can assist in the retrieval process. More recently, too, mechanical aids, starting with photography, then developing through vocal recording into silent and then talking films, have facilitated a process of at least partial recovery as well as in themselves extending the written word as the medium through which the achievements of theatre are best appreciated. Happily, those who have written about theatre in English include some exceptionally fine prose stylists. Art has generated art, with the result that an anthology of theatre criticism may itself stimulate the imagination rather than simply record facts about performance.

My aims in compiling this anthology have been varied. I have tried to give a sense of the evolution of Shakespeare's plays in theatrical performance over the centuries from his time to ours. For this reason the arrangement is chronological. I have tried to select accounts that give a clear sense of what happened in the theatre and of the effect it had upon the spectator. My choice has been circumscribed by the availability of material worth including; it favours the plays most frequently performed, but I have tried to represent the less popular ones, too. Some performances that I should like to have included are absent because I could find no account that did them justice; we know from scattered comments, for instance, that Dorothy (Dora) Jordan (1761–1816) gave great performances of heroines of Shakespeare's comedies, but there is no way of telling exactly how she played them. Even in recent times there are productions I have seen myself, such as the *Troilus and Cressida* directed by Peter Hall and John Barton at Stratford-upon-Avon in 1960, and their great cycle of the history plays under the title of *The Wars of the Roses* (initially given in 1963), which seem to me to be inadequately represented by any surviving individual pieces of criticism. I include some retrospective accounts but for the sake of immediacy of impression have preferred ones written close to the event, and with one exception have avoided composite discussions based on multiple sources.[2]

No criticism is objective. Anyone accustomed to reading reviews of productions in more than one newspaper will know how differently individuals may react to a single performance. The predictable polarities of opinion expressed by Harold Hobson and Kenneth Tynan which amused readers of their reviews when they were writing respectively for the *Sunday Times* and *The Observer* in the 1960s were only an extreme example of a recurrent phenomenon.[3] I have tried not to give prominence to accounts that clearly misrepresent the overall impact a production or performance made at the time. Even the greatest performers have had their detractors. This is especially true of innovators: Granville-Barker's Savoy Theatre productions of 1912 to 1914, for example, were attacked as well as eulogized. Occasionally (as with Beerbohm Tree's production of *Julius Caesar*) I offer alternative views (pp. 152–60), but readers seeking a broader conspectus of opinions than I can offer may find guidance in the Further Reading (pp. 326–30).[4] On the whole I have preferred accounts that convey enthusiasm, if only because admiration for a performance tends to stimulate vivid criticism. Inevitably, then, I have tried to choose pieces that are well written; only a writer who can handle language skilfully can hope to arouse interest and stimulate the imagination.

I have generally confined my choice to performances in the English language, not because of any lack of appreciation of the work of foreign directors and actors but partly because translation inevitably poses different challenges than performance in English, and also because of the understandable scarcity of good reviews written in English, and for limitations of space. As a result most of the performances represented here were given initially in England and, from the middle of the nineteenth century onwards, America.

Even the more conservative productions of our own time rarely use complete, unaltered texts (Peter Brook's of *A Midsummer Night's Dream* and Deborah Warner's of *Titus Andronicus*, discussed on pp. 277–9 and 303–7, though not in other respects conservative, are virtual exceptions), and some of the greatest performances by actors such as David Garrick, Sarah Siddons, Edmund Kean, and Henry Irving have been given in texts that were either radically altered or at least extensively re-arranged and shortened. For the twentieth century, at least, I have generally preferred productions that attempt to face the challenges of Shakespeare's texts head-on, without major adaptation, while also attempting to give some impression of the diversities of meaning that have emerged from the interaction of these texts with their interpreters and the social and intellectual circumstances prevailing at the time of performance.

Early Responses

The practice of formal theatre criticism was slow to evolve and is closely linked with the development of periodical journalism and of the essay as a literary form. Only fragmentary accounts of reactions to performances of Shakespeare's plays survive from the first two centuries and more of their existence; moreover, description and evaluation of the performance, which we associate with theatre criticism from the later part of the eighteenth century onwards, is rarely if ever part of the writers' aim. Gāmini Salgādo, in his valuable collection *Eyewitnesses of Shakespeare: First Hand Accounts of Performances 1590–1890* (1975), offers what he describes as 'an attempt to include everything that can reasonably be called an eyewitness account, a memory, or even an allusion to a Shakespearean performance' for the period up to 1700, but his selections occupy only fifty pages, in spite of including merely factual references such as extracts from the Revels Accounts simply naming plays performed at court, accounts of the burning of the Globe during a performance of *All is True* (*Henry VIII*), and the intriguing but sadly uninformative records of performances of *Hamlet* and *Richard II* at sea in 1607 and 1608. I have chosen not to reprint any of the early evidence in full, but will offer a brief analysis of it before introducing the accounts of performances that form the body of this book.

On the whole, allusions to performances in Shakespeare's time and up to the Restoration tell us more about reactions of audiences than about the theatre and what went on there. They give some indication of the qualities that spectators most valued in actors, and of the emotional impact made by their performances, but the only actor they name is the great tragedian Richard Burbage; they supply just a little information that either supplements or clarifies what we can derive from the texts;

and they provide clues as to which plays, and parts of plays, were most popular.

The longest accounts surviving from Shakespeare's lifetime are those written by Simon Forman, an astrologer, doctor, and almost professional womanizer, who in his voluminous and fascinating notebooks and other papers records seeing *Macbeth*, *The Winter's Tale*, and *Cymbeline*, the first two certainly and the last quite possibly at the Globe, in 1611. Forman's main interest seems to lie in noting features of the plots of the plays and in drawing lessons in behaviour from them: so, for example, he ends his account of *The Winter's Tale* with the words 'Beware of trusting feigned beggars or fawning fellows'. He names no performers (perhaps an interesting piece of negative evidence) and does not comment explicitly on their abilities, but his statements that 'when Macbeth had murdered the King, the blood on his hands could not be washed off by any means, nor from his wife's hands, which handled the bloody daggers in hiding them, by which means they became both much amazed and affronted', and that Macbeth 'fell into a great passion of fear and fury' on seeing Banquo's ghost, certainly suggest that he was impressed by the emotional impact of these stretches of the action, as well as not merely confirming that Banquo's ghost really did appear, but providing a detailed description of the episode:

The next night, being at supper with his noblemen whom he had bid to a feast to the which also Banquo should have come, he began to speak of 'Noble Banquo', and to wish that he were there. And as he thus did, standing up to drink a carouse to him, the ghost of Banquo came and sat down in his chair behind him. And he turning about to sit down again saw the ghost of Banquo, which fronted him so that he fell into a great passion of fear and fury, uttering many words about his murder, by which when they heard that Banquo was murdered they suspected Macbeth.

One could wish that many later critics had been as precise in describing stage action. In his account of *Cymbeline*, Forman's use of the name 'Innogen' for the heroine supports emendation from 'Imogen', the form found in the Folio.[5]

Stronger evidence that audiences could identify closely with the emotions of the characters portrayed comes as early as 1592, when Thomas Nashe, writing it would seem about *Henry VI, Part One*, exclaims how it would 'have joyed brave Talbot, the terror of the French, to think that after he had lien two hundred years in his tomb he should triumph again on the stage, and have his bones new-embalmed with the tears of ten thousand spectators at least, at several times, who in the tragedian that represents his person imagine they behold him fresh bleeding!'[6] And in 1610 a don called Henry Jackson wrote of performances given by the King's Men in Oxford that in tragedies the players 'moved some to tears not only by their words but even by their actions'[7]—an indication that gesture played an important part in attaining tragic effect—and particularly that in *Othello* Desdemona, although the entire role was played supremely well, was especially moving in death, when 'by her very countenance she invoked the tearful pity of those who saw her.'[8] Jackson's identification with the role is shown by his referring to the character rather than the actor.

Although we know the names of many of the actors who performed in early productions of Shakespeare's plays, the only one to break through the barrier of anonymity of comment is Richard Burbage, who probably played Othello when Jackson saw the play; an elegy on the actor's death in 1619 praises particularly his capacity to persuade those who saw him that he really was the character he represented; with his death, we are told, 'young Hamlet', Kyd's Hieronimo, 'Kind [or should it be King?] Lear', and

> the grieved Moor, and more beside
> That lived in him have now for ever died;

when he played a mad (or, in an alternative version, sad) lover,

> . . . I would have sworn he meant to die;
> Oft have I seen him play this part in jest
> So lively that spectators and the rest
> Of his sad crew, whilst he but seemed to bleed,
> Amazed, thought even then he died indeed.[9]

Comments like these suggest a naturalistic acting style rather than the formalistic which is often supposed to have prevailed—but styles of acting may have varied from one performer to another, and may have altered over the years, in part to suit the style in which plays were written.

Praise of the acting company as a whole comes in Thomas Platter's comments on seeing *Julius Caesar* 'very pleasingly performed' at the Globe in 1599, in which he also praises the skill of the actors in performing a graceful dance 'at the end of the play'.[10] Platter was a Swiss visitor to England, a physician, and his remarks come in a letter written back home: English acting was literally something to write home about.

More general praise of the *mise en scène* appears in Sir Henry Wotton's account of the burning of the Globe in 1613 during a performance of the play published in 1623 as *Henry VIII*, where he tells how the 'new play called *All is True*...was set forth with many extraordinary circumstances of pomp and majesty, even to the matting of the stage; the Knights of the Order, with their Georges and Garter, the Guards with their embroidered coats and the like'.[11] One of the most intriguing facts about this play is that the trial of Queen Katharine dramatized by Shakespeare and Fletcher had taken place in the very room in the Blackfriars that the King's Men used as a winter house. It would be touching to think of the mimic representation of the scene in this identical space, but Wotton's and other accounts indicate that the earliest performances, at least, were given in the Globe, not the Blackfriars.

What may be, but is not certainly, the most specific account of staging comes in the second version, dating from 1607, of Samuel Daniel's play *Cleopatra*, which includes a description of how Cleopatra 'draws' up Antony 'in rolls of taffaty | T'a window at the top' of her monument, and how Charmian and Iras

> Tugged at the pulley, having n'other aids,
> And up they hoise the swooning body there
> Of pale Antonius, show'ring out his blood
> On th'underlookers, which there gazing stood...

This may well be influenced by performance of Shakespeare's play, but it has to be treated with caution, if only because Daniel may have let his imagination play over his memories of what he had seen.[12]

Caution should perhaps also be exercised in heeding evidence derived from memorial verses in which the intention is to praise the deceased, but Leonard Digges conveys apparent enthusiasm in his lines printed first in the Shakespeare First Folio of 1623 and then, in amplified form and four years after their author's death, in John Benson's heavily edited collection of the *Poems* of 1640, where he exclaims 'how the audience | Were ravished' by the tent scene in *Julius Caesar*, 'with what wonder they went thence', and comments on the drawing power of 'Honest Iago, or the jealous Moor...Falstaff...Hal, Poins, the rest', of 'Beatrice | And Benedick', and of 'Malvolio, that cross-gartered gull'.[13]

From Cibber on Betterton to Lichtenberg on Garrick

Professional theatrical activity in England came to an abrupt halt in 1642 with the fall of the monarchy, and when theatres reopened on the restoration to the throne of Charles II in 1660, conditions were very different. The major theatres were roofed, unlike the public theatres of Shakespeare's time; women's roles were taken by female performers; fashions in drama changed, with the result that Shakespeare's plays came to seem dated and either fell out of the repertory or were played, often, in radically adapted form; and the social composition of audiences, too, changed. Instead of plays being taken to court, the court came to the theatre. Theatregoing became a still more fashionable activity, and courtiers paid court to actors and, especially, to actresses. The journals of Samuel Pepys bear witness to the extensive theatregoing of an intelligent and socially adept man about town who responded to the glamour of the theatre in all senses of the word. Regrettably, his references to Shakespeare plays are couched in very general terms of approbation or distaste, which may be exemplified by his comment on *A Midsummer Night's Dream* in 1662:

We saw *Midsummers nights dreame*, which I have never seen before, nor shall ever again, for it is the most insipid ridiculous play that ever I saw in my life. I saw, I confess, some good dancing and some handsome women, which was all my pleasure.[14]

Only fragmentary accounts remain even of Thomas Betterton, undoubtedly the greatest and most highly regarded actor of the period, but some impression of his power as Hamlet may be gleaned from one of the earliest autobiographies of a man of the theatre, the *Apology for the Life of Mr Colley Cibber* which, although it did not appear until 1740, some thirty years after Betterton's death at an advanced age, gives a vivid account of what Betterton actually did during part of the play's action, as well as of the impact he had on the spectators (pp. 18–19).[15]

Cibber's praise of Betterton is typical of accounts of Shakespearian performances from much of the rest of the eighteenth century in its concentration on an individual actor. Increasingly the reading public were being offered books of theatre reminiscence, but the general assumption seems to be that readers would be familiar with the way plays were put on, and would be interested mainly in an evocation of performances that either they might have enjoyed or they might regret not having seen. Few actors of any period have been so universally and passionately admired as David Garrick. The date—19 October 1741—of his London début, as Richard III, at the minor theatre of Goodman's Fields, is as much of a landmark in theatre history as that of Edmund Kean as Shylock, at Drury Lane on 26 January 1814; each of them came at exactly the right moment, at a point when tragic acting seemed in danger of ossifying into the 'classical' stateliness associated with, respectively, James Quin and John Philip Kemble; and each was short and fiery rather than dignified and physically impressive. Regrettably, although many tributes, both formal and informal, to Garrick's excellence reached print, few if any of them attempt to place his performances in relation to those of the rest of his company, or to give an impression of the overall impact of the plays' staging. Most of them still derive from books of memoirs or accounts of travellers, such as the marvellous letters written (for publication) by G. C. Lichtenberg, whose descriptions of Garrick as Hamlet (pp. 24–8) have rarely been bettered for accuracy of observation (or so it appears, for of course we have no means of putting it to the test) combined with a sense of what it felt like to be there. And there is a large body of pamphlet literature which often deals in detail with theatrical politics and performances.

The first English journal specifically devoted to the theatre is Richard Steele's *The Theatre*, which first appeared in 1720, and journals with similar aims came and—some very rapidly—went in increasing numbers as the century wore on, with a proliferation at the turn of the century reflecting the popularity of actors such as Sarah Siddons, John Philip Kemble, and, later, Edmund Kean.[16] Newspapers with broader coverage also grew in number—*The Times* was founded in 1775—and took an increasing interest in theatrical matters. To an extent newsworthiness was—as it has always continued to be—a criterion for attention, so that for example David Garrick's final performances received special coverage (pp. 28–9), and the amorous and alcoholic scandals surrounding Kean's public as well as his private life (in so far as actors can expect to have a private life) came as grist to the journalists' mills.

Romantics and Early Victorians

Much of the early periodical criticism is anonymous, and some of it far from disinterested. The first figure of literary distinction to undertake systematic theatre criticism was Leigh Hunt, who was only twenty years old when, in 1805, he began writing regularly for his brother John's paper *The News*. In his *Autobiography* written many years later he castigated the state of theatre criticism at that time, describing it as 'an interchange of amenities over the dinner-table; a flattery of power on the one side, and puns on the other', adding that 'what the public took for a criticism on a play was a draft upon the box-office, or reminiscences of last Thursday's salmon and lobster sauce'.[17] Hunt, a somewhat mischievous man, was not averse to exposing his own prejudices in the public press, and to writing with satirical irony. He pursued what was virtually a private feud with John Philip Kemble, criticizing him for 'the clap-provoking frivolities of ending every speech with an energetic dash of the fist, or of running off the stage after a vehement declamation, as if the actor was in haste to get his pint of wine'—and Hunt no doubt expected his readers to know that Kemble was a heavy drinker. And Mrs Faucit, after playing Volumnia, cannot have been pleased to be told that 'A Roman matron did not think it essential to her dignity to step about with her head thrown half a yard back, as if she had a contempt for her own chin.' Nevertheless, during over a quarter of a century of activity as a theatre critic Hunt won many expressions of respect from theatre people, and, more importantly, wrote analytical notices of their performances which display a connoisseur's appreciation of the finer points of their acting along with a deeply sensitive responsiveness to their speaking of Shakespeare's lines and to visual effects of appearance, gesture, stage business, and the like. As Hunt is the first, so he is in some ways the best of our professional theatre critics above all because of a literary power that combines apparently objective description with a capacity for imaginative reconstruction which creates in the reader a sense, if not of what it was actually like to be witnessing the performance, at least of what Hunt himself saw, heard, and felt when he did.

Many other versatile men of letters of Hunt's time took a passionate interest in the theatre and wrote vividly about performances while not necessarily practising formal theatre criticism. Perhaps the best-known sentence in the whole of theatre criticism is one spoken by a man who never formally practised the art: Coleridge's throwaway remark that to see Kean was 'like reading Shakespeare by flashes of lightning' (not an unqualified compliment).[18] Charles Lamb, though he wrote a few reviews, was at his best in writing long after the event, reminiscing about perform-ances that had passed through the filter of his imagination, as in his essay 'On Some of the Old Actors' (pp. 29–32). Sir Walter Scott's admirable recollections of Kemble (pp. 33–7) come from a review of the actor's biography published three years after Kemble's death. John Keats's letters display his interest in the theatre, and especially his profound admiration for Kean; Keats aspired to become a playwright, but wrote formally about the theatre only as a stand-in for his friend John Hamilton Reynolds, himself a good critic (pp. 52–5). But William Hazlitt, like Hunt, counted theatre criticism among his professional activities. Fortunate enough to be present at the first of Edmund Kean's great performances at

Drury Lane (as Shylock), Hazlitt wrote with especial eloquence about this actor.

Like Hunt and many later theatre critics, Hazlitt was a literary as well as a theatre critic. Indeed the two activities are often hard to distinguish. A theatre critic, at least in writing about new plays, is expected to discuss the qualities and merits of texts as well as performances. And even when writing about established classics, such as the works of Shakespeare, the critic needs to relate performance to interpretation. It is significant that when, in 1817, Hazlitt came to publish his book *Characters of Shakespear's Plays*, for long a classic of literary (or dramatic) criticism, he incorporated into his studies of individual plays many paragraphs that he had previously published in his notices of performances. There is no clear-cut distinction between Hazlitt the reviewer of Shakespeare in the theatre, and Hazlitt the literary critic of Shakespeare. Fine critic of performance though he is, Hazlitt's writing about theatre can seem more studied than Hunt's, less immersed in the theatrical experience. And his literary sensibility is often at odds with the way Shakespeare was presented in his time, to such an extent that he can even express the belief that 'Poetry and the stage do not agree together.'[19] Leigh Hunt was more capable of an unbuttoned response to adaptations of Shakespeare. Even so, Hazlitt's descriptions of Kean's death scene in *Richard III* (pp. 38–41) and of the way in which Kean played the scene with Ophelia in *Hamlet* (pp. 41–3) are among the classics of English prose.

Biographies and autobiographies of actors continued to appear, often including valuable descriptions of performances such as that of Mrs Siddons's Volumnia in Julian Charles Young's life of his father, Charles Mayne Young, written long after the event (pp. 37–8), and occasionally too performers themselves ventured into criticism, such as Helena Faucit's book *On Some of Shakespeare's Female Characters* with its rapturous account of Macready's Leontes (pp. 67–72).

The Later Victorians

As century wore on, newspapers allowed more space for theatre reviews, and more distinguished reviewers emerged. John Forster was not only a successful journalist but also the first professional biographer of the century and a close associate of many of the most eminent literary and theatrical figures of his time, including Charles Dickens and W. C. Macready, of whose performances he wrote with special sympathy (pp. 72–84). G. H. Lewes (1817–78, not represented here) was a playwright, an actor, a novelist, an historian of philosophy and of science, and the author of a major biography of Goethe as well as a theatre critic. Forster and Lewes were writing about theatre mainly during the heyday of Macready, the later years of Edmund Kean and the earlier career of his son Charles. In mid-century, during the period of Charles Kean's management of the Princess's Theatre and Samuel Phelps's of Sadler's Wells, Henry Morley, first Professor of English at University College London and a prolific literary historian and biographer who, as a popular educator, had special sympathy with the ideals of Phelps, was reviewing theatre for *The Examiner* (pp. 87–94). During the same period too the German novelist Theodor Fontane visited London and wrote for German newspapers fascinating and so far little-known reports on the London theatrical scene, frequently attempting to indicate ways in which the German theatre might profit from the English in its Shakespeare productions.[20] I include Fontane's account of Charles Kean's *Winter's Tale* (pp. 95–9).

In the later part of the nineteenth century newspapers allowed more space to their theatre correspondents than at any other time before or since. This results sometimes in redundancy and verbosity; notices often start with paragraphs that give the impression of having been written before the event; but it also offered exceptional opportunities for detailed analysis of performance, as can be seen in the best notices of, for instance, Clement Scott (pp. 106–12) Joseph Knight (pp. 112–17), William Archer (pp. 152–6), and J. T. Grein (not represented here). It provided opportunities too for Bernard Shaw, the most coruscatingly brilliant of theatre critics whose capacities as an entertainer, often apparent in corrosively unfavourable but illuminatingly informative notices of the follies of directors such as Augustin Daly (pp. 132–44), and even in attacks on aspects of Shakespeare's plays that he did not wholly admire, should not be allowed to obscure his capacity to respond with sensitive and well informed appreciation and analytical power to the work of performers whom he admired, such as Ada Rehan, Ellen Terry, and Johnston Forbes-Robertson (pp. 144–52), and even to those, such as Henry Irving, about whom his feelings were equivocal.

Shaw's successor on *The Saturday Review*, Max Beerbohm, wrote more briefly, rather perhaps because of his fastidiousness as a stylist and of his affectation of lassitude than because of editorial constraints, but again the surface of his work—its urbanity, its delicate wit understated at times almost to the point of imperceptibility, its disdain of emotional display—should not be mistaken for an absence of a fundamentally serious engagement with drama and its interpreters. Beerbohm's theatre criticism demonstrates that it is possible to be a member of the avant-garde without stridency; he was, for example, one of the earliest critics to champion the scenic innovations of Gordon Craig (pp. 171–4, etc.).

Earlier Twentieth-Century Criticism

Until the twentieth century most of the important British work on Shakespeare originated in London, even though leading actors often performed in other British, European, and American centres, sometimes with local companies but at other times, at least from fairly early in the nineteenth century, taking their own companies and productions with them. Most of the critics, too, were London-based, but the *Manchester Guardian* (founded as a daily paper in 1855), the leading provincial newspaper of its time, employed distinguished critics, among them C. E. Montague (pp. 165–70), and the rise of the repertory movement in the early twentieth century increased the amount of significant work originating in the provinces—but, although modern-dress Shakespeare began with Barry Jackson's *Cymbeline* in Birmingham in 1923, he chose to open his influential *Hamlet* in London (pp. 204–6). One of the most prolific of twentieth-century critics, J. C. Trewin (not represented here) wrote extensively for the *Birmingham Post* as well as for London-based journals such as *The Illustrated London News*, and although many of the best productions were given in London by the Old Vic Company from 1914 to 1963, the increasing importance of Stratford-upon-Avon as a centre of Shakespearian production has done much to shift the centre of balance. And not all companies have been theatre-based. F. R. Benson toured extensively in the early years of the century, so later did Donald Wolfit (pp. 224–30, 239–43), and, more recently, the English Shakespeare Company (pp. 297–300), Cheek by Jowl (pp. 316–17), and Northern Broadsides (pp. 318–20).

Between the Wars the leading London critic was James Agate, well-read in English and French literature and in theatre history, a voluminous, professional diarist, a conscious wit, a man of strong prejudices who was nevertheless, at his best, a stylish analyst of acting (pp. 210–19, etc.). Other prominent critics of this period include Herbert Farjeon (pp. 201–3) and, not represented here, Ivor Brown, and Desmond MacCarthy who, like T. C. Worsley (pp. 244–8) and others before and since, found publishers for volumes reprinting their notices, many of which are listed in the Further Reading.[21] As in the past, creative writers occasionally wrote about theatre, as Virginia Woolf did (reluctantly) in her essay on *Twelfth Night* at the Old Vic (pp. 207–10).

The Moderns: from Tynan on Olivier to Kitchin on Scofield

From around the middle of the twentieth century onwards criticism of classical theatre in England increasingly becomes the province of university-educated writers employed often by periodicals with a comparatively limited circulation. Admittedly the precocious and immensely gifted Kenneth Tynan (pp. 230–43), having established his credentials at the age of twenty-three with the publication in 1950 of *He that Plays the King: A View of the Theatre* and in the same year been appointed theatre critic of *The Spectator*, graduated, via the *Evening Standard* and *The Daily Sketch*, to *The Observer*, in whose columns he conducted his flytings with Hobson from 1954 to 1963; as a special admirer of heroic acting he found it easier to admire Olivier than Gielgud. Ronald Bryden (pp. 270–7) wrote mainly for *The New Statesman*. Large-circulation newspapers have increasingly devoted less space to theatre reviews, or have required their critics to cover several productions in one review, so that even serious critics such as Irving Wardle (author of a fine book on theatre criticism[22]), Michael Billington (pp. 301–3), Benedict Nightingale, John Peter, Paul Taylor (pp. 313–17) and many others have often lacked adequate space to do justice even to major productions. Laurence Kitchin contributed to *The Times*, but his essays reprinted here were written for publication in book form (pp. 260–9).

The Growth of Academic Criticism

The most important development in the postwar period has been the growth of academic interest in performance criticism. From its earliest years *Shakespeare Survey*, founded in 1948, has included articles on plays in performance whose authors have usually been able to see productions more than once and to write about them at comparative leisure. Richard David (pp. 248–52), academic publisher and editor of the Arden edition (1951) of *Love's Labour's Lost*, wrote regularly for *Shakespeare Survey*, basing a number of his essays on lectures given to the Royal Shakespeare Theatre's annual Summer School, and using both as the basis for his book *Shakespeare in the Theatre* (1978). Other academic writers for *Survey* represented here include John Russell Brown (pp. 256–9), Peter Thomson (pp. 279–82), Roger Warren (pp. 283–9, 294–7), Nicholas Shrimpton (pp. 292–4), Peter Holland (pp. 318–20), and Robert Smallwood (pp. 307–13, 320–5). In America, too, *Shakespeare Quarterly*, founded in 1950, has increasingly published notices of Shakespeare productions in America, Britain, and elsewhere. Since 1974 the *Times Literary Supplement* has regularly opened its columns to the arts of performance, and it too has stimulated criticism with a scholarly basis.

American Criticism

From the early nineteenth century there has often been fruitful inter-change of actors and productions between England and America. I include a brief account of a little-known performance of Posthumus by Charles Kean in Philadelphia (pp. 64–6) as well as a review of John Barrymore's Hamlet when he played it in England after his great success on Broadway (pp. 195–201). A prolific American writer on theatre was William Winter, who had close personal links with, among other practi-tioners, Edwin Booth, Ada Rehan, and Augustin Daly. His professional involvement with, especially, Daly detracts from his objectivity, and he sometimes writes uncritically, but at his best, as in his remarkably detailed account of Irving as Shylock (pp. 117–26), he can be a highly perceptive observer. Henry Austin Clapp, who wrote about theatre in Boston from 1868 to 1904, had a high reputation for incorruptibility; I include his account of the extraordinary Charlotte Cushman, who played men even more successfully than she played women, as Queen Katharine in *Henry VIII* (pp. 103–5). Both Stark Young (pp. 195–201) and John Mason Brown (pp. 220–3) wrote with distinction on American theatre from the 1920s to the 1940s.

The performances and productions discussed in this volume represent only a tiny proportion of the enormous quantity of theatrical work on Shakespeare. It would be possible to fill many more volumes with accounts of performances not only in the English language, wherever it is spoken, but also in translation in most countries of the world, repre-sented here principally by Granville-Barker's review (pp. 187–94) of Jacques Copeau's *Twelfth Night* (though it would not always be at all easy to find worthwhile reviews in English). My Further Reading provides a pointer to additional sources of information.

Whereas performances until the middle of the nineteenth century are memorialized only by the written word, from then onwards mechanical recordings become available. It is possible, for instance, to hear fragments of Edwin Booth's performance of Othello, of Ellen Terry's as Ophelia, of Beerbohm Tree's as Mark Antony and Falstaff and of Johnston Forbes-Robertson's as Hamlet. Silent film exists of Tree as King John, Benson as Richard III, Forbes-Robertson as Hamlet, and the American Frederick Warde as Lear and Richard III. More recently entire performances have been recorded in sound and on film and video—always with some degree of textual adaptation to the different medium. Among stage performances reviewed here, we can see Olivier as Richard III and Othello, Ian McKellen as Macbeth and Iago, Judi Dench as Lady Macbeth. Such performance records are of immense interest, but they do not supplant the written word. Partly this is because of technical inadequacies in the earlier period—crackly sound, deteriorating film, poor techniques of film-making, failure to adapt styles of performance to a new medium—but it is also inherent in the very nature of performance. Every production, however 'traditional' in style, belongs inescapably to its time. No actor can act, no director can direct, for posterity. As the years pass, as styles of acting and production change, as the intellectual, social, and aesthetic context in which they were created recedes into the past, emotional reality drains away, quaintness supervenes, and an ever-increasing exercise of the historical imagination is demanded if we are to have any sense of what they meant to their contemporaries. It is only through the reactions of those who experienced these performances that we can sense not simply what they sounded like, or what they looked like, but what it meant to be present at them. It is not the microphone or the camera but the seeing eye and the listening ear, the responsive imagination and the analysing brain, and the power to wield words that confer what passes for immortality on those who practise the arts of the theatre.

1. From *Hymenaei* (1606).

2. The exception is Ronald Harwood's account (pp. 224–30) of Donald Wolfit as Lear, which gives a fuller account of the performance than any single review I could find.

3. See Dominic Shellard, *Harold Hobson: Witness and Judge* (Keele, 1995), p. 8, etc.

4. Much work remains to be done on listing and assessing theatre criticism that has not been reprinted. While relying mainly on reviews that have already appeared in collections of one sort or another, I include some accounts that so far as I know have not been previously reprinted or are available only in scarce volumes.

5. A. L. Rowse's *Simon Forman: Sex and Society in Shakespeare's Age* (1974) offers a racy account of Forman's activities, but there is room for a much fuller study of Forman's voluminous papers.

6. From *Pierce Penniless his Supplication to the Devil* (1592), in *Thomas Nashe: Selected Writings*, ed. Stanley Wells (1964), p. 65.

7. 'non solum dicendo, sed etiam faciendo quaedam lachrymas movebant.'

8. 'spectantium misericordiam ipso vultu imploraret'; Geoffrey Tillotson, '*Othello* and *The Alchemist* at Oxford in 1610', *TLS* 20 July 1933, p. 494; quoted by Salgãdo, p. 30.

9. E. K. Chambers, *The Elizabethan Stage*, 4 vols. (Oxford, 1923), ii. 309.

10. The most satisfactory transcript and translation of Platter is by Ernest Schanzer in 'Thomas Platter's Observations on the Elizabethan Stage', *Notes and Queries*, 201 (1956), 465–7.

11. Wotton's letter, with other documents relating to the burning down of the Globe, is quoted in my *Shakespeare: A Dramatic Life* (1994), pp. 374–6.

12. The suggestion is made in 'An Elizabethan Eyewitness of *Antony and Cleopatra*', by Joan Rees, *Shakespeare Survey 6* (1953), pp. 91–3.

13. Reprinted in *William Shakespeare: The Complete Works*, General Editors Stanley Wells and Gary Taylor (Oxford, 1986, etc.), p. xlviii.

14. *The Diary of Samuel Pepys*, ed. Robert Latham and William Matthews, 11 vols. (1970–83), iii. 208.

15. Betterton's performance as Hamlet is studied in the opening chapter of *Shakespearian Players and Performances*, by Arthur Colby Sprague (Cambridge, Mass., 1953).

16. C. V. Stratman's *British Theatrical Periodicals 1720–1967: A Bibliography* (1972) is an invaluable guide.

17. Cited in my article 'Shakespeare in Leigh Hunt's Theatre Criticism', *Essays and Studies*, 33 (1980), pp. 119–38.

18. *Table Talk*, 23 April 1823.

19. In the review of *A Midsummer Night's Dream* reprinted on pp. 43–5.

20. An edition of these reports collected as *Shakespeare in the London Theatre* is to be published by the Society for Theatre Research in a translation by Russell Jackson.

21. Most of these volumes cover a wide spread of plays, but Farjeon's Shakespeare notices, one of which is reprinted on pp. 201–3, are gathered together in his *The Shakespearean Scene: Dramatic Criticisms, 1913–44* (1949). It can be recommended particularly for his enthusiastic appreciations of the work of Edith Evans.

22. *Theatre Criticism* (1992).

TEXT

[*c.*1700], Colley Cibber (1671–1757) on Thomas Betterton
(1635–1710) as Hamlet, from *An Apology for the Life of Mr Colley
Cibber* (1740), ed. Robert W. Lowe, 2 vols. (1889), i. 100–2.

OVER his fifty-year career Thomas Betterton was by all accounts the greatest
actor after Richard Burbage and before David Garrick, and Hamlet was one of
his greatest roles. Samuel Pepys noted in 1661, when Betterton was twenty-six,
that he 'did the Prince's part beyond imagination'; he was still playing it at the age
of seventy-four, when, according to a report in *The Tatler*, 'he acted youth; and by
the prevalent power of proper manner, gesture, and voice, appeared throughout
the whole drama a young man of great expectation, vivacity, and enterprise'. He
appears to have used a somewhat truncated but not substantially adapted text.
We lack detailed accounts of his performances, but a vivid glimpse of his Hamlet,
along with a sense of the technical means by which he achieved his effects, is
preserved by the actor, playwright, and theatre manager Colley Cibber in his
autobiography, an invaluable source of information about the theatre of his time.

YOU have seen a Hamlet perhaps, who, on the first appearance of his
father's Spirit, has thrown himself into all the straining vociferation
requisite to express rage and fury, and the house has thundered with
applause; though the misguided actor was all the while (as Shakespeare
terms it) tearing a passion into rags—I am the more bold to offer you this
particular instance because the late Mr. Addison,[1] while I sat by him to see
this scene acted, made the same observation, asking me, with some
surprise, if I thought Hamlet should be in so violent a passion with the
Ghost, which, though it might have astonished, it had not provoked
him?—for you may observe that in this beautiful speech the passion
never rises beyond an almost breathless astonishment, or an impatience,
limited by filial reverence, to enquire into the suspected wrongs that may
have raised him from his peaceful tomb and a desire to know what a spirit
so seemingly distressed might wish or enjoin a sorrowful son to execute
towards his future quiet in the grave? This was the light into which
Betterton threw this scene; which he opened with a pause of mute
amazement, then rising slowly to a solemn, trembling voice, he made
the Ghost equally terrible to the spectator as to himself, and in the
descriptive part of the natural emotions which the ghastly vision gave
him, the boldness of his expostulation was still governed by decency,
manly, but not braving, his voice never rising into that seeming outrage
or wild defiance of what he naturally revered. But alas! to preserve this
medium, between mouthing and meaning too little, to keep the attention
more pleasingly awake by a tempered spirit than by mere vehemence of

voice, is of all the master-strokes of an actor the most difficult to reach. In this none yet have equalled Betterton.

1. **Addison**, Joseph (1672–1719), essayist and poet.

༺✿༻

[*c*.1738–9], Thomas Davies (*c*.1712–85) on Colley Cibber (1671–1757) at the Theatre Royal, Drury Lane, London, as Justice Shallow in *Henry the Fourth, Part Two*, from *Dramatic Micellanies* [*sic*], 3 vols. (1784), i. 306–7.

THOMAS DAVIES was an actor turned bookseller and publisher whose *Dramatic Micellanies, consisting of critical observations on several plays of Shakespeare, with a review of his principal characters and those of various eminent writers, as represented by Mr Garrick and other celebrated comedians*, appeared first in 1784. Justice Shallow in *Henry the Fourth, Part Two* was one of Cibber's best roles. He ostensibly retired from the stage in 1733 but reappeared later, playing Shallow with great success at Drury Lane in the 1738–9 season. Davies's account suggests how Cibber capitalized on his own appearance to create an impression of individual character.

WHETHER he was a copy or an original in Shallow, it is certain that no audience was ever more fixed in deep attention, at his first appearance, or more shaken with laughter in the progress of the scene, than at Colley Cibber's exhibition of this ridiculous justice of peace. Some years after he had left the stage, he acted Shallow for his son's[1] benefit—I believe in 1737, when Quin[2] was the Falstaff, and Milward[3] the king. Whether it was owing to the pleasure the spectators felt on seeing their old friend return to them again, *though for that night only*, after an absence of some years, I know not; but, surely, no actor or audience were better pleased with each other. His manner was so perfectly simple, his look so vacant, when he questioned his Cousin Silence about the price of ewes, and lamented, in the same breath, with silly surprise, the death of Old Double, that it will be impossible for any surviving spectator not to smile at the remembrance of it. The want of ideas occasions Shallow to repeat almost every thing he says. Cibber's transition from asking the price of bullocks, to trite, but grave, reflections on mortality, was so natural, and attended with such an unmeaning roll of his small pig's-eyes, accompanied with an important utterance of tick! tick! tick! not much louder than the balance of a watch's pendulum, that I question if any actor was ever superior in the conception or expression of such solemn insignificancy.

1. **son**, Theophilus (1703–58), also an actor and manager. The performance referred to is probably that given at Drury Lane on 13 October 1738.
2. **Quin**, James (1693–1766), leading English actor between Betterton and Garrick; Falstaff was his most famous role.
3. **Milward**, William (1702–42), a prominent actor.

⟪⟫

[1744–68], Thomas Davies on David Garrick (1719–79) and Mrs Pritchard (1711–68) in *Macbeth*, from *Dramatic Micellanies* [*sic*], 3 vols. (1784), ii. 140–1, 148–9, 166–7; with James Boaden, *Life of Mrs Siddons*, 2 vols. (1827), ii. 140–2.

THE meteoric rise to fame of David Garrick was signalled by his performance of Richard III, in Colley Cibber's adaptation, at the minor theatre in Goodman's Fields, London, on 19 October 1741. He became Shakespeare's greatest champion, playing in and adapting (sometimes drastically) many of his plays, and organizing in 1769 the Jubilee at Stratford-upon-Avon which inaugurated the Romantic deification of the dramatist.

Garrick first played Macbeth, with great success, on 7 January 1744; Hannah Pritchard was his Lady Macbeth, and he relinquished the role when she died, in 1768. William Davenant's considerably rewritten version (published in 1674) had held the stage. It elaborated the witch scenes (incorporating the songs, apparently by Thomas Middleton, which seem to have been used by Shakespeare's company), enhanced the role of Lady Macduff, and watered-down the dialogue. Garrick used a version of his own, closer to the original though retaining the singing witches and adding, for instance, a moralistic death speech. The passages described here were not much altered; they are from Act 2, Scenes 1 and 2, and Act 3, Scene 4 in standard editions. Though Davies offers a vivid impression of the third of these, James Boaden pours scorn on it: I reproduce his comments as a possible corrective. Pl. 1 reproduces Zoffany's painting of Mrs Pritchard in the play.

1. Thomas Davies

(*a*) Is this a dagger which I see before me!

MANY stage critics suppose this to be one of the most difficult situations in acting. The sudden start on seeing the dagger in the air,—the endeavour of the actor to seize it,—the disappointment,—the suggestion of its being only a vision of the disturbed fancy,—the seeing it still in form most palpable, with the reasoning upon it,—these are difficulties which the mind of Garrick was capable of encountering and subduing. So happy did he think himself in the exhibition of this scene, that, when he was in Italy, and requested by the duke of Parma to give a proof of his skill in action, to the admiration of that prince, he at once threw himself into the attitude of Macbeth's seeing the air-drawn dagger. The duke desired no farther proof of Garrick's great excellence in his profession, being perfectly convinced, by this specimen, that he was an absolute master of it.

(*b*) The representation of this terrible part of the play, by Garrick and Mrs. Pritchard, can no more be described than I believe it can be equalled. I will not separate these performers, for the merits of both were transcendent. His distraction of mind and agonizing horrors were finely contrasted by her seeming apathy, tranquillity, and confidence. The beginning of the scene after the murder was conducted in terrifying whispers. Their looks and action supplied the place of words. You heard what they spoke, but you learned more from the agitation of mind displayed in their action and deportment. The poet here gives only an outline to the consummate actor.—*I have done the deed!—Didst thou not hear a noise?—When?—Did you not speak?*—The dark colouring, given by the actor to these abrupt speeches, makes the scene awful and tremendous to the auditors! The wonderful expression of heartful horror, which Garrick felt when he shewed his bloody hands, can only be conceived and described by those who saw him!

(*c*) This admirable scene was greatly supported by the speaking terrors of Garrick's look and action. Mrs Pritchard shewed admirable art in endeavouring to hide Macbeth's frenzy from the observation of the guests, by drawing their attention to conviviality. She smiled on one, whispered to another, and distantly saluted a third; in short, she practised every possible artifice to hide the transaction that passed between her husband and the vision his disturbed imagination had raised. Her reproving and angry looks, which glanced towards Macbeth, at the same time were mixed with marks of inward vexation and uneasiness. When, at last, as if unable to support her feelings any longer, she rose from her seat, and seized his arm, and, with a half-whisper of terror, said, '*Are you a man!*' she assumed a look of such anger, indignation, and contempt, as cannot be surpassed.

2. James Boaden

I SHOULD think Mr. Davies, from his minuteness of observation, must have figured there as one of the nobles, only a few covers from the royal state. But the truth is, a great deal of this is impossible—there has been *no time* for it—the lords *observe* as soon as anything occurs to excite attention, as the text shews us.

> '*Macb.*—The table's full.
> *Len.*—Here is a place reserv'd, Sir.
> *Macb.*—Where?
> *Len.*—Here, my good lord. What is't that moves your highness?
> *Macb.*—Which of you have done this?
> *Lords*—What, my good lord!'

On Rosse's calling upon them to *rise*, his highness not being well, Lady Macbeth desires them to keep their seats—explains his malady, which notice only augments; begs them to feed, and regard him not; and *then* coming down to Macbeth, endeavours to *baffle* his terrors. Davies closes the eulogium thus: 'When, *at last*, as if unable to support her feelings any longer, she rose from her seat, and with a half-whisper of terror, said "are you a man?" she assumed a look of anger, indignation, and contempt, not to be surpassed.'

This is very far from being clearly put; a half-whisper of *terror*, attended by a look of *anger, indignation,* and *contempt,* is a rather singular mode of encouraging *dismay.* The whisper is for concealment of what is said from others; but the words whispered are a reproach, and something *more,* incompatible with TERROR. She is so much mistress of herself, as even to assail him with ridicule. His conviction is '*proper stuff,*' the 'painting of fear'—the 'air-drawn dagger, which, he *said,* led him to Duncan'—Such *flaws* and *starts,* as became only a story told by a *woman* at a *winter's fire,* under the wise authority of a *grandam.* 'When *all's done,* he look'd but on a stool.' But so it is, without perfect recollection of the scenes, praise is drawn from the imagination rather than the fact, and much is imputed which was never done by the actress; and if it had been done, would have merited no commendation.

[1742–76], Thomas Davies on David Garrick as King Lear, from *Dramatic Micellanies* [*sic*], 3 vols. (1784), ii. 318–20.

GARRICK acted in a modified version of the adaptation by Nahum Tate published in 1681 and described by John Forster on pp. 72–7 below.

THEY, who have had the exquisite pleasure to see Mr. Garrick in King Lear, will most unfeignedly wish that his action and elocution could have been perpetuated. A Reynolds[1] could have faithfully transcribed a look and an attitude; but, alas! this would have been but an imperfect representation. The wonders of his voice and multiplied expression could not have been preserved!

In the preceding scenes of Lear, Garrick had displayed all the force of quick transition from one passion to another: he had, from the most violent rage, descended to sedate calmness; had seized, with unutterable sensibility, the various impressions of terror, and faithfully represented all the turbid passions of the soul; he had pursued the progress of agonizing feelings to madness in its several stages. Yet, after he had done all this, he exhibited himself, in this fine scene, in such a superior taste, as to make it more interesting than any thing the audience had already enjoyed. But indeed the incident itself is very striking.—Every spectator feels for himself and common humanity, when he perceives man, while living, degraded to the deprivation of sense and loss of memory! Who does not rejoice, when the creative hand of the poet, in the great actor, restores him to the use of his faculties!

Mrs. Cibber,[2] the most pathetic of all actresses, was the only Cordelia of excellence. The discovery of Lear, in prison, sleeping with his head on her lap, his hand closed in hers, whose expressive look spoke more than the most eloquent language, raised the most sympathising emotions.

1. **Reynolds**, Sir Joshua (1732–92), portrait painter who in 1764 founded a Literary Club with Garrick and other distinguished figures as members. He painted Garrick several times.

2. **Cibber**, Mrs Susanna (1714–66), sister of the composer Thomas Arne (1710–78), actress and singer, married Theophilus Cibber as his second wife in 1734. A fine painting of her by Van Bleeck in the role of Cordelia is in the Paul Mellon Collection.

[1774–5], Georg Christoph Lichtenberg (1742–99) on David Garrick as Hamlet in his own adaptation at the Theatre Royal, Drury Lane, London, from the *Deutsches Museum*, translated in *Lichtenberg's Visits to England*, edited by M. L. Mare and W. H. Quarrell (Oxford, 1938), pp. 9–11, 15–17.

GARRICK first played Hamlet in 1742, the year following his London début, with Peg Woffington as Ophelia, and continued in the role until his retirement, in 1776.

Georg Lichtenberg, German scientist and philosopher, paid two visits to England towards the end of Garrick's career, in 1770 and 1774–5; his accounts of visits to the theatre in letters written in October and November 1775 for publication in a literary periodical, the *Deutsches Museum*, provide some of the most vivid and detailed descriptions of individual stretches of action in Shakespearian performances ever written. They may be supplemented by entries from Lichtenberg's diary for 2 and 12 December 1774, on which the letters are based, translated with a commentary by R. B. Sutton, 'Further Evidence of David Garrick's Portrayal of Hamlet from the Diary of Georg Christoph Lichtenberg', *Theatre Notebook*, 50 (1996), pp. 8–14.

HAMLET appears in a black dress, the only one in the whole court, alas! still worn for his poor father, who has been dead scarce a couple of months. Horatio and Marcellus, in uniform, are with him, and they are awaiting the ghost; Hamlet has folded his arms under his cloak and pulled his hat down over his eyes; it is a cold night and just twelve o'clock; the theatre is darkened, and the whole audience of some thousands are as quiet, and their faces as motionless, as though they were painted on the walls of the theatre; even from the farthest end of the playhouse one could hear a pin drop. Suddenly, as Hamlet moves towards the back of the stage slightly to the left and turns his back on the audience, Horatio starts, and saying: 'Look, my lord, it comes,' points to the right, where the ghost has already appeared and stands motionless, before anyone is aware of him. At these words Garrick turns sharply and at the same moment staggers back two or three paces with his knees giving way under him; his hat falls to the ground and both his arms, especially the left, are stretched out nearly to their full length, with the hands as high as his head, the right arm more bent and the hand lower, and the fingers apart; his mouth is open: thus he stands rooted to the spot, with legs apart, but no loss of dignity, supported by his friends, who are better acquainted with the apparition and fear lest he should collapse. His whole demeanour is so expressive of terror that it made my flesh creep even before he began to speak. The almost terror-struck silence of the audience, which preceded this appearance and filled one with a sense of insecurity, probably did much to enhance this effect. At last he speaks, not at the beginning, but at the end of a breath, with a trembling voice: 'Angels and ministers of grace defend us!' words which supply anything this scene may lack and make it one of the greatest and most terrible which will ever be played on any stage. The ghost beckons to him; I wish you could see him, with eyes fixed on the ghost, though he is speaking to his companions, freeing himself from their restraining hands, as they warn him not to follow and hold him back. But at length, when they have tried his patience too far, he turns his face towards them, tears himself with great violence from their grasp, and draws his sword on them with a swiftness that makes one shudder, saying: 'By Heaven! I'll make a ghost of him that lets me.' That is enough for them. Then he stands with his sword upon guard against the spectre, saying: 'Go on, I'll follow thee,' and the ghost goes off the stage. Hamlet still remains motionless, his sword held out so as to make him keep his distance, and at length, when the spectator can no longer see the ghost, he begins slowly to follow him, now standing still and then going on, with sword still upon guard, eyes fixed on the ghost, hair disordered, and out of breath, until he too is lost to sight. You can well imagine what loud applause accompanies this exit. It begins as soon as the ghost goes off the stage and lasts until Hamlet also disappears. What an amazing triumph it is. One might think that such applause in one of the first playhouses in the world and from an audience of the greatest sensibility would fan into flame every spark of dramatic genius in a spectator. But then one perceives that to act like Garrick and to write like Shakespeare are the effects of very deep-seated causes. They are certainly imitated; not they, but rather their phantom self, created by the imitator according to the measure of his own powers. He often attains to and even surpasses this phantom, and nevertheless falls far short of the true original. The house-painter thinks his work as perfect as, or even more so than that of the artist. Not every player who can always command the applause of a couple of hundred people or so is on that account a Garrick; and not every writer who has learnt the trick of blabbing a few so-called secrets of human nature in archaic prose, outraging language and propriety by his bombast, is on that account a Shakespeare.

The ghost was played by Mr. Bransby.[1] He looked, in truth, very fine, clad from head to foot in armour, for which a suit of steel-blue satin did duty; even his face is hidden, except for his pallid nose and a little to either side of it....

In the excellent soliloquy: 'O that this too, too solid flesh would melt,' &c., he again applies, to make use of astronomical terms, a number of small equations, by which he heightens the actions of an average man, giving them individuality by touches of truth and exactitude. Garrick is completely overcome by tears of grief, felt with only too good cause, for a virtuous father and on account of a light-minded mother, who not only wears no mourning, but feels no sorrow, at a time when all the toadies should still be wearing black; tears which flow all the more unrestrainedly, perhaps, since they are the sole relief of an upright heart in such a conflict of warring duties. The last of the words: 'So excellent a King', is utterly lost; one catches it only from the movement of the mouth, which quivers and shuts tight immediately afterwards, so as to restrain the all too distinct expression of grief on the lips, which could easily tremble with unmanly emotion. This manner of shedding tears, which betrays both the heavy burden of grief on his heart and the manly spirit which suffers under it, is irresistibly poignant. But as soon as one is attuned to Shakespeare's mind, each word, as Garrick speaks it, pierces one's heart. At the end of the soliloquy his grief is mingled with righteous anger, and on one occasion, when he brings his arm down sharply in a single movement, so as to lend emphasis to one word of invective, his voice is choked with emotion, when the audience is not expecting it, and he can only bring out this word after some moments amidst his tears. At this point I and my neighbour, to whom I had not as yet uttered a word, looked at each other and spoke. It was quite irresistible.

The famous soliloquy: 'To be or not to be,' &c., does not naturally make the same impression on the auditor, and cannot, in truth, do so. But it produces an infinitely greater effect than could be expected of an argument on suicide and death in a tragedy; and this is because a large part of the audience not only knows it by heart as well as they do the Lord's Prayer, but listens to it, so to speak, as if it were a Lord's Prayer, not indeed with the profound reflections which accompany our sacred prayer, but with a sense of solemnity and awe, of which some one who does not know England can have no conception. In this island Shakespeare is not only famous, but holy; his moral maxims are heard everywhere; I myself heard them quoted in Parliament on 7 February,[2] a day of importance. In this way his name is entwined with most solemn thoughts; people sing of him and from his works, and thus a large number of English children know him before they have learnt their A.B.C. and creed.

Hamlet, who is in mourning, as I have already reminded you, appears here, having already begun to feign madness, with his thick hair dishevelled and a lock hanging over one shoulder; one of his black stockings has slipped down so as to show his white socks, and a loop of his red garter is hanging down beyond the middle of the calf. Thus he comes on to the stage sunk in contemplation, his chin resting on his right hand, and his right elbow on his left, and gazes solemnly downwards. And then, removing his right hand from his chin, but, if I remember right, still supporting it with his left hand, he speaks the words 'To be or not to be,' &c., softly, though, on account of the absolute silence (not because of some particular talent of the man's, as they say even in some of the newspapers), they are audible everywhere.

Here I must make a short comment on the language. In the fourth line of this soliloquy some suggest[3] the reading 'against assailing troubles', instead of 'against a sea of troubles', because one cannot take arms against the sea. In spite of this Mr. Garrick says 'against a sea of troubles'. I merely quote Garrick's opinion, and do not go into the question of the authorities he follows. It would not be easy to do so here, and you can settle the matter in a moment in the Library at Göttingen.

Ophelia's dress, likewise, after she has lost her reason, is disordered, as far as propriety allows. She was played by Mrs. Smith,[4] a young woman and a good singer, who is admirably suited to the part (although she has not enough vivacity for several others that she takes). Her long flaxen hair hung partly down her back, and partly over her shoulders; in her left hand she held a bunch of loose straw, and her whole demeanour in her madness was as gentle as the passion which caused it. The songs, which she sang charmingly, were fraught with such plaintive and tender melancholy that I fancied that I could still hear them far into the night, when I was alone. Shakespeare makes this whole scene so moving as to cause one actual pain and leave a sore place in the heart, which goes on throbbing until one could wish never to have seen poor, unhappy Ophelia. I wish that Voltaire[5] might have been here and heard Mrs. Smith's interpretation of Shakespeare! This remarkable man would, I believe, almost have repented of what he said against these scenes. I am sure that if I had written any such thing—of course with the wit of a Voltaire and his influence on weak minds—and had afterwards seen what I have been seeing, I should, forsooth, have asked the forgiveness of Shakespeare's spirit in the newspapers. Voltaire has, however, gained one victory at Drury Lane. The gravediggers' scene is omitted. They retain it at Covent Garden. Garrick should not have done this. To represent so ancient and superb a piece in all its characteristic rude vigour in these insipid times, when even in this country the language of nature is beginning to yield to fine phrases and conventional twaddle, might have arrested this decline, even if it could not put a stop to it.

I must pass by some of the finest scenes, as, for instance, that in which he instructs the players, and the one where he pierces his mother's heart by his comparison of his uncle and his father, and the ghost appears forthwith; one blow after another, before one has had time to recover from the first. But one could go on for ever, so I will here conclude the tragedy and give you only a short farce....

1. **Bransby**, Astley (died 1789), a tall actor, first heard of in 1745, who played many supporting roles at Drury Lane and, during 1749–53, Covent Garden. He retired in 1777.

2. **7 February**. On this date in 1775 the House of Lords debated the proposition that an Address on the situation in North America should be sent by both houses to George III; in effect this was a request that force be used against the rebellious colonies, and what was perceived as a declaration of war was hotly debated. Lord Camden is reported as saying 'When compared with several of the great powers of Europe, England, in the words of Shakespeare, being no more than a bird's nest floating on a pool.'

3. **some suggest**. The reading originated with Sir Thomas Hanmer, whose Oxford edition appeared in 1743–44.

4. **Smith**, Mrs Theodore, Maria, née Harris (*fl.* 1772–96), singer and actress. (In its entry for her the *Actors' Dictionary* states that Lichtenberg is writing 'of the 23 October 1775 performance . . . with William "Gentleman" Smith in the title role', but his remarks clearly refer to Garrick.)

5. **Voltaire** (François-Marie Arouet, 1694–1778). The French philosopher published a harsh criticism (reprinted in the New Variorum edition, ed. H. H. Furness, 2 vols., 1877, ii. 381), of *Hamlet*, which offended his neoclassical critical principles, describing it as 'a vulgar and barbarous drama', while conceding that it contains 'some sublime passages, worthy of the greatest genius'. He particularly disapproved of the gravediggers.

---

22 May 1776, Henry Bate (Sir Henry Bate Dudley, 1745–1824), on David Garrick as Lear at the Theatre Royal, Drury Lane, London, from *The Morning Post*, reprinted by James Agate in *The English Dramatic Critics 1660–1932* (n.d. [1932]), p. 61.

HENRY BATE DUDLEY, journalist, man-about-town, librettist and clergyman, known as 'The Fighting Parson', was a close friend of Garrick and editor of *The Morning Post* at the time he wrote this piece. The emotionalism of both audience and performers was no doubt enhanced by the knowledge that this was Garrick's farewell season—he was to play Lear only once more—but additional testimony to the greatness of this particular performance comes from the theatre journal of William Hopkins, the prompter at Drury Lane, who noted that 'Human nature cannot arrive at greater excellence in acting than Mr Garrick was possessed of this night. All words must fall far short of what he did and none but his spectators can have an idea of how great he was—the applause was unbounded.'

MR. GARRICK last night repeated his capital representation of Lear, and in consequence thereof drew together a most crowded audience, principally composed of the first people of distinction, who seem resolved to let no opportunity escape them of enjoying the remainder of his inimitable performances. However difficult it may be to prevail upon the absentees to admit it, yet it will be readily confessed by those who were fortunate enough to be present last night, that he never appeared so great in the character before.

The curse at the close of the first act,—his phrenetic appeal to heaven at the end of the second on Regan's ingratitude, were two such enthusiastic scenes of human exertion, that they caused a kind of momentary petrefaction through the house, which he soon dissolved as universally into tears.—Even the unfeeling Regan and Goneril, forgetful of their characteristic cruelty, played through the whole of their parts with aching bosoms and streaming eyes.—In a word, we never saw before so exquisite a theatrical performance, or one so loudly and universally applauded.

[*c*.1790–6], Charles Lamb (1775–1834) on Robert Bensley (1742–1817) as Malvolio and James William Dodd (?1740–96) as Sir Andrew Aguecheek in *Twelfth Night*, from 'On Some of the Old Actors', reprinted from *The London Magazine* (1822) in his *Essays of Elia* (1823).

LAMB was never a regular drama critic but wrote from time to time about theatrical topics. Although Malvolio was one of Bensley's most successful parts, Lamb's eloquent account of his performance seems to be heavily coloured by his own conception of the role. Dodd, who specialized in foppish parts, frequently played Sir Andrew with great success. Lamb, a versatile man of letters, is here writing nostalgically about performances he had seen in the past—Dodd had died, and Bensley retired, in 1796, when the critic was only twenty-one years old.

THE part of Malvolio, in the *Twelfth Night*, was performed by Bensley, with a richness and a dignity, of which (to judge from some recent castings of that character) the very tradition must be worn out from the stage. No manager in those days would have dreamed of giving it to Mr. Baddeley,[1] or Mr. Parsons;[2] when Bensley was occasionally absent from the theatre, John Kemble[3] thought it no derogation to succeed to the part. Malvolio is not essentially ludicrous. He becomes comic but by accident. He is cold, austere, repelling; but dignified, consistent, and, for what appears, rather of an over-stretched morality. Maria describes him as a sort of Puritan; and he might have worn his gold chain with honour in one of our old round-head families, in the service of a Lambert,[4] or a Lady Fairfax.[5] But his morality and his manners are misplaced in Illyria. He is opposed to the proper *levities* of the piece, and falls in the unequal contest. Still his pride, or his gravity (call it which you will) is inherent, and native to the man, not mock or affected, which latter only are the fit objects to excite laughter. His quality is at the best unlovely, but neither buffoon nor contemptible. His bearing is lofty, a little above his station, but probably not much above his deserts. We see no reason why he should not have been brave, honourable, accomplished. His careless committal of the ring to the ground (which he was commissioned to restore to Cesario), bespeaks a generosity of birth and feeling. His dialect on all occasions is that of a gentleman, and a man of education. We must not confound him with the eternal old, low steward of comedy. He is master of the household to a great Princess; a dignity probably conferred upon him for other respects than age or length of service. Olivia, at the first indication of his supposed madness, declares that she 'would not have him miscarry for half of her dowry.' Does this look as if the character was meant to appear little or insignificant? Once, indeed, she accuses him to his face—of what?—of being 'sick of self-love,'—but with a gentleness and considerateness which could not have been, if she had not thought that this particular infirmity shaded some virtues. His rebuke to the knight, and his sottish revellers, is sensible and spirited; and when we take into consideration the unprotected condition of his mistress, and the strict regard with which her state of real or dissembled mourning would draw the eyes of the world upon her house-affairs, Malvolio might feel the honour of the family in some sort in his keeping; as it appears not that Olivia had any more brothers, or kinsmen, to look to it—for Sir Toby had dropped all such nice respects at the buttery hatch. That Malvolio was meant to be represented as possessing estimable qualities, the expression of the Duke in his anxiety to have him reconciled, almost infers. 'Pursue him, and entreat him to a peace.' Even in his abused state of chains and darkness, a sort of greatness seems never to desert him. He argues highly and well with the supposed Sir Topas, and philosophises gallantly upon his straw. There must have been some shadow of worth about the man; he must have been something more than a mere vapour—a thing of straw, or Jack in office—before Fabian and Maria could have ventured sending him upon a courting-errand to Olivia. There was some consonancy (as he would say) in the undertaking, or the jest would have been too bold even for that house of misrule.

Bensley, accordingly, threw over the part an air of Spanish loftiness. He looked, spake, and moved like an old Castilian. He was starch, spruce, opinionated, but his superstructure of pride seemed bottomed upon a sense of worth. There was something in it beyond the coxcomb. It was big and swelling, but you could not be sure that it was hollow. You might wish to see it taken down, but you felt that it was upon an elevation. He was magnificent from the outset; but when the decent sobrieties of the character began to give way, and the poison of self-love, in his conceit of the Countess's affection, gradually to work, you would have thought that the hero of La Mancha[6] in person stood before you. How he went smiling to himself! with what ineffable carelessness would he twirl his gold chain! what a dream it was! you were infected with the illusion, and did not wish that it should be removed! you had no room for laughter! if an unseasonable reflection of morality obtruded itself, it was a deep sense of the pitiable infirmity of man's nature, that can lay him open to such frenzies—but in truth you rather admired than pitied the lunacy while it lasted—you felt that an hour of such mistake was worth an age with the eyes open. Who would not wish to live but for a day in the conceit of such a lady's love as Olivia? Why, the Duke would have given his principality but for a quarter of a minute, sleeping or waking, to have been so deluded. The man seemed to tread upon air, to taste manna, to walk with his head in the clouds, to mate Hyperion.[7] O! shake not the castles of his pride— endure yet for a season bright moments of confidence—'stand still ye watches of the element,'[8] that Malvolio may be still in fancy fair Olivia's lord—but fate and retribution say no—I hear the mischievous titter of Maria—the witty taunts of Sir Toby—the still more insupportable triumph of the foolish knight—the counterfeit Sir Topas is unmasked—and 'thus the whirligig of time,' as the true clown hath it, 'brings in his revenges.' I confess that I never saw the catastrophe of this character, while Bensley played it, without a kind of tragic interest. There was good foolery too. Few now remember Dodd. What an Aguecheek the stage lost in him! Lovegrove,[9] who came nearest to the old actors, revived the character some few seasons ago, and made it sufficiently grotesque; but Dodd was *it*, as it came out of nature's hands. It might be said to remain *in puris naturalibus*. In expressing slowness of apprehension this actor surpassed all others. You could see the first dawn of an idea stealing slowly over his countenance, climbing up by little and little, with a painful process, till it cleared up at last to the fulness of a twilight conception— its highest meridian. He seemed to keep back his intellect, as some have had the power to retard their pulsation. The balloon takes less time in filling, than it took to cover the expansion of his broad moony face over all its quarters with expression. A glimmer of understanding would appear in a corner of his eye, and for lack of fuel go out again. A part of his forehead would catch a little intelligence, and be a long time in communicating it to the remainder.

1. **Baddeley**, Robert (1733–94), a popular actor who bequeathed £100 to provide actors at Drury Lane with cakes and ale on 12 November, a custom still observed.

2. **Parsons**, William (1736–95), a popular actor who appeared in many roles at Drury Lane over thirty-two seasons.

3. **Kemble**, John Philip (1757–1823); the great actor first played Malvolio in London during the 1788–9 season at Drury Lane.

4. **Lambert**, John (1619–83), soldier, commissary-general of Sir Thomas Fairfax's army in 1644, prominent as a supporter of Oliver Cromwell.

5. **Lady Fairfax** (Anne Vere), wife of Sir Thomas.

6. **hero of La Mancha**, Don Quixote, hero of the novel (1605) by Miguel de Cervantes (1547–1616).

7. **Hyperion**, in Greek myth, a Titan, father of the sun, or the sun itself.

8. **'stand still ye watches of the element'**, from *Edward II* by Christopher Marlowe (1564–93), 5.1.66.

9. **Lovegrove**, William (1778–1816), actor who joined the Drury Lane company in 1810.

[1789–*c*.1817], Sir Walter Scott (1771–1832) on John Philip Kemble (1757–1823) as Macbeth (pp. 218–19) and on Coriolanus' death scene (p. 224); from Scott's review of James Boaden's *Memoirs of the Life of John Philip Kemble*, in *The Quarterly Review*, 34 (June, 1826), pp. 196–248.

JOHN PHILIP KEMBLE, actor, manager, and play adapter, was the leading figure of the English theatre between the death of Garrick and the emergence of Edmund Kean, whose fiery genius threw him into eclipse in his final years. Kemble managed Drury Lane from 1788 to 1802, and Covent Garden from 1803 till he retired in 1817. He often played Macbeth with his sister, Sarah Siddons, as his Lady. Sir Walter Scott was a favourite drinking companion who helped him to write a farewell speech in verse, delivered after his last performance, as Macbeth, in Edinburgh during his final season. Scott's long review of Boaden's biography gave him the opportunity to assess the actor's qualitities with affectionate but judicious nostalgia. He also provides interesting comments on changes in production methods. The concluding anecdote is told elsewhere of more than one actor (W. Clark Russell, *Representative Actors* (1869), pp. 178–9.

IN Lear, Kemble must, we think, have been decidedly inferior to Garrick.[1] In Hamlet he was not more than the equal of Garrick, and a most formidable rival arose in his own time in Charles Young.[2] But in Macbeth, Kemble has been as yet unapproachable; nor can we conceive that the bold and effective manner of Garrick, touching on the broad points of the character with a hand however vigorous, could at all compare with Kemble's exquisitely and minutely elaborate delineation of guilty ambition, drawn on from crime to crime, while the avenging furies at once scourge him for former guilt, and urge him to further enormities. We can never forget the rueful horror of his look, which by strong exertion he endeavours to conceal, when on the morning succeeding the murder he receives Lennox and Macduff in the ante-chamber of Duncan. His efforts to appear composed, his endeavours to assume the attitude and appearance of one listening to Lennox's account of the external terrors of the night, while in fact he is expecting the alarm to arise within the royal apartment, formed a most astonishing piece of playing. Kemble's countenance seemed altered by the sense of internal horror, and had a cast of that of Count Ugolino[3] in the dungeon, as painted by Reynolds.[4] When Macbeth felt himself obliged to turn towards Lennox and reply to what he had been saying, you saw him, like a man awaking from a fit of absence, endeavour to recollect at least the general tenor of what had been said, and it was some time ere he could bring out the general reply, ''Twas a rough night.' Those who have had the good fortune to see Kemble and Mrs. Siddons[5] in Macbeth and his lady, may be satisfied they have witnessed the highest perfection of the dramatic art....

When he condescended—we must give it that term—to play the part of Percy in the Castle Spectre,[6] he used, in the scene where Percy drops back on the couch, just as when rising to make his spring from the window, to discover all the address and activity of the most able panto-mimist. The same command of muscle and limb was far more strikingly exemplified when the Volscian assassins approaching him from behind in the very midst of the triumphant vaunt of his repeated victories over their countrymen, seemed to pass their swords through the body of Coriolanus. There was no precaution, no support; in the midst of the exclamation against Tullus Aufidius, he dropped as dead and as flat on the stage as if the swords had really met within his body. We have repeatedly heard screams from the female part of the audience when he presented this scene, which had the most striking resemblance to actual and instant death we ever witnessed, and saved all that rolling, gasping and groaning which generally takes place in our theatres, to the scandal of all foreigners, until at length a stout fellow, exhausted by his apparent efforts and agonies, lies on his back, puffing like a grampus, and is to be received as a heroic corpse....

During his whole life Kemble was intent on improving, by all means which occurred, the accuracy of the dresses which he wore while in character. Macbeth was one of the first plays in which the better system of costume was adopted, and he wore the highland dress, as old Macklin[7] had done before him. Many years afterwards he was delighted when, with our own critical hands, which have plucked many a plume besides, we divested his bonnet of sundry huge bunches of black feathers which made it look like an undertaker's cushion, and replaced them with the single broad quill feather of an eagle sloping across his noble brow; he told us afterwards that the change was worth to him three distinct rounds of applause as he came forwards in this improved and more genuine head-gear.

With the subject of dress, modes of disposing and managing the scenes are naturally connected; and here also, Kemble, jealous of the dignity of his art, called in the assistance of able artists, and improved in a most wonderful degree the appearance of the stage and the general effect of the piece in representation. Yet, in our opinion, the Muse of Painting should be on the stage the handmaid not the rival of her sisters of the drama. Each art should retain its due predominance within its own proper region. Let the scenery be as well painted and made as impressive as a moderate sized stage will afford: but when the roof is raised to give the scene-painter room to pile Pelion upon Ossa; when the stage is widened that his forests may be extended, or deepened that his oceans may flow in space apparently interminable, the manager who commands these decorations is leaving his proper duty, and altering entirely the purpose of the stage. Meantime, as the dresses ought to be suited to the time and country, the landscape and architecture should be equally coherent. Means may, besides, be discovered from time to time tending to render the scenic deception more effective, and the introduction of such must be advantageous, provided always that this part of theatrical business be kept in due subordination to that which is strictly dramatic.

Processions and decorations belong to the same province as scenes and dresses, and should be heedfully attended to, but at the same time kept under, that they may relieve the action of the scene instead of shouldering aside the dramatic interest. Kemble carried his love of splendour rather to the extreme, though what he introduced was generally tasteful and splendid. He sacrificed perhaps his own opinion to the humour of the audience, and to the tempting facilities which the size of the modern theatres afford for what is called spectacle.

Macbeth was, as has been hinted, one of the first of the old stock plays which he brought forward in this splendid manner, and in many respects it was admirably suited for such a purpose. The distant approach of Macbeth's army, as well as the apparitions of the cavern, were very well managed. By causing the descendants of the murdered thane to pass behind a screen of black crape, he diminished their corporeal appearance, and emulated the noble lines of Collins:

> 'From thence he sung how, mid his bold design,
>   Before the Scot afflicted and aghast,
> The shadowy kings of Banquo's fated line
>   Through the dark cave in gleamy pageant passed.'[8]

Things occurred, however, even in this fine spectacle, which show that matters of show and pageantry have their own peculiar risques. At first Kemble had introduced four bands of children, who rushed on the stage at the invocation of the witches, to represent the

> 'Black spirits and white,
> Blue spirits and grey.'

There was perhaps little taste in rendering these aërial beings visible to the bodily eye, especially when the same manager had made an attempt to banish even the spectre of Banquo. But he was obliged to discard his imps for an especial reason. Mr. Kelly[9] informs us that, egged on, and encouraged by one of their number, a blackeyed urchin, ycleped *Edmund Kean*,[10] they made such confusion on the stage that Kemble was fain to dismiss them to the elements. Another failure we ourselves witnessed—a whimsical failure—in this piece, which we may mention as a warning to those managers who put too much faith in such mechanical aids. It occurred when the armed head ought to have arisen, but when, though the trap-door gaped, no apparition arose. The galleries began to hiss; whereupon the scene-shifters in the cellarage, redoubling their exertions, and overcoming, perforce, the obstinacy of the screw which was to raise the trap, fairly, out of too great and urgent zeal, overdid their business, and produced before the audience, at full length, the apparition of a stout man, his head and shoulders arrayed in antique helmet and plate, while the rest of his person was humbly attired after the manner of a fifth-rate performer of these degenerate days,—that is to say, in a dimity waistcoat, nankeen breeches, and a very dirty pair of cotton stockings. To complete the absurdity, the poor man had been so hastily promoted that he could not keep his feet, but prostrated himself on his nose before the audience, to whom he was so unexpectedly introduced.

The effect of this accident was not recovered during the whole evening, though the play was performed with transcendant ability.

1. **Garrick**, David. See p. 20.

2. **Young**, Charles. See p. 37.

3. **Ugolino**, Count Ugolino della Gherardesca (*c.*1220–89), Pisan nobleman. Dante, in the *Divine Comedy, Inferno*, Canto xxxiii, tells how Ugolino and his four sons were imprisoned and died in horrific circumstances. Reynolds's painting of 1774 shows the Count with staring eyes, transfixed with horror.

4. **Reynolds**, Sir Joshua. See p. 23.

5. **Siddons**, Mrs (Sarah). See p. 37.

6. **Castle Spectre**, The, a popular Gothic melodrama by Matthew 'Monk' Lewis (1775–1818) in which Kemble appeared at Drury Lane in spite of regarding it as 'a vile thing', and in which he had a spectacular fall.

7. **Macklin**, Charles (*c.*1697–1797), Irish actor and playwright whose best-known role was Shylock.

8. **Collins**, William (1721–59), pre-Romantic poet. The quotation is from his 'Ode on the Popular Superstitions of the Highlands of Scotland, Considered as the Subject of Poetry', ll. 179–82.

9. **Kelly**, Michael (?1762–1826), singer and composer who was in charge of the music for Kemble's *Macbeth* and whose delightful *Reminiscences* (1826) Scott reviews along with Boaden's biography of Kemble.

10. **Kean**, Edmund. See p. 38.

[1789–*c*.1812], Julian Charles Young (died 1873) on J. P. Kemble as Coriolanus and Sarah Siddons (1755–1831) as Volumnia in *Coriolanus* at the Theatre Royal, Drury Lane, London, from his *Memoirs of Charles Mayne Young* (1840), pp. 40–1.

THE first performances of Kemble's version of *Coriolanus* were given at Drury Lane in 1789, with great success. Kemble based his version on one by Thomas Sheridan which borrowed from a play on the same subject by James Thomson. The title role, in which Kemble was finely portrayed by Sir Thomas Lawrence (see Pl. 2), was especially suited to his talents as a heroic actor in classical parts, and Volumnia gave great opportunities, too, to Sarah Siddons, who played with him on these and later occasions. The Reverend Julian Charles Young (vicar of Ilmington, Warks.), son of one of Kemble's disciples, the actor Charles Mayne Young (1777–1856), offers his account of Mrs Siddons's performance in support of what he calls his 'theory of the mute eloquence of gait and movement', remarking that his father 'used to speak in terms of almost wanton admiration, of a boldly conceived point he saw Mrs Siddons once make, while playing the comparatively inferior part of Volumnia for her brother's benefit'.

IN the second scene of the second act of *Coriolanus*, after the victory of the battle of Corioli, an ovation in honour of the victor was introduced with great and imposing effect by John Kemble.[1] On reference to the stage directions of my father's interleaved copy, I find that no fewer than 240 persons marched, in stately procession across the stage. In addition to the recognised dramatis personae, thirty-five in number, there were vestals, and lictors with their fasces, and soldiers with the spolia opima, and sword-bearers, and standard-bearers, and cup-bearers, and senators, and silver eagle-bearers, with the S.P.Q.R. upon them, and trumpeters, and drummers, and priests, and dancing-girls, &c., &c.

Now, in this procession, and as one of the central figures in it, Mrs. Siddons had to walk. Had she been content to follow in the beaten track of her predecessors in the part, she would have marched across the stage, from right to left, with the solemn, stately, almost funeral, step conventional. But, at the time, as she often did, she forgot her own identity. She was no longer Sarah Siddons, tied down to the directions of the prompter's book—or trammelled by old traditions—she was Volumnia, the proud mother of a proud son and conquering hero. So that, when it was time for her to come on, instead of dropping each foot at equi-distance in its place, with mechanical exactitude, and in cadence subservient to the orchestra; deaf to the guidance of her woman's ear, but sensitive to the throbbings of her haughty mother's heart, with flashing eye and proudest smile, and head erect, and hands pressed firmly on her bosom, as if to repress by manual force its triumphant swellings, she towered above all around, and rolled, and almost reeled across the stage; her very soul, as it were, dilating, and rioting in its exultation; until her action lost all grace, and, yet, became so true to nature, so picturesque, and so descriptive, that pit and gallery sprang to their feet electrified by the transcendent execution of an original conception.

1. **Kemble,** John. See p. 33.

꧁꧂

15 February 1814, William Hazlitt (1778–1830) on Edmund Kean (1787 or 1789–1833) as Richard III at the Theatre Royal, Drury Lane, London, from *The Morning Chronicle*; reprinted in e.g. *Hazlitt on Theatre*, ed. William Archer and Robert Lowe (1895; repr. New York, n.d. [1957]), pp. 3–5.

EDMUND KEAN made a sensational London debut at Drury Lane as Shylock in *The Merchant of Venice* on 26 January 1814. Though the audience was sparse it included the versatile man of letters William Hazlitt who wrote enthusiastically about the performance in *The Morning Chronicle*. He wrote later 'I had been told to give as favourable an account as I could: I gave a true one. I am not one of those who, when they see the sun breaking from behind a cloud, stop to ask others whether it is the moon. Mr Kean's appearance was the first gleam of genius breaking athwart the gloom of the stage.' This may seem unfair to Kean's immediate predecessors, but Kean's vivid, direct, apparently spontaneous style came as a contrast to the declamatory manner of actors of the school of Kemble, whose genius Hazlitt could also appreciate while welcoming a breaking of the mould. Kean's style had in fact been anticipated by the brilliant but erratic George Frederick Cooke (1756–1811). Hazlitt's account of Kean's Richard III, in the Colley Cibber adaptation, has become one of the most famous pieces of theatre criticism.

M R. KEAN'S manner of acting this part has one peculiar advantage; it is entirely his own, without any traces of imitation of any other actor. He stands upon his own ground, and he stands firm upon it. Almost every scene had the stamp and freshness of nature. The excellences and defects of his performance were in general the same as those which he discovered in Shylock; though, as the character of Richard is the most difficult, so we think he displayed most power in it. It is possible to form a higher conception of this character (we do not mean from seeing other actors, but from reading Shakespeare) than that given by this very admirable tragedian; but we cannot imagine any character represented with greater distinctness and precision, more perfectly *articulated* in every part. Perhaps, indeed, there is too much of this; for we sometimes thought he failed, even from an exuberance of talent, and dissipated the impression of the character by the variety of his resources. To be perfect, it should have a little more solidity, depth, sustained, and impassioned feeling, with somewhat less brilliancy, with fewer glancing lights, pointed transitions, and pantomimic evolutions.

The Richard of Shakespeare is towering and lofty, as well as aspiring; equally impetuous and commanding; haughty, violent, and subtle; bold and treacherous; confident in his strength, as well as in his cunning; raised high by his birth, and higher by his genius and his crimes; a royal usurper, a princely hypocrite, a tyrant and a murderer of the House of Plantagenet.

> But I was born so high;
> Our airy buildeth in the cedar's top,
> And dallies with the wind, and scorns the sun.

The idea conveyed in these lines (which are omitted in the miserable medley acted for *Richard III*) is never lost sight of by Shakespeare, and should not be out of the actor's mind for a moment. The restless and sanguinary Richard is not a man striving to be great, but to be greater than he is; conscious of his strength of will, his powers of intellect, his daring courage, his elevated station, and making use of these advantages, as giving him both the means and the pretext to commit unheard-of crimes, and to shield himself from remorse and infamy.

If Mr. Kean does not completely succeed in concentrating all the lines of the character, as drawn by Shakespeare, he gives an animation, vigour, and relief to the part, which we have never seen surpassed. He is more refined than Cooke; more bold, varied, and original than Kemble,[1] in the same character. In some parts, however, we thought him deficient in dignity; and particularly in the scenes of state business, there was not a sufficient air of artificial authority. The fine assumption of condescending superiority, after he is made king—'Stand all apart—Cousin of Buckingham,' &c., was not given with the effect which it might have received. There was also at times a sort of tip-toe elevation, an enthusiastic rapture in his expectations of obtaining the crown, instead of a gloating expression of sullen delight, as if he already clutched the bauble, and held it within his grasp. This was the precise expression which Mr. Kean gave with so much effect to the part where he says that he already feels

> The golden rigol bind his brows.

In one who *dares* so much, there is little indeed to blame. The only two things which appeared to us decidedly objectionable, were the sudden letting down of his voice when he says of Hastings, 'Chop off his head,'[2] and the action of putting his hands behind him, in listening to Buckingham's account of his reception by the citizens. His courtship scene with Lady Anne was an admirable exhibition of smooth and smiling villainy. The progress of wily adulation, of encroaching humility, was finely marked throughout by the action, voice, and eye. He seemed, like the first tempter, to approach his prey, certain of the event, and as if success had smoothed the way before him. We remember Mr. Cooke's manner of representing this scene was more violent, hurried, and full of anxious uncertainty. This, though more natural in general, was, we think, less in character. Richard should woo, not as a lover, but as an actor—to show his mental superiority, and power to make others the playthings of his will. Mr. Kean's attitude in leaning against the side of the stage before he comes forward in this scene, was one of the most graceful and striking we remember to have seen. It would have done for Titian[3] to paint. The opening scene in which Richard descants on his own deformity, was conceived with perfect truth and character, and delivered in a fine and varied tone of natural recitation. Mr. Kean did equal justice to the beautiful description of the camps the night before the battle, though, in consequence of his hoarseness, he was obliged to repeat the whole passage in an under-key. His manner of bidding his friends good-night, and his pausing with the point of his sword drawn slowly backward and forward on the ground, before he retires to his tent, received shouts of applause. He gave to all the busy scenes of the play the greatest animation and effect. He filled every part of the stage. The concluding scene, in which he is killed by Richmond, was the most brilliant. He fought like one drunk with wounds: and the attitude in which he stands with his hands stretched out, after his sword is taken from him, had a preternatural and terrific grandeur, as if his will could not be disarmed, and the very phantoms of his despair had a withering power.

1. **Kemble,** John. See p. 33.
2. **'Chop off his head'** (by Cibber).
3. **Titian** (?1490–1576), the great Italian painter.

---

14 **March 1814,** William Hazlitt on Edmund Kean as Hamlet at the Theatre Royal, Drury Lane, London, from the *Morning Chronicle*, reprinted in *Hazlitt on Theatre*, ed. William Archer and Robert Lowe (1895; repr. New York, n.d. [1957]), pp. 10–14.

IN the opening paragraphs, omitted here, Hazlitt writes in general terms of Shakespeare and of the play, remarking that, though 'This character is probably of all others the most difficult to personate on the stage', 'Mr Kean's representation of the character' which 'had the most brilliant success', 'was a most striking and animated rehearsal [i.e. rendition, performance] of the part.'

HIGH as Mr. Kean stood in our opinion before, we have no hesitation in saying that he stands higher in it (and, we think, will in that of the public), from the powers displayed in this last effort. If it was less perfect as a whole, there were parts in it of a higher cast of excellence than any part of his Richard. We will say at once in what we think his general delineation of the character wrong. It was too strong and pointed. There was often a severity, approaching to virulence, in the common observations and answers. There is nothing of this in Hamlet. He is, as it were, wrapped up in the cloud of his reflections, and only *thinks aloud*. There should, therefore, be no attempt to impress what he says upon others by any exaggeration of emphasis or manner, no talking *at* his hearers. There should be as much of the gentleman and scholar as possible infused into the part, and as little of the actor. A pensive air of sadness should sit unwillingly upon his brow, but no appearance of fixed and sullen gloom. He is full of 'weakness and melancholy,' but there is no harshness in his nature. Hamlet should be the most amiable of misanthropes. There is no one line in this play which should be spoken like any one line in Richard, yet Mr. Kean did not appear to us to keep the two characters always distinct. He was least happy in the last scene with Guildenstern and Rosencrantz. In some of these more familiar scenes, he displayed more energy than was requisite, and in others, where it would have been appropriate, did not rise equal to the exigency of the occasion. In particular, the scene with Laertes, where he leaps into the grave, and utters the exclamation, ''Tis I, Hamlet the Dane,' had not the tumultuous and overpowering effect we expected from it. To point out the defects of Mr. Kean's performance of the part, is a less grateful but a much shorter task than to enumerate the many striking beauties which he gave to it, both by the power of his action and by the true feeling of nature. His surprise when he first sees the Ghost, his eagerness and filial confidence in following it, the impressive pathos of his action and voice in addressing it, 'I'll call thee Hamlet, *Father*, Royal Dane,' were admirable.

Mr. Kean has introduced in this part a *new reading*, as it is called, which we think perfectly correct. In the scene where he breaks from his friends to obey the command of his father, he keeps his sword pointed behind him, to prevent them from following him, instead of holding it before him to protect him from the Ghost. The manner of his taking Guildenstern and Rosencrantz under each arm, under pretence of communicating his secret to them, when he only means to trifle with them, had the finest effect, and was, we conceive, exactly in the spirit of the character. So was the suppressed tone of irony in which he ridicules those who gave ducats for his uncle's picture, though they would 'make mouths at him' while his father lived. Whether the way in which Mr. Kean hesitates in repeating the first line of the speech in the interview with the player, and then, after several ineffectual attempts to recollect it, suddenly hurries on with it, 'The rugged Pyrrhus,' &c., is in perfect keeping, we have some doubts; but there was great ingenuity in the thought, and the spirit and life of the execution was beyond everything. Hamlet's speech in describing his own melancholy, his instructions to the players, and the soliloquy on death, were all delivered by Mr. Kean in a tone of fine, clear, and natural recitation. His pronunciation of the word 'contumely' in the last of these is, we apprehend, not authorised by custom, or by the metre.

Both the closet scene with his mother, and his remonstrances to Ophelia, were highly impressive. If there had been less vehemence of effort in the latter, it would not have lost any of its effect. But whatever nice faults might be found in this scene, they were amply redeemed by the manner of his coming back after he has gone to the extremity of the stage, from a pang of parting tenderness to press his lips to Ophelia's hand. It had an electrical effect on the house. It was the finest commentary that was ever made on Shakespeare. It explained the character at once (as he meant it), as one of disappointed hope, of bitter regret, of affection suspended, not obliterated, by the distractions of the scene around him! The manner in which Mr. Kean acted in the scene of the Play before the King and Queen was the most daring of any, and the force and animation which he gave to it cannot be too highly applauded. Its extreme boldness 'bordered on the verge of all we hate,'[1] and the effect it produced was a test of the extraordinary powers of this extraordinary actor.

1. **'bordered on the verge of all we hate'**, a misquotation of Epistle 2, 'To a Lady', of Alexander Pope's 'Moral Essays': 'Yet ne'er so sure our passion to create, | As when she touched the brink of all we hate' (ll. 51–2).

21 January 1816, William Hazlitt on *A Midsummer Night's Dream*, adapted by Frederic Reynolds (1764–1841) with music composed and arranged by Sir Henry Bishop , at the Theatre Royal, Covent Garden, London, from *The Examiner*, reprinted in *Hazlitt on Theatre*, ed. William Archer and Robert Lowe (1895; repr. New York, n.d. [1957]), pp. 73–6.

THE play was given in a musical and spectacular adaptation by Frederic Reynolds, who went on to produce similar quasi-operatic versions of several other comedies by Shakespeare. G. C. D. Odell describes *A Midsummer Night's Dream* in his *Shakespeare, from Betterton to Irving*, 2 vols. (New York, 1920), ii. 111–14. The theatre is illustrated in Pl. 3.

WE hope we have not been accessory to murder, in recommending a delightful poem to be converted into a dull pantomime; for such is the fate of the *Midsummer Night's Dream*. We have found to our cost, once for all, that the regions of fancy and the boards of Covent Garden are not the same thing. All that is fine in the play, was lost in the representation. The spirit was evaporated, the genius was fled; but the spectacle was fine: it was that which saved the play. Oh, ye scene-shifters, ye scene-painters, ye machinists and dressmakers, ye manufacturers of moon and stars that give no light, ye musical composers, ye men in the orchestra, fiddlers and trumpeters and players on the double drum and loud bassoon, rejoice! This is your triumph; it is not ours: and ye full-grown, well-fed, substantial, real fairies, Messieurs Treby, and Truman, and Atkins, and Misses Matthews, Carew, Burrell, and MacAlpine,[1] we shall remember you: we shall believe no more in the existence of your fantastic tribe. Flute the bellows-mender, Snug the joiner, Starveling the tailor, farewell! you have lost the charm of your names; but thou, Nic Bottom, thou valiant Bottom, what shall we say to thee? Thou didst console us much; thou didst perform a good part well; thou didst top the part of Bottom the weaver! He comes out of thy hands as clean and clever a fellow as ever. Thou art a person of exquisite whim and humour; and thou didst hector over thy companions well, and fall down flat before the Duke, like other Bullies, well; and thou didst sing the song of the Black Ousel well; but chief, thou didst noddle thy ass's head, which had been put upon thee, well; and didst seem to say, significantly, to thy new attendants, Peaseblossom, Cobweb, Moth, and Mustardseed, 'Gentlemen, I can present you equally to my friends, and to my enemies!'[2]

All that was good in this piece (except the scenery) was Mr. Liston's[3] Bottom, which was an admirable and judicious piece of acting. Mr. Conway[4] was Theseus. Who would ever have taken this gentleman for the friend and companion of Hercules? Miss Stephens[5] played the part of Hermia, and sang several songs very delightfully, which, however, by no means assisted the progress or interest of the story. Miss Foote[6] played Helena. She is a very sweet girl, and not at all a bad actress; yet did anyone feel or even hear her address to Hermia? To show how far asunder the closet and the stage are, we give it here once more entire:

> Injurious Hermia! most ungrateful maid!
> Have you conspir'd, have you with these contriv'd
> To bait me with this foul derision?
> Is all the counsel that we two have shar'd,
> The sister-vows, the hours that we have spent,
> When we have chid the hasty-footed time
> For parting us, O! is it all forgot?
> All school-days' friendship, childhood innocence?
> We, Hermia, like two artificial gods,
> Created with our needles both one flower,
> Both on one sampler, sitting on one cushion,
> Both warbling of one song, both in one key,
> As if our hands, our sides, voices, and minds,
> Had been incorporate. So we grew together,
> Like to a double cherry, seeming parted,

But yet an union in partition;
. . . . .

And will you rent our ancient love asunder,
To join with men in scorning your poor friend?
It is not friendly, 'tis not maidenly:
Our sex, as well as I, may chide you for it,
Though I alone do feel the injury.

In turning to Shakespeare to look for this passage, the book opened at the *Midsummer Night's Dream*, the title of which half gave us back our old feeling; and in reading this one speech twice over, we have completely forgot all the noise we have heard and the sights we have seen. Poetry and the stage do not agree together. The attempt to reconcile them fails not only of effect, but of decorum. The *ideal* has no place upon the stage, which is a picture without perspective; everything there is in the foreground. That which is merely an airy shape, a dream, a passing thought, immediately becomes an unmanageable reality. Where all is left to the imagination, every circumstance has an equal chance of being kept in mind, and tells according to the mixed impression of all that has been suggested. But the imagination cannot sufficiently qualify the impressions of the senses. Any offence given to the eye is not to be got rid of by explanation. Thus Bottom's head in the play is a fantastic illusion, produced by magic spells: on the stage it is an ass's head, and nothing more; certainly a very strange costume for a gentleman to appear in. Fancy cannot be represented any more than a simile can be painted; and it is as idle to attempt it as to personate Wall or Moonshine. Fairies are not incredible, but fairies six feet high are so. Monsters are not shocking, if they are seen at a proper distance. When ghosts appear in midday, when apparitions stalk along Cheapside, then may the *Midsummer Night's Dream* be represented at Covent Garden or at Drury Lane; for we hear that it is to be brought out there also, and that we have to undergo another crucifixion.

Mrs. Faucit[7] played the part of Titania very well, but for one circumstance—that she is a woman. The only glimpse which we caught of the possibility of acting the imaginary scenes properly, was from the little girl who dances before the fairies (we do not know her name), which seemed to show that the whole might be carried off in the same manner—by a miracle.

1. Treby ... Truman ... Atkins ... Matthews ... Carew ... Burrell ... MacAlpine, I have not identified these performers, but it would appear that, like Peter Brook's fairies in 1970 (see pp. 277–9), they were 'full-grown'.

2. 'Gentlemen . . . enemies!' Hazlitt notes that Louis XVIII of France (1755–1824) said this to his new National Guards.

3. **Liston**, John (1776–1846), a popular comic actor.

4. **Conway**, William Augustus (1789–1828), actor known as 'Handsome Conway'.

5. **Stephens**, presumably Catherine (1794–1882), later Countess of Essex.

6. **Foote**, Maria (?1797–1867), made her first appearance at Covent Garden in 1814. She became notorious because of a breach-of-promise case in 1824. Her successful stage career ended in 1831 with her marriage to the 4th Earl of Harrington.

7. **Faucit**, Harriet, first appeared in London as Desdemona in 1813, retired in 1824; mother of Helena Faucit (see p. 67).

---

4 November 1816, Leigh Hunt (1784–1859) on Edmund Kean as Timon of Athens at the Theatre Royal, Drury Lane, London, from *The Examiner*, reprinted in *Leigh Hunt's Dramatic Criticism 1808–1831*, ed. L. H. and C. W. Houtchens (New York, 1949), pp. 134–9.

James Henry Leigh Hunt, essayist, critic, and poet, is described by his editors, William Archer and Robert W. Lowe, as 'the first English dramatic critic' in the sense that he was 'the first writer of any note who made it his business to see and report upon all the principal theatrical events of the day'. He wrote theatre criticism for *The News* from May 1805 till the end of 1807, for his own paper, *The Examiner*, from January 1808 till February 1813, and for *The Tatler* from September 1830 till February 1832. His reviews for *The News* appeared as *Critical Essays on the Performers of the London Theatres* in 1807.

Kean performed Timon in a shortened adaptation by the Hon. George Lamb (1784–1834) which has no female characters; it is described by G. C. D. Odell in *Shakespeare, from Betterton to Irving*, 2 vols. (New York, 1920), ii. 77–9. The production had only seven performances.

THE tragedy of *Timon of Athens*, after a lapse of several years, was revived at this theatre on Monday. The Managers, we suppose, were led to their choice of it, not only by their general desire to bring forward what is good, but by the great success of Mr. Kean in characters of a certain caustic interest; yet although the selection is honourable to both parties, and the performance was received and given out for repetition with great applause, we doubted and still doubt whether it will have what is called a run. . . .

The whole play indeed abounds in masterly delineations of character, and in passages equally poetical and profound; though the latter unfortunately reduced the adapter of the piece to an awkward dilemma; for they constitute its main beauty, and yet he seems to have felt himself obliged to cut them short, either for fear of making it drag with the spectators, or in compliance with a sophisticated decorum. Thus many of the most striking pieces of satire are left out; and we see nothing of the two females who come in upon *Timon's* retreat with *Alcibiades*. Yet the character of *Alcibiades* himself survives and furnishes a singular sort of cooler to the two burning, theoretical spirits of *Timon* and *Apemantus*. Shakspeare seems to have well appreciated this celebrated pupil of Socrates, at least the better part of him, and perhaps to have liked him. He makes him utterly careless of pretension of any sort, brave, open, generous, pleasurable, making allowances for other people, and revenging himself of his enemies rather out of contempt for their not being generous, also, than from any graver self-love of his own, though still he does not affect to be exempt from it. He takes the world as he finds it; and though he kicks a little at the meaner part, enjoys the generous; and is not to be put out, as the phrase is, even by difference of opinion. He has all the knowledge of humanity to which the military profession naturally contributes, and which renders a cheerful and intelligent soldier one of the most amiable men in the world, making the best of evil, and the very best of good. Of all the persons who visit *Timon* in his misery, *Alcibiades* is the only one whom the misanthrope seems puzzled how to abuse. When he came to him in his prosperity, it was not as a flatterer like the others, but as a cheerful friend; and when he sees him in his adversity, he would do him service if *Timon* would suffer it, bears his contumely with silent commiseration, and at last tells the drums to strike up for the march, because 'We but offend him.'

The play, upon the whole, was well performed. Mr. Kean, as usual, gave touches of natural excellence, such as no other living actor could produce. We suspect however that *Timon* will not rank as one of his first performances; it wants sufficient variety and flexibility of passion for him. Neither do we think that he succeeded in the first part of the play, where *Timon* is prosperous and indulges his credulous generosity. He was too stately and tragic. It is true this may appear reconcilable with the ostentation which is charged *Timon*; but as we have before observed, the charge appears to us to be unfounded, as far as the leading passion is concerned; and *Timon* is a man of ardent animal spirits, whose great enjoyment is the sense of a certain glorious fellowship, upon which he thinks he could equally reckon in a time of adversity, and the disappointment of which drives him, in a manner, distracted. He smiles at first, when his steward talks to him of cold friends; finds a reason for the first disappointment he encounters from the senators in the cold-bloodedness of their time of life; and, during the banquet in the second scene, the fullness of his trusting heart fairly runs over into tears of delight. From all this, it appears to us that the actor's representation of him in his prosperity should be more easy and cordial, and that he should receive and entertain his visitors, not like a prince with a diadem, but like a companion who has the happy art of being heartily though gracefully one's equal. If *Timon* had been only ostentatious, he would hardly have been so willing to borrow, and to think all his friends as generous as himself: he would have run mad for pride; whereas his misanthropy is really owing, as in almost all instances, to an unexpected and extreme conviction of the hollowness of the human heart. We think Mr. Kean also had too great a tendency in some parts to be violent, or rather to carry the paroxysms of *Timon* to a pitch beyond true rage, and too often to mistake vehemence for intenseness. *Timon's* curses in general should have been 'not loud, but deep':[1] and, where Mr. Kean's acting was of this description, it certainly had the greatest effect out of the pale of the galleries, though some of his passionate starts were deservedly admired also. The finest scene in the whole performance was the one with *Alcibiades*. We never remember the force of contrast to have been more truly pathetic. *Timon*, digging in the woods with his spade, hears the approach of military music; he starts, waits its approach sullenly, and at last in comes the gallant *Alcibiades* with a train of splendid soldiery. Never was scene more effectively managed. First, you heard a sprightly quick march playing in the distance; Kean started, listened, and leaned in a fixed and angry manner on his spade, with frowning eyes, and lips full of the truest feeling, compressed but not too much so; he seemed as if resolved not to be deceived, even by the charm of a thing inanimate; the audience were silent; the march threw forth its gallant note nearer and nearer; the Athenian standards appear, then the soldiers come treading on the scene with that air of confident progress which is produced by the accompaniment of music; and at last, while the squalid misanthrope still maintains his posture and keeps his back to the strangers, in steps the young and splendid *Alcibiades*, in the flush of victorious expectation. It is the encounter of hope with despair.

Alcibiades luckily had a representative in Mr. Wallack[2] who, besides performing the rest of his part with good credit, dressed and looked it uncommonly well. He seemed to have been studying the bust of his hero, as well as the costume of the Greek soldier. Mr. Bengough,[3] in *Apemantus*, made as good a Cynic philosopher as we wished to see; he did not look quite so shrewd or beggarly as Diogenes, but he was wise enough for the part. As to Mr. Holland[4] in the kind and lamenting Steward, he seemed quite inspired. We do not know that we ever saw him in so much advantage: but Mr. Kean's acting, we suspect, has given a great fillip to all the minor performers now-a-days.

With respect to the scenery and other mechanical matters, the piece was excellently got up. One of the scenes was a striking view of Athens, composed perhaps, from the picture in *Hobhouse's Travels*.[5] Timon's solitude also was very leafy and to the purpose; and the splendour of the banquet-scene obtained great applause. We must protest however against the dance of young Amazons, clashing their swords and shields. Shakspeare, we allow, has specified Amazons for the occasion; but if Amazons there must be, they should at least have had lutes in their hands, which he has specified also, instead of weapons. We are at a loss to conjecture why Shakspeare introduced Amazons at all, which seem to be no more to his taste in general than they were to old Homer's; but did he find, anywhere, that an Amazon with a lute was *Timon's* device? We have not the commentators at hand to refer to; but *Timon* in thanking the dancers, tells them that they have entertained him with his 'own device'; and devices of this kind were common from time immemorial. A dramatic mask, it is true, was called a device; but the host in the present instance seems to have been taken unawares, and could hardly have spoken as he did, had he himself invented the subject of the dance. At all events, we should like to have as little of these unfeminine feminines as possible: lutes would make them more human, and might act as a sort of compliment to *Alcibiades*, who is one of the guests, or to the spirit of sociality in general, as much as to say—a spirit of harmony corrects what is barbarous. We doubt also the propriety of the diadem and fillet worn by Mr. Kean, as well as the want of another sort of wreath to the heads of him and his guests during the banquets. They should undoubtedly, as was the custom, wear roses, myrtles, or other flowers mentioned by Anacreon[6] and Plutarch,[7] which besides being proper, would also have a pleasing effect, and contribute to the luxury of the scene: not that all this is necessary to Shakspeare, or demanded by him, but that it is as well to complete the costume in all instances, where it is undertaken in most.

We thank the Managers for *Timon*, which for our part we could see over again, were it only for the fine scene before mentioned; though we are afraid they have miscalculated the chances of its long run. We hope their next reproduction will be equally creditable to their taste, and more likely to reward it.

1. 'not loud, but deep', *Macbeth*, 5.3.29.
2. **Wallack**, James William (?1791–1864; misidentified by Houtchens); actor who emigrated to America in 1845 and established Wallack's Theatre, New York, in 1852.
3. **Bengough**, Mr, described in the *Thespian Dictionary* (1805) as a 'favourite at Manchester... a married man, and reckoned a useful actor'.
4. **Holland**, Charles (1768–?1849), a frequent performer at Drury Lane.
5. *Hobhouse's Travels*. John Cam Hobhouse (1786–1869), who became Baron Broughton de Gyffordd, travelled with Byron and published *A Journey through Albania and other Provinces of Turkey in Europe and Asia* (1813).
6. **Anacreon** (*c.*6th century BC), Greek lyric poet.
7. **Plutarch** (*c.*46–*c.*120), Greek historian whose *Lives of the Noble Grecians and Romans* in the translation (1579, etc.) by Sir Thomas North provided Shakespeare with material for *Timon of Athens*.

꧁꧂

21 December 1817, John Keats (1795–1821) on Edmund Kean as a Shakespearian actor, and John Hamilton Reynolds (1796–1852) on Kean at the Theatre Royal, Drury Lane, London, as Richard, Duke of York in the play of that name adapted by John Herman Merivale (1779–1844) from *Henry the Sixth*, Parts One, Two, and Three; from *The Champion*, reprinted in *The Poetical Works and Other Writings of John Keats*, ed. H. Buxton Forman, revised with additions by Maurice Buxton Forman (Hampstead edition), 8 vols. (New York, 1939), v. 227–46.

THE first of the reviews cited here was written by the poet Keats to help out his friend Reynolds, who at the time was reviewing for *The Champion*. A great admirer of Kean, Keats wrote a play, *Otho the Great*, in collaboration with his friend George Brown, and started another, *King Stephen*, in 1818, hoping that Kean would play the central roles in both; they abandoned *King Stephen* on hearing that Kean was planning an American tour.

The second review has usually been attributed to Keats, but Leonidas Jones demonstrates that it is virtually certain to be by Reynolds ('Keats's Theatrical Reviews in the *Champion*', *Keats–Shelley Journal*, III [1954], 55–65)—though the sentence 'The very eyelid dies' sounds quintessentially Keatsian. The play, which was published, uses non-Shakespearian material; Reynolds surmises that it might have been put together by Kean, but in fact the adaptation is by John Herman

Merivale, a barrister, who however may well have worked very much to Kean's orders. Odell describes it as 'a frightful, unintelligible hodge-podge', and in spite of Reynolds's praise it met with little success. The review is of interest as a description of an early example of the kind of telescoping that has often been applied to the early histories, as well as for its description of Kean's performance.

1. Keats on Edmund Kean as a Shakespearian Actor

M R. K E A N's two characters of this week, comprising as they do, the utmost of quiet and turbulence, invite us to say a few words on his acting in general. We have done this before, but we do it again without remorse. Amid his numerous excellencies, the one which at this moment most weighs upon us, is the elegance, gracefulness, and music of elocution. A melodious passage in poetry is full of pleasures both sensual and spiritual. The spiritual is felt when the very letters and points of charactered language show like the hieroglyphics of beauty;—the mysterious signs of an immortal freemasonry! 'A thing to dream of, not to tell!'[1] The sensual life of verse springs warm from the lips of Kean, and to one learned in Shakespearian hieroglyphics,—learned in the spiritual portion of those lines to which Kean adds a sensual grandeur: his tongue must seem to have robbed 'the Hybla bees, and left them honeyless.'[2] There is an indescribable gusto in his voice, by which we feel that the utterer is thinking of the past and the future, while speaking of the instant. When he says in Othello 'put up your bright swords, for the dew will rust them,' we feel that his throat had commanded where swords were as thick as reeds. From eternal risk, he speaks as though his body were unassailable. Again, his exclamation of 'blood, blood, blood!' is direful and slaughterous to the deepest degree, the very words appear stained and gory. His nature hangs over them, making a prophetic repast. His voice is loosed on them, like the wild dog on the savage relics of an eastern conflict; and we can distinctly hear it 'gorging, and growling o'er carcase and limb.'[3] In Richard, 'Be stirring with the lark to-morrow, gentle Norfolk!' comes from him, as through the morning atmosphere, towards which he yearns. We could cite a volume of such immortal scraps, and dote upon them with our remarks; but as an end must come, we will content ourselves with a single syllable. It is in those lines of impatience to the night who, 'like a foul and ugly witch, doth limp so tediously away.'[4] Surely this intense power of anatomizing the passion of every syllable—of taking to himself the wings of verse, is the means by which he becomes a storm with such fiery decision; and by which, with a still deeper charm, he 'does his spiriting gently.'[5] Other actors are continually thinking of their sum-total effect throughout a play. Kean delivers himself up to the instant feeling, without a shadow of a thought about any thing else. He feels his being as deeply as Wordsworth,[6] or any other of our intellectual monopolists. From all his comrades he stands alone, reminding us of him, whom Dante has so finely described in his Hell:

'And sole apart retir'd, the Soldan fierce.'[7]

Although so many times he has lost the battle of Bosworth Field, we can easily conceive him really expectant of victory, and a different termination of the piece. Yet we are as moths about a candle in speaking of this great man. 'Great, let us call him, for he conquered us!'[8] We will say no more. Kean! Kean! have a carefulness of thy health, an in-nursed respect for thy own genius, a pity for us in these cold and enfeebling times! Cheer us a little in the failure of our days! for romance lives but in books. The goblin is driven from the heath, and the rainbow is robbed of its mystery!

2. Reynolds on Kean in 'Richard Duke of York'

T HE play, as it is compressed, is most interesting, clear, and
• • • vigorous. It bears us from the beginning to the middle of that tremendous struggle,—and very properly stops at the death of the first of the *Richards*. *Richard, Duke of York*, has all the quickness, resolution, and ability,—which would naturally exist in a man that was inwardly stirred to wrestle for the crown. He has not that rushing stream of thoughts and purposes which characterized *Richard the Third*, his son, who was born in the cause;—of an aspiring father; and with all the excitement of a parent's and a brother's death, urging him on. The individuality of Shakespeare's characters is most strongly exemplified in the two *Richards*:—but in what is it not?—perhaps the faults of the compilation are these;—first, the characters are too hastily introduced and despatched and their language clipped too closely. They are 'curtailed of their fair proportions.' *Jack Cade* and his rabble are put into strait-waistcoats, as a body might say,—and the armourer and his man are cut short in their dispute most abruptly and unsatisfactorily. We see nothing of *Talbot*,—and missing him is like walking among the Elgin Marbles,[9] and seeing an empty place where the Theseus had reclined. In the next place, the poetry is too much *modernized*. We speak of it as we heard it. Again, the events are not harmonized well,—and Shakespeare felt that they could not be put together in less than fifteen acts,—'and we would

take the ghost's word for a thousand pounds."[10] The present play appears to go on by fits and starts,—and to be made up too much of unmatchable events. It is inlaid with facts of a different colour,—and we can see the cracks which the joiner's hand could not help leaving. After these little objections, all our observations on the compilation are full of praise. Great ingenuity is displayed,—and we should think Kean had a hand in it. The author has extracted veins of gold from a huge mine,—and he is liberal enough to share it with other people. The workings of *Richard's* mind are brought out as it were by the hand of the anatomist,—and all the useless parts are cut away and laid aside.—But with all, we fear the public will not take the obligation as it is meant, and as it ought to be received. The English people do not care one fig about Shakespeare,—only as he flatters their pride and their prejudices:—we are not sure that this has not been remarked before, though we do not remember where; nevertheless, it is our firm opinion. But let us say a few words of the actors.—

Kean stands like a tower. He is 'all power, passion, self-will.'[11] His insinuations flow from his lips as 'musical as is Apollo's lute.'[12] It is impossible to point out any peculiar and little felicities,—where the whole piece of acting is of no mingled web. If we were to single a favourite part, we should chuse that in which he parts with his son, *Young Rutland*, just before the battle. It was pathetic to oppression. Our hearts swelled with the feeling of tears, which is a deeper feeling than the starting of them in the eye. His tongue lingered on the following passage as fondly as his eyes clung to the object which occasioned them; and as tenderly as the heart dwells and doats on some long loved object.

> Bring in my dear boy, Rutland.
>
> *(Enter* RUTLAND *with attendants.)*
>
> My darling! let me kiss thee ere I go—
> I know not if I e'er shall see thee more.
> If I should fall, I leave thee to thy brothers,
> All valiant men; and I will charge them all,
> On my last blessing, to take care of thee,
> As of their souls.

His death was very great:—but Kean always 'dies as erring men do die.'[13] The bodily functions wither up,—and the mental faculties hold out, till they crack. It is an extinguishment, not a decay. The hand is agonized with death; the lip trembles, with the last breath,—as we see the autumn leaf thrill in the cold wind of evening. The very eye-lid dies. The acting of Kean is Shakesperian;—he will fully understand what we mean. There is little to be said of the rest. Pope[14] as a *Cardinal* (how aptly chosen) balances a red hat. Holland[15] wears insipid white hair, and is even more insipid than the hair which he carries. Rae[16] plays the adulterous *Suffolk*, and proves how likely he is to act amiss. Wallack,[17] as *Young Clifford*, 'towers above his sex.' Mr. Maywood[18] is more miserable in *Henry the Sixth* than winter, or wet nights, or Death on a pale horse,[19] or want of money, or deceitful friends, or any other crying evil. The comic parts are sadly mangled, owing to illness of Munden[20] and Oxberry.[21] *Jack Cade* dies of a locked jaw;—and *Dick* the butcher is become a grave man. Mrs. Glover[22] chews the blank verse past all endurance:—her Comedy is round and comfortable; her Tragedy is worse than death.

One thing we are convinced of, on looking over the three parts of *Henry*, from which this play is gleaned;—which is,—that Shakespeare was the only lonely and perfectly happy creature God ever formed. He never could have had a mate,—being most unmatchable.

1. '**A thing to dream of, not to tell!**' A description of the naked Geraldine in 'Christabel', by Samuel Taylor Coleridge (1772–1834), l. 253 ('sight', not 'thing').

2. **robbed 'the Hybla bees...**' Based on *Julius Caesar*, 5.1.34–5.

3. '**gorging, and growling o'er carcase and limb**', from 'The Siege of Corinth' (1816) by George Gordon, Lord Byron (1788–1824): l. 411.

4. '**like...away**', *Henry V*, 4.0.21–2.

5. '**does...gently**', *The Tempest*, 1.2.299.

6. **Wordsworth**, William (1770–1850). Keats, as his letters show, had a profound distaste for what he calls 'the Wordsworthian sublime'.

7. '**And sole apart...**', from Dante's *Inferno*, translated by Henry Francis Cary (1772–1844), 1805, Canto iv, l. 126.

8. '**Great...us!**' Adapted from 'Great let me call him, for he conquered me', 1.1.30 of *The Revenge* (1721), a tragedy by Edward Young (1683–1765) popular with Romantic actors including Kemble and Kean.

9. **Elgin Marbles** These marble sculptures from the Parthenon in Athens, bought by the government for the British Museum in 1816, profoundly impressed Keats and members of his circle.

10. '**and we would...pounds**', *Hamlet*, 3.2.274–5: 'I'll take the Ghost's word for a thousand pound.'

11. '**all power, passion, self-will**' [not identified].

12. '**musical as is Apollo's lute**', from *Comus*, by John Milton (1608–74), l. 476, which is itself influenced by *Love's Labour's Lost* 4.3.318–19: 'as sweet and musical | As bright Apollo's lute...'

13. '**dies as erring men do die**' [not identified].

14. **Pope**, Alexander (1762–1835), actor and playwright who had a long career on the London stage; he was also a distinguished painter of miniatures.

15. **Holland**, Charles, see p. 50.

16. **Rae**, Alexander (1782–1829), acted at Drury Lane from 1812 to 1820.

17. **Wallack**, James William. See p. 50.

18. **Maywood**, Robert Campbell (died in 1856 aged 70).

19. **Death on a pale horse**. 'And I looked, and behold a pale horse: and his name that sat on him was Death': Revelation 4: 8—the subject and title of a vast painting by Benjamin West (1738–1820), born in America, but settled in England in 1763; it is now in the Pennsylvania Academy of Arts. Keats writes about it in his 'negative capability' letter (21 December 1817).

20. **Munden**, Joseph Shepherd (1758–1832), comic actor with a special talent for drunken scenes.

21. **Oxberry**, William (1784–1824), comic actor, editor, and publisher.

22. **Glover**, Julia (1779–1850), a leading performer in comic roles.

---

4 October 1818, Leigh Hunt on Edmund Kean as Othello at the Theatre Royal, Drury Lane, London, from *The Examiner*, reprinted in *Leigh Hunt's Dramatic Criticism 1808–1831*, ed. L. H. and C. W. Houtchens (New York, 1949), pp. 201–2.

OTHELLO was considered by many to be Kean's greatest role, though he acted in a shortened and partly expurgated version. Marvin Rosenberg devotes a chapter to the performance in *The Masks of Othello* (1961).

MR. KEAN has returned from his tour to France and Italy—a very proper relaxation for a man of his talents—and has performed in the course of the week *Richard the Third* and *Othello*. We saw the latter on Thursday evening; and with all our experience of the stage, and with all our scepticism as to the powers of the very best actors in characters from Shakspeare, we never witnessed a performance that struck us so forcibly. It brought back upon us the earnestness and implicit attention of our younger days. We have admired Mrs. Siddons, been infinitely amused with Lewis,[1] been sore with laughing at Munden,[2] been charmed with Mrs. Jordan;[3] but we never saw anything that so completely held us suspended and heart-stricken, as Mr. Kean's *Othello*. In all parts it is as complete as actor can shew it—in the previous composure of its dignity, in its soldier-like repression of common impulse, in the deep agitation of its first jealousy, in the low-voiced and faltering affection of occasional ease, in the burst of intolerable anguish, in the consciousness that rage has hurt its dignity and ruined the future completeness of its character, in the consequent melancholy farewell to its past joys and greatness, in the desperate savageness of its revenge, in its half-exhausted reception of the real truth, and lastly, in the final resumption of a kind of moral attitude and dignity, at the moment when it uses that fine deliberate artifice and sheathes the dagger in its breast.

If we might venture to point out any parts the most admirable in this performance, it would be the low and agitated affectation of quiet discourse, in which he first canvasses the subject with *Iago*, the mild and tremulous farewell to 'the tranquil mind, the plumed troop,' &c. in which his voice occasionally uttered little tones of endearment, his head shook, and his visage quivered; and thirdly, those still more awfully mild tones in which he trembles and halts through those dreadful lines beginning—

> Had it pleased heaven
> To try me with affliction; had he rained
> All kinds of sores and shames on my bare head.

His louder bitterness and his rage were always fine; but such passages as these, we think, were still finer. You might fancy you saw the water quivering in his eyes.

And here two things struck us very forcibly; first, how impossible it is for actor and audience to be both as they ought to be in such large theatres,[4] since Mr. Kean's quietest and noblest passages could certainly not have been audible in the galleries; and second, how much an actor's talent must be modified by his own character off the stage, an observation we may reasonably make when it leans to the favourable side; for we conjecture from anecdotes that are before the public, that Mr. Kean's temper is hasty, and his disposition excellent and generous; and it is of passion and natural generosity that *Othello's* character is made up. For this reason we can never help being sceptical about Garrick's[5] excellence in characters of deep and serious interest; since, off the stage, he was little better than a quick-eyed trifler, full of phrases of gabbling jargon, and coarse-minded withal.

Of the two new performers—Mrs. West,[6] who repeated *Desdemona*, and Mr. Cleary,[7] who changed from *Othello* to *Iago*—we have nothing to add to our former observations, except that the lady performed still better than before.

There is a new afterpiece here, which is below criticism.

Mr. Kean's *Othello* is the masterpiece of the living stage.

---

1. **Lewis**, William Thomas (1749–1811), comic actor, known as 'Gentleman Lewis'.
2. **Munden**, Joseph Shepherd. See p. 55.
3. **Jordan**, Dorothy (1761–1816), one of the greatest of comic actresses.

4. **such large theatres**. The theatre still stands. Built in 1812, it originally had a capacity of around 3,120. (See Pl. 5.)It replaced a theatre which held around 3,900—more than any other European theatre of the time. Covent Garden, built in 1732 to hold 1,897, was rebuilt after a fire in 1809 to hold 2,800.

5. **Garrick**, David. See p. 20.

6. **West**, Sarah (1790–1876), played leading roles, mainly in tragedy, at Drury Lane from 1818 to 1828.

7. **Cleary** [not identified].

---

31 October 1819, Leigh Hunt on William Charles Macready (1793–1873) as Richard III at the Theatre Royal, Covent Garden, London, from *The Examiner*, reprinted in *Leigh Hunt's Dramatic Criticism 1808–1831*, ed. L. H. and C. W. Houtchens (New York, 1949), pp. 219–21.

MACREADY had made his first appearance on the stage in 1810 playing Romeo in Birmingham. In spite of his distaste for the profession, which he never overcame, he rapidly developed to become Kean's only real rival.

A NEW and unexpected circumstance has taken place here, which promises to rescue the character of the house from the pantomimic degradation into which it was fast falling. Mr. Macready has performed *Richard* twice in the course of the week, with the greatest applause. We must confess we went to see him with no sort of expectations at all commensurate with the greatness of the part. We thought him a man of feeling, but little able to give a natural expression to it, and so taking the usual refuge in declamation. He appeared to us one of the best readers of a part we had seen, according to the received notions of good reading; but with the exception of a character now and then bordering on the melodramatic, like *Rob Roy*[1]—that was all.

We are bound to say that we found our anticipations completely erroneous. A proper sense of the greatness of the part, and of the honorable rank as an actor which he now had to sustain, seems to have roused up all his intelligence to give fit companionship to his sensibility. We expected to find vagueness and generality, and we found truth of detail. We expected to find declamation, and we found thoughts giving a soul to words. We expected to find little more than shewy gestures and a melodious utterance, and we found expression and the substantial *Richard*.

A critic on these particular occasions is forced upon comparisons. However, they sometimes enable him to give his readers a more exact idea of a performance. Compared then with Mr. Kean,[2] we should say that a division of merits usual enough with the performance of such comprehensive characters as Shakspeare's, has taken place in the *Richards* of these two actors. Mr. Kean's *Richard* is the more sombre and perhaps deeper part of him; Mr. Macready's the livelier and more animal part—a very considerable one nevertheless. Mr. Kean's is the more gloomy and reflective villain, rendered so by the united effect of his deformity and subtle-mindedness; Mr. Macready's is the more ardent and bold-faced one, borne up by a temperament naturally high and sanguine, though pulled down by mortification. The one has more of the seriousness of conscious evil in it, the other of the gaiety of meditated success. Mr. Kean's has gone deeper even than the relief of his conscience—he has found melancholy at the bottom of the necessity for that relief; Mr. Macready's is more sustained in his troubled waters by constitutional vigour and buoyancy. In short, Mr. Kean's *Richard* is more like *King Richard*, darkened by the shadow of his very approaching success, and announcing the depth of his desperation when it shall be disputed; Mr. Macready's *Richard* is more like the *Duke of Gloucester*, brother to the gay tyrant *Edward the 4th*, and partaking as much of his character as the contradiction of the family handsomeness in his person would allow.

If these two features in the character of *Richard* could be united by any actor, the performance would be a perfect one: but when did the world ever see a perfect performance of a character of Shakspeare's? When did it ever see the same *Macbeth's* good and ill nature worn truly together, the same *King John* looking mean with his airs of royalty, the same *Hamlet* the model of a court and the victim of melancholy? Mr. Kean's *Othello* is perhaps the most perfect performance on the modern stage; but it is not a perfect *Othello* nevertheless. The union of such a variety of tones of feeling as prevails in the great humanities of Shakspeare seems as impossible to be found in an actor, as the finest musical instrument is insufficient to supply all the effect of a great writer for a band.

At the same time when we thus compare Mr. Macready with Mr. Kean, it is to be recollected that Mr. Kean first gave the living stage that example of a natural style of acting, on which Mr. Macready has founded his new rank in the theatrical world. Nor must we omit that the latter falls into some defects which the former is never betrayed into; and those too of a description inconsistent with the general style of his performance. We allude to some over-soft and pathetic tones towards the conclusion of the part, where *Richard* is undergoing remorse of conscience. *Richard* might lament and even be pathetic; but he would certainly never whine, or deal in anything approaching to the lack-a-daisical. We think both performers occasionally too violent; but this may be partly a stage-necessity. Mr. Macready (and he is evidently quite capable of doing it) should reflect that all depth of feeling in reflecting minds requires a proportionate depth and quietness of expression. It may be as imaginative as he pleases; but it has no taste or leisure for dallying with the gentilities of grief.

Upon the whole, Mr. Macready's *Richard* is a very great addition indeed to his reputation, and no small one to the stock of theatrical pleasure. The Covent-Garden stage was thirsty for a little more genius to refresh it; and he has collected all his clouds, and burst down upon it in a sparkling shower. We certainly never saw the gayer part of *Richard* to such advantage. His very step, in the more sanguine scenes, had a princely gaiety of self-possession, and seemed to walk off to the music of his approaching triumph.

1. **Rob Roy.** Macready played in a musical adaptation of Sir Walter Scott's novel by Isaac Pocock (1782–1835) at Covent Garden in 1818.
2. **Kean**, Edmund. See p. 38.

5 December 1819, Leigh Hunt on William Charles Macready as Coriolanus at the Theatre Royal, Covent Garden, London, from *The Examiner*, reprinted in *Leigh Hunt's Dramatic Criticism 1808–1831*, ed. L. H. and C. W. Houtchens (New York, 1949), pp. 223–5.

THESE were Macready's earliest performances in the role, given in response to his triumph as Richard III. His own later staging of the play is discussed on pp. 77–84.

MR. MACREADY has appeared twice during the past week in the character of *Coriolanus*; and is to repeat it tomorrow. It is another unquestionable addition to his repute, though not so high a one as his *Richard*. In *Richard*, Mr. Macready seized one particular side of the character—the gayer and more sanguine—and appropriated it to himself. In *Coriolanus* he rather gives additional proof that he deserves to have good parts allotted him in general, than exhibits anything particularly characteristic of the part. Yet it is well worth seeing him in; and this is no mean praise for any performer. In one respect, his *Coriolanus* would have surprised us almost as much as *Richard* did, if we had not seen him in the latter; we mean that the temptation which all such characters hold out to be declamatory did not seduce him back, generally speaking, to that former contentedness of monotonous elocution which we should now perhaps rather conclude to have been discontentedness. Let Mr. Macready take what character he pleases now; we venture to say that since his talents have got an opportunity of shewing themselves, and have been acknowledged, he will never again be found rolling forth that mere melodious declamation which he used to deal out, sentence after sentence, like a machine turning ivory balls.

If Mr. Macready did not touch all the keys of *Coriolanus's* passions truly, he touched them for the most part variously; and often with truth, if not the completest truth. His voice is the finest and most heroical on the stage; not sweeter, we think, occasionally, than Mr. Kean's; which however hoarse in the long run, is as melodious, and finely tempered with passion as any man's in the gentler tones, and before it has been over-exerted; but more according to the old requisites of a hero's utterance, when the general shouted to his army, and the chiefs could be distinguished above the tumult by their respective voices, as they were by their crests and cognizances. As far also as height and figure go, he will have no rival in the part: for though it is curious enough that heroes and great political chiefs have for the most part been short rather than tall (as in the instances of Alexander,[1] Agesilaus,[2] Caesar,[3] Charles the 5th,[4] Frederick the 2nd,[5] and Bonaparte[6]), yet this is not the poetical or sculptural idea of a hero; and the *altae moenia Romae*—the loftiness of Roman domination—has instinctively heightened to our mind's eye the very bodies of the Roman people.

But we doubt whether Mr. Macready's graceful gestures and shapely movements are not somewhat too elegant for *Coriolanus*; perhaps we should say, too softly elegant and swimming. It is true, he holds his head up loftily and looks disdainfully; but even here again we doubt whether there is not a something of ideal grace beyond what Shakspeare intended. *Coriolanus*, though a haughty patrician, was after all a soldier, whose friends found excuses for his unaccommodating temper and style of language in the rudeness of military habits. He could look grand on grand occasions, as in the instance of his sudden and godlike appearance at the hearth of *Aufidius*, but then the circumstance constituted its own grandeur. At other times, especially in his reluctant applications to the people for the consulship, and still more so in the impatience he expressed on that subject to his friends in private, we suspect he was intended to be more short, impatient, and familiar; always haughty indeed, but more plain and soldier-like in his haughtiness, with less of the graceful ungraciousness of the mere patrician.

Again, Mr. Macready would be too loud occasionally even for a hot rude soldier; much more is he so for the elegant personage which he makes him. He is also apt to be too sudden and theatrical in his contrasts, from a loud utterance to a low one; nor must it be concealed that his finest touch of all, where he literally casts in *Aufidius's* teeth the scornful word Boy! was toned and gestured too obviously, however unintentionally, in the manner of Mr. Kean. Still his quarrel with *Aufidius* is altogether a noble scene, and deserved the great applause with which the curtain dropt upon his assassination.

The reader may judge what we think of Mr. Macready's *Coriolanus* with all its drawbacks, when at the same time that we think it worth going to see, we are compelled to say that the rest of the performance of this play is beneath criticism. Miss Foote[7] is a clever as well as handsome actress, and very pleasant to see in such parts as the one in *A Roland for an Oliver,*[8] which we take this opportunity of instancing because we omitted the proper notice of it last Sunday in our comparative list of a week's performances at both houses; but though suitable enough to *Coriolanus's* young wife, with her few unassuming speeches and 'those dove's eyes,' she cannot be said to give any important addition to the performance. Mr. Blanchard[9] is the only other performer worth noticing; and he is well enough in *Menenius.* Mrs. Faucit[10] belongs to melodrama. A Roman matron did not think it essential to her dignity to step about with her head thrown half a yard back, as if she had a contempt for her own chin.

1. **Alexander** the Great (356–323 BC), King of Macedonia.
2. **Agesilaus** (444–360 BC), King of Sparta.
3. **Caesar,** Julius (*c.*100–44 BC), Roman Emperor and military leader.
4. **Charles the 5th** (1500–58), Holy Roman Emperor.
5. **Frederick the 2nd** ('the Great', 1712–86), King of Prussia, military commander.
6. **Bonaparte,** Napoléon (1769–1821), French emperor and military leader.
7. **Foote,** Maria, see p. 46.
8. *A Roland for an Oliver* by Thomas Morton (*c.*1764–1838).
9. **Blanchard,** William (1769–1835), comic and character actor.
10. **Faucit,** Harriet. See p. 46.

25 April 1820, anonymous review of Edmund Kean as King Lear
   at the Theatre Royal, Drury Lane, London, from *The Times*,
   reprinted in *Eyewitnesses of Shakespeare*, edited by Gāmini
   Salgādo (1975), pp. 280–2.

IN this performance Kean played in a modification of Nahum Tate's 1681
adaptation which deprived him of the tragic conclusion. Hazlitt, writing for
The London Magazine, was less enthusiastic than the anonymous critic of *The
Times*. Kean returned to Shakespeare in 1823, but failed and reverted to Tate after
three performances.

PUBLIC expectation has seldom been raised to a greater height than by
the announcement of Kean's appearance in *King Lear*, which, after
numerous delays, took place yesterday evening. The admirers of this
highly-gifted actor, confident in the extent and diversity of his talents,
have long anticipated this trial as the last seal to his theatrical renown;
while his enemies, on the other hand (for Kean, like other men of genius,
has encountered the extremes of hostility as well as of admiration), have
not scrupled to predict failure and loss of reputation. Such was the anxiety
of all parties to witness the experiment, that a crowd was collected at the
doors long before the period of admission; and the first rush filled the pit,
with a great portion of those boxes where seats had not been secured.
When the curtain rose, it was evident that a large majority of the
spectators consisted of the friends of Kean, and he was received on his
first appearance with a burst of applause truly enthusiastic. It soon ceased,
however, and the play was listened to throughout, but especially in the
scenes where Lear is present, with the most profound attention. The first
scene contains nothing prominent; yet it was apparent, even then, that the
actor, as if fully aware of the ordeal through which he had to pass, had
tasked his powers to the utmost, and was resolved to let no occasion pass
of making an impression. This was shown in his quick susceptibility to
the reluctance of Cordelia to echo the professions of her sisters. The first
symptoms of distrust of Goneril were beautifully developed, where he
retains the disguised Kent in his service; and when distrust is changed
into certainty by her behaviour, his manner denoted that the first inroads
were already made on his reason. The passage containing the recollection
of Cordelia, and remorse for his conduct—

> 'How small, Cordelia, was thy fault! O Lear,
> Beat at this gate that let thy folly in,
> And thy dear judgment out!'

was beautifully expressed. The curse on Goneril, which follows, can scarcely be contemplated without pain, but, aided by his action and manner, became truly terrific. On the arrival at Gloster's castle, as the interest increased, the actor rose in power. One of the finest passages in that scene was the appeal to Regan—

> 'Dear daughter, I confess that I am old;
> Age is unnecessary; on my knees I beg
> That you'll vouchsafe me raiment, bed, and food'

where to unite the tone of sarcasm with the dignified sorrow of the monarch forms so remarkable a difficulty. Kean, however, expressed it with truth and feeling. Nothing could evince greater judgment in this part of the play than the manner in which he represented the gradual aberration of reason under the repeated shocks to which it was exposed. Its last light seemed to be extinguished in this passage—

> No, you unnatural hags,
> I will have such revenges on you both,
> That all the world shall—I will do such things—
> What they are yet I know not; but they shall be
> The terrors of the earth.—You think I'll weep;
> No, I'll not weep;—
> I have full cause of weeping; but this heart
> Shall break into a hundred thousand flaws
> Or ere I'll weep.
> O gods, I shall go mad.

We cannot, without quoting more largely than our space will permit, follow the actor through the manifestations of genius he displayed in the character. The scene of the storm was less effective than many others, because the manager,[1] by a strange error, had caused the tempest to be exhibited with so much accuracy that the performer could scarcely be heard amidst the confusion. He should have recollected that it is the bending of Lear's mind under his wrongs that is the object of interest, and not that of a forest beneath the hurricane. The machinery may be transferred to the next new pantomime. In the interview of Lear with Edgar, and the scene where he is carried off by the emissaries of Cordelia, the picture of mental alienation was completed, and we believe that a scene more perfect or pathetic has never been represented on the stage. The scene in the beginning of the 5th act, where the unhappy King is restored to reason, was the most masterly of the whole performance, there was scarcely a dry eye in the theatre. While it lasted, the silence would have rendered the fall of a pin audible; and it was followed by a burst of applause, unanimous, long, and enthusiastic. Whatever study Kean may have bestowed on the character of Lear, he has not been able to free it wholly from its prevailing faults; but they are as dust in the balance, in the consideration of a scene so highly wrought as that we have mentioned and, indeed, with his general conception and execution of this difficult part. It will be quoted as the *chef-d'oeuvre* of the English drama, and must be handed down to the emulation of future actors.

    1. **the manager**, Robert Elliston (1774–1831), actor who managed Drury Lane from 1819 to 1826.

[1832], James E. Murdoch (1811–93) on Charles Kean (1811–68) as Posthumus in *Cymbeline* at the Arch Street Theatre, Philadelphia, from his *The Stage, or Recollections of Actors and Acting from an Experience of Fifty Years: A Series of Dramatic Sketches* (Philadelphia, 1880; repr. New York, 1969), pp. 146–8.

JAMES MURDOCH was a versatile and successful American actor and lecturer. Charles, son of Edmund Kean, first visited America in 1830 and played Post-humus in late October 1832, when he was twenty-one. He seems never to have played it again. He returned to England in 1833. Murdoch was writing some fifty years after the event, but his account is interesting as one professional's descrip-tion of what another did during a precise stretch of action.

THE occasion which first called my attention to young Kean's peculiar method was his acting of Posthumus in the play of *Cymbeline* at the Arch Street Theatre in Philadelphia about 1832. The character is one which requires quick perception and acute sensibility in conception and portraiture, the prominent traits being scepticism on the one hand, and obstinate adhesion to conviction on the other. Throughout the play Mr. Kean sustained his reputation for artistic excellence. There was nothing in the performance above or below the requirements of the language and situation until the last scene of the last act. Here the actor sprang, as it were, from his previous still-life with the most astounding abruptness of vehement fury I ever remember to have seen upon the stage. It was indeed art, but it was the perfection of art; it was fiery passion and melting tenderness. In that one outburst I fully realized all that tradition had said of the father's power. Throughout the play the fire of emotion had been kept smouldering under restraint, in order that it might burst forth in one dazzling flash, to die out as suddenly as it had been kindled. Had such an exhibition of force been displayed in a character requiring a repetition of such effects, I question whether the actor would not have failed in attempting to meet such a demand.

I will endeavor to bring before the mental vision of my readers a bird's-eye view of the scene to which I have referred. In Act V. Scene v. of *Cymbeline*, Iachimo, the villain of the play, is called upon by Imogen to tell how he became possessed of the ring of her husband, who is supposed to be dead. While the repentant culprit tells his story of cold-blooded fraud Posthumus stands hidden behind the groups of courtiers and attendants, listening to that 'which ran like poison through his blood.' Iachimo, finishing the recital of his villainy, says, 'Methinks I see him now.' At this Kean suddenly darted from his concealment, and dashing down the stage struck his attitude and exclaimed, with a wild outburst of passion, sharp, harsh, and rattling in tone—

> Ay, so thou dost,
> Italian fiend!

As the instantaneous flash and bolt startle the beholder, so the actor seemed to electrify his auditors; they broke out into the most determined and prolonged applause. Then came, in tones of mingled rage and remorse, the choking utterance of self-reproach:

> Ay me! most credulous fool,
> Egregious murderer, thief, anything
> That's due to all the villains past, in being,
> To come!

Here a sudden transition brought out the next lines in bold, ringing notes of adjuration:

> Oh give me cord, or knife, or poison,
> Some upright justicer!

Now the voice was changed to impetuous command, fierce and imperious denunciation, high, strong, and full-toned:

> Thou, king, send out
> For torturers ingenious; it is I
> That all the abhorred things o' the earth amend

> By being worse than they. I am Posthumus,
> That killed thy daughter:—villain-like, I lie;
> That caused a lesser villain than myself,
> A sacrilegious thief, to do 't.

This was followed by a mingling of the tearful tones of pity and pathetic admiration on the words—

> The temple
> Of virtue was she; yea, and she herself.

Choking sobs now gave way to vehement utterance and piercing tones that seemed to penetrate the brain with the wild notes of insanity:

> Spit, and throw stones, cast mire upon me, set
> The dogs o' the street to bay me; every villain
> Be called Posthumus Leonatus.

Here the climax of passion and fury culminated, while the words,

> And
> Be villainy less than 'twas,

formed a forcible cadence. Then, as if all the elements of indignant reproach and self-condemnation had spent themselves, the actor poured forth a flood of tenderness that seemed to upheave the very depths of his soul, exclaiming in an ecstasy of love and grief—

> O Imogen!
> My queen, my life, my wife! O Imogen,
> Imogen, Imogen!

From the wonderful effect of this lava-like flood of passion exhibited by the son I caught a glimpse of that power which, when a mere boy, listening to the elder Kean in Othello, overwhelmed me with a kind of bewildering idea that the little 'black man' in the Moorish dress was acting like a lunatic and ought to be chained up.

[*c*.1837], Helena Faucit (1817–98), on herself as Hermione, with
  W. C. Macready as Leontes, in *The Winter's Tale*, from her *On
  Some of Shakespeare's Female Characters* (1885, revised 1891; sixth
  edn., 1899), pp. 385–91 (extracts).

HELENA (or Helen) Faucit often acted with Macready until he retired in 1851, in
which year she married Theodore Martin (knighted in 1880 for his biography of
Prince Albert), after which she rarely performed. Her book *On Some of Shakespeare's Female Characters* appeared in 1885, with an enlarged edition in 1891. She
first appeared as Hermione during Macready's Covent Garden season in 1837,
when she was only twenty years old. Her account of the role is written in the
form of a letter to Alfred, Lord Tennyson; her memories of performing it with
Macready are remarkable not least for what she tells us about the audience's
reactions. Before the first extract printed she describes her dress, 'composed of
soft white cashmere, the draperies and edges bordered with the royal purple
enriched with a tracery in gold, and thus harmonising with the colouring of the
lips, eyes, hair, etc., of the statue'.

A T the back of the stage, when I acted in this play, was a dais which
was led up to by a flight of six or eight steps, covered with rich cloth
of the same material and crimson colour as the closed curtains. The
curtains when gradually opened by Paulina disclosed, at a little distance
behind them, the statue of Hermione, with a pedestal of marble by her
side.

Here, let me say, that I never approached this scene without much
inward trepidation. You may imagine how difficult it must be to stand in
one position, with a full light thrown upon you, without moving an eyelid
for so long a time. I never thought to have the time measured, but I
should say that it must be more than ten minutes—it seemed like *ten*
times ten. I prepared myself by picturing what Hermione's feelings would
be when she heard Leontes' voice, silent to her for so many years, and
listened to the remorseful tender words addressed to what he believed to
be her sculptured semblance. Her heart hitherto has been full only of her
lost children. She has thought every other feeling dead, but she finds
herself forgetting all but the tones of the voice, once so loved, now broken
with the accents of repentance and woe-stricken desolation. To her own
surprise her heart, so long empty, loveless, and cold, begins to throb again,
as she listens to the outpourings of a devotion she had believed to be
extinct. She would remember her own words to him, when the familiar
loving tones were turned to anger and almost imprecation, 'I never wished
to see you sorry, now I trust I shall.'

Of the sorrow she had thus wished for him she is now a witness, and it all but unnerves her. Paulina had, it seemed to me, besought Hermione to play the part of her own statue, in order that she might hear herself apostrophised, and be a silent witness of the remorse and unabated love of Leontes before her existence became known to him, and so be moved to that forgiveness, which, without such proof, she might possibly be slow to yield. She is so moved; but for the sake of the loving friend, to whom she has owed so much, she must restrain herself, and carry through her appointed task.

But, even although I had fully thought out all this, it was impossible for me ever to hear unmoved what passes in this wonderful scene. My first Leontes was Mr Macready, and, as the scene was played by him, the difficulty of wearing an air of statuesque calm became almost insuperable. As I think over the scene now, his appearance, his action, the tones of his voice, the emotions of that time, come back. There was a dead awe-struck silence, when the curtains were gradually drawn aside by Paulina. She has to encourage Leontes to speak.

> 'I like your silence, it the more shows off
> Your wonder. But yet speak—first you, my liege,
> Comes it not something near?'

Then with what wonderful tenderness of tone Mr Macready answered—

> 'Her natural posture!
> Chide me, dear stone; that I may say, indeed,
> Thou art Hermione; *or, rather, thou art she*
> *In thy not chiding; for she was as tender*
> *As infancy and grace.*'

His eyes seemed to devour the figure before him, as the scene proceeded, and he said—

> 'Oh, thus she stood,
> Even with such life of majesty,—warm life,
> As now it coldly stands, when first I woo'd her!
> I am ashamed. Does not the stone rebuke me,
> For being more stone than it? Oh, royal piece,
> There's magic in thy majesty, which has
> My evils conjured to remembrance, and
> From thy admiring daughter took the spirits,
> Standing like stone with thee.
>   *Per.*   And give me leave,
> And do not say, 'tis superstition, that

> I kneel, and then implore her blessing. Lady,
> Dear queen, that ended when I but began,
> Give me that hand of yours to kiss.'

But the time for this has not arrived, and Paulina prevents her, saying, the colour on the statue is not yet dry. Leontes stands so broken down with the bitter remembrances the statue calls up, that he is urged by Polixenes and Camillo to subdue his grief. Paulina, also deeply moved, exclaims—

> 'Indeed, my lord,
> If I had thought the sight of my poor image
> Would thus have wrought you,—for the stone is mine,—
> I'd not have show'd it.'

And is about to close the curtain. Never can I forget the manner in which Mr Macready here cried out, 'Do not draw the curtain!' and, afterwards, when Paulina says,

> 'No longer shall you gaze on't, lest your fancy
> May think anon it moves'—

'*Let be, let be!*' in tones irritable, commanding, and impossible to resist. 'Would I were dead,' he continues, 'but that, methinks already—' Has he seen something that makes him think the statue lives? Mr Macready indicated this, and hurriedly went on—

> 'What was he that did make it? See, my lord,
> Would you not deem it breathed? And that those veins
> Did verily bear blood.…
> The fixture of her eye has motion in't,
> As we are mocked with art.
>   *Paul.*   I'll draw the curtain.
> My lord's almost so far transported, that
> He'll think anon it lives.
>   *Leon.*   Oh sweet Paulina,
> Make me to think so twenty years together;
> No settled senses of the world can match
> The pleasure of that madness. *Let it alone!*
>   *Paul.* I am sorry, sir, I have thus far stirr'd you: but
> I could afflict you further.
>   *Leon.*   Do, Paulina,
> For this affliction has a taste as sweet
> As any cordial comfort.'

His eyes have been so riveted upon the figure, that he sees, what the others have not seen, that there is something about it beyond the reach of art. He continues—

> 'Still methinks,
> There is an air comes from her: What fine chisel
> Could ever yet cut breath? Let no man mock me,
> For I will kiss her.'

Paulina again interposes with the same suggestion as before, that 'the ruddiness on the lip being wet,' 'he would mar the work,' adding, 'Shall I draw the curtain?'

> '*Leon.* No, not these twenty years.
> *Per.*   So long could I
> Stand by a looker on.'

Paulina sees that the strain upon Hermione and all present must not be prolonged; and she tells them—

> 'If you can behold it,
> I'll make the statue move indeed. . . .
> . . . . It is required
> You do awake your faith. Then, all stand still.
> . . . Music awake her, strike! (*Music.*)
> 'Tis time, descend, be stone no more: approach!
> Strike all that look upon with marvel; come.'

You may conceive the relief I felt, when the first strain of solemn music set me free to breathe! There was a pedestal by my side on which I leant. It was a slight help during the long strain upon the nerves and muscles, besides allowing me to stand in that 'natural posture' which first strikes Leontes, and which therefore could not have been rigidly statuesque. By imperceptibly altering the poise of the body, the weight of it being on the forward foot, I could drop into the easiest position from which to move. The hand and arm still resting quietly on the pedestal materially helped me. Towards the close of the strain the head slowly turned, the 'full eyes' moved, and at the last note rested on Leontes.

This movement, together with the expression of the face, transfigured as we may imagine it to have been by years of sorrow and devout meditation,—speechless, yet saying things unutterable,—always produced a startling, magnetic effect upon all—the audience upon the stage as well as in front of it. After the burst of amazement had hushed down, at a sign from Paulina the solemn sweet strain recommenced. The arm and hand were gently lifted from the pedestal; then, rhythmically following the music, the figure descended the steps that led up to the dais, and advancing slowly, paused at a short distance from Leontes. Oh, can I ever forget Mr Macready at this point! At first he stood speechless, as if turned to stone; his face with an awe-struck look upon it. Could this, the very counterpart of his queen, be a wondrous piece of mechanism? Could art so mock the life? He had seen her laid out as dead, the funeral obsequies performed over her, with her dear son beside her. Thus absorbed in wonder, he remained until Paulina said, 'Nay, present your hand.' Tremblingly he advanced, and touched gently the hand held out to him. Then, what a cry came with, 'O, she's warm!' It is impossible to describe Mr Macready here. He was Leontes' very self! His passionate joy at finding Hermione really alive seemed beyond control. Now he was prostrate at her feet, then enfolding her in his arms. I had a slight veil or covering over my head and neck, supposed to make the statue look older. This fell off in an instant. The hair, which came unbound, and fell on my shoulders, was reverently kissed and caressed. The whole change was so sudden, so overwhelming, that I suppose I cried out hysterically, for he whispered to me, 'Don't be frightened, my child! don't be frightened! Control yourself!' All this went on during a tumult of applause that sounded like a storm of hail. Oh, how glad I was to be released, when, as soon as a lull came, Paulina, advancing with Perdita, said, 'Turn, good lady, our Perdita is found.' A broken trembling voice, I am very sure, was mine, as I said—

> 'You gods, look down,
> And from your sacred vials pour your graces
> Upon my daughter's head! Tell me, mine own,
> Where hast thou been preserved? Where lived? How found
> Thy father's court? For thou shalt hear, that I,—
> Knowing by Paulina, that the oracle
> Gave hope thou wast in being,—have preserved
> Myself to see the issue.'

It was such a comfort to me, as well as true to natural feeling, that Shakespeare gives Hermione no words to say to Leontes, but leaves her to assure him of her joy and forgiveness by look and manner only, as in his arms she feels the old life, so long suspended, come back to her again. . . .

My first appearance as Hermione is indelibly imprinted on my memory by the acting of Mr Macready as I have described it in the statue scene. Mrs Warner[1] had rather jokingly told me, at one of the rehearsals, to be *prepared* for something extraordinary in his manner, when Hermione

71

returned to life. But prepared I was not, and could not be, for such a display of uncontrollable rapture. I have tried to give some idea of it; but no words of mine could do it justice. It was the finest burst of passionate speechless emotion I ever saw, or could have conceived. My feelings being already severely strained, I naturally lost something of my self-command, and as Perdita and Florizel knelt at my feet I looked, as the gifted Sarah Adams[2] afterwards told me, 'like Niobe, all tears.' Of course, I behaved better on the repetition of the play, as I knew what I had to expect and was somewhat prepared for it; but the intensity of Mr Macready's passion was so real, that I never could help being moved by it, and feeling much exhausted afterwards.

1. **Warner**, Mrs, formerly Mary Amelia Huddart. She married in 1837 and later acted under her married name; see p. 84. Faucit says she 'had been for years the recognised Hermione of the London stage'.
2. **Adams**, Sarah (*c*.1805–48), poet remembered for the hymn 'Nearer my God to thee'.

14 February 1838, John Forster on W. C. Macready as King Lear at the Theatre Royal, Covent Garden, London from *The Examiner*, 14 February, reprinted in *Dramatic Essays by John Forster, George Henry Lewes*, ed. William Archer and Robert W. Lowe (1896), pp. 48–54.

JOHN FORSTER (1812–76) was theatre critic of *The Examiner* from 1833 to 1838, and later became its editor. He was a close friend of Charles Dickens, to whom this review has often been mistakenly attributed (for example, by Edgar and Eleanor Johnson in their *The Dickens Theatrical Reader* (1964), J. C. Trewin, in his *Theatre Bedside Book* (1974), and Gāmini Salgādo in *Eyewitnesses of Shakespeare* (1975)). John Forster's authorship is conclusively demonstrated in an article by W. J. Carlton, *The Dickensian*, September 1965, who shows that Forster copied into it long passages from two earlier reviews of *King Lear* which he had published in the *Weekly True Sun*, 26 January 1834, of an actor called Samuel Butler as Lear, and in the *New Monthly Magazine*, June 1834, of Macready's first London performances as Lear, at Drury Lane and Covent Garden. A review by Dickens of a later Macready performance as Lear at the Haymarket Theatre appeared in *The Examiner* on 27 October 1849; the manuscript survives and is printed by Leslie C. Staples in 'Dickens and Macready's Lear', *The Dickensian*, March 1948, pp. 78–80.

Forster's essay is largely devoted to the contribution made to the play by the Fool, omitted by Tate; Macready restored the character only after great hesitation, and had the role played by a young woman, Priscilla Horton, later Mrs German Reed (1815–95), who sang as well as acted.

W HAT we ventured to anticipate when Mr. Macready assumed the management of Covent Garden Theatre,[1] has been every way realised. But the last of his well-directed efforts to vindicate the higher objects and uses of the drama, has proved the most brilliant and the most successful. He has restored to the stage Shakespeare's true *Lear*, banished from it, by impudent ignorance, for upwards of a hundred and fifty years.

A person of the name of Boteler[2] has the infamous repute of having recommended to a notorious poet laureate, Mr. Nahum Tate,[3] the 'new modelling' of *Lear*. 'I found the whole,' quoth Mr. Tate, addressing the aforesaid Boteler in his dedication, 'to answer your account of it; a heap of jewels unstrung and unpolished, yet so dazzling in their disorder, that I soon perceived I had seized a treasure.' And accordingly to work set Nahum, very busily indeed; strung the jewels and polished them with a vengeance; omitted the grandest things, the Fool among them, polished all that remained into commonplace; inter-larded love-scenes; sent Cordelia into a comfortable cave with her lover, to dry her clothes and get warm, while her distracted and houseless old father was still left wandering without, amid all the pelting of the pitiless storm; and finally rewarded the poor old man in his turn, and repaid him for all his suffering, by giving him back again his gilt robes and tinsel sceptre!

Betterton was the last great actor who played Lear before the commission of this outrage. His performances of it between the years 1663 and 1671, are recorded to have been the greatest efforts of his genius.[4] Ten years after the latter date Mr. Tate published his disgusting version, and this was adopted successively by Boheme,[5] Quin,[6] Booth,[7] Barry,[8] Garrick,[9] Henderson,[10] Kemble,[11] Kean.[12] Mr. Macready has now, to his lasting honour, restored the text of Shakespeare, and we shall be glad to hear of the actor foolhardy enough to attempt another restoration of the text of Tate! Mr. Macready's success has banished that disgrace from the stage for ever.

The Fool in the tragedy of *Lear* is one of the most wonderful creations of Shakespeare's genius. The picture of his quick and pregnant sarcasm, or his loving devotion, of his acute sensibility, of his despairing mirth, of his heartbroken silence—contrasted with the rigid sublimity of Lear's suffering, with the huge desolation of Lear's sorrow, with the vast and outspread image of Lear's madness—is the noblest thought that ever entered into the mind and heart of man. Nor is it a noble thought alone. Three crowded audiences in Covent Garden Theatre have now proved by something better than even the deepest attention that it is for action—for representation: that it is necessary to an audience as tears are to an overcharged heart; and necessary to Lear himself as the recollection of his kingdom, or as the worn and faded garments of his power. We predicted some years since that this would be felt, and we have the better right to repeat it now. We take leave again to say that Shakespeare would have as soon consented to the banishment of Lear from the tragedy, as to the banishment of his Fool. We may fancy him, while planning his immortal work, feeling suddenly, with an instinct of divinest genius, that its gigantic sorrows could never be presented on the stage without a suffering too frightful, a sublimity too remote, a grandeur too terrible—unless relieved by quiet pathos, and in some way brought home to the apprehensions of the audience by homely and familiar illustration. At such a moment that Fool rose to his mind, and not till then could he have contemplated his marvellous work in the greatness and beauty of its final completion.

The Fool in *Lear* is the solitary instance of such a character, in all the writings of Shakespeare, being identified with the pathos and passion of the scene. He is interwoven with Lear—he is the link that still associates him with Cordelia's love, and the presence of the regal state he has surrendered. The rage of the wolf Goneril is first stirred by a report that her favourite gentleman had been struck by her father 'for chiding of his fool'—and the first impatient questions we hear from the dethroned old man are 'Where's my knave—my fool? Go you and call my fool hither.'—'Where's my fool? ho! I think the world's asleep.'—'But where's my fool? I have not seen him this two days.'—'Go you and call hither my fool.' All which prepare us for that affecting answer stammered forth at last by the Knight in attendance—'Since my young Lady's going into France, sir, the fool hath much pined away.' Mr. Macready's manner of turning off at this with an expression of half impatience, half ill-repressed emotion—'No more of that—*I have noted it well*'—was inexpressibly touching. We saw him, in the secret corner of his heart, still clinging to the memory of her who used to be his best object, the argument of his praise, balm of his age, 'most best, most dearest.' And in the same noble and affecting spirit was his manner of fondling the Fool when he sees him first, and asks him with earnest care—'How now, my pretty knave? *How dost thou?*' Can there be a doubt, after this, that his love for the Fool is associated with Cordelia, who had been kind to the poor boy, and for the loss of whom he pines away? And are we not even then prepared for the sublime pathos of the close, when Lear, bending over the dead body of all he had left to love upon the earth, connects with her the memory of that other gentle, faithful, and loving being who had passed from his side—unites, in that moment of final agony, the two hearts that had been broken in his service—and exclaims—'And my poor fool is hanged!'

Mr. Macready's Lear, remarkable before for a masterly completeness of conception, is heightened by this introduction of the Fool to a surprising degree. It accords exactly with the view he seeks to present of Lear's character. The passages we have named, for instance, had even received illustration in the first scene, where something beyond the turbulent greatness or royal impatience of Lear had been presented—something to redeem him from his treatment of Cordelia. The bewildered pause giving his 'father's heart' away—the hurry yet hesitation of his manner as he orders France to be called—'Who stirs? Call Burgundy'—had told us at once how much consideration he needed, how much pity, of how little of himself he was indeed the master, how crushing and irrepressible was the strength of his sharp impatience. We saw no material change in his style of playing the first great scene with Goneril, which fills the stage with true and appalling touches of nature. In that scene he ascends indeed with the heights of Lear's passion; through all its changes of agony, of anger, of impatience, of turbulent assertion, of despair, and mighty grief; till on his knees, with arms upraised and head thrown back, the tremendous curse bursts from him amid heaving and reluctant throes of suffering and anguish. The great scene of the second act had also its old passages of power and beauty—his self-persuading utterance of 'hysterica passio'—his anxious and fearful tenderness to Regan—the elevated grandeur of his appeal to the Heavens—his terribly suppressed efforts, his pauses, his reluctant pangs of passion, in the speech 'I will not trouble thee, my child'—and surpassing the whole, as we think, in deep simplicity as well as agony of pathos, that noble conception of shame as he *hides his face* on the arm of Goneril and says—

> I'll go with thee—
> Thy fifty yet doth double five and twenty,
> And thou art twice her love!'

The Fool's presence then enabled him to give an effect, unattempted before, to those little words which close the scene, when, in the effort of bewildering passion with which he strives to burst through the phalanx of amazed horrors that have closed him round, he feels that his intellect is shaking, and suddenly exclaims, 'O, Fool! I shall go mad!' This is better than hitting the forehead and ranting out a self-reproach.

But the presence of the Fool in the storm-scene! The reader must witness this to judge its power, and observe the deep impression with which it affects the audience. Every resource that the art of the painter and the mechanist can afford is called in aid in this scene—every illustration is thrown on it of which the great actor of Lear is capable—but these are nothing to that simple presence of the Fool! He has changed his character there. So long as hope existed he had sought by his hectic merriment and sarcasm to win Lear back to love and reason—but that half of his work is now over, and all that remains for him is to soothe and lessen the certainty of the worst. Kent asks who is with Lear in the storm, and is answered—

> 'None but the *Fool*, who labours to outjest
> His heart-struck injuries!'

When all his attempts have failed, either to soothe or outjest these injuries, he sings, in the shivering cold, about the necessity of 'going to bed at noon.' He leaves the stage to die in his youth, and we hear of him no more till we hear the sublime touch of pathos over the dead body of the hanged Cordelia.

The finest passage of Mr. Macready's scenes upon the heath is his remembrance of the 'poor naked wretches,' wherein a new world seems indeed to have broken upon his mind. Other parts of these scenes wanted more of tumultuous extravagance, more of a preternatural cast of wildness. We should always be made to feel something beyond physical distress predominant here. The colloquy with Mad Tom, however, was touching in the last degree—and so were the two last scenes, the recognition of Cordelia and the death, which elicited from the audience the truest and best of all tributes to their beauty and pathos. Mr. Macready's representation of the father at the end, broken down to his last despairing struggle, his heart swelling gradually upwards till it bursts in its closing sigh, completed the only perfect picture that we have had of Lear since the age of Betterton.

1. **assumed . . . Theatre** (in 1837).

2. **Boteler,** Thomas; the otherwise unknown dedicatee of Tate's adaptation.

3. **Tate,** Nahum (1652–1715), poet and playwright, librettist of Henry Purcell's opera *Dido and Aeneas* (1689), published his adaptation of *King Lear* in 1681; it held the stage, with partial restorations of Shakespeare's words, until well into the nineteenth century.

4. **Betterton.** These statements lack authority.

5. **Boheme**, Anthony (died 1731), played Lear at Lincoln's Inn Fields from 1720.

6. **Quin**, James. See p. 20.

7. **Booth**, Barton (?1679–1733), played Lear from 1714 onwards.

8. **Barry**, Spranger (?1717–77), contemporary and rival of David Garrick, he played Lear from 1756; he was described as 'every inch a king' while Garrick was 'every inch King Lear'.

9. **Garrick**, David. See p. 20.

10. **Henderson**, John (1747–85), acted Lear for the first time in London in 1779.

11. **Kemble**, John Philip. See p. 33. He played Lear at Drury Lane in 1788 with Sarah Siddons as Cordelia, using his own revision of Tate's text.

12. **Kean**, Edmund. See p. 38.

꧁ꆜ꧂ꆜ꧁ꆜ꧂ꆜ꧁ꆜ꧂ꆜ꧁ꆜ꧂ꆜ꧁ꆜ꧂ꆜ꧁ꆜ꧂ꆜ꧁ꆜ꧂ꆜ꧁ꆜ꧂ꆜ꧁ꆜ꧂ꆜ꧁ꆜ꧂ꆜ꧁ꆜ꧂ꆜ꧁ꆜ꧂ꆜ꧁ꆜ꧂ꆜ꧁ꆜ꧂ꆜ꧁ꆜ꧂ꆜ꧁ꆜ꧂ꆜ

18 March 1838, John Forster on W. C. Macready as Coriolanus at the Theatre Royal, Covent Garden, London, from *The Examiner*, reprinted in *Dramatic Essays by John Forster, George Henry Lewes*, ed. William Archer and Robert W. Lowe (1896), pp. 54–65.

MACREADY's first Coriolanus is reviewed on pp. 59–61. By the time he came to present the play under his own management, in 1838, historically based pictorialism had begun to exert the influence on Shakespeare production that was to dominate the rest of the century and beyond. The opening paragraph of Forster's review helps to explain the growing appeal of this kind of staging.

THE presentation of this play at Covent Garden Theatre on Monday night last may be esteemed the worthiest tribute to the genius and fame of Shakespeare that has been yet attempted on the English stage. We have had nothing to compare with it, even in Mr. Macready's management. Magnificent as the revivals of *Hamlet, Othello, Lear*, and *Macbeth* have been, this of *Coriolanus* surpasses them all, in the opportunity it has afforded of presenting together upon the stage those striking characteristics, material no less than intellectual, which render a correct knowledge of great times past superior to every other sort of knowledge— not less an instructive picture of noble or heroic manners, than an exercise of reason, and a school of philosophy.

Rome has been presented on the theatrical scene before, but never this Rome; the rude city of the rude age of the Conqueror of Corioli. That is the first distinction which claims notice. The pictures which Kemble[1] gave when he revived the play might be splendid, but they were utterly unreal—they clustered fine buildings together with equal disregard to the proprieties of place or time—the arch of Severus or Constantine, the Coliseum, the pillar of Trajan, all the grandeurs of imperial Rome, flaunted away within three hundred years of the first birth of the city— and even men of scholarship could find no bounds to the satisfaction they expressed. We can scarcely blame them. It was natural that they should prefer even that to the wilder absurdity of a picture of Grosvenor Square; and it must be confessed that the effect of solid long lines and triumphant-looking arches is so very Roman, generally speaking, and the idea of Rome in the mind of posterity possesses so mighty and enduring a grandeur analogous to its stone and marble, that one of these Kemble misrepresentations might be almost hailed as even the just substitution of a general truth for a particular one—a moral and characteristic, if not a chronologic, truth. Nevertheless, truth itself, as a plain-spoken old Roman would have said, is the best of all truths; and upon this wiser principle Mr. Macready has proceeded; with what effect let the reader judge who goes to see the play. To what infinitely higher purpose is the moral grandeur of the place and of the men set off by a comparatively rude and barren city!

The first scene (all are painted with consummate skill and exactness) presents Rome from the skirt of Mount Aventine across a bend of the Tiber (which would bear, by-the-bye, an additional tinge of yellow)— taking in a view of the Capitoline hill, a glimpse of the porticoes of the forum, the temple of Vesta, the Cloaca Maxima, and the Palatine covered with its patrician dwellings. It is by an exquisite arrangement of art that, throughout the play, and in the rudest streets of the city, the Capitol is kept in view, and still presents, under varying aspects, the never-changed old Roman form (no matter that the materials were afterwards more splendid) of the three temples to Jupiter, Juno, and Minerva. As a chord in music pervading the entire composition, this awakens and sustains in the spectator's mind grand associations of the later with those of the earlier Rome. The second scene is the interior of the house of Coriolanus, with its earthen vases, its bronze candelabra, its exquisite and almost pathetic simplicity. We have then pictures of the country between Rome and the Volscian territory—a distant view of the square camp entrenched—a field of battle covered with dead, and in the distance Corioli. We are afterwards brought back to Rome, and placed in the interior of the forum, with, above, a glimpse of the still proud Capitol, and the little 'thatched house of Romulus,' while on our right stands the rostrum, and, terrifying us even yet from the very thought of litigation, the transfixed and ghastly image of the miserable Marsyas.[2] Then follows Coriolanus' triumphant entrance into Rome. The emotion of the vast crowds as the passage of the procession through the gate brings nearer and nearer its renowned hero—the forest of laurel boughs rustling through the air as each hand seeks to contribute something to the glory of the scene—the 'stalks, bulks, windows' of the old and rude brick buildings of the city 'smother'd up'—

> 'Leads fill'd, and ridges hors'd
> With variable complexions, all agreeing
> In earnestness to see him'—

and more touching still, the triumph, surpassing all this, of the mother and wife of the great soldier, as standing apart in the crowd (not coldly and absurdly, as in Kemble's time, arranged as figures in the procession),[3] they see him enter at last covered with the light purple and crowned with the oaken garland—these were the elements of a picture of life and excitement at once the noblest, and produced by the simplest and most striking means, we ever witnessed in a theatre. Every attempt at a stage 'triumph' we happen to have seen before, compared with this, was as the gilt gingerbread of a Lord Mayor's show—the gorgeous tinsel of an ill-imitated grandeur. *This* was the grandeur itself, the rudeness and simplicity, the glory and the truth, of Life. The next scene was that of the assembled senate of Rome, and perhaps in simple and majestic beauty this scene surpassed every other. The senators, in number between one and two hundred, occupy three sides of the stage in triple rows of benches—all in their white robes; with every point of the dress, no less than of the grave and solemn bearing, that distinguished the Roman senator, duly and minutely rendered. The Consul occupies the chief seat in the middle of the back row—before him burns the sacred fire on an altar—and behind him, overhead, is the only other ornament of the place, the famous brazen wolf suckling Romulus and Remus. We defy any one, scholar or not, to look at this scene without emotion. It is not simply the image of power, but a reflection of the great heart, of Rome. It does not strike the senses, but appeals at once to the imagination. It breathes into the cold and statue-like associations of our youthful studies the passionate spirit of humanity and life. It is, as it were, the actual presence of the *genius* of Rome—not of her turbulent and wilful days, nor of those grim, ghastly, long-robed, heartless figures, that too often usurp her memory—but of that high-souled thought and temper, which, whenever the few great minds of the earth have since her fall made a stand against violence and fraud in the cause of liberty and reason, has still in the midst of them conjured up her image—the comfort of the battlefield of Hampden,[4] the glory and consolation of the scaffolds of More[5] and Vane and Sydney![6]

When Kemble played Coriolanus, his first appearance after his banishment was under worthy James Thomson's[7] statue of Mars in the house of Aufidius. This was to the text of Shakespeare as a declamation to a feeling. When the curtain withdrew upon the first scene of the fourth act on Monday night, it disclosed a view of the city of Antium, by starlight— a truly grand and imaginative yet real scene—and in the centre of the stage Macready stood alone, the muffled, disguised, banished Coriolanus. This realised Shakespeare and Plutarch. Behind him were the moles running out into the sea, and at the back of the scene the horizon drawn beyond the sea in one long level line, interrupted only by a tall, solitary tower, the pharos, or watchtower of Antium. The strict truth, and lofty moral effect, of this scene, are surpassingly beautiful. Its wide and barren aspect presents the simplicity and large-minded poverty of those old times, and the tower looks like Coriolanus himself in a less mortal shape, rising in lonely grandeur, but with still unextinguished light, above the melancholy of his exile and the level sternness of his contemporaries. The pathetic effect is suddenly and startlingly increased by the intrusion of music on the air, as the door of Aufidius' house, where the General feasts his nobles, opens on the left of the stage. The next scene shows Coriolanus (an image of Themistocles[8]) seated by the wide hearth of Aufidius, around which are the household gods, and in its centre a burning fire. In all this Shakespeare's text is illustrated by the text of Shakespeare's own original, North's Plutarch.[9] 'It was even twilight when he entered the city of Antium, and many people met him in the streets, but no man knew him. So he went directly to Tullus Aufidius' house, and when he came thither, *he got him up straight to the chimney harth, and sate him downe*, and spake not a word to any man, his face all muffled ouer. They of the house spying him, wondred what he should be, and yet they durst not bid him rise. For il fauouredly muffled and disguised as he was, yet there appeared a certaine maiestie in his countenance, *and in his silence.*'

The last scene was a worthy climax to this series of triumphant effects—(among which, by the way, we should have mentioned the striking simplicity of the tent of Coriolanus). The entire Volscian army is shown under the walls of Rome, which are presented, with the proud Capitol still visible above them, in the distance, while we see in various moving towers and battering-rams vivid preparations for a siege. The number of brilliantly equipped soldiers on the stage in this scene is truly startling, and as their serried ranks open for the advance of the suppliants from Rome, we might fancy them thousands instead of hundreds. The appearance—the black apparition rather—of Coriolanus' mother and family with the other Roman matrons, stretching obliquely across the stage, in the midst of these brilliant warrior-files, one long, dreary, sable line of monotonous misery—was in the best and deepest taste. The last effect of all is a simple adherence to Shakespeare's own stage directions. The tragedy, as it were, does not end. Its action is only removed to Antium or Rome. 'Exeunt, bearing the body of Coriolanus.' As Aufidius mourns his treachery, the warriors around lift up the dead body of the conqueror on their shields, hang around it the splendidest trophies of war, and trailing their steel pikes in sorrow, move with it slowly up the stage to the sound of mournful music. The curtain falls, and, thinking of the scene about to be enacted in Antium, we imagine the sorrow which will break some hearts in Rome!

Such are the pictorial effects alone in this magnificent revival, in themselves most beautiful always, and yet in every case kept strictly subservient to the conduct of the action and story of Coriolanus—not standing, as it were, apart from it, picture-like—but forming an actual portion of the lofty purposes and passions of the play. This profoundest effect of all is created throughout by the masterly arrangement and grouping of the persons engaged in each scene, and above all by the management of the formidable mob of the tragedy, the starving, discon-tented, savage, cowardly, fickle, tumultuous Roman people. The last alone would have sufficiently demonstrated the power of the artist-actor to grasp the entire conception of the poet's genius. The mob in *Coriolanus* were now for the first time shown upon the stage, on a level with the witches in *Macbeth*, as agents of the tragic catastrophe. 'First mob' (as the list of *dramatis personae* calls a plebeian speaker with his 'Many') was personated with singular skill and energy by Mr. Meadows,[10] and never before, we dare assert, felt himself in such lively and multitudinous condition. He was something like a mob. His numerousness gave due effect to his will. He was not the one, or two, or half-dozen inefficient *sawnies*[11] of former times, when John Kemble stalked and *thin-voiced* it among them, like the ghost of the Roman State; but a proper massy crowd of dangerous, violent fellows, fit to hustle Macready's flesh and blood. Those first and second mobs hitherto proper to the stage, and whose 'voices' Coriolanus might reasonably scorn to ask for, were fitter to have represented the nine tailors who make one married man in Mr. Beresford's[12] laughable appendix to his *Miseries of Human Life*; where *their wife*, hearing *him-them* coming upstairs, meets him on the stair-case, and says, 'I knew it was you, my love; for I heard your *voices.*' It was really formidable to see these Covent Garden mobs of Monday night. They fluctuated to and fro, as their violent assent or dissent impelled them, with a loud and overwhelming suddenness, and one-minded ponderosity, truly fearful to think of encountering; and the mere recollection of which gives more heroic breadth to the courage of Coriolanus. Their dresses, we may add, varying in every degree from the complete toga to the savage strip,[13] were in the highest degree accurate and effective, as indeed the dresses were throughout. Old Menenius, who, when his zeal has betrayed him on one occasion into an appearance in armour, complains that he can hardly bear it, does not, as in Kemble's time, wear nothing else throughout the tragedy; nor does Coriolanus himself (wisely recollecting the Tarpeian rock) venture out in the fluttering scarlet which Kemble took such perverse delight in.

We have left ourselves less room than we could have wished, in closing our notice of this memorable revival, to speak of what has equal beauty, though less novelty, with these noble illustrations we have so long dwelt upon. Mr. Macready's Caius Marcius (we do not express this opinion for the first time) makes what we believe to be the nearest approach the stage has ever presented to the intention Shakespeare had in view. Coriolanus is not an ideal abstraction of the dignities and graces, but a soldier of the early republic of Rome, a man of rough manners, but of fiery and passionate sincerity. His friends are driven in the course of the tragedy to find many excuses for his unaccommodating temper and style of language in the rudeness of military habits, and it must be admitted that his style and temper are much the same, whether he addresses Patricians or People. He objects that the senate should 'monster' his nothings, and he begs of the Consul Cominius, 'for that he hath not wash'd his nose that bled,' that he will not diet the little he has been able to accomplish 'in praises sauc'd with lies.' Plutarch (after whom Shakespeare modelled his tragedy) observes distinctly of him that for 'lack of education' he was 'so cholericke and impatient, that he would yeeld to no liuing creature: which made him churlish, *vnciuill*, and altogether vnfit for any man's conuersation.' And again, the historian observes of him: 'He was a man *too ful of passion and choller*, and too much giuen ouer to self-wil and opinion, and *one of a high mind* and great courage, that *lacked the grauitie and affabilitie* that is gotten with iudgment of learning and reason.' This is the original sketch which Shakespeare has filled up with so much power and grandeur, with all the truth, the greatness, and the majesty of man. It is the silliest of mistakes to suppose that Coriolanus is an abstraction of Roman-nosed grandeur[14]—an embodiment of dignified contempt against the poor common people. Let not aristocrats suppose it. The scorn which he gives vent to, wrong and misplaced as it often is, has its unfailing source in what his own heart believes to be noble in thought and just in action. He has none of the characteristics of an oppressor or scorner of the poor. 'He would not,' as his friend tells us, 'flatter Neptune for his trident, or Jove for his power of thunder.' A thing has no charms for him because it is a thing of custom—for of 'Custom' he holds 'mountainous Error' to have been born. He opposes the people because he does not believe them to be trustworthy—he sides with the Patricians, only (as Plutarch says) because he hopes to persuade them to 'show themselues no lesse forward and willing to fight for their country, then the common people were: and to let them know by their deeds and acts, *that they did not so much passe the people in power and riches, as they did exceed them in true nobility and valiantnesse*'—and not succeeding in this, he stigmatises them as 'dastard nobles.' Yet were all these glorious gifts made vain by an unhappy temper, and an education still more unhappy— his own strong natural passions and intense sensibility thwarted every way by the Spartan severity of Volumnia, his mother. The people had their faults no less, and as the passionate soldier refused to acknowledge the fairness of their simple claim, of exacting as the price of the Consulship that it should be asked for kindly—so, on the other hand, they would not see an anti-patrician simplicity and beauty in the claim of Coriolanus from *them*, that they should account him the more virtuous that he had not been common in his love and attachment to men.

This is the Coriolanus of Mr. Macready—not merely an ideal picture of one intense sentiment, but the reality of various and conflicting passion. He does not work up dignified contempt to an extraordinary pitch of intensity with a view to have it on the minds of the audience as one great ideal abstraction—he gives nature full and various play; he calls in other passions to harmonise and redeem; he suffers as much as he sways, and, conflicting with opposite emotions in his soul, sinks at last beneath the struggle. After the preternatural excitement in the quarrel with Aufidius we feel that he is for the Earth no more. His scene with his mother and friends in the third act—his banishment in the forum—the claim of protection from Aufidius—the agonies of his yielding resolution in the last scene—all are exquisite illustrations of the view of the character we have attempted to describe. He was well supported by Miss Huddart[15] in Volumnia (who was only a little too vehement sometimes) and by Mr. Anderson[16] and Mr. Warde[17] in Aufidius and Cominius. Mr. Bartley's[18] Menenius is well known as an accurate and delightful picture of that honest and humorous patrician.

1. **Kemble**, J. P. See p. 33.

2. **Marsyas**, mythical flute-player flayed alive for beating Apollo in a contest. A statue of him at the entrance of the Forum was intended to deter litigants.

3. **arranged as figures**. This does not accord with Charles Mayne Young's account of Mrs Siddons in Kemble's production: see pp. 37–8.

4. **Hampden**, John (1594–1643), republican killed in the Civil War.

5. **More**, Thomas, Sir (1478–1535), writer, and Lord Chancellor to Henry VIII, executed for treason.

6. **Vane**, Sir Henry (1613–62), **Sydney**, Algernon (1622–83), republican leaders executed after the Restoration of the monarchy.

7. **Thomson**. James Thomson (1700–48), poet and playwright, wrote a play about Coriolanus (acted 1749) on which Kemble drew in his acting text. Kemble calls for a statue of Mars, but does not appear to be indebted to Thomson for this. In Nahum Tate's adaptation, *The Ingratitude of a Commonwealth* (1681), however, one of Aufidius' servants tells him that 'One of exalted port, his visage hid, | Has placed himself beneath the statue of | The mighty Mars, and there majestic stands | In solemn silence.'

8. **Themistocles** (*c*.523–*c*.458 BC), Athenian statesman and hero ostracized after falling from favour.

9. **North's Plutarch**, translation (1579) by Sir Thomas North (?1531–?1601) of Plutarch's *Lives of the Noble Grecians and Romans*, Shakespeare's main source for his Roman plays.

10. **Meadows**, Drinkwater (1799–1869), best known as a comic actor.

11. *sawnies*, simpletons, fools.

12. **Beresford**, James (1764–1840), author of *The Miseries of Human Life; or, the Groans of Samuel Sensitive and Timothy Testy, with a few Supplementary Sighs from Mrs Testy. In Twelve Dialogues* (1806).

13. **savage strip**, presumably a rudimentary piece of clothing as worn by savages.

14. **Roman-nosed grandeur**, an allusion to Kemble (see p. 33), whose nose was notable, which, as Archer and Lowe note, drew from the humorist James Smith (1775–1839) the epigram 'What scenes of grandeur does this play disclose, | Where all is Roman—save the Roman's nose!'

15. **Huddart**, Mary Amelia (1804–54); she became Mrs Warner in 1837 (see p. 72).

16. **Anderson**, James (1811–95), an actor, engaged by Macready as 'juvenile lead', who went on to play many leading roles in both England and America.

17. **Warde**, James Prescott (1792–1840); actor who played many leading roles without achieving the highest distinction.

18. **Bartley**, George (1784–1858), an experienced comic actor and stage manager.

[1844], James Robinson Planché (1796–1880), description of Ben Webster's neo-Elizabethan production of *The Taming of the Shrew*, from his *Recollections and Reflections*, 2 vols. (1872), ii. 83–6.

AFTER the Restoration of the monarchy, in 1660, performances of *The Taming of the Shrew* were normally given in heavily adapted texts, such as John Lacy's *Sauny the Scot* (1667), Christopher Bullock's *The Cobbler of Preston* (1716), and, above all, David Garrick's *Catharine and Petruchio* (1754), which held the stage until the late nineteenth century with the exception of the production given at the Haymarket Theatre in 1844 and 1847 under the auspices of its manager, Benjamin Webster (1797–1873) and the playwright and antiquarian James Robinson Planché which, uniquely for its time, also attempted a reconstruction of Elizabethan staging methods. Planché wrote retrospectively about this in his autobiography; he appears not to have known the early play *The Taming of a Shrew*, printed in 1594, in which the Sly framework is briefly rounded out. Contemporary reactions to the production are cited in '*The Taming of the Shrew* at the Haymarket Theatre, 1844 and 1847', by Jan Macdonald, in *Nineteenth-Century British Theatre*, ed. K. Richards and P. Thomson (1971), pp. 157–70.

THE season 1846–47 was signalised by the return to the stage of that charming woman and actress, Mrs. Nisbett,[1] then Lady Boothby, and for the second time a widow but slenderly provided for. During her brief sojourn in Derbyshire she had endeared herself to all classes, particularly the poor, in the neighbourhood of Ashbourne, by whom her memory was cherished long after her leaving it, as I can avouch from personal experience when visiting in that locality in 1851.

Her engagement suggested the idea to me of reviving 'The Taming of the Shrew,' not in the miserable, mutilated form in which it is acted under the title of 'Katherine and Petruchio,' but in its integrity, with the Induction, in which I felt satisfied that excellent actor Strickland[2] would, as Christopher Sly, produce a great effect. It also occurred to me to try the experiment of producing the piece with only two scenes— 1. The outside of the little ale-house on a heath, from which the drunken tinker is ejected by the hostess, and where he is found asleep in front of the door by the nobleman and his huntsmen; and, 2. The nobleman's bedchamber, in which the strolling players should act the comedy, as they would have done in Shakespeare's own time under similar circumstances—viz., without scenery, and merely affixing written placards to the wall of the apartment to inform the audience that the action is passing 'in a public place in Padua,'—'a room in Baptista's house,'—'a public road,' &c.

Mr. Webster, to whom of course I proposed this arrangement, sanctioned it without hesitation. I prepared the comedy for representation, gave the necessary instructions for painting the two scenes, and made the designs for the dresses. One difficulty was to be surmounted. How was the play to be finished. Schlegel[3] says that the part 'in which the tinker, in his new state, again drinks himself out of his senses, and is transformed in his sleep into his former condition, from some accident or other, is lost.' Mr. Charles Knight[4] observes upon this: 'We doubt whether it was ever produced, and whether Shakespere did not exhibit his usual judgment in letting the curtain drop upon honest Christopher, when his wish was accomplished, at the close of the comedy, which he had expressed very early in its progress—

'Tis a very excellent piece of work, Madame Lady—would 't were done.

Had Shakespeare brought him again on the scene in all the richness of his first exhibition, perhaps the patience of the audience would never have allowed them to sit through the lessons of 'the taming school.' We have had farces enough *founded* upon the legend of Christopher Sly, but no one has ever ventured to *continue* him. I was the last person who would have been guilty of such presumption, but after studying the play carefully, I hit upon the following expedient:—Sly was seated in a great chair in the first entrance, O.P.,[5] to witness the performance of the comedy. At the end of each act no drop scene came down, but music was played while the servants brought the bewildered tinker wine and refreshments, which he partook of freely. During the fifth act he appeared to fall gradually into a heavy drunken stupor, and when the last line of the play was spoken, the actors made their usual bow, and the nobleman, advancing and making a sign to his domestics, they lifted Sly out of his chair, and as they bore him to the door, the curtain descended slowly upon the picture. Not a word was uttered, and the termination, which Schlegel supposes to have been lost, was *indicated* by the simple movement of the *dramatis personae*, without any attempt to *continue* the subject.

The revival was eminently successful, incontestably proving that a good play, well acted, will carry the audience along with it, unassisted by scenery; and in this case also, remember, it was a comedy in *five* acts, without the curtain once falling during its performance.

No such Katherine as Mrs. Nisbett had been seen since Mrs. Charles Kemble[6] had acted it in the pride of her youth and beauty. Strickland justified all my expectations. As powerful and unctuous as Munden,[7] without the exaggeration of which that glorious old comedian was occasionally guilty. Buckstone[8] was perfectly at home in Grumio, and Webster, although the part was not in his line, acted Petruchio like an artist, as he acts everything.

Of the 'Induction,' which had been for so many years neglected, that intelligent critic, Charles Knight, says: 'We scarcely know how to speak without appearing hyperbolical in our praise. It is to us one of the most precious gems in Shakespeare's casket. If we apply ourselves to compare it carefully with the earlier Induction upon which Shakespeare formed it, and with the best of the dramatic poetry of his contemporaries, we shall in some degree obtain a conception not only of the qualities in which he equalled and excelled the highest things of other men, and in which he could be measured with them, but of those wonderful endowments in which he differed from all other men, and to which no standard of comparison can be applied.' My restoration of this 'gem' is one of the events in my theatrical career on which I look back with the greatest pride and gratification.

1. **Nisbett**, Louisa Cranston (?1812–58), known especially for her comic roles. Writing long after the event, Planché confuses the 1844 and 1847 productions.

2. **Strickland**, Robert (died in 1845 aged 47).

3. **Schlegel**, August Wilhelm von (1767–1845), German Romantic translator of Shakespeare. This passage is quoted by Charles Knight in the work referred to below.

4. **Knight**, Charles (1791–1873), author and publisher. This and the later quotation are from p. 328 of his edition of the play (1839) in *The Pictorial Edition of Shakspere*.

5. O. P., 'Opposite Prompt', a term usually used in British theatre to mean stage right, although sometimes stage left.

6. **Kemble**, Mrs Charles (1774–1838), born Maria Theresa de Camp, one of the best comic actresses of her day.

7. **Munden**, Joseph. See p. 55.

8. **Buckstone**, John Baldwin (1802–79), comic actor and author of many farces.

꧁꧂

15 October 1853, Henry Morley (1822–94) on *A Midsummer Night's Dream*, produced by Samuel Phelps (1804–78) at the Sadler's Wells Theatre, London, in his *The Journal of a London Playgoer* (1866; repr. 1891), pp. 56–61.

HENRY MORLEY was a prolific writer and editor and an indefatigable lecturer who became Professor of English in the University of London in 1865. He wrote theatre reviews for *The Examiner* from 1851 to 1866, when he reprinted most of them in collected form. His mission as a popular educator matched the ideals of

Samuel Phelps, who acted with Macready at Covent Garden and later co-managed Sadler's Wells Theatre from 1844 to 1862 where he staged over thirty of Shakespeare's plays, a total of 1,632 performances, often playing leading roles himself, and paying exceptional attention to *mise en scène* and to the improvement of the theatrical texts. Morley's reaction to Phelps's production of *A Midsummer Night's Dream* forms an interesting contrast to Hazlitt's 1816 review of a performance at Covent Garden (see pp. 43–6). The development of Sadler's Wells as a home of 'legitimate' drama had been made possible by the Theatres' Licensing Act of 1843, which abolished the monopoly of the Theatres Royal, Covent Garden and Drury Lane. As Morley makes clear, the suburban theatre attracted more earnestly attentive audiences than the patent houses.

EVERY reader of Shakespeare is disposed to regard the 'Midsummer Night's Dream' as the most essentially unactable of all his plays. It is a dramatic poem of the utmost grace and delicacy; its characters are creatures of the poet's fancy that no flesh and blood can properly present—fairies who 'creep into acorn-cups,' or mortals who are but dim abstractions, persons of a dream. The words they speak are so completely spiritual that they are best felt when they are not spoken. Their exquisite beauty is like that of sunset colours which no mortal artist can interpret faithfully. The device of the clowns in the play to present Moonshine seems but a fair expression of the kind of success that might be achieved by the best actors who should attempt to present the 'Midsummer Night's Dream' on the stage. It was, therefore, properly avoided by managers as lying beside and above their art; nor was there reason to be disappointed when the play some years ago furnished Madame Vestris' with a spectacle that altogether wanted the Shakespearian spirit.

In some measure there is reason for a different opinion on these matters in the 'Midsummer Night's Dream' as produced at Sadler's Wells by Mr. Phelps. Though stage fairies cannot ride on bluebells, and the members of no theatrical company now in existence can speak such poetry as that of the 'Midsummer Night's Dream' otherwise than most imperfectly, yet it is proved that there remains in the power of the manager who goes with pure taste and right feeling to his work, enough for the establishment of this play as a most charming entertainment of the stage.

Mr. Phelps has never for a minute lost sight of the main idea which governs the whole play, and this is the great secret of his success in the presentation of it. He knew that he was to present merely shadows; that spectators, as *Puck* reminds them in the epilogue, are to think they have slumbered on their seats, and that what appeared before them have been visions. Everything has been subdued as far as possible at Sadler's Wells to this ruling idea. The scenery is very beautiful, but wholly free from the meretricious glitter now in favour; it is not so remarkable for costliness as for the pure taste in which it and all the stage arrangements have been planned. There is no ordinary scene-shifting; but, as in dreams, one scene is made to glide insensibly into another. We follow the lovers and the fairies through the wood from glade to glade, now among trees, now with a broad view of the sea and Athens in the distance, carefully but not at all obtrusively set forth. And not only do the scenes melt dream-like one into another, but over all the fairy portion of the play there is a haze thrown by a curtain of green gauze placed between the actors and the audience, and maintained there during the whole of the second, third, and fourth acts. This gauze curtain is so well spread that there are very few parts of the house from which its presence can be detected, but its influence is every-where felt; it subdues the flesh and blood of the actors into something more nearly resembling dream-figures, and incorporates more completely the actors with the scenes, throwing the same green fairy tinge, and the same mist, over all. A like idea has also dictated certain contrivances of dress, especially in the case of the fairies.

Very good taste has been shown in the establishment of a harmony between the scenery and the poem. The main feature—the Midsummer Night—was marked by one scene so elaborated as to impress it upon all as the central picture of the group. The moon was just so much exaggerated as to give it the required prominence. The change, again, of this Mid-summer Night into morning, when Theseus and Hippolyta come to the wood with horn and hound, was exquisitely presented. And in the last scene, when the fairies, coming at night into the hall of Theseus, 'each several chamber bless,' the Midsummer moon is again seen shining on the palace as the curtains are drawn that admit the fairy throng. Ten times as much money might have been spent on a very much worse setting of the 'Midsummer Night's Dream.' It is the poetical feeling prompting a judicious but not extravagant outlay, by aid of which Mr. Phelps has produced a stage-spectacle more refined and intellectual, and far more absolutely satisfactory, than anything I can remember to have seen since Mr. Macready was a manager.

That the flesh and blood presentments of the dream-figures which constitute the persons of the play, should be always in harmony with this true feeling, was scarcely to be expected. A great deal of the poetry is injured in the speaking. Unless each actor were a man who combined with elocutionary power a very high degree of sensibility and genius, it could hardly be otherwise. Yet it cannot be said even here that the poet's effects entirely failed. The 'Midsummer Night's Dream' abounds in the most delicate passages of Shakespeare's verse; the Sadler's Wells pit has a keen enjoyment for them; and pit and gallery were crowded to the farthest wall on Saturday night with a most earnest audience, among whom many a subdued hush arose, not during, but just before, the delivery of the most charming passages. If the crowd at Drury Lane is a gross discredit to the public taste, the crowd at Sadler's Wells more than neutralizes any ill opinion that may on that score be formed of playgoers. The Sadler's Wells gallery, indeed, appeared to be not wholly unconscious of the contrast, for, when *Bottom* volunteered to roar high or roar low, a voice from the gallery desired to know whether he could 'roar like Brooke.'[2] Even the gallery at this theatre, however, resents an interruption, and the unexpected sally was not well received.

A remarkably quick-witted little boy, Master F. Artis,[3] plays *Puck*, and really plays it with faithfulness and spirit as it has been conceived for him by Mr. Phelps. His training has evidently been most elaborate. We see at once that his acts and gestures are too perfect and mature to be his own imaginings, but he has been quick-witted enough to adopt them as his own, and give them not a little of the charm of independent and spontaneous production. By this thoughtfulness there is secured for the character on the stage something of the same prominence that it has in the mind of closet-readers of the play.

Of Miss Cooper's[4] *Helena* we cannot honestly say very much. In that as in most of the other characters the spirit of the play was missed, because the arguing and quarrelling and blundering that should have been playful, dreamlike, and poetical, was much too loud and real. The men and women could not fancy themselves shadows. Were it possible so far to subdue the energy of the whole body of actors as to soften the tone of the scenes between *Theseus, Hippolyta, Lysander, Demetrius, Hermia*, and *Helena*, the latter character even on the stage might surely have something of the effect intended by the poem. It is an exquisite abstraction, a pitiful and moving picture of a gentle maid forlorn, playfully developed as beseems the fantastic texture of the poem, but not at all meant to excite mirth; and there was a very great mistake made when the dream was so worked out into hard literalness as to create constant laughter during those scenes in which *Helena*, bewildered by the change of mood among the lovers, shrinks and complains 'Wherefore was I to this keen mockery born?' The merriment which Shakespeare connected with those scenes was but a little of the poet's sunlight meant to glitter among tears.

It remains for us only to speak of the success of Mr. Phelps as *Bottom*, whom he presented from the first, with remarkable subtlety and spirit, as a man seen in a dream. In his first scene, before we know what his conception is, or in what spirit he means the whole play to be received, we are puzzled by it. We miss the humour, and we get a strange, elaborate, and uncouth dream-figure, a clown restless with vanity, marked by a score of little movements, and speaking ponderously with the uncouth gesticulation of an unreal thing, a grotesque nightmare character. But that, we find, is precisely what the actor had intended to present, and we soon perceive that he was right. Throughout the fairy scenes there is a mist thrown over *Bottom* by the actor's art. The violent gesticulation becomes stillness, and the hands are fixed on the breast. They are busy with the unperceived business of managing the movements of the ass's head, but it is not for that reason they are so perfectly still. The change of manner is a part of the conception. The dream-figure is dreaming, there is dream within dream, *Bottom* is quiet, his humour becomes more unctuous, but *Bottom* is translated. He accepts all that happens, quietly as dreamers do; and the ass's head we also accept quietly, for we too are in the middle of our dream, and it does not create surprise. Not a touch of comedy was missed in this capital piece of acting, yet *Bottom* was completely incorporated with the Midsummer Night's Dream, made an essential part of it, as unsubstantial, as airy and refined as all the rest. Quite masterly was the delivery by Mr. Phelps of the speech of *Bottom* on awakening. He was still a man subdued, but subdued by the sudden plunge into a state of an unfathomable wonder. His dream clings about him, he cannot sever the real from the unreal, and still we are made to feel that his reality itself is but a fiction. The preoccupation continues to be manifest during his next scene with the players, and his parting 'No more words; away; go away,' was in the tone of a man who had lived with spirits and was not yet perfectly returned into the flesh. Nor did the refinement of this conception, if we except the first scene, abate a jot of the laughter that the character of *Bottom* was intended to excite. The mock play at the end was intensely ludicrous in the presentment, yet nowhere farcical. It was the dream. *Bottom* as *Pyramus* was more perfectly a dream-figure than ever. The contrast between the shadowy actor and his part, between *Bottom* and *Pyramus*, was marked intensely; and the result was as quaint a phantom as could easily be figured by real flesh. Mr. Ray's[5] *Quince* was very good indeed, and all the other clowns were reasonably well presented.

It is very doubtful whether the 'Midsummer Night's Dream' has yet, since it was first written, been put upon the stage with so nice an interpretation of its meaning. It is pleasant beyond measure to think that an entertainment so refined can draw such a throng of playgoers as I saw last Saturday sitting before it silent and reverent at Sadler's Wells.

1. **Vestris**, Lucia Elizabeth (1797–1856), singer and actor-manager, married Charles James Mathews in 1838. Her production of *A Midsummer Night's Dream* at Covent Garden in 1840, in which she played Oberon, returned to Shakespeare's text, heavily abbreviated to make room for musical additions. It was more popular with the public than with the critics.

2. **Brooke**, Gustavus Vaughan (1818–66), tragedian noted for his fine voice.

3. **Artis**, F. Not otherwise known, so far as I can discover.

4. **Cooper**, Frances, later Mrs T. H. Lacy (1819–72), was Leading Comic Actress for Macready and performed many of Shakespeare's heroines with Phelps.

5. **Ray**, J. W., actor engaged by Phelps in 1840 as 'First Old Man'.

21 October 1854, Henry Morley on Samuel Phelps's production of *Pericles* at the Sadler's Wells Theatre, London, in his *The Journal of a London Playgoer* (1866; repr. 1891), pp. 78–84.

PHELPS'S production of *Pericles* illustrates his missionary zeal; the play had remained unperformed since 1738, when it had been given with little success in a heavily adapted version, *Marina*, by George Lillo (1693–1739). As Morley's account makes clear, Phelps, too, considerably altered the play, adding passages of his own composition, and making the most of the opportunities for spectacle. I omit Morley's lengthy summary of the plot.

OCTOBER 21.—'Pericles, Prince of Tyre,' that Eastern romance upon which Shakespeare first tried his power as a dramatist,[1] and which he may have re-adapted to the stage even while yet a youth at Stratford, has been produced at Sadler's Wells by Mr. Phelps, with the care due to a work especially of interest to all students of Shakespeare, and with the splendour proper to an Eastern spectacle....

[I]n the revival of the play Mr. Phelps was left to choose between two difficulties. The omission of Gower would be a loss to the play, in an artistic sense, yet the introduction of Gower before every act would very probably endanger its effect in a theatrical sense, unless the part were spoken by an actor of unusual power. The former plan was taken; and in adding to certain scenes in the drama passages of his own writing, strictly confined to the explanation of those parts of the story which Shakespeare represents Gower as narrating between the acts, Mr. Phelps may have used his best judgment as a manager. Certainly, unless he could have been himself the Gower as well as the *Pericles* of the piece, the frequent introduction of a story-telling gentleman in a long coat and long curls would have been an extremely hazardous experiment, even before such an earnest audience as that at Sadler's Wells.

The change did inevitably, to a certain extent, disturb the poetical effect of the story; but assuming its necessity, it was effected modestly and well. The other changes also were in no case superfluous, and were made with considerable judgment. The two scenes at Mitylene, which present *Marina* pure as an ermine which no filth can touch, were compressed into one; and although the plot of the drama was not compromised by a false delicacy, there remained not a syllable at which true delicacy could have conceived offence. The calling of *Blount* [*sic*] and his Mistress was covered in the pure language of *Marina* with so hearty a contempt, that the scene was really one in which the purest minds might be those which would take the most especial pleasure.

The conception of the character of *Pericles* by Mr. Phelps seemed to accord exactly with the view just taken of the play. He was the Prince pursued by evil fate. A melancholy that could not be shaken off oppressed him even in the midst of the gay court of King Simonides, and the hand of *Thaisa* was received with only the rapture of a love that dared not feel assured of its good fortune. Mr. Phelps represented the Prince sinking gradually under the successive blows of fate, with an unostentatious truthfulness; but in that one scene which calls forth all the strength of the artist, the recognition of *Marina* and the sudden lifting of the Prince's bruised and fallen spirit to an ecstasy of joy, there was an opportunity for one of the most effective displays of the power of an actor that the stage, as it now is, affords. With immense energy, yet with a true feeling for the pathos of the situation that had the most genuine effect, Mr. Phelps achieved in this passage a triumph marked by plaudit after plaudit. They do not applaud rant at Sadler's Wells. The scene was presented truly by the actor and felt fully by his audience.

The youthful voice and person, and the quiet acting of Miss Edith Heraud,[2] who made her *début* as *Marina*, greatly helped to set forth the beauty of that scene. The other parts had also been judiciously allotted, so that each actor did what he or she was best able to do, and did it up to the full measure of the ability of each. Miss Cooper[3] gave much effect to the scene of the recovery of *Thaisa*, which was not less well felt by those who provided the appointments of the stage, and who marked that portion of the drama by many delicacies of detail.

Of the scenery indeed it is to be said that so much splendour of decoration is rarely governed by so pure a taste. The play, of which the text is instability of fortune, has its characteristic place of action on the sea. *Pericles* is perpetually shown (literally as well as metaphorically) tempest-tost, or in the immediate vicinity of the treacherous waters; and this idea is most happily enforced at Sadler's Wells by scene-painter and machinist. They reproduce the rolling of the billows and the whistling of the winds when *Pericles* lies senseless, a wrecked man on a shore. When he is shown on board ship in the storm during the birth of *Marina*, the ship tosses vigorously. When he sails at last to the temple of Diana of the Ephesians, rowers take their places on their banks, the vessel seems to glide along the coast, an admirably-painted panorama slides before the eye, and the whole theatre seems to be in the course of actual transportation to the temple at Ephesus, which is the crowning scenic glory of the play. The dresses, too, are brilliant. As beseems an Eastern story, the events all pass among princes. Now the spectator has a scene presented to him occupied by characters who appear to have stepped out of a Greek vase; and presently he looks into an Assyrian palace and sees figures that have come to life and colour from the stones of Nineveh. There are noble banquets and glittering processions, and in the banquet-hall of King Simonides there is a dance which is a marvel of glitter, combinations of colour, and quaint picturesque effect. There are splendid trains of courtiers, there are shining rows of vestal virgins, and there is Diana herself in the sky.

We are told that the play of 'Pericles' enjoyed, for its own sake, when it first appeared, a run of popularity that excited the surprise and envy of some playwrights, and became almost proverbial. It ceased to be acted in the days of Queen Anne; and whether it would attract now as a mere acted play, in spite of the slight put upon it by our fathers and grandfathers, it is impossible to say, since the 'Pericles' of Sadler's Wells may be said to succeed only because it is a spectacle.

1. **first ... dramatist.** *Pericles* was often thought of as Shakespeare's first play, mainly because of lines referring to it by John Dryden (1631–1700) which speak of 'a first good play' (Prologue to *Circe*, 1677).

2. **Heraud,** Edith (born *c.*1836), went on to make a successful career as actor and reader.

3. **Cooper,** Fanny (Frances). See p. 92.

[1856], Theodor Fontane (1819–98) on Charles Kean's production of *The Winter's Tale* at the Princess's Theatre, London, translated by Russell Jackson from Fontane's pamphlet *Die Londoner Theater, mit besondere Rücksicht auf Shakespeare* (1858), reprinted in his collected *Causerien über Theater*, vols. 22–3, pp. 7–117, ed. Edgar Gross and Rainer Bachmann, in collaboration with Kurt Schreinert. The appended diary entry is from vol. 17 of the same edition, pp. 556–7.

CHARLES KEAN (1811–68), Eton-educated, respectable, earnest, scholarly—he became a Fellow of the Society of Antiquaries in 1857—was in many ways the antithesis of his disreputable genius of a father, Edmund. Along with his wife, the actress formerly known as Ellen Tree (1805–80), he managed the Princess's Theatre, London, from 1850 to 1859, putting on with great popular success elaborate productions of eighteen Shakespeare plays along with spectacular historical dramas that have not maintained their place in the repertoire.

Kean expended great effort on the visual and historical aspects of Shakespeare, going to enormous pains in the large, lengthy and detailed programmes offered to his audiences to cite precise historical sources for scenery and properties; on the bear in *The Winter's Tale*, for instance, he wrote 'The existence of bears in the East is exemplified in the 2nd chapter of the Second Book of Kings, in the 23rd, 24th, and 25th verses: "And he [Elisha] went up from thence unto Bethel . . . And there came forth two she bears out of the wood."' But his emphasis on spectacle was achieved at the expense of textual adaptation and abbreviation. The ponderous aspects of his work did not go unremarked by his contemporaries; an entertaining travesty of both play and production, *Perdita, or The Royal Milkmaid*, by William Brough, opened at the Lyceum less than a month after the last of the 102 consecutive performances of Kean's production, in which Ellen Terry, aged nine, played Mamillius. (Brough's piece is reprinted in *Shakespeare Burlesques*, ed. Stanley Wells, 5 vols. (1977), iii. 151–203.)

Fontane is best known for a series of realist novels published late in his long and varied career. During the 1850s he worked in London for a press agency set up by the Prussian government and reported for Berlin journals on Shakespeare productions, often drawing comparisons with German theatre practice. It seems particularly useful to have a foreign view on Kean as many reviews by his fellow countrymen seem uncritically adulatory. The account given here is taken from a short book which Fontane based on his reviews which is to be published in a translation by Russell Jackson by the Society for Theatre Research. It is supplemented by a diary entry recording additional details.

1. From *Die Londoner Theater*

T HIS play, as performed at the Princess's, is not satisfying. It is not easy to explain quite why this should be, though I think it is mainly to do with the *production*: but the play itself is partly to blame. Things that do not disturb in reading may present insurmountable problems in performance. We see too much of the babe in arms, which the jealous, demented Leontes[1] has cast away as the presumed illegitimate offspring of Hermione[2] and Polixenes,[3] for its effect to be anything other than comic. This giant doll is seen first in the arms of the lady-in-waiting, then laid at the feet of Leontes *in the centre of the stage*, and finally in the hands of old Antigonus[4] amid thunder and lighting. It is a source of merriment throughout, but the more pathetic the frantic Leontes becomes in his gestures, the more we laugh. It is not whole-hearted laughter. One cannot free oneself from the sensation of disruption, of a loss of aesthetic pleasure, and even as we laugh we feel discomfited. There is no point in discussing the bear at the end of the third act, which stalks across the stage in such a frighteningly natural manner. It is neither gruesome nor comic and only increases the discontent that the first three acts have done so much to arouse. I would have these misgivings about any production of *The Winter's Tale*, and indeed I would hardly recommend that it be attempted by our German theatres. On the other hand it goes without saying that Kean's production of the play, with its finicky way of doing just a little too much of a good thing, provokes particular reservations as well as these general ones. There is no question that the final two acts are superbly staged. One could see nothing more charming or skilful than the sheep-shearing in the fourth act, and nothing more magical than Hermione's descent from her pedestal in the final scene, as white as marble, but gradually suffused again with the blush of life. But these final acts are so rich in beauties that they have sufficient power in retrospect to make us forget what we have suffered during the greater part of the play. The smell of Kean's lamp is there throughout the course of the first three acts, and I am afraid I have to attest that this heaviness and deliberation—the pretentiousness that attaches itself to everything—frankly torments the spectator and makes him fidget with impatience.

The very first impression is decidedly unfortunate. The curtain rises, and we see a hall set out for a feast. Polixenes speaks, and we want to overhear the conversation that ensues, but meanwhile wine is mixed in golden vessels at the front of the stage. I have nothing against that, but the wine is mixed in a manner never seen before on any stage. Boys come in with terracotta vases on their shoulders, hold them high in the air with outstretched arms and pour the wine into the mixing-bowl in two long, glistening red streams. This wine-mixing takes at least five minutes, and for the whole time one is forced to pay attention to the streams of wine rather than the progress of the dialogue. The production is packed with with clumsy business of this kind. The presence of little Mamillius[5] is an embarrassment, and he ruins a whole scene with his affectedness. England is, generally speaking, the land of spoiled children, and being brought up behind the scenes is the least likely way of putting a stop to all affectation. 'Play, child!' says the jealous Leontes to his son, shuddering with emotion, and Mamillius needs no second bidding. He stands by his father's throne, leaning on its arm with his left arm. With his right hand he pulls backwards and forwards a little cart (a *duodecimo* edition of a victory chariot) dozens of times, like one of those little squirrels that have been trained to feed themselves. These are small details, but although they may not altogether ruin the performance, they are enough to spoil one's enjoyment. It must remain an open question whether this enjoyment would have been any greater if such annoyances as I have described above were removed. I never had the pleasure of becoming really engaged with the poetry itself. There are so many incidental felicities, that the effect of the whole escaped me. I only became involved when Perdita[6] and Florizel[7] appeared, but that is like a love-affair that begins in the very hour of parting. The first three acts have only *one* oasis, which is the great trial scene, where the pronouncement of the Delphic oracle testifies to Hermione's innocence. This scene was full of dramatic power.

The performances were for the most part unremarkable. Perdita and Florizel were effective largely because of the situation and the charm of their appearance. Only Autolycus[8] was outstanding. The English really do excel now in comic parts.

The person sitting next to me summed up his judgement in the words 'It is too heavy'. That hit the nail on the head. Everything in this production is overloaded, and perhaps no play has more claim than this to 'travel light'. The poetry collapses under the burden of stage effect imposed on it.

2. Diary Entry for 20 August 1856

(Fontane's diary records his immediate impressions of Kean's production. He refers to the appearance of the Moon in the allegorical interlude with which Kean marked the lapse of time between the third and fourth acts of the play: clouds filled the stage, then 'Luna' appeared in her chariot, accompanied by the stars (personified); after they sank into the ocean, Time appeared, sitting atop a huge sphere.)

I WATCHED the performance with my mind already made up. After everything I had heard about it, especially from those who could not admire all this colour and splendour enough, I had taken most decidedly against it. Up to the fourth act this prejudice was fully justified, 'boring—affected nonsense' I murmured to myself alternately. But my opinion changed with the fourth act. I could resist no longer... From the very moment when *Luna* appeared in the clouded sky and shone her magic light through the theatre, the play was no longer the same for me. Humour, sincere joy, unaffected love, poetic wonder, and the rediscovery that is so fraught with the spirit of reconciliation—all break in upon us in a heady succession, and our heart laughs and bounds in continual joy.

The last scene: Hermione as a stone statue, suddenly achieving life and speech, is magical, but the most entrancing part is still the pastoral scene in the fourth act. I have never seen anything more delightful. The radiant landscape, the joy of Southern life, the colourful yet simple costumes, the carefree love of the young shepherd folk, the simple sounds of the music, the beautiful gestures of the maidens, who lead the dance up and down; then suddenly a loud noise in the air, satyrs and fauns capering and leaping, children cheering, tambourines jingling, and then everyone dancing, laughing, singing—conjured up the beautiful South to me, the South that I now have an indescribable longing for. I want to see no more of this *money-making* nation: there is nothing at all in it to warm the heart.

How touched I was by this simple scene between Perdita (Miss Charlotte [*sic*] Leclercq) and Florizel (Miss Heath)! The two girls were good enough to eat, though Miss Leclercq is a coquette, and might have spoiled the whole scene. But she had adopted a childish manner to go with the childish role. Nothing disturbed the magic of this delightful pastoral scene. Now, for the first time, I understand how the best brains of a whole century can take pleasure in such representations. One sees an ideal world, and one believes in it. One believes, because the heart of man needs this belief. After all we did once live in a paradise, or will live in one again: this longing is either a puzzling memory or a sense of what is to come. Happiness lies not in passion, but in peace. The man who is out of breath has different notions of heaven from the madcap. In the hustle and bustle of the world one comes to believe that there is pleasure in simply *watching*, and being a mere spectator is not 'boring' as in younger days one laughed and swore it would be. O Shakespeare, O Kean, O

Miss Charlotte Leclercq, what have you done?—You have read me a sermon, more effectively than any preacher, and the impression cannot be erased by imagining that Miss Charlotte possibly has three illegitimate children and twice as many lovers. In the end, it is all no more than a longing for the South. And when I have seen the South, what then?!

1. **Leontes** was played by Kean.
2. **Hermione** was played by Mrs Kean.
3. **Polixenes** was played by John Ryder (1814–85), a declamatory actor who worked with Macready as well as Charles Kean.
4. **Antigonus** was played by John Cooper (died 1870 aged 77), who also acted with Vestris and Phelps.
5. **Mamillius**. (Alice) Ellen Terry (1847–1928; Dame of the British Empire 1925) went on to become one of England's greatest Shakespearian actresses, famous for her performances with Henry Irving. She writes touchingly and illuminatingly about this production in her book *The Story of My Life* (1908). A photograph of her with the cart and Charles Kean is reproduced as Pl. 4.
6. **Perdita** was played by Carlotta Leclercq (1840–93), a child performer who went on to make a successful career acting especially with Charles Fechter in England and America; Clement Scott called her 'the sweetest Perdita ... ever seen'.
7. **Florizel** was played by a young woman, Caroline Heath (1833–87), who had made her début at the Princess's in 1852 and went on to play in a number of Kean's productions.
8. **Autolycus** was played by John Pritt Harley (1786–1858), a successful actor in character roles, and a close friend of Kean.

---

24 April 1858, Charles Kean's production of (and performance in) *King Lear*, anonymous review from *The Illustrated London News*, reprinted in *Eyewitnesses of Shakespeare*, edited by Gāmini Salgādo (1975), pp. 287–90.

THE revival of the 'Lear,' as we had previously announced, took place on Saturday evening at this theatre, and fully justified the expectations that had been formed: we may add, more than justified them, and in ways that had not been previously imagined. There is always danger in scenic illustration, pictorially carried out and archaeologically conducted, that the spectacular will overlay the dramatic, and thus the poetic and histrionic suffer from too violent a contrast with the stage appointments. In this case nothing of the kind happens. The subordination of the mechanist and the painter to the poet and actor is duly maintained throughout, and yet the widest scope has been accorded to their talents. The action of the drama being placed in the mythic period, there is, of course, no authority that can be appealed to; the manager is consequently left at liberty to select the epoch that may best answer the purpose of theatrical interpretation. The earliest that could be taken would of course be the most preferable, and therefore we think Mr. Kean has acted judiciously in choosing the Anglo-Saxon era of the eighth century 'for the regulation of the scenery and dresses, as affording a date sufficiently remote, while it is at the same time associated with the British soil.' His details are in all respects picturesque, and nothing finer in this way was ever done than the second scene of the first act, representative of the Room of State in the palace of the old Monarch. The Saxon adornments of spear, shield, shaft, and skin, antlers and body of the deer, with other trophies of the battle and the chase, the primitive hearthstone and the blazing yule-log, and similar accessories too numerous to record or to remember, gave to the long and slanting apartment a romantic appearance that could not be exceeded for its barbaric gorgeousness of state and ceremonial splendour. Then the grouping of the old King and his three daughters was admirable; and the motion of the scene, including the exits and entrances, was actualised in the most ingenious manner. The whole was full of invention, original, suggestive, and vitally pleasing. The next scene was the courtyard in the Duke of Albany's palace, rendered still more significant by the return of Lear from the boar-chase, attended by his knights and huntsmen. But this was far excelled by the scene that opened the second act, representing the exterior of the Earl of Gloster's castle by night, fortified, in the manner of the Anglo-Saxons' camps, by pallisades. Nevertheless, greater excellence was attained, both in the mechanist's and scene-painter's department, in the second scene of the third act—that of the heath, with the storm of thunder and lightning. The clouds and electric fluid travelling rapidly across the sky in the distance, and with a lurid gloom investing the entire landscape, were grandly terrific; and, when associated by the mind with the animated figures in the foreground—the raving Lear, the exhausted Fool, and the provident Kent—composed a picture that was truly sublime. But art had yet something else in store; for in the scene of the hovel some Druidical remains are introduced, and the wind through the roofless columns blows its organ-notes, that sound like music. In act four there is also a fine picture—'the country near Dover, showing a Roman road and an ancient obelisk;' to which may be added the last scene of the fifth act, which is also near Dover, and exhibits the camp of the British forces, with the distant view of a Saxon castle. All these scenes were exquisitely painted; each had also some special merit of its own, but so judiciously introduced that the action was in no wise interfered with by its illustrative accessory.

The dominant excellence of the revival consisted in the histrionic *genius* by which it was supported. Mr. Walter Lacy[1] as Edmund, Mr. Ryder[2] as Edgar, Mr. Graham as the Earl of Gloster, Mr. Cooper[3] as the Earl of Kent, and Miss Poole[4] as the Fool, had each parts specially suited to their several aptitudes. More especial commendation still may be accorded to Miss Kate Terry,[5] whose Cordelia was in all respects excellent—innocent and animated, intelligent and pathetic, modest and yet expressive. Miss Heath[6] and Miss Buften[7] were the Goneril and Regan, and both played with exemplary care these two most ungrateful parts. There was also a little part which, for its *vraisemblance*, should be mentioned: we mean Gloster's Old Tenant, impersonated by a Mr. Morris.[8] In all these points we recognise the care of the manager equally present in the minute as in the large, in the least as well as the most demonstrative. Thus, there was a unity and a harmony between part and part, and a common relation between the different effects, conducting to a common origin, and answering one and the same intelligent purpose.

Mr. C. Kean had prepared us by his Louis XI.[9] for a display of elaboration and finish in which the minutest points of character and dialogue should be profusely interpreted; but that part, thoroughly stage-eligible as it is, left yet the highest dramatic and poetic elements unvisited. In *Lear* these are the all-in-all. Every portion of it thoroughly demonstrates the most complete mastery over the wonderful language in which every conception and feeling of this magnificent tragedy is clothed.

Mr. Kean made good his impression right early in the play. No sooner does poor Cordelia falter in her utterance than the overloving King, feeling his heart rebuked by an unsatisfactory response, is constrained to give decided indications of the most grievous disappointment that he has undergone. The revulsion of feeling is as natural as it is powerful. When we next see him, Lear has recovered his serenity. He has returned cheerful and weary from the chase, his appetite awakened, and his desire for dinner urgent. But now come the signs of a change of mood; for neglect has usurped the place of observance, and the old King is purposely insulted by Goneril's menials; at last, by Goneril herself. This is too much. Astonishment seizes on the King; then for a while he collects himself, but at length he gives the full tide of passion way, and utters the wronged father's bitter malediction. Mr. Kean's delivery of the curse was perfect: the suppressed emotion, the irrepressible exclamatory impulse, and the passionate emphasis, were alike admirable.

At the end of the second act Lear is worked up to a similar state of mind in regard to Regan; and again the actor achieved an unparalleled triumph. At length nature, that always sympathises with the mind of man, represents by an external tempest the inward rage that consumes the outcast father and discrowned monarch; and the true actor is required to rise to the sublimity of the highest poetic conception, and the vigour of the boldest histrionic delineation. Mr. Kean's success was complete. With Lear's madness began a series of new triumphs. 'Reason in madness': that was the poet's problem, that is the actor's test. In the blending of these opposites the highest skill was exhibited. In the fourth and fifth acts Shakspeare, as his manner is, has diverted his subject into the calmer regions of fancy and feeling; and there revelling, mitigated the pain that the mere circumstantial horror of his story would else have inflicted. Fantastic frenzy succeeds to fierce madness; and restoration to sanity, preceding a catastrophe that crushes the heart, demonstrates that the world is no place for the pure affections, but one of probation only, where compromises of all sorts are needed—

> Vex not his ghost. O, let him pass! He hates him
> That would upon the rack of this tough world
> Stretch him out longer.

The triumphant development of genius displayed by Mr. Kean in his embodiment of Shakspeare's sublime creation places beyond doubt his supremacy as a histrionic artist. We have only to add that the audience testified their sense of its excellence by repeated plaudits and frequent summons before the curtain.

1. **Lacy**, Walter (1809–98), a successful comic and character actor.

2. **Ryder**, John, see p. 99, n. 2.

3. **Cooper**, John, see p. 99, n. 4.

4. **Poole**, Miss (died in 1906 aged 85).

5. **Terry**, Kate (1844–1924), eldest sister of Ellen; she had made her first stage appearance aged three, and was a young Cordelia.

6. **Heath**, Caroline. See p. 99, n. 7.

7. **Buften** (or Bufton), Eleanor (1840–93). After working with Charles Kean she went on to take leading roles in comedies and burlesques at the Strand Theatre.

8. **Morris**, Mr. [unidentified].

9. **Louis XI**, central character of a melodrama by Casimir Delavigne, translated by Dion Boucicault (?1820–90), in which Kean scored a great hit in 1855.

[*c.*1850–*c.*1860], Henry Austin Clapp (1841–1904), on Charlotte
Cushman (1816–76) as Queen Katharine in *Henry VIII*, from his
Reminiscences of a Dramatic Critic (Boston and New York, 1902),
pp. 86–92.

CLAPP was theatre critic for the *Boston Daily Advertiser* from 1868 to 1902, and
for the *Boston Herald* from 1902 to 1904. He had a high reputation for fairness
and incorruptibility. The American Charlotte Cushman began her career as an
opera singer, unsuccessfully playing the Countess in *The Marriage of Figaro* in
her nineteenth year; the following year she acted Lady Macbeth, and she went on
to become the leading American actress of her time, often playing with Macready. She made her London début at the Princess's Theatre with Edwin Forrest
in 1845. She frequently played men, and was especially fine as Romeo. Her first
performance as Queen Katharine was in 1839; in 1857 she added Cardinal Wolsey,
in the same play, to her list of roles.

MISS CUSHMAN's impersonation of the Queen Katharine of *Henry
VIII*. must be accounted her crowning achievement, and, therefore, the highest histrionic work of any American actress. I shall merely
note, with little detailed comment, the grandeur and simplicity of the
character as she presented it in the first three acts of the play. Here, her
Katharine was a document in human flesh, to show how a heavenly
minded humility may be a wellspring of dignity, how true womanly
sensibility may exalt the queenliness of a sovereign. The bearing of
Katharine at the trial, in the second act, has been discussed till the
theme is trite, and Mrs. Siddons's[1] interpretation of the scene and of its
most famous line has been enforced, I suppose, upon her successors. The
great daughter of the house of Kemble may, perhaps, have made the
attack upon Wolsey, in 'Lord Cardinal, | To you I speak,' more prepotent
and tremendous than it was possible for her transatlantic sister-in-art to
make it; but it is not to be believed that any player could have surpassed
Miss Cushman in the unstudied eloquence of the appeal of the wife and
mother to the hard heart of the Royal Voluptuary, who sat 'under the
cloth of state,' his big red face, as Mademoiselle de Bury[2] says, almost
'bursting with blood and pride.'

It was in the second scene of the fourth act that Miss Cushman's genius
and art found their loftiest and most exquisite expression. Katharine—
now designated in the text as 'dowager,' since Anne Bullen wears the
crown—is led in, 'sick,' by her two faithful attendants, Griffith and
Patience. The careful reader of the text will mark the transition from

the previous scene, filled with the pomp and throng of Anne's coronation and with sensuous praises of the young queen's beauty, to the plain room at Kimbolton, whence a homely, discarded wife of middle age is passing into the Valley of the Shadow of Death. Nothing of its kind that I have heard surpassed the actress's use of the 'sick' tone of voice through all of Katharine's part of the fine dialogue. 'Querulous' is the only adjective that will describe that tone, and yet 'querulous' is rude and misdescriptive. The note was that which we all recognize as characteristic of sufferers from sickness, after many days of pain, or when an illness has become chronic. In Katharine this tone must not be so pronounced as to imply mental or moral weakness or a loss of fortitude: it was but one of the symptoms of the decay of the muddy corporal vesture in which her glorious soul was closed. Miss Cushman avoided excess with the nicest art, but quietly colored the whole scene with this natural factor of pathos. A finely appealing touch was made on the words in her first speech,—

> 'Reach a chair:
> So; now, methinks, I feel a little ease,'—

which were spoken first with the breaks and halts of an invalid, then with a slight comfortable drop in pitch, succeeded by a little sigh or grunt of relief at the period. All that followed was exceedingly noble,—her pity for Wolsey in his last humiliations, her pious prayer for his soul, her just, intuitive comment upon his grievous faults, her magnanimous acceptance of Griffith's attributions of merit to her implacable foe. As the shadows deepened about the sick woman, Miss Cushman's power took on an unearthly beauty and sweetness which keenly touched the listener's heart, often below the source of tears. Her cry, out of the depths of her great storm-beaten heart, of infinite longing for the rest of paradise, after her vision of the 'blessed troop,' who invited her to a banquet,—

> 'Spirits of peace, where are ye? are ye all gone,
> And leave me here in wretchedness behind ye?'—

will be recalled to-day by thousands of men and women, and at this mere mention the lines will echo and reëcho through the chambers of their memories. Katharine's one flash of indignation at the rudeness of a messenger—queenly wrath, for an instant clearing her voice and lifting her form—made more effective the rapid lapse in strength which naturally followed. Capucius, the gentle envoy of her 'royal nephew,' the Emperor Charles V., has entered with messages of 'princely commendations' and comfort from King Henry. To him she gave her last charges, all for deeds of loving-kindness to those about her, with an eagerness of desire which carried through her broken voice. Her messages of meekness and unfaltering affection to her false husband were, of all her touching words, the most poignant. In her commendation of her daughter Mary to the king, who is besought 'a little to love' the child,—

> 'for her mother's sake that lov'd him,
> *Heaven knows how dearly,'*—

and in her word of farewell to Henry,—

> 'Remember me
> In all humility unto his highness:
> *Say his long trouble now is passing*
> *Out of this world: tell him, in death I bless'd him,*
> *For so I will,'*—

the supreme point of pathos was reached. The throb and thrill of her voice in the italicized lines deserve never to be forgotten. After the word 'say' there was a second's hesitation, then the phrase descriptive of herself, 'his long trouble,' was breathed in a sort of sob, into which was concentrated with meek unconsciousness a damning indictment of her cruel lord.

Throughout the final fifty verses of the scene Miss Cushman caused Katharine's voice to grow gradually thicker, as the night of death closed in upon sight and speech. But Katharine's last command, that she 'be used with honour' after her death, and, 'although unqueen'd,' be interred 'yet like a queen, and daughter to a king,' given slowly and with the clutch of the Destroyer upon her throat, was superb and majestic. The queenly soul had prevailed, and wore its crown despite the treason of king, prelates, and courts. After Miss Cushman, all recent attempts, even by clever actresses, to impersonate Katharine of Aragon seem to me light, petty, and ineffectual.

1. **Siddons**, Sarah. See p. 37.
2. **de Bury**, Mademoiselle [not identified].

November 1874, Clement Scott (1841–1904) on Henry Irving
(1838–1905) as Hamlet, at the Lyceum Theatre, London; from his
'The Bells' to 'King Arthur' (1896), pp. 61–7.

SCOTT was a prolific writer who worked for many journals and was especially
associated with the *Daily Telegraph*, for which he wrote on theatre from 1871 to
1899. He also wrote plays, and published extensively on the theatre.

Irving (originally John Henry Brodribb) first appeared on stage in 1856. The
production reviewed here gave him his first major success as Hamlet; it ran for
200 nights. In 1879 he inaugurated his managership of the Lyceum, which lasted
till 1899, in the same role. For all his idiosyncrasies, he became a legend in his
lifetime. I omit Scott's opening paragraphs.

ALL present longed to see Hamlet. Bernardo and Marcellus, the
Ghost, the platform, the grim preliminaries, the prologue or introduction to the wonderful story, were, as usual, tolerated—nothing more.
Away go the platform, the green lights, the softly-stepping spirit, the
musical-voiced Horatio. The scene changes to a dazzling interior, broken
in its artistic lines, and rich with architectural beauty; the harps sound, the
procession is commenced, the jewels, and crowns, and sceptres, dazzle,
and at end of the train comes Hamlet. Mark him well, though from this
instant the eyes will never be removed from his absorbing figure. They
may wander, but they will soon return. The story may interest, the
characters may amuse, the incidents may vary, but from this moment
the presence of Hamlet will dwarf all else in the tragedy. How is he
dressed, and how does he look? No imitation of the portrait of Sir
Thomas Lawrence,[1] no funereal velvet, no elaborate trappings, no Order
of the Danish Elephant, no flaxen wig after the model of M. Fechter,[2] no
bugles, no stilted conventionality. We see before us a man and a prince, in
thick robed silk and a jacket, or paletot, edged with fur; a tall, imposing
figure, so well dressed that nothing distracts the eye from the wonderful
face; a costume rich and simple, and relieved alone by a heavy chain of
gold; but, above and beyond all, a troubled, wearied face displaying the
first effects of moral poison.

The black, disordered hair is carelessly tossed about the forehead,
but the fixed and rapt attention of the whole house is directed to the
eyes of Hamlet: the eyes which denote the trouble—which tell of the
distracted mind. Here are 'the windy suspiration of forced breath,'
'the fruitful river in the eye,' the 'dejected 'haviour of the visage.' So subtle
is the actor's art, so intense is his application, and so daring his disregard

of conventionality, that the first act ends with comparative disappointment. Those who have seen other Hamlets are aghast. Mr. Irving is missing his points, he is neglecting his opportunities. Betterton's[3] face turned as white as his neck-cloth, when he saw the Ghost. Garrick[4] thrilled the house when he followed the spirit. Some cannot hear Mr. Irving, others find him indistinct. Many declare roundly he cannot read Shakespeare. There are others who generously observe that Hamlets are not judged by the first act; but over all, disputants or enthusiasts, has already been thrown an indescribable spell. None can explain it; but all are now spell-bound. The Hamlet is 'thinking aloud,' as Hazlitt[5] wished. He is as much of the gentleman and scholar as possible, and 'as little of the actor.'

We in the audience see the mind of Hamlet. We care little what he does, how he walks, when he draws his sword. We can almost realise the workings of his brain. His soliloquies are not spoken down at the footlights to the audience. Hamlet is looking into a glass, into 'his mind's eye, Horatio!' His eyes are fixed apparently on nothing, though ever eloquent. He gazes on vacancy and communes with his conscience. Those only who have closely watched Hamlet through the first act could adequately express the impression made. But it has affected the whole audience— the Kemble[6] lovers, the Kean[7] admirers, and the Fechter rhapsodists. They do not know how it is, but they are spell-bound with the incomparable expression of moral poison.

The second act ends with nearly the same result. There is not an actor living who on attempting Hamlet has not made his points in the speech, 'Oh! what a rogue and peasant slave am I!' But Mr. Irving's intention is not to make points, but to give a consistent reading of a Hamlet who 'thinks aloud.' For one instant he falls 'a-cursing like a very drab, a scullion;' but only to relapse into a deeper despair, into more profound thought. He is not acting, he is not splitting the ears of the groundlings; he is an artist concealing his art: he is talking to himself; he is thinking aloud. Hamlet is suffering from moral poison, and the spell woven about the audience is more mysterious and incomprehensible in the second act than the first.

In the third act the artist triumphs. No more doubt, no more hesitation, no more discussion. If Hamlet is to be played like a scholar and a gentleman, and not like an actor, this is the Hamlet. The scene with Ophelia turns the scale, and the success is from this instant complete. But we must insist that it was not the triumph of an actor alone: it was the realisation of all that the artist has been foreshadowing. Mr. Irving made no sudden and striking effect, as did Mr. Kean. 'Whatever nice faults might be found on this score,' says Hazlitt, 'they are amply redeemed by the manner of his coming back after he has gone to the extremity of the stage, from a pang of parting tenderness to press his lips to Ophelia's hand. It had an electrical effect on the house.' Mr. Irving did not make his success by any theatrical *coup*, but by the expression of the pent-up agony of a harassed and disappointed man. According to Mr. Irving, the very sight of Ophelia, is the keynote of the outburst of his moral disturbance. He loves this woman; 'forty thousand brothers' could not express his overwhelming passion, and think what might have happened if he had been allowed to love her, if his ambition had been realised. The more he looks at Ophelia, the more he curses the irony of fate. He is surrounded, overwhelmed, and crushed by trouble, annoyance, and spies.

They are watching him behind the arras. Ophelia is set on to assist their plot. They are driving him mad, though he is only feigning madness. What a position for a harassed creature to endure! They are all against him. Hamlet alone in the world is born to 'set it right.' He is in the height and delirium of moral anguish. The distraction of the unhinged mind, swinging and banging about like a door; the infinite love and tenderness of the man who longs to be soft and gentle to the woman he adores: the horror and hatred of being trapped, and watched, and spied upon, were all expressed with consummate art. Every voice cheered, and the points Mr. Irving had lost as an actor were amply atoned for by his earnestness as an artist. Fortified with this genuine and heart-stirring applause, he rose to the occasion. He had been understood at last. To have broken down here would have been disheartening; but he had triumphed.

The speech to the players was Mr. Irving's second success. He did not sit down and lecture. There was no affectation or princely priggishness in the scene at all. He did not give his ideas of art as a prince to an actor, but as an artist to an artist. Mr. Irving, to put it colloquially, buttonholed the First Player. He spoke to him confidentially, as one man to another. He stood up and took the actor into his confidence, with a half deferential smile, as much as to say, 'I do not attempt to dictate to an artist, but still these are my views on art.' But with all this there was a princely air, a kindly courtesy, and an exquisite expression of refinement which astonished the house as much from its daring as its truth. Mr. Irving was gaining ground with marvellous rapidity. His exquisite expression of friendship for Horatio was no less beautiful than his stifled passion for Ophelia. For the one he was the pure and constant friend, for the other the baffled lover.

Determined not to be conquered by his predecessors, he made a signal success in the play scene. He acted it with an impulsive energy beyond all praise. Point after point was made in a whirlwind of excitement. He lured, he tempted, he trapped the King, he drove out his wicked uncle conscience-stricken and baffled, and with an hysterical yell of triumph he sank down, 'this expectancy and rose of the fair State,' in the very throne which ought to have been his, and which his rival had just vacated. It is difficult to describe the excitement occasioned by the acting in this scene. When the King has been frighted, the stage was cleared instantaneously. No one in the house knew how the people got off. All eyes were fixed on Hamlet and the King; all were forgetting the real play and the mock play, following up every move of the antagonists, and from constant watching they were almost as exhausted as Hamlet was when he sank a conqueror into the neglected throne.

It was all over now. Hamlet had won. He would take the ghost's word for a thousand pounds. The clouds cleared from his brow. He was no longer in doubt or despair. He was the victor after this mental struggle. The effects of the moral poison had passed away, and he attacked Rosencrantz and Guildenstern in the Recorder scene with a sarcasm and a withering scorn which were among the results of a reaction after pent-up agony. But this tremendous act was even now not yet over. There was the closet-scene still to come—a scene which still further illustrates the daring defiance of theatrical tradition exhibited by Mr. Irving. If the Hamlet was to be a mental study it should be one to the last. The actor who could conquer prejudices so far, was bound to continue, and when the audience looked at the arras for the pictures, or round the necks of the actors and actresses for the counterfeit presentment of two brothers, they found nothing.

Mr. Irving intended to conjure up the features of the dead King by a mental struggle, not by any practical or painted assistance. Speaking of David Garrick, Mr. Percy Fitzgerald[8] says, 'it was a pity he did not break through the stale old tradition of Hamlet's pulling out the two miniatures instead of the finer notion suggested by Davies of having them on the tapestry—*or the better idea still of seeing them with his mind's eye only.*'

It is this idea which Mr. Irving adopts, and with so striking a success that the audience could scarcely believe that they had for so many years been misled. It is unquestionably the correct view to take, and it can be done with the best possible effect. An act which was such an intellectual strain as this for both actor and audience could not fail to be felt. It was exhausting, overpowering. The play ought to have ended here. It was too much for one night.

The nervousness and paralysing excitement occasioned by such an evening, made its mark on the actors. It was too great an effort. The fear of being shut out from a glass of beer before midnight frightened the audience, and there were a few minutes of doubt and anxiety. But art conquered, and the audience obeyed. Miss Isabel Bateman[9] came on to play the mad scene of Ophelia, at the very moment when the house was longing for reaction, and was hungry to be free. She conquered at the most important instant of the evening, and she crushed down cruel scoffs by her true artistic impulse. It was a great sight to see the young lady—a true artist—sitting down, playing with the flowers, and acting the most difficult scene that was ever written, at a moment when it required the greatest discipline to keep peace. But Miss Bateman conquered, with the rest of the artists, mainly owing to the admirable taste and assistance of an audience loyal to, and appreciative of, art. Not all the heresies of Garrick, nor the sarcasms of Voltaire,[10] would permit Mr. Bateman[11] to remove, either the King's praying scene, or the churchyard ceremonies. Poor Mr. Swinbourne[12] went through the first, to a chorus of hammering and shouting from behind; and Mr. Compton,[13] as the First Gravedigger, had not time to remove his ten waistcoats. Still the audience, true to its purpose, never ventured to interfere. The strain upon the nervous system of Mr. Irving upon so important an occasion, the growing lateness of the hour, and the wealth of beauty in the play, prevented the success which will yet be obtained by Ophelia's mad scene, by Mr. Compton's acting of the Clown, or Gravedigger, and by Hamlet's churchyard passion. But let it not for a moment be supposed that Hamlet ended in an anti-climax. A fencing scene between Hamlet and Laertes, which would have rejoiced the heart of M. Angelo,[14] and which will, owing to the practice and industry of both Mr. Irving and Mr. Leathes,[15] make us forget the tradition of Charles Kean[16] and Alfred Wigan[17] in the 'Corsican Brothers';[18] to say nothing of the murder of the King by Hamlet, which, as regards impulse, determination, and effect, has never been equalled, put the final touches to this overwhelming work.

It may be, that the intellectual manager will yet have to see how far 'Hamlet' can be curtailed to suit this luxurious and selfish age. There are not many audiences which will relinquish their beer for the sake of art. This was a very special occasion. But the supreme moment for the audience had come when the curtain fell. If they had sacrificed their refreshment, waiting there, as many of them had done, since three o'clock in the afternoon, they had done something for art. They had, at least, deserved the pleasure of cheering the artist who had inspired them. It was no *succès d'estime*. The actor of the evening had, in the teeth of tradition, in the most unselfish manner, and in the most highly artistic fashion convinced his hearers. William Hazlitt, the critic, was right. Here was the Hamlet who *thinks aloud*; here was the scholar, and so little of the actor. So they threw crowns, and wreaths, and bouquets, at the artist, and the good people felt that this artistic assistance had come at a turning point in the history of English dramatic art. 'A pensive air of sadness should sit reluctantly on his brow, but no appearance of fixed and sullen gloom. He is full of weakness and melancholy; but there is no harshness in his nature. He is the most amiable of misanthropes.' So wrote William Hazlitt of Hamlet.[19] It might have been written to-day of Henry Irving. 'I have acted Ophelia three times with my father, and each time, in that beautiful scene where his madness and his love gush forth together, like a torrent swollen with storms, that bears a thousand blossoms on its troubled waters, I have experienced such deep emotion, as hardly to be able to speak. The letter and jewel cases I was tendering him, were wet with tears.' So wrote Fanny Kemble[20] of her father, Charles Kemble.[21] The words might have been spoken of Henry Irving, whose scene with Ophelia will never be forgotten. This is not a critical essay on the distinguished merit of a most valuable performance, but a necessarily brief comment on the impressions registered by a remarkable evening at the play. Time will not allow one to linger as one might on the distinguished and loyal assistance of such artists and favourite actors as Mr. Thomas Mead,[22] Mr. Chippendale,[23] Mr. Swinbourne, and Miss Pauncefort.[24] The effect of Mr. Mead's splendid elocution, and of Miss Pauncefort's facial agony cannot be overrated. It would be highly pleasant also to congratulate such genuine young enthusiasts of another and more modern school, as Mr. George Neville,[25] Mr. Leathes, Mr. Beveridge,[26] and Miss Isabel Bateman. But our efforts, without prejudice, have been devoted to the actor who will be valued by his fellows, and to a performance which will make its mark in the dramatic history of our time. The position of Mr. Irving, occasionally wavering and pleasantly hesitating in the balance, has now been firmly established. The Hamlet of Henry Irving is a noble contribution to dramatic art.

1. **Lawrence**, Sir Thomas (1769–1830), painted numerous portraits of the Kemble family; the allusion is to his famous painting of John Philip as Hamlet, now in the Tate Gallery.

2. **Fechter**, Charles (1824–79); born in England of French parents and brought up partly in France, he played Hamlet with great success in England and America.

3. **Betterton**. See p. 18.

4. **Garrick**. See p. 20.

5. **Hazlitt**. See p. 38, and the later reference in this review.

6. **Kemble** (i.e. J. P.). See p. 33.

7. **Kean**. The reference could be to either Edmund or Charles (see pp. 38 and 64).

8. **Fitzgerald**, Percy (1834–1925). This is a slightly inaccurate quotation from his *The Life of David Garrick* (1868, revised 1899), pp. 256–7.

9. **Bateman**, Isabel(la) (1854–1934), an American, frequently performed with Irving.

10. **Voltaire**. See p. 28.

11. **Bateman**, H. W. (1813–75), lessee of the Lyceum; Isabel's father.

12. **Swinbourne**, Thomas (1823–95). Claudius in this production. He played many leading roles in London and the provinces.

13. **Compton**, Henry (1805–77), regarded as the best Shakespearian clown of his time.

14. **Angelo**, M., Domenico Angelo Malevolti (1716–1802), author of the classic *École d'Armes* (1763), translated as *The School of Fencing* (1787). His son Henry (?1760–1839) was also a distinguished fencing teacher.

15. **Leathes**, Edmund (1847–78), actor and manager.

16. **Kean**, Charles. See p. 64.

17. **Wigan**, Alfred (1817–78), actor and manager.

18. *The Corsican Brothers*, enormously successful melodrama by Dion Boucicault (?1820–90) in which Kean and Wigan fought a famous duel.

19. **Hazlitt . . . Hamlet**. These are the closing sentences of his essay on *Hamlet* in *Characters of Shakespere's Plays* (1817).

20. **Kemble**, Fanny (1809–93), actress, reader and abolitionist.

21. **Kemble**, Charles (1775–1854), younger brother of John Philip.

22. **Mead**, Thomas (1820–89), played the Ghost.

23. **Chippendale**, W. H. (1801–88), played Polonius; he was best known for playing old men.

24. **Pauncefort**, Georgina (1820–95), played Gertrude.

25. **Neville**, George (dates unknown), played Horatio, and Ross in Irving's 1875 *Macbeth*.

26. **Beveridge**, George (1845–1926), played First Player.

---

10 April 1875, Joseph Knight (1829–1907) on Tommaso Salvini (1829–1915) as Othello, from his *Theatrical Notes* (1875), pp. 19–25.

KNIGHT was appointed theatre critic of *The Literary Gazette* in 1860, and wrote for *The Athenaeum* from 1867 until he died. He edited *Notes and Queries* from 1883 until 1907. Salvini was a great Italian actor who won international acclaim as, especially, Hamlet and Othello. He toured extensively, usually (as in the production reviewed here) playing in Italian with his own company, but sometimes from 1880 playing in Italian while his fellow-actors spoke English. Among other reviews of his Othello is one by Henry James, reprinted in *The Scenic Art*, ed. Allan Wade (1949), pp. 173–5, but Knight gives the more vivid account.

IN coming before the public...as Othello, Signor Salvini has to fear little competition, either actual or retrospective. So unlike anything that the present generation has seen is, however, his impersonation of the Moor, that opportunity is scarcely offered for comparison. It is splendid alike in its qualities and its defects, in virtues which raise it to something like supremacy in tragic art, and in defects powerful enough to mar its beauty, and leave the prevalent impression on the mind one not far from disappointment. Much as English actors may learn from the distinguished stranger who now comes among us, it will be an evil day for art when young actors begin to train themselves in the school of which he is the most illustrious exponent.

Few physical advantages are wanting to Signor Salvini. His frame is manly and robust, his stature tall, his face handsome and expressive, and his voice powerful. These gifts have, of course, been cultivated to the utmost: the bearing is perfect in simplicity and nobility, the features are singularly mobile, and the music of the voice is as remarkable as its power.

Signor Salvini's conception of Othello is that we expect from a thoughtful, perceptive, and cultivated man. Othello with him is a barbarian, whose instincts, savage and passionate, are concealed behind a veneer of civilisation so thick that he is himself scarcely conscious he can be other than he appears. Friendly, loving, and courteous, he can, as Iago says:—

> As tenderly be led by the nose
> As asses are.

When the poison of jealousy ferments in his blood, the strife between the animal nature and the civilising influences of custom is long and sharp. In the end the barbarian triumphs, the concluding scene, if not wholly savage, exhibiting mere glimpses of those restraints which in the third act, though sorely tested, remain dominant. The picture is exact of a noble animal turning piteously in the toils in which it has been enmeshed, and finding its efforts at escape serve only to render its position more desperate.

In dwelling upon some salient features in the interpretation, it is well to note the gradual conquest of the intellectual nature and its disappearance before the rising passion and fury.

To the counsel of the Duke, in the first act, Othello listens with dignified attention. As Brabantio enters, uttering exclamations concerning his daughter's loss, mixed with charges against Othello, the face of the Moor exhibits a variety of emotions, of which pity is the most conspicuous. His address to the senators is delivered with calm and sustained dignity, and with less aid of gesture than is common. The first revelation of his true nature occurs upon the appearance of Desdemona, whom he covers with a glance of indescribable tenderness. As she claims from the Duke permission to go with her husband to the wars his gaze becomes burning. Forgetful of all restraints, he approaches and almost folds her in his arms; but awaking in time to recollections of the august presence in which he stands, he turns from her with a gesture of apology. The start with which he receives Brabantio's caution—

> Look to her, Moor; have a quick eye to see;
> She has deceived her father, and may thee—

shows not only his quickness in receiving a hint which, taken in conjunction with other matters, works afterwards 'like madness in the brain,' but his fiery and impetuous disposition.

His delivery of the speech in the second act, on rejoining Desdemona at Cyprus, is steeped in Southern voluptuousness, for which the words afford warrant, since words can scarcely depict more profound contentment or more burning love. The interruption of the brawl begotten of Cassio's drunkenness is noticeable only inasmuch as it exhibits Othello as the commander of men, and reveals the qualities which have raised a Moor to a position of trust in a republic so intolerant of strangers as that of Venice. A noteworthy touch of uxoriousness is found in the manner in which Othello, after limiting the punishment of Cassio to dismissal, grows more angered upon Desdemona's appearance:—

> Look, if my gentle love be not raised up!
> (*To* CASS.) I'll make thee an example.

Supreme beatitude is evinced in the look which accompanies the delivery in the next act of the well-known speech, 'Excellent wench,' etc. The duel with Iago commences, and uneasiness is gradually communicated to the mind of Othello by the 'leprous distilment' which Iago drops in his ear. Sitting at the table, Othello, at the first word, suspends his work, his attention becomes gradually close, until at the words, 'Thou dost mean something,' he rises from his chair, throwing down impatiently the pen he has been using. Few gestures are subsequently employed until the meaning of Iago's accusation is made plain. The slowness of his mind to drink in suspicion, and the manner in which presentiment of evil is transfigured into horror and rage, are the most striking and original characteristics of the interpretation. Iago's repetition of the charge previously brought against Desdemona of deceiving her father pains him, but communicates no downright mistrust, and the words 'Not a jot, not a jot' (*Punto, punto*) seem an attempt at self-encouragement. With uneasy steps he now paces about the room, drinking in the words of Iago, until slowly the foul accusation takes shape in his mind. Shortly and sharply, and with tones of authority, he bids his antient farewell. He would fain be alone and hide his struggles from all observation; the injunction, 'Set on thy wife to observe,' comes as an afterthought. A brief episode of the loss by Desdemona of the handkerchief and its transfer to Iago separates the two portions of the duel. When with mind almost distracted he re-enters, he gazes gloomily back through the door which he holds open. Then follows the most impressive scene of the play. The famous farewell to his former occupation is delivered with much pathos. It is virtually a farewell also to his better self. When the voice of Iago breaks the thread of his reflections, the animal nature springs to assert itself. Seizing fiercely Iago by the throat, he crushes the cowering miscreant to the ground, and in the whirlwind of his passion lifts his foot to stamp the heel upon his head, it might even be to stamp out his brains. Recalled, however, to reason, he turns away, and with averted head he stretches out his hand, and penitently, yet with a species of loathing, raises the prostrate wretch from the ground. In this scene, the one profoundly electrical effect of the interpretation is reached. Quitting Iago, he sits at the very back of the stage, until as the tempter deals the poison in stronger doses, and speaks of Cassio's sleeping words, he comes again forward to kneel and swear a terrible revenge.

Little opportunity is offered in the fourth act. His illworn courtesy to Desdemona renders more marked the menace of his eye, in which burns a lurid light of resolution. The blow before the messengers from Venice is well given, and the speech, 'She can turn, and turn,' is spoken with suppressed passion and enforced politeness, strikingly contrasted. The speech, 'Had it pleased Heaven,' etc., is delivered at the back of the stage. It has pathos, though scarcely in an eminent degree. When the interview with Desdemona is over, Othello shakes savagely the money in his purse in the ear of Emilia, and departs throwing it at her feet with a fine expression of scorn and indignation.

Thus far, though there are points on which we have doubts, the merits of the impersonation so completely overpower its defects, we have not stayed to hint censure. In the concluding scenes of the last act the conquest of the civilised being by the barbarian is carried out at the sacrifice of Shakspeare's intentions and at that of Art. After delivering the speech, 'It is the cause,' slowly, the first lines being spoken close to the door by which he enters, Othello kisses his sleeping wife, then goes to the window, and stands with the lightning playing upon his face. Desdemona wakes, sees him, and approaches. His recoil, expressive partly of unwillingness to embrace one who has so foully wronged him, next of fear lest the sweet seductive influence of her caress might yet unman him, is fine. After the short dialogue of supplication on the one side, and refusal on the other, he seizes her by the hair of the head, and, dragging her on to the bed, strangles her with a ferocity that seems to take a delight in its office. The murder committed, Othello walks agitatedly backwards and forwards, not answering the cry of Emilia. When she tells him of the death of Roderigo by the hand of Cassio he starts, then relapses into sullen fury of discontent. He remains motionless for a while, with eye glazing, as he learns how mightily he has been abused, then staggers forward with open mouth and with a countenance charged with tragic passion. The following words are delivered in a wild abandonment of grief, that in the end becomes inarticulate in utterance, and with an accompaniment of beating of his head with his hands which, according to English canons of art, is excessive. Suddenly the thought of the tempter comes to him. Crouching low like a wild beast, he prepares for a spring. A sword is in the girdle of one of the attendants. Upon this he seizes, and passes it with one thrust through the traitor's body. Staggering then to a seat, he commences, sitting and weeping, the final speech. Nearing the end, he rises, and at the supreme moment cuts his throat with a short scimitar, hacking and hewing with savage energy, and imitating the noise that escaping blood and air may together make when the windpipe is severed.

Nothing in art so terribly realistic as this death-scene has been attempted. It is directly opposed to Shakspeare, who makes Othello say—

> I took by the throat the circumcised dog,
> And smote him—thus.

A man does not take by the neck one whose throat he is going to cut, since he would cut his own fingers in so doing. He seizes one, on the contrary, into whose heart he is about to plunge a dagger. The word 'smote' in Shakspeare is, indeed, sufficiently clear to leave no room for doubt or misconception. The effect on the audience is repellent to the last degree. This kind of death-scene needs only such slight and easily provided additions as the rupture of a bladder of blood, which the actor might place within reach, the exhibition of a bleeding throat, and a stream of blood serpenting upon the floor, to reach the limits of attainable realism. Tendencies in the direction of this kind of so-called art were seen in Signora Ristori,[1] and marred her marvellously artistic impersonations. In the present case their effect is singularly detrimental to the artistic value of the performance. A movement in the same direction is, moreover, noticeable in other arts. When we instance the famous picture of Regnault,[2] 'An Execution in a Moorish Palace,' the reader will at once see the parallel we draw. It is a different matter even to give realistic effects in pictures and to introduce them into Shakspearian tragedy. Aristotle's definition of Tragedy has never been surpassed. Its aim is to give the pleasure which arises from pity and terror through imitation—τὴν ἀπὸ ἐλέου καὶ φόβου διὰ μιμήσεως ἡδονὴν παρασκευάζειν.[3] Terror is, indeed, the aim of all tragic art. When for this is substituted horror, and even commonplace horror, the degradation of art has commenced. Here is the one blot upon an interpretation which otherwise would command our warmest admiration. We have left ourselves no space to dwell on the version presented, which differs, in some respects, from that ordinarily adopted, upon the general cast, or upon any other features of interest. It may be mentioned that the get-up of Signor Salvini is always admirable, the most striking appearance being that assumed in the second act, when he is dressed in chain armour, with a steel helmet and hauberk.

1. **Ristori**, Adelaide (1822–1906), great Italian actress and manager, famous for her Lady Macbeth which she performed in English in London in 1882.
    2. **Regnault**, Henri Alexandre Georges (1843–71), French history and genre painter.
    3. **Aristotle** (384–322 BC), Greek philosopher; the quotation, translated in what goes before, is from his *Poetics*, 14, l. 5 in the Loeb Classical Library edition.

<hr/>

[1879–1905], William Winter (1836–1919) on Henry Irving as Shylock, from his *Shakespeare on the Stage* (1912), pp. 179–97.

WINTER was theatre critic of the *New York Tribune* from 1865 to 1909. He prepared acting versions of plays by Shakespeare for Edwin Booth and Augustin Daly, and published extensively on the theatre of his time. Irving first played Shylock in 1879 and is said to have given over 1,000 performances of the role in England and America. He used a severely shortened text, sometimes omitting the last act. The interpretation apparently darkened over the years. Winter's exceptionally detailed account is based on later performances; he is reported as having heard Irving say that Shylock was 'a bloody-minded monster—but you mustn't play him so, if you wish to succeed; you must get some sympathy with him'.

IRVING'S *Shylock* entered, for the first time, preceding *Bassanio*, who, obviously, had found him in the mart and spoken to him about a loan of money. He was seen to be a man stricken in years—his shoulders a little bowed, his knees a little bent, his face lined and wrinkled, his hair gray,— '*old* Shylock' in every detail,—but hardy, resolute, formidable, possessing the steel-sinewy, nervous vitality of the Hebrew race, and animated by indomitable will. His aspect was distinctively Jewish, and it was Orientally pictorial. His demeanor revealed a mind intensely interested, veiling that interest by a crafty assumption of indifference. His detested enemy had applied to him, to borrow money: that fact was singular, was astonishing; there might be no consequence in it, or there might proceed from it the opportunity, for which he had long hungered and thirsted, to strike that enemy dead. *Bassanio* must be made to repeat his request, and the matter must be carefully considered. One skirt of the *Jew's* gabardine,—a garment of rich material but of sober hue and well-worn,—was caught up at the side and held in the right hand, which also held a black crutch-stick, grasping it near the middle and more as though it were a weapon than a prop. Throughout the opening scene the mention by *Shylock* of the ducats desired by *Antonio* was made in a lingering, caressing tone, involuntarily expressive of his love of money, and the thumb and first two fingers of whichever hand happened to be free,—for he shifted his staff occasionally from one hand to the other,—were, from time to time, moved slowly, as though in the act of counting coins. The first speech, 'Three thousand ducats—Well?' only noted the sum, with an accent of inquiry; the second speech, 'For three months:—Well?' indicated watchful expectation of something to follow; but the third speech, '*Antonio* shall become *bound*,' was uttered with a strong emphasis on the merchant's name and on the word 'bound,' accompanied by a momentary flash of lurid fire in the dark, piercing, baleful eyes, a quick contraction of the muscles of arms and hands, instantly succeeded by a perfect resumption of self-control, as the calm, cold voice, reiterated the recurring question, 'Well?' The utterance of the declaration 'I *will* be *assured* I may' was sharp, incisive, almost fierce, but the tone quickly softened in delivery of the words that immediately follow. The rebuff beginning 'Yes, to smell pork,' was ejaculated in a bitter tone of contemptuous protest, till the close, when the words 'nor *pray* with you' were spoken in accents of deep solemnity. Then *Shylock* saw and recognized the approaching figure of *Antonio*,—a fact signified in the expression of his face, before he asked, with an entire change of manner, in a nonchalant, indifferent way, 'What news on the Rialto?' He then raised his left hand, as though to shade his eyes, and gazed intently into the distance, saying 'Who is he comes here?' There was in the action of Irving's *Shylock*, at that and at some other points, a viperous impartment of the *Jew's* inherent treachery and deep-seated malice—the duplicity which is characteristically false in circumstances in which it would be much easier to be true. *Bassanio* left the scene, to meet his friend *Antonio*, while *Shylock*, alone, delivered the self-communing speech which follows, not as an 'aside,' but as a soliloquy, gazing malevolently at the Christian friends, and contemptuously mimicking their greeting of one another. The line 'How like a *fawning publican* he looks!' was spoken with a loathing sneer, a peculiar long, soft emphasis of contempt and scorn being laid on the word 'fawning,' but that sneer instantly gave place to a glare of reptile hate, as the avowal of bitterest animosity was harshly snarled forth, with significant and appropriate stress on the second word of the second line:

> 'I *hate* him, for he is a Christian,
> But MORE, for that, in low simplicity,
> He lends out money *gratis*.'

Shylock was shown to be aware of the *Merchant's* approach, but also he was shown to assume, because of sheer, innate duplicity, an air of preoccupation, as though ignorant of the contiguity of the man whom thus he hated and denounced. His greeting to *Antonio* was that of cringing humility, and when he mentioned the feasibility of borrowing money from *Tubal*, 'a *wealthy* Hebrew' of his tribe, he lapsed into the condition of the sordid, specious, wily money-lender, incapable, from force of the habit of trickery, of anything like fair and open dealing. His manner became formal and his articulation sharply incisive, when saying 'I had forgot—three months,'— a pause, and then an intent look at *Bassanio*,—'*You* told me so.' The *Jew's* defence of usury was made with a slow, ruminative insistence on the details of the Biblical story of Jacob's thrift. The trenchant rebuke to *Antonio* was begun with an assumption of judicial restraint, a certain dignity, but, as the delivery of it proceeded, the feeling became intense, the utterance bitter, mordant, and fiery, such as might well incite the *Merchant's* angry retort; but at 'Why, look you, how you storm,' the manner of the *Jew*,—his rage repressed by a sudden exertion of will,—became meek and ingratiating. When he said, 'Your single bond,' *Shylock*, over-eager, touched the breast of *Antonio*, who thereupon drew back, wrapping his cloak around him, as though the touch of the *Jew* were a contamination, and in the brief pause which ensued *Shylock* was seen to curb his resentful exasperation at being treated as if he were a leper, the obvious effort being followed by a copious glow of cordiality, in the offer of 'kindness' and in the insidious proposal of the 'merry bond.' There was, in Irving's peculiar intonation and manner, when his *Shylock* said, 'An equal pound of *your fair flesh*,' a suggestion of latent, sinister meaning, as if his secret thought were, 'If my touch contaminates you, perhaps I shall soon give you reason, indeed, to dread it!' His delivery of 'O father Abraham, what these Christians are!' was so convincingly honest and earnest, in its apparent candor, that it might have beguiled even the most distrustful of hearers. At the close of the scene, *Antonio* and *Bassanio* having parted from him, *Shylock* turned away, moved a few steps, paused, turned back, glared after his foes, raised his crutch-stick and shook it, in menace, with a look of frightful hatred, making such an illuminative picture of the character as only the brush of inspired genius could convey.

In Irving's arrangement of the comedy the Second Act contained three scenes, the second being devoted to *Lorenzo's* love affairs, and the third, exceptionally picturesque and illuminative, devoted to *Shylock*, in his relation to the incident of *Jessica's* elopement. In this latter scene the place represented was a street in front of *Shylock's* house. At the back a finely painted drop afforded a spacious view of romantic Venice, in the dim starlight. A high bridge, spanning a canal, extended across the stage, from the upper left-hand corner to a point forward on the right. The bridge was accessible by steps. At the right of and below it was a building, fashioned with a projecting hood above the door,—the 'pent house' mentioned by *Lorenzo*. At the left of the stage, in the foreground, bordering the canal, was placed the house of *Shylock*, on the front of which was a prominent balcony. *Launcelot* and *Shylock* entered from that dwelling, the former in haste and perturbation, as if retreating from his harsh employer. *Shylock's* speech of dismissal to him,—'Well, thou shalt see,'—was spoken by Irving in a strain of censorious sarcasm, and the *Jew's* parting from his daughter, immediately before her flight, was effected in a mood of querulous anxiety, *Shylock* showing himself oppressed by presentiment of impending disaster: 'There is some ill a-brewing towards my rest.' At mention of *Bassanio*, when *Launcelot* said, 'My young master doth expect your reproach,' there was a quick accession of severity in *Shylock's* face and demeanor, and the tone in which, to the menial's blundering speech, he replied 'So do I—*his*'—was grim with expectancy of revenge. When he ended his authoritative delivery of the mandate, to *Jessica*, 'Lock up my doors,' he entered the house, was absent for a moment, and then returned, wearing a cloak and an orange-tawny, turban-like head-dress, and carrying a lantern and a staff. Hearing the voice of *Launcelot*, who was speaking in a hurried undertone to *Jessica*, but not hearing the words, he swiftly advanced to his daughter, as *Launcelot* sped away, seized her by the wrist, looked suspiciously upon her face and harshly put the question to her,— pointing with his stick after the departed servant,—'*What says* that fool of Hagar's offspring—ha?' Reassured by *Jessica's* ready lie, he turned from her, murmuring, 'The patch is kind enough,' and then, with the old proverb about the wisdom of precaution on his lips, ascended to the bridge and passed across it, out of sight. The elopement of *Jessica* with *Lorenzo* was then effected, in a gondola, which moved smoothly away in the canal, and the scene became tumultuous with a revel of riotous maskers, who sang, danced, frolicked, and tumbled in front of *Shylock's* house, as though obtaining mischievous pleasure in disturbing the neighborhood of the *Jew's* decorous dwelling. Soon that clamorous rabble streamed away; there was a lull in the music, and the grim figure of *Shylock*, his staff in one hand, his lantern in the other, appeared on the bridge, where for an instant he paused, his seamed, cruel face, visible in a gleam of ruddy light, contorted by a sneer, as he listened to the sound of revelry dying away in the distance. Then he descended the steps, crossed to his dwelling, raised his right hand, struck twice upon the door with the iron knocker, and stood like a statue, waiting—while a slow-descending curtain closed in one of the most expressive pictures that any stage has ever presented.

Irving did not follow the Macklin[1] tradition as to the acting of *Shylock* in the tremendous Street Scene of the Third Act,—the stage tradition, that is, which prescribes as imperative in that scene almost incessant movement, explosive vociferation, and lamentable and furious delirium. His reason, probably, was that he did not consider himself physically equal to the effort required by that method of treating the situation, or he may have deemed, and probably did deem, another method more effective upon the feelings of an audience. The treatment which he devised and employed was wonderfully potent. The convulsive passion, liberating the man from every restraint of prudence and every expedient of duplicity and bursting forth in torrid eloquence, the derascinating conflict between outraged parental authority and the animal instinct of paternity, the overwhelming access of religious fanaticism, the terrific wrath of despoiled avarice, and the savage determination to have a hellish revenge—all those shattering forces were implicated and displayed in Irving's acting of *Shylock*, in this tempestuous scene, with a spasmodic energy of natural emotion, transcending, in its power to excite pity while diffusing a sense of terror, any possible manifestation of mere physical excitement. When he entered, the 'outrageous passion' immediately consequent on his daughter's thievery and flight had somewhat abated. His dress was disordered. His gown (the cloak or gabardine had not been put on) was torn open at the throat, his hair was dishevelled, his hands were clenched, his movements were swift,—the mental tempest venting itself in physical agitation,—and as he approached, the jeers of his Christian persecutors being faintly audible in the distance, he was snarling and muttering to himself. When he perceived the Christians, *Salanio* and *Salarino*, the comrades of *Lorenzo* and *Bassanio*, his fury flamed forth again, and the glare of hatred which he bent upon them was shocking in its infernal intensity. The exclamation, 'My own flesh and blood *to rebel!*' commingled relentless anger with astounded incredulity. There was comparatively little movement on the part of *Shylock*, throughout this scene,—there was no yelling, and there was no rushing to and fro. The utterance of 'There I have another—*bad match*' expressed the infinite of loathing. The ominous words, 'Let him look to his bond,' were spoken in a lower tone than was used in speaking the associated sentences, and in the final iteration every word was uttered separately. 'Let—him—look—to—his—*bond!*' The furious response to *Salarino's* question about the flesh, 'What's that good for?' came like a lightning flash,—'To bait fish withal!' and then, after a pause of suspense, ensued the torrid invective, the greatest of all *Shylock's* speeches, uttered at first in an almost suffocated voice,—'If it will feed nothing else it will feed my revenge,'—but presently in the fluent tones of completely liberated passion. As the infuriated *Jew* proceeded the Christians involuntarily shrank from him and he slowly moved toward them, until he had fiercely enunciated the reply to his own question, 'Why, revenge!'—at which point he whirled away and came down the stage in the opposite direction, twice ejaculating the word 'Revenge,' as if convulsed with delirium, and then he stopped and again turned on his enemies. Throughout that exacting scene Irving never lost control equally of the situation and the audience, but held both in complete thrall, not pausing to allow the destructive interjection of applause, after the word 'Revenge,'—an interruption frequently permitted by performers of *Shylock*,—but commanding his auditors till the superbly rounded close, 'It shall go hard but *I* will *better* the *instruction!*' which always elicited a tremendous burst of enthusiastic fervor. The awful picture of wrath which he had thus created was held by him for a moment, and then *Shylock* seemed to become oblivious of the Christians, and, turning from them, encountered his associate and emissary, *Tubal*. That person came from the left of the stage, as *Salanio* and *Salarino* vanished at the right, and *Shylock*, meeting him, laid his left hand on *Tubal's* right arm, at the elbow, and his right hand on *Tubal's* left shoulder, and, so holding him and leaning on him, three times spoke his name: 'How now, Tubal, Tubal, Tubal,—*what* news from Genoa?' Then, holding him off at arm's length, he asked, 'Hast thou found *my daughter?*' The revelation of the indurated selfishness of *Shylock's* nature, in Irving's utterance of 'The *curse* never fell upon our nation *till now*—*I* NEVER *felt* it till now,' was so complete as to be absolutely shocking. There could be no doubt relative to his perception of the character. When *Shylock*, in the overwhelming anguish of self-pity, dwelt on the magnitude of his losses, he plucked open his robe, with the left hand, while with the right, firmly clenched, he convulsively smote himself, many times, delivering slow, heavy blows, on his naked breast. The momentary revulsion of feeling that Irving permitted the *Jew* to indicate, after his frenzied invective relative to *Jessica's* ignominious robbery of his treasure and flight from his home, seemed to be an involuntary impulse not so much of human nature as of the animal propension toward its young. A kindred emphasis was placed on 'No tears but of my shedding'; but the tears of *Shylock* are those of rancorous rage and furious desperation, not of wounded affection or grief, and that was the meaning Irving conveyed. The ejaculation, 'What, what, what? *ill* luck, *ill luck?*' was given with ferocious animation and joyous expectancy, and the wicked outcry, 'I thank God, I thank God,' with a horrible exuberance of delight, immediately succeeded by almost piteous doubt, at '*is* it true? *is it*— TRUE?' An effect of contemptuous amusement followed his agonized groan, at *Tubal's* mention of *Jessica's* extravagance and the abject meanness of the accents in which he moaned, 'I shall never see my gold again.' The repetition, 'fourscore ducats,' was spoken in a semi-bewildered undertone, as though the *Jew* could not credit the possibility of such wanton waste by his child. The supreme climax of the situation was reached and shown by means of sudden contrast,—fury abruptly succeeding lamentation, in the thrilling celerity with which he cried, 'I am very glad of it:—I'll *plague* him: I'll *torture* him: I am *glad* of it,' and the subsequent, 'I will have the *heart* of him, if he forfeit.' Persons who truly saw that frightful figure,—an authentic and terrific image of tragedy,—can never forget it,—the tall, attenuated form, the ghastly, pallid face, the deep-sunken, dark eyes, blazing with wrath, the jaws champing, the left hand turning the sleeve up on the right arm as far back as the elbow, and the fingers of the right hand stretched forth and quivering, as if already they were tearing out the heart of his hated enemy. The scene was rapidly rounded. Irving, although exceptional among actors for the perfect poise and massive authority which take fully and exactly the time required, be it ever so long, for the accomplishment of a purposed artistic result, never marred effect, whether great or small, by lingering unduly on an achievement once completed.

Some time had been supposed to elapse prior to the scene of the *Jew's* colloquy with the *Merchant*, when *Antonio* walks abroad, in the *Jailer's* custody. *Shylock's* excitement had given place to cold, concentrated determination of murder. In that scene Irving was incarnate cruelty. His attire was orderly, sober, correct; his demeanor obdurate. He evinced a calm, revolting pleasure in the rejection and suppression of the miserable *Antonio's* appeals, together with hectoring censure of the *Jailer's* clemency, in allowing his prisoner 'to come abroad' for exercise. Throughout the Trial Scene his acting was perfect in symmetry, particularity of expressive detail, cumulative power, and tragic effect. All indication of passion had disappeared from his visage and person. He seemed the authentic personification of the Mosaic Law, the righteous minister of Justice; the ordained avenger. In the presence of that majestic Hebrew the observer became, for a moment, completely oblivious that *Shylock* is not only a villain but a trickster; that his nature, like his quest, is abhorrent; that the 'bond' to which he appeals, and by virtue of which he so ostentatiously craves 'the law,' was obtained by the hypocritical pretence of friendship and magnanimity; and that he is now proceeding in his actual character, that of a dissembling scoundrel, to do a murder, under the compulsory sanction of a Court of Justice. The illusion, however, was only momentary. Every evil passion poisons the mind that harbors it, till, if the inevitable degradation be not stayed, the character is vitiated, the body is ravaged, the soul is polluted. That truth was legibly written in the countenance of Irving's *Shylock*, and as the *Jew* stood there, in the Courtroom, no thoughtful observer could fail to read it. There was a horrible yellow pallor of the skin. The lines in the face had been deepened. The cheeks were hollow. There was a faint glow of hectic color around the sunken, burning eyes. The body was emaciated. On entering the Court *Shylock* advanced a little way, paused, and slowly gazed around until his eyes found *Antonio*, upon whom his look then settled, with evident gloating satisfaction,—a cruel, deadly look of sanguinary hatred,—and then he stepped a little forward and gravely bowed toward the *Duke's* throne. The address of that magistrate was heard by him with patient but wholly unmoved attention, and his reply was spoken with dignity and decisive force. The words, 'What judgment shall I dread, doing no wrong?' were so spoken that they seemed those of honesty, and almost carried conviction of right intent. The contempt with which *Gratiano's* appeal was answered was of withering indifference. That voluble inter-cessor's denunciation was totally disregarded, except that, after it had ended, *Shylock*, with the point of his naked knife, touched the bond, which had been thrust into his girdle in the form of a roll, and made his curt answer in a cold, level, sinister tone, expressive of a scorn so profound as to be devoid of all feeling. In the peculiar emphasis that he laid on the word 'law' there was a latent sarcastic mockery, as if, in his thought, he were deriding the folly of a law that could be made to serve such a purpose as the murder which he intended to commit. There was bland simplicity in his question, 'On *what* "compulsion" *must* I?' and he listened with weariness and growing impatience to the speech about 'The quality of mercy,' feeling it to be irrelevant, futile, and tedious: his answer to it was abrupt and decisive. When *Portia*, in pitiful entreaty, said, 'Bid me *tear* the bond,' he laid his left hand heavily on both of her hands, to stay the action, and answered, without even a tremor, 'When it is *paid*, according to the tenor.' At 'So says the bond—doth it not, noble judge?' he laid the point of his knife on the words in that document, held open by *Portia*, and when she inquired, 'Are there balance' here, to weigh the flesh?' he caused an hysterical laugh, by the grisly promptitude with which he brought forth the 'balance' from his bosom,—an action which seemed to imply that he had carried the implement there, to comfort him by its touch, with assurance of his certain revenge. The relentless statement ''Tis not *in* the bond' was horrible in its icy implacable resolve, and he uttered with infernal exultation the summons to the *Merchant*, 'A sen-tence!—*Come!* PREPARE!' In the subsequent resolute, persistent effort to extricate himself with at least financial profit from the ruins of his defeated scheme of murder the stalwart force of the *Jew's* character was splendidly maintained, and at the final catastrophe, the collapse, both physical and mental, was denoted with consummate skill. In making his exit from the Court *Shylock* moved slowly and with difficulty, as if he had been stricken by fatal weakness and were opposing it by inveterate will. At the door he nearly fell, but at once recovered himself, and with a long, heavy sigh he disappeared. The spectacle was intensely pathetic, awakening that pity which naturally attends upon despoiled greatness of character and broken, ruined power, whether that character and that power be malignant or benign.

Irving's dress, for *Shylock*, comprised a brown gabardine, girdled by a parti-colored shawl, a black, flat-topped cap with a yellow band across it, and square-toed shoes, of soft leather. He dressed the head with gray hair, long behind, the crown of the skull being bald. One lock of hair, being brushed forward, appeared on the brow, projecting from beneath the hat. He carried a black crutch-stick. In the Second Act he slightly changed the costume,—as already noted. In the Third Act he wore a long robe, but neither hat nor gabardine. In the Trial Scene, his dress was scrupulously correct, neat, and formal, his hair carefully smoothed and arranged, his aspect that of a priest going to the altar, to offer sacrifice: a more composed aspect could not be imagined,—the aspect of a lethal monster, sure of his prey, because bulwarked behind the pretence of religion and law,—and nothing at once as imposing and terrible had before been shown on our stage by any actor of *Shylock*. When Irving first presented 'The Merchant of Venice,' in London, it had a run of two hundred and fifty consecutive performances, a record never equalled with any play of Shakespeare's. He restored the Fifth Act, which, after the time of Edmund Kean, had frequently been omitted.

1. **Macklin**, Charles. See p. 36.

༄༅

8 November 1880, anonymous review from *The Times* on Edwin Booth (1833–93) as Hamlet at the Princess's Theatre, London, reprinted in *Shakespearean Criticism*, vol. 21, ed. Joseph C. Tardiff (Detroit, Gale Research, 1993), pp. 69–70.

BOOTH, member of a famous American acting family, was the finest American tragedian of his time. He toured extensively, and was to alternate the roles of Othello and Iago with Irving at the Lyceum in 1881. I omit the opening paragraphs of the review, which include the information that Booth 'first essayed Hamlet in 1853 in San Francisco', that he had played the role 'in Australia, after the gold-rushes, and in the Sandwich Islands, where for two months Mr Booth "ran" the Hawaiian Theatre Royal, under the patronage of His Majesty King Kameeyah IV', and that 'In New York Mr Booth played Hamlet for 100 nights at the Winter Garden.'

Every distinguished tragedian has now his own edition of *Hamlet*. Mr. Booth departs less than we are accustomed to from the text of the great dramatist, and is so much the more acceptable. Much is omitted, but care has been taken to preserve all that is 'essential to the exposition of Hamlet's madness and of the mental condition that leads him to assume it.' The quotation is from the authorized prompt-book of '*Hamlet* as presented by Edwin Booth,' edited by Mr. W. Winter[1] of New York, and marks the spirit in which the actor views the part. Nor can one have any doubt in the matter after hearing his confession to Guildenstern before the courtier has lost his confidence:—

I am but mad north-north-west: when the wind is southerly, I know a hawk from a handsaw.

In Mr. Booth's view the Prince of Denmark is neither wholly mad nor wholly sane. 'Hamlet's wildness,' he thinks with Coleridge,[2] 'is but half false; he plays that subtle trick of pretending to act only when he is very near really being what he acts.' This being the general conception of the part, it is carried out with scholarly attention to detail. If Mr. Booth is a less picturesque Hamlet in appearance than we have seen, his declamation has the effect (although sometimes deformed by an exuberance of gesture) of being beautifully musical and distinct, no slight advantage in a play which is so thickly set with gems of thought, and as essential to this one of Shakespeare's plays as the most vivid representation of passion. His expression of fear at the first appearance of the ghost of Hamlet's father offered rather a bad augury in the beginning: his acting here was laboured and tricky. But as he went on Mr. Booth quite dispelled the apprehensions raised by the scene that he was about to give a mere conventional picture of Shakespeare's most famous hero. His voice has the quality of sympathy, and there were tears in it when Hamlet commented on the wrongs done to his father, and when, devoting his own life to a purpose which left no space for love, he bade farewell to Ophelia in assumed madness and with a pretence of such raillery at women as his mother's conduct suggested, but in real heart-pity for Ophelia and himself. The wit of the part was effectively brought out, and the dry conceits which have become familiar as household words seemed novel from the way in which they were uttered. It was the quiet, unconscious, method of American humour. Hamlet bantered Polonius and the courtiers without a smile, as Bret Harte[3] in a lecture makes jokes with a grave face. The tension of the tragedy is at once relieved and (by contrast) heightened by preserving some of the quaint jests of the old play. Hamlet, when the ghost says

'Swear,' speaks the line often omitted, but useful as indicating his necessity for finding relief to his pent-up feelings—

Ah, ha, boy! say'st thou so? art thou there, true penny?

Other speeches in the same spirit are, in deference to modern taste, left out. In the curious old play of *Hamlet* in German, printed by Mr. Albert Cohen,[4] the humour was carried so far that the ghost is made to give the sentinel a box on the ear from behind and cause him to drop his musket. A fine scene was the interview between Hamlet and his mother (Mrs. Hermann Vezin[5]), in which Polonius is stabbed. The Prince's pathos and his mother's terror when he pronounced the line

My father, in his habit as he lived!

were very affecting. Mr. Booth's way of solving the problem of the pictures is a combination of the method adopted by Fechter[6] and Rossi[7] with that suggested by a note of Malone[8] on Betterton's practices in the scene. A portrait of the father is hung on the wall, and the portrait of the usurper is worn on her neck in a medallion by Hamlet's mother. The courtiers wear similar medallions, which Hamlet touches in reciting the words—

It is not strange; for my uncle is King of Denmark, and those that would make mows at him while my father lived, give twenty, forty, fifty, a hundred ducats a-piece for his picture in little.

Mr. Booth had a reception of the warmest kind, and was called before the curtain at the end of every act amid enthusiastic applause from all parts of the house.

1. **Winter**, W. See p. 117.

2. **Coleridge**, Samuel Taylor (1772–1834), poet and philosopher; the quotation, from one of his lectures of 1818, is cited in H. H. Furness's New Variorum edition (2 vols., 1877), p. 109.

3. **Harte**, Bret (1836–1902), American writer.

4. **Cohen** (i.e. Cohn), Albert, author of *Shakespeare in Germany in the sixteenth and seventeenth centuries* (1865), which reprints *Der Bestrafte Brudermord* (*Fratricide Punished*), also included in the New Variorum edition, ii. 121–42; the reference is to 1.2.

5. **Vezin**, Mrs H. (1827–1902). She had a special aptitude for Shakespeare and other poetic drama.

6. **Fechter**, Charles. See p. 112.

7. **Rossi**, Ernesto (1827–96), Italian actor-manager who toured widely in Shakespearian and other roles.

8. **Malone**, Edmond (1741–1812), scholar; the allusion is to a note in his edition of Shakespeare reprinted in H. H. Furness's New Variorum edition of *Hamlet*, i. 290.

[1887–*c*.1900], William Winter on Ada Rehan (1860–1916) as Kate in *The Taming of the Shrew*, from his *Shakespeare on the Stage* (1912), pp. 520–7.

WINTER (see p. 117) was so deeply involved with Daly's productions that he may not be regarded as an entirely objective witness, but his admiration for Ada Rehan was shared by some of the best critics of the time, including Shaw, as is clear from the following review. She had made her début at the age of 13, and was Daly's leading lady from 1878 until he died in 1899.

The American Augustin Daly opened his London theatre, Daly's, in 1893 with a performance of *The Taming of the Shrew* starring Ada Rehan, to whom he owed much of his success, as Kate.

ACCORDING to Miss Rehan's ideal, the shrewishness of *Katharine* is largely superficial. She is externally a virago, but the loveliest qualities of womanhood are latent in her. She is at war with herself; a termagant in temper; haughty; self-willed; imperious; resentful of control; still more resentful of the thought of submission to love, yet, at heart, ardently desirous of it, and secretly impelled to seek for it. Her spirit is high and fiery, and while she longs for the triumph and the endearments of love, she rages against herself, contemning the weakness which permits her longing, but which really is her, as yet unrecognized, power. That ideal was implied by Miss Rehan's treatment of the character, and her art, in the implication and expression of it, was as nearly perfect as anything of human fabric can be. The vitality, sympathy, and delicious bloom of her *Katharine* could not be too freely extolled. By precisely what means she imparted a sense of *Katharine's* charm it would be difficult to say. Perhaps it would be exact to suggest that her latent loveliness was signified not by action but by condition,—by the personality of the actress, and by the feeling, relative to the character, with which she was wholly possessed and animated. The method and execution of her acting can be precisely described: Her appearance was magnificent. The raiment that she wore and the make-up of her face were exactly correspondent with the complex temperament of the ideal *Shrew* she had determined to represent. She wore ruddy golden hair, short and curly. Her first dress, dark red in color, consisted of a short skirt of velvet; an over-skirt of stiff, heavy, flowered silk, looped up at the left side, with a gold cord, so as to expose the velvet skirt; a short train; a long-bodied waist; inner sleeves, fitted close to the arms; and over-sleeves, depending from the shoulders almost to the knees, with flame-colored lining. Around her neck she wore a single, close-fitting string of large, heavy, dark-ruddy beads. On her head was a small red cap, and from her ears depended massy gold ornaments. Her shoes were of satin, dark red in color, to match the dress. Her first entrance on the scene, as she swept in, driving *Bianca* along with her, affected her audience like the rush of a whirlwind. Her impetuosity was terrific, and yet she was majestic. Her every movement, lithe, graceful, and splendid, showed the abounding health and affluent energy of youthful womanhood. As she moved to and fro, in tempestuous rage, it became easy to appreciate the dread of her which had previously been expressed, by *Gremio* and *Hortensio*. After a moment, as *Bianca* ended her speech of supplication, she suddenly came to a menacing stand, towering over the frightened girl, and, in her first, deep-throated, tremulous, angry query, struck the key-note of *Katharine's* raging discontent:

> '*Of all thy suitors*, here I charge thee, tell
> Whom thou lov'st best: see thou dissemble not!'

In *Katharine's* subsequent scene with her father she was effectively rebellious and sullen. The sound of her voice, outside, exclaiming 'Out of the house, you scraping fool!' plainly and comically signified the sorry plight of the unlucky *Music-Master*, and there was an expressive blending of rage and curiosity in the tone of her remonstrance, 'Sir—father—surely—' spoken outside to *Baptista*, and by him curtly interrupted, with 'Hence, Kate! ne'er tell *me!*' just before her entrance to meet *Petruchio*. In *Katharine's* first scene with that impudent wooer she evinced extraordinary vigor and variety of feeling and action, and, notwithstanding the intensity of her struggle with him and her fierce defiance of him, there was underlying her violence of demeanor and effervescence of wrath, a subtle denotement of resentful consciousness of being interested in and even attracted by him, and with this was mingled an agitation not unlike the tremor of fear. A gleam of gratified vanity showed itself in her face when *Petruchio* said:

> 'For by this light whereby I see thy beauty—
> Thy beauty that doth make me love thee well!'

The threatening speech at the end of the act, already mentioned, was delivered with such magnificent savagery that sometimes I used to wonder whether *Petruchio*, if he had heard it, would have had the hardihood to make his appearance, according to promise, 'on Sunday next.' In the Third Act *Katharine* did not appear till the moment of the tumultuous return of the guests and bridegroom, after the marriage service, when, distracted between fear and fury, she was half dragged upon the scene by *Petruchio*, who compelled her to dance with him. Her imperative ejaculation to *Baptista*, 'Father, *be quiet!*', instead of offending, merely amused. There was a singular blending of dread and supplication in her entreaty to *Petruchio*, spoken as though intended for his hearing only, 'Now, if you love me, *stay!*' And there was a fiery 'now or never' spirit in the 'Nay, then, do what thou wilt, *I* will not hence to-day!' and in the mocking repetition, 'No-o-o-o-o-o!' of *Petruchio's* interjected query. From that point onward, through the trial and tribulation of the Taming episode, the actress steadily held the sympathy of every spectator, largely by virtue of the potent charm of her natural womanly feeling. This was deftly used, as involuntary, to show *Katharine's* gradual change from turbulence to serenity, and from shrewishness to loveliness. Throughout the closing scenes, in illustrating the ideal which she had formed, Miss Rehan depicted the unfolding of a woman's nature under the stress of widely varied emotions,—showing pride, scorn, sarcasm, anger, bewilderment, terrified amazement, and, at the last, sweetly feminine tenderness. Her appearance was continuously lovely. *Katharine*, finally, was shown as indeed changed 'as she had never been' from what she was at the opening of the play, yet, as indicative of the uniformity of the impersonation, she was seen to be unmistakably the same woman, only now her actual self.

The description which *Grumio* gives of the mishap of her fall with her horse, in the journey from Padua to *Petruchio's* house, was, for some inscrutable reason, ignored,—her dress remaining undamaged and in perfect condition: this was a blemish on almost perfect stage management. Another neglect of the prescription of the text occurred in the Last Act,—Miss Rehan wearing not a 'cap,' but a handsome wreath of dark green leaves, though *Petruchio* always spoke the lines,

> 'Katharine, that *cap* of yours becomes you not;
> Off with that bauble, throw it under foot!'

In the acting of Ada Rehan there were many charming qualities;—obvious purpose, clearly seen and steadily pursued; complete identification with assumed character; unerring, responsive intelligence, which answers every look and word of others; ample breadth and fine denotement of gesture; prescient purpose; exact performance; invariable authority; that art which conceals art, producing an effect of perfect spontaneity; melodious, flexible elocution, which flows from deep feeling; and the refined physical luxuriance which at once pleased the imagination and satisfied the eye: but the most delightful of all its qualities was its healthful vitality,—an impartment of freshness and purity, as of roses in their morning bloom. No taint infected it; no element of morbidity underlaid it; no hint of coarseness ever defaced it; and the observer was conscious of a large, fine, breezy, vigorous nature, a lovely temperament, diffusive of happiness and stimulative of noble thoughts and genial feelings. The figure of her *Katharine,*—splendid with beauty, stormy with arrogant passion, diversified with continuous fluctuation of mood, subtle with revelations of the woman's true heart, and beautiful with symmetry of treatment and melody of speech,—stood out with royal prominence, and it has rightly passed into theatrical history as one of the few really great and perfect dramatic creations of its time. It was all that could have been in Shakespeare's mind when he wrote, and it *far transcended* what is depicted in his text of 'The Shrew.' That performance, fine as it was, did not mark the highest range of Ada Rehan's achievement. Her *Rosalind, Lady Teazle,[1] Portia,* and *Beatrice* were all works of art of at least equal beauty, of greater variety, and illustrative of higher ideals of womanhood: but her *Katharine* was an epitome of her powers, and, being condensed, concise, and continually active, it was widely popular. Moreover, its great *brilliancy* gave it an emphasis that public observation could not mistake.

1. **Lady Teazle**, in Richard Brinsley Sheridan's popular play *The School for Scandal.*

---

6 July 1895, Bernard Shaw (1856–1959) on *The Two Gentlemen of Verona,* produced by Augustin Daly (1838–99) at Daly's Theatre, London; from *The Saturday Review,* reprinted in *Shaw on Shakespeare,* pp. 192–7.

WILLIAM WINTER (p. 117) had arranged the text as a vehicle for Rehan. The production lasted only a week. Shaw reviewed for *The Saturday Review* from 1895 to 1898.

THE piece founded by Augustin Daly on Shakespear's Two Gentlemen of Verona, to which I looked forward last week, is not exactly a comic opera, though there is plenty of music in it, and not exactly a serpentine dance,[1] though it proceeds under a play of changing colored lights. It is something more old-fashioned than either: to wit, a vaudeville. And let me hasten to admit that it makes a very pleasant entertainment for those who know no better. Even I, who know a great deal better, as I shall presently demonstrate rather severely, enjoyed myself tolerably. I cannot feel harshly towards a gentleman who works so hard as Mr. Daly does to make Shakespear presentable: one feels that he loves the bard, and lets him have his way as far as he thinks it good for him. His rearrangement of the scenes of the first two acts is just like him. Shakespear shews lucidly how Proteus lives with his father (Antonio) in Verona, and loves a lady of that city named Julia. Mr. Daly, by taking the scene in Julia's house between Julia and her maid, and the scene in Antonio's house between Antonio and Proteus, and making them into one scene, convinces the unlettered audience that Proteus and Julia live in the same house with their father Antonio. Further, Shakespear shews us how Valentine, the other gentleman of Verona, travels from Verona to Milan, the journey being driven into our heads by a comic scene in Verona, in which Valentine's servant is overwhelmed with grief at leaving his parents, and with indignation at the insensibility of his dog to his sorrow, followed presently by another comic scene in Milan in which the same servant is welcomed to the strange city by a fellow-servant. Mr. Daly, however, is ready for Shakespear on this point too. He just represents the two scenes as occurring in the same place; and immediately the puzzle as to who is who is complicated by a puzzle as to where is where. Thus is the immortal William adapted to the requirements of a nineteenth-century audience.

In preparing the text of his version Mr. Daly has proceeded on the usual principles, altering, transposing, omitting, improving, correcting, and transferring speeches from one character to another. Many of Shakespear's lines are mere poetry, not to the point, not getting the play along, evidently stuck in because the poet liked to spread himself in verse. On all such unbusinesslike superfluities Mr. Daly is down with his blue pencil. For instance, he relieves us of such stuff as the following which merely conveys that Valentine loves Silvia, a fact already sufficiently established by the previous dialogue:

> My thoughts do harbor with my Silvia nightly;
>   And slaves they are to me, that send them flying:
> Oh, could their master come and go as lightly,
>   Himself would lodge where senseless they are lying.
> My herald thoughts in thy pure bosom rest them,
>   While I, their king, that thither them importune,
> Do curse the grace that with such grace hath blessed them,
>   Because myself do want my servant's fortune.

I curse myself, for they are sent by me,
    That they should harbor where their lord would be.

Slaves indeed are these lines and their like to Mr. Daly, who 'sends them flying' without remorse. But when he comes to passages that a stage manager can understand, his reverence for the bard knows no bounds. The following awkward lines, unnecessary as they are under modern stage conditions, are at any rate not poetic, and are in the nature of police news. Therefore they are piously retained:

What halloing, and what stir, is this today?
These are my mates, that make their wills their law,
Have some unhappy passenger in chase.
They love me well; yet I have much to do,
To keep them from uncivil outrages.
Withdraw thee, Valentine; whos this comes here?

The perfunctory metrical character of such lines only makes them more ridiculous than they would be in prose. I would cut them out without remorse to make room for all the lines that have nothing to justify their existence except their poetry, their humor, their touches of character—in short, the lines for whose sake the play survives, just as it was for their sake it originally came into existence. Mr. Daly who prefers the lines which only exist for the sake of the play, will doubtless think me as great a fool as Shakespear; but I submit to him, without disputing his judgment, that he is, after all, only a man with a theory of dramatic composition, going with a blue pencil over the work of a great dramatist, and striking out everything that does not fit his theory. Now, as it happens, nobody cares about Mr. Daly's theory; whilst everybody who pays to see what is, after all, advertised as a performance of Shakespear's play entitled The Two Gentlemen of Verona, and not as a demonstration of Mr. Daly's theory, does care more or less about the art of Shakespear. Why not give them what they ask for, instead of going to great trouble and expense to give them something else?

In those matters in which Mr. Daly has given the rein to his own taste and fancy: that is to say, in scenery, costumes, and music, he is for the most part disabled by a want of real knowledge of the arts concerned. I say for the most part, because his pretty fifteenth-century dresses, though probably inspired rather by Sir Frederic Leighton[2] than by Benozzo Gozzoli,[3] may pass. But the scenery is insufferable. First, for 'a street in Verona' we get a Bath bun colored operatic front cloth with about as much light in it as there is in a studio in Fitzjohn's Avenue in the middle of October. I respectfully invite Mr. Daly to spend his next holiday looking at a real street in Verona, asking his conscience meanwhile whether a manager with eyes in his head and the electric light at his disposal could not advance a step on the Telbin (senior) style. Telbin[4] was an admirable scene painter; but he was limited by the mechanical conditions of gas illumination; and he learnt his technique before the great advance made during the Impressionist movement in the painting of open-air effects, especially of brilliant sunlight. Of that advance Mr. Daly has apparently no conception. The days of Macready[5] and Clarkson Stanfield[6] still exist for him; he would probably prefer a water-color drawing of a foreign street by Samuel Prout[7] to one of Mr. T. M. Rooke;[8] and I daresay every relic of the original tallow candlelight that still clings to the art of scene-painting is as dear to him as it is to most old playgoers, including, unhappily, many of the critics.

As to the elaborate set in which Julia makes her first entrance, a glance at it shews how far Mr. Daly prefers the Marble Arch to the loggia of Orcagna. All over the scene we have Renaissance work, in its genteelest stages of decay, held up as the perfection of romantic elegance and beauty. The school that produced the classicism of the First Empire, designed the terraces of Regent's Park and the façades of Fitzroy Square, and conceived the Boboli Gardens and Versailles as places for human beings to be happy in, ramps all over the scenery, and offers as much of its pet colonnades and statues as can be crammed into a single scene, by way of a compendium of everything that is lovely in the city of San Zeno and the tombs of the Scaligers. As to the natural objects depicted, I ask whether any man living has ever seen a pale green cypress in Verona or anywhere else out of a toy Noah's Ark. A man who, having once seen cypresses and felt their presence in a north Italian landscape, paints them lettuce color, must be suffering either from madness, malice, or a theory of how nature should have colored trees, cognate with Mr. Daly's theory of how Shakespear should have written plays.

Of the music let me speak compassionately. After all, it is only very lately that Mr. Arnold Dolmetsch,[9] by playing fifteenth-century music on fifteenth-century instruments, has shewn us that the age of beauty was true to itself in music as in pictures and armor and costumes. But what should Mr. Daly know of this, educated as he no doubt was to believe that the court of Denmark should always enter in the first act of Hamlet to the march from Judas Maccabaeus?[10] Schubert's setting of Who is Silvia? he knew, but had rashly used up in Twelfth Night as Who's Olivia. He has therefore had to fall back on another modern setting, almost supernaturally devoid of any particular merit. Besides this, all through the drama the most horribly common music repeatedly breaks out on the slightest pretext or on no pretext at all. One dance, set to a crude old English popular tune, sundry eighteenth and nineteenth century musical banalities, and a titivated plantation melody in the first act which produces an indescribably atrocious effect by coming in behind the scenes as a sort of coda to Julia's curtain speech, all turn the play, as I have said, into a vaudeville. Needless to add, the accompaniments are not played on lutes and viols, but by the orchestra and a guitar or two. In the forest scene the outlaws begin the act by a chorus. After their encounter with Valentine they go off the stage singing the refrain exactly in the style of La Fille de Madame Angot.[11] The wanton absurdity of introducing this comic opera convention is presently eclipsed by a thunderstorm, immediately after which Valentine enters and delivers his speech sitting down on a bank of moss, as an outlaw in tights naturally would after a terrific shower. Such is the effect of many years of theatrical management on the human brain.

Perhaps the oddest remark I have to make about the performance is that, with all its glaring defects and blunders, it is rather a handsome and elaborate one as such things go. It is many years now since Mr. Ruskin[12] first took the Academicians of his day aback by the obvious remark that Carpaccio and Giovanni Bellini[13] were better painters than Domenichino and Salvator Rosa.[14] Nobody dreams now of assuming that Pope[15] was a greater poet than Chaucer,[16] that Mozart's Twelfth Mass[17] is superior to the masterpieces of Orlandus Lassus[18] and Palestrina,[19] or that our 'ecclesiastical Gothic' architecture is more enlightened than Norman axe work. But the theatre is still wallowing in such follies; and until Mr. Comyns Carr[20] and Sir Edward Burne-Jones,[21] Baronet, put King Arthur on the stage more or less in the manner natural to men who know these things, Mr. Daly might have pleaded the unbroken conservatism of the playhouse against me. But after the Lyceum scenery and architecture I decline to accept a relapse without protest. There is no reason why cheap photographs of Italian architecture (sixpence apiece in infinite variety at the book-stall in the South Kensington Museum) should not rescue us from Regent's Park Renaissance colonnades on the stage just as the electric light can rescue us from Telbin's duncolored sunlight. The opera is the last place in the world where any wise man would look for adequate stage illusion; but the fact is that Mr. Daly, with all his colored lights, has not produced a single Italian scene comparable in illusion to that provided by Sir Augustus Harris[22] at Covent Garden for Cavalleria Rusticana.[23]

Of the acting I have not much to say. Miss Rehan provided a strong argument in favor of rational dress by looking much better in her page's costume than in that of her own sex; and in the serenade scene, and that of the wooing of Silvia for Proteus, she stirred some feeling into the part, and reminded us of what she was in Twelfth Night, where the same situations are fully worked out. For the rest, she moved and spoke with imposing rhythmic grace. That is as much notice as so cheap a part as Julia is worth from an artist who, being absolute mistress of the situation at Daly's Theatre, might and should have played Imogen for us instead. The two gentlemen were impersonated by Mr. Worthing[24] and Mr. Craig.[25] Mr. Worthing charged himself with feeling without any particular reference to his lines; and Mr. Craig struck a balance by attending to the meaning of his speeches without taking them at all to heart. Mr. Clarke,[26] as the Duke, was emphatic, and worked up every long speech to a climax in the useful old style; but his tone is harsh, his touch on his consonants coarse, and his accent ugly, all fatal disqualifications for the delivery of Shakespearean verse. The scenes between Launce and his dog brought out the latent silliness and childishness of the audience as Shakespear's clowning scenes always do: I laugh at them like a yokel myself. Mr. Lewis[27] hardly made the most of them. His style has been formed in modern comedies, where the locutions are so familiar that their meaning is in no danger of being lost by the rapidity of his quaint utterance; but Launce's phraseology is another matter: a few of the funniest lines missed fire because the audience did not catch them. And with all possible allowance for Mr. Daly's blue pencil, I cannot help suspecting that Mr. Lewis's memory was responsible for one or two of his omissions. Still, Mr. Lewis has always his comic force, whether he makes the most or the least of it; so that he cannot fail in such a part as Launce. Miss Maxine Elliot's[28] Silvia was the most considerable performance after Miss Rehan's Julia. The whole company will gain by the substitution on Tuesday next of a much better play, A Midsummer Night's Dream, as a basis for Mr. Daly's operations. No doubt he is at this moment, like Mrs. Todgers,[29] 'a dodgin' among the tender bits with a fork, and an eatin' of 'em'; but there is sure to be enough of the original left here and there to repay a visit.

1. **serpentine dance**, an undulating dance popularized by the American Loie Fuller.
2. **Leighton**, Sir Frederic, later Lord Leighton (1830–96), painter and sculptor of classical subjects.
3. **Gozzoli**, Benozzo (c.1421–97), painter and sculptor of classical subjects.
4. **Telbin**, William (1813–73), scene painter whose son, William Lewis Telbin (1846–1931), worked for Irving at the Lyceum.

5. **Macready**, William. See p. 57.

6. **Stanfield**, Clarkson (1783–1867), scenic artist who worked with Macready and later became an independent artist.

7. **Prout**, Samuel (1783–1852), water-colourist known especially for drawings of continental scenes.

8. **Rooke**, Thomas Matthew (1842–1942), water-colourist noted for drawings of ancient buildings.

9. **Dolmetsch**, Arnold (1858–1940), pioneer in the revival of ancient music and the reconstruction of early instruments.

10. **Judas Maccabaeus**, oratorio (1747) by G. F. Handel (1685–1759).

11. **La Fille de Madame Angot**, operetta by Charles Lecocq (1832–1918), French composer, first performed in 1872.

12. **Ruskin**, John (1819–1900), artist and writer who exercised a major influence on taste.

13. **Carpaccio**, Vittore (*c.*1460/5–1523/6), and Giovanni **Bellini** (*c.*1431–1516), Venetian painters.

14. **Domenichino** (1581–1641), Italian landscape painter, and Salvator **Rosa** (1615–73), Neapolitan painter with a taste for the bizarre.

15. **Pope**, Alexander (1688–1744), poet.

16. **Chaucer**, Geoffrey (?1340–1400), poet.

17. **Twelfth Mass**, a spurious but long-popular composition.

18. **Lassus**, Orlando (*c.*1532–94), Flemish composer of, especially, choral music.

19. **Palestrina**, Giovanni Pierluigi da (*c.*1525–94), Italian composer of vocal music.

20. **Comyns Carr**, J. (1849–1916), art critic and writer, author of *King Arthur*, a play with music by Arthur Sullivan (1842–1900) starring Irving which had opened with great popular success on 12 June.

21. **Burne-Jones**, Edward (1833–98), pre-Raphaelite painter, designer for *King Arthur*; he received a baronetcy in 1894.

22. **Harris**, Augustus (1851–96), manager of Drury Lane and other theatres; knighted 1891.

23. **Cavalleria Rusticana**, popular opera by Pietro Mascagni (1863–1945), first performed in 1890.

24. **Worthing**, Frank (1866–1910), Scottish-born actor who became a popular member of Daly's company; played Proteus.

25. **Craig**, John (died in 1932 aged 64).

26. **Clarke**, George (1844–1906), one of Daly's leading actors who withdrew from the company in 1874 on refusing to shave off his moustache, but returned later and became stage-manager.

27. **Lewis**, James (1837–96), a leading actor for Daly. An American, he was especially successful as Toby Belch and Touchstone.

28. **Elliot**, Maxine (1871–1940), American actress and theatre manager; she played Sylvia.

29. **Mrs Todgers**, boarding-house keeper in Charles Dickens's novel *Martin Chuzzlewit* (1843–4); the (slightly erroneous) quotation is from Chapter 9.

15 July 1895, Bernard Shaw on Augustin Daly's production of *A Midsummer Night's Dream* at Daly's Theatre, London, from *The Saturday Review*, reprinted in *Shaw on Shakespeare*, pp. 125–31.[1]

T HE Two Gentlemen of Verona has been succeeded at Daly's Theatre by A Midsummer Night's Dream. Mr. Daly is in great form. In my last article I was rash enough to hint that he had not quite realized what could be done with electric lighting on the stage. He triumphantly answers me by fitting up all his fairies with portable batteries and incandescent lights, which they switch on and off from time to time, like children with a new toy. He has trained Miss Lillian Swain in the part of Puck until it is safe to say that she does not take one step, strike one attitude, or modify her voice by a single inflexion that is not violently, wantonly and ridiculously wrong and absurd. Instead of being mercurial, she poses academically, like a cheap Italian statuette; instead of being impish and childish, she is elegant and affected; she laughs a solemn, measured laugh, like a heavy German Zamiel;[2] she announces her ability to girdle the earth in forty minutes in the attitude of a professional skater, and then begins the journey awkwardly in a swing, which takes her in the opposite direction to that in which she indicated her intention of going: in short, she illustrates every folly and superstition that still clings round what Mr. Daly no doubt calls 'the legitimate.' Another stroke of his is to make Oberon a woman. It must not be supposed that he does this solely because it is wrong, though there is no other reason apparent. He does it partly because he was brought up to do such things, and partly because they seem to him to be a tribute to Shakespear's greatness, which, being uncommon, ought not to be interpreted according to the dictates of common sense. A female Oberon and a Puck who behaves like a page-boy earnestly training himself for the post of footman recommend themselves to him because they totally destroy the naturalness of the representation, and so accord with his conception of the Shakespearean dramas as the most artificial of all forms of stage entertainment. That is how you find out the man who is not an artist. Verse, music, the beauties of dress, gesture, and movement are to him interesting aberrations instead of being the natural expression which human feeling seeks at a certain degree of delicacy and intensity. He regards art as a quaint and costly ring in the nose of Nature. I am loth to say that Mr. Daly is such a man; but after studying all his Shakespearean revivals with the thirstiest desire to find as much art as possible in them, I must mournfully confess that the only idea I can see in them is the idea of titivation. As to his slaughterings of the text, how can one help feeling them acutely in a play like A Midsummer Night's Dream, in which Shakespear, having to bring Nature in its most enchanting aspect before an audience without the help of theatrical scenery, used all his power of description and expression in verse with such effect that the utmost any scene-painter can hope for is to produce a picture that shall not bitterly disappoint the spectator who has read the play beforehand? Mr. Daly is, I should say, one of those people who are unable to conceive that there could have been any illusion at all about the play before scenery was introduced. He certainly has no suspicion of the fact that every accessory he employs is brought in at the deadliest risk of destroying the magic spell woven by the poet. He swings Puck away on a clumsy trapeze with a ridiculous clash of the cymbals in the orchestra, in the fullest belief that he is thereby completing instead of destroying the effect of Puck's lines. His 'panoramic illusion of the passage of Theseus's barge to Athens' is more absurd than anything that occurs in the tragedy of Pyramus and Thisbe in the last act. The stage management blunders again and again through feeble imaginative realization of the circumstances of the drama. In the first act it should be clear to any stage manager that Lysander's speech, beginning, 'I am, my lord, as well derived as he,' should be spoken privately and not publicly to Theseus. In the rehearsal scene in the wood, Titania should not be conspicuously exhibited under a limelight in the very centre of the stage, where the clowns have, in defiance of all common sanity, to pretend not to see her. We are expected, no doubt, to assume that she is invisible because she is a fairy, though Bottom's conversation with her when she wakes and addresses him flatly contradicts that hypothesis. In the fourth act, Theseus has to enter from his barge down a bank, picking his way through the sleeping Lysander and Hermia, Demetrius and Helena. The four lions in Trafalgar Square are not more conspicuous and unoverlookable than these four figures are. Yet Theseus has to make all his hunting speeches in an impossible unconsciousness of them, and then to look at them amazedly and exclaim, 'But soft, what nymphs are these?' as if he could in any extremity of absence of mind have missed seeing them all along. Most of these absurdities are part of a systematic policy of sacrificing the credibility of the play to the chance of exhibiting an effective 'living picture.'

> I swear to thee by Cupid's strongest bow,
> By his best arrow with the golden head,
> By the simplicity of Venus' doves,
> By that which knitteth souls and prospers loves, etc.

Mr. Daly's powerful mind perceived at a glance that the second and third lines are superflous, as their omission does not destroy the sense of the passage. He accordingly omitted them. In the same sense, Shakespear makes the two star-crossed lovers speak in alternate lines with an effect which sets the whole scene throbbing with their absorption in one another:

> LYSANDER. The course of true love never did run smooth.
> But either it was different in blood—
> HERMIA. O cross! too high to be enthralled to low!
> LYSANDER. Or else misgraffed in respect of years,
> HERMIA. O spite! too old to be engaged to young!
> LYSANDER. Or else it stood upon the choice of friends,
> HERMIA. O hell! to choose love by another's eye!
> LYSANDER. Or if there were a sympathy in choice,
> War, death, or sickness did lay siege to it, etc.

With a Hermia who knew how to breathe out these parentheses, the duet would be an exquisite one; but Mr. Daly, shocked, as an American and an Irishman, at a young lady using such an expression as 'Oh hell!' cuts out the whole antiphony, and leaves Lysander to deliver a long lecture without interruption from the lady. At such moments, the episode of the ass's head rises to the dignity of allegory. From any other manager I should accept the excuse that the effects of verse for which I am pleading require a virtuosity of delivery on the part of the actor which is practically not to be had at present. But Mr. Daly has Miss Rehan,[3] who is specially famous for just this virtuosity of speech; and yet her lines are treated just as the others are. The fact is, beautiful elocution is rare because the managers have no ears.

The play, though of course very poorly spoken in comparison with how it ought to be spoken, is tolerably acted. Mr. George Clarke,[4] clad in the armor of Alcibiades and the red silk gown of Charley's Aunt,[5] articulates most industriously, and waves his arms and flexes his wrists in strict accordance, not for a moment with the poetry, but with those laws of dramatic elocution and gesture which veteran actors are always willing to impart to novices at a reasonable price per dozen lessons. Mr. Lewis[6] as Bottom is not as funny as his part, whereas in modern plays he is always funnier than his part. He seemed to me to miss the stolid, obstinate, self-sufficient temperament of Bottom altogether. There is a definite conception of some particular sort of man at the back of all Shakespear's characters. The quantity of fun to be got out of Bottom and Autolycus, for instance, is about the same; but underneath the fun there are two widely different persons, of types still extant and familiar. Mr. Lewis would be as funny in Autolycus as he is in Bottom; but he would be exactly the same man in both parts.

As to Miss Rehan, her scenes in the wood with Demetrius were very fine, although, in the passage where Hermia frightens her, she condescends to arrant clowning. Her treatment of Shakespearean verse is delightful after the mechanical intoning of Sarah Bernhardt.[7] She gives us beauty of tone, grace of measure, delicacy of articulation: in short, all the technical qualities of verse music, along with the rich feeling and fine intelligence without which those technical qualities would soon become monotonous. When she is at her best, the music melts in the caress of the emotion it expresses, and thus completes the conditions necessary for obtaining Shakespear's effects in Shakespear's way. When she is on the stage, the play asserts its full charm; and when she is gone, and the stage carpenters and the orchestra are doing their best to pull the entertainment through in Mr. Daly's way, down drops the whole affair into mild tedium. But it is impossible to watch the most recent developments of Miss Rehan's style without some uneasiness. I wonder whether she is old enough to remember the late Barry Sullivan[8] when he was still in his physical prime. Those who do will recall, not an obsolete provincial tragedian, trading on the wreck of an unaccountable reputation, but an actor who possessed in an extraordinary degree just the imposing grace, the sensitive personal dignity of style, the force and self-reliance into which Miss Rehan's style is settling. Miss Rehan's exit in the second act of A Midsummer Night's Dream, with the couplet,

> I'll follow thee, and make a heaven of hell
> To die upon the hand I love so well,

is an exact reproduction of the Barry Sullivan exit. Again, in the first act, when Miss Rehan, prone on a couch, raises herself on her left hand, and, with her right raised 'to heaven,' solemnly declaims the lines:

> For ere Demetrius look'd on Hermia's eyne
> He hailed down oaths, that he was only mine;
> And when this hail some heat from Hermia felt,
> So he dissolved, and showers of oaths did melt,

you are, once more, not forward with Duse,[9] but back with Barry Sullivan, who would in just the same way, when led into it by a touch of stateliness and sonority in the lines, abandon his part, and become for the moment a sort of majestic incarnation of abstract solemnity and magnificence. His skill and intense belief in himself gave him the dangerous power of doing so without making himself ridiculous; and it was by this power, and by the fascination, the grace, and the force which are implied by it, that he gave life to old-fashioned and mutilated representations of Shakespear's plays, poorly acted and ignorantly mounted. This was all very well whilst the fascination lasted; but when his voice lost its tone, his figure its resilience and grace, and his force its spontaneity and natural dignity, there was nothing left but a mannered, elderly, truculent, and, except to his old admirers, rather absurd tragedian of the palmy school. As I was a small boy when I first saw Barry Sullivan, and as I lost sight of him before his waning charm had quite vanished, I remember him, not as he is remembered by those who saw him only in the last ten years of his life, but as an actor who was in his day much further superior in pictorial, vocal, and rhetorical qualities to his next best rival than any actor or actress can easily be nowadays. And it strikes me forcibly that unless Miss Rehan takes to playing Imogen instead of such comparatively childish stuff as Julia or even Helena, and unless she throws herself into sympathy with the contemporary movement by identifying herself with characteristically modern parts of the Magda[10] or Nora[11] type, she may find herself left behind in the race by competitors of much less physical genius, just as Barry Sullivan did. Miss Rehan is clearly absolute mistress of the situation at Daly's Theatre: nobody can persuade me that if she says Cymbeline, Mr. Daly can say The Two Gentlemen of Verona, or that if she says Sudermann or Ibsen, Mr. Daly can insist on the author of Dollars and Cents.[12] But the self-culture which has produced her superb graces of manner and diction seems to have isolated her instead of quickening her sympathy and drawing closer her contact with the world. Every woman who sees Duse play Magda feels that Duse is acting and speaking for her and for all women as they are hardly ever able to speak and act for themselves. The same may be said of Miss Achurch[13] as Nora. But no woman has ever had the very faintest sensation of that kind about any part that Miss Rehan has yet played. We admire, not what she is doing, but the charm with which she does it. That sort of admiration will not last. Miss Rehan's voice is not henceforth going to grow fresher, nor her dignity less conscious, nor her grace of gesture less studied and mannered, nor her movements swifter and more spontaneous. Already I find that young people who see her for the first time cannot quite agree that our raptures about her Katharine and her Rosalind are borne out by her Julia and Helena. Five years hence she will be still more rhetorical and less real:

further ahead I dare not look with Barry Sullivan in my mind. There is only one way to defy Time; and that is to have young ideas, which may always be trusted to find youthful and vivid expression. I am afraid this means avoiding the company of Mr. Daly; but it is useless to blink the fact that unless a modern actress can and will force her manager, in spite of his manly prejudices, to produce plays with real women's parts in them, she had better, at all hazards, make shift to manage for herself. With Grandfather Daly to choose her plays for her, there is no future for Ada Rehan.

1. The production is illustrated in Pl. 6.

2. **Zamiel**, a melodramatic representation of the Devil in the opera *Der Freischütz*, by Carl Maria von Weber (1786–1826).

3. **Rehan**, Ada. See p. 129.

4. **Clarke**, George, see p. 138; presumably played Theseus.

5. **Charley's Aunt**, eponymous central character of the farce by W. Brandon Thomas (1856–1914), first performed in 1892.

6. **Lewis**, James, see p. 138.

7. **Bernhardt**, Sarah (1844–1923), great French actress who frequently appeared in London.

8. **Sullivan**, Barry (1821–91), actor especially popular in the provinces and in his native Ireland, best-known in tragic roles.

9. **Duse**, Eleanora (1859–1924), great Italian actress and manager who toured extensively and first appeared in London in 1893.

10. **Magda**, central character of *Die Heimat* (1893), also known as *Magda*, by Hermann Sudermann (1857–1928), German realist dramatist influenced by Ibsen. Duse played the role in London in 1895.

11. **Nora**, central character in *A Doll's House* by Henrik Ibsen (1828–1906).

12. **Dollars and Cents**. Actually *Dollars and Sense* (1883), a German farce adapted by Daly and his brother Joseph, played in London in 1893; they originally called it by the title Shaw uses.

13. **Achurch**, Janet (1864–1916), English actress, the first to play Nora in London, known especially for her roles in Ibsen and Shaw.

<hr />

2 October 1897, Bernard Shaw on Johnston Forbes-Robertson (1853–1937) as Hamlet at the Lyceum Theatre, London, from *The Saturday Review*, reprinted in e.g. *Shaw on Shakespeare*, pp. 80–8.

FORBES-ROBERTSON was a disciple of Samuel Phelps and acted at the Lyceum with Henry Irving. He had a fine voice (as can be heard in recordings: see p. 14), and was especially successful as Hamlet; he made a silent film of the play, lasting one hour and forty minutes, in 1913, the year when he officially retired (he made a few later appearances) and received a knighthood. Shaw wrote for him the role of Julius Caesar in *Caesar and Cleopatra*. Shaw's expressions of surprise at Forbes-Robertson's textual restorations are disingenuous, as he had privately advised on the production (see W. A. Armstrong, 'Bernard Shaw and Forbes-Robertson's *Hamlet*', *Shakespeare Quarterly*, 15 (1964), pp. 27–31).

THE Forbes Robertson Hamlet at the Lyceum is, very unexpectedly at that address, really not at all unlike Shakespear's play of the same name. I am quite certain I saw Reynaldo in it for a moment; and possibly I may have seen Voltimand and Cornelius; but just as the time for their scene arrived, my eye fell on the word 'Fortinbras' in the program, which so amazed me that I hardly know what I saw for the next ten minutes. Ophelia, instead of being a strenuously earnest and self-possessed young lady giving a concert and recitation for all she was worth, was mad— actually mad. The story of the play was perfectly intelligible, and quite took the attention of the audience off the principal actor at moments. What is the Lyceum coming to? Is it for this that Sir Henry Irving has invented a whole series of original romantic dramas, and given the credit of them without a murmur to the immortal bard whose profundity (as exemplified in the remark that good and evil are mingled in our natures) he has just been pointing out to the inhabitants of Cardiff[1] and whose works have been no more to him than the word-quarry from which he has hewn and blasted the lines and titles of masterpieces which are really all his own? And now, when he has created by these means a reputation for Shakespear, he no sooner turns his back for a moment on London than Mr. Forbes Robertson competes with him on the boards of his own theatre by actually playing off against him the authentic Swan of Avon. Now if the result had been the utter exposure and collapse of that imposter, poetic justice must have proclaimed that it served Mr. Forbes Robertson right. But alas! the wily William, by literary tricks which our simple Sir Henry has never quite understood, has played into Mr. Forbes Robertson's hands so artfully that the scheme is a prodigious success. The effect of this success, coming after that of Mr. Alexander's[2] experiment with a Shakespearean version of As You Like It, makes it almost probable that we shall presently find managers vying with each other in offering the public as much of the original Shakespearean stuff as possible, instead of, as heretofore, doing their utmost to reassure us that everything that the most modern resources can do to relieve the irreducible minimum of tedium inseparable from even the most heavily cut acting version will be lavished on their revivals. It is true that Mr. Beerbohm Tree[3] still holds to the old scepticism, and calmly proposes to insult us by offering us Garrick's[4] puerile and horribly caddish knock-about farce of Katharine and Petruchio for Shakespear's Taming of the Shrew; but Mr. Tree, like all romantic actors, is incorrigible on the subject of Shakespear.

Mr. Forbes Robertson is essentially a classical actor, the only one, with the exception of Mr. Alexander, now established in London management. What I mean by classical is that he can present a dramatic hero as a man whose passions are those which have produced the philosophy, the poetry, the art, and the statecraft of the world, and not merely those which have produced its weddings, coroners' inquests, and executions. And that is just the sort of actor that Hamlet requires. A Hamlet who only understands his love for Ophelia, his grief for his father, his vindictive hatred of his uncle, his fear of ghosts, his impulse to snub Rosencrantz and Guildenstern, and the sportsman's excitement with which he lays the 'mouse-trap' for Claudius, can, with sufficient force or virtuosity of execution, get a great reputation in the part, even though the very intensity of his obsession by these sentiments (which are common not only to all men but to many animals) shews that the characteristic side of Hamlet, the side that differentiates him from Fortinbras, is absolutely outside the actor's consciousness. Such a reputation is the actor's, not Hamlet's. Hamlet is not a man in whom 'common humanity' is raised by great vital energy to a heroic pitch, like Coriolanus or Othello. On the contrary, he is a man in whom the common personal passions are so superseded by wider and rarer interests, and so discouraged by a degree of critical self-consciousness which makes the practical efficiency of the instinctive man on the lower plane impossible to him, that he finds the duties dictated by conventional revenge and ambition as disagreeable a burden as commerce is to a poet. Even his instinctive sexual impulses offend his intellect; so that when he meets the woman who excites them he invites her to join him in a bitter and scornful criticism of their joint absurdity, demanding 'What should such fellows as I do crawling between heaven and earth?' 'Why wouldst thou be a breeder of sinners?' and so forth, all of which is so completely beyond the poor girl that she naturally thinks him mad. And, indeed, there is a sense in which Hamlet is insane; for he trips over the mistake which lies on the threshold of intellectual self-consciousness: that of bringing life to utilitarian or Hedonistic tests, thus treating it as a means instead of an end. Because Polonius is 'a foolish prating knave,' because Rosencrantz and Guildenstern are snobs, he kills them as remorselessly as he might kill a flea, shewing that he has no real belief in the superstitious reason which he gives for not killing himself, and in fact anticipating exactly the whole course of the intellectual history of Western Europe until Schopenhauer[5] found the clue that Shakespear missed. But to call Hamlet mad because he did not anticipate Schopenhauer is like calling Marcellus mad because he did not refer the Ghost to the Psychical Society. It is in fact not possible for any actor to represent Hamlet as mad. He may (and generally does) combine some notion of his own of a man who is the creature of affectionate sentiment with the figure drawn by the lines of Shakespear; but the result is not a madman, but simply one of those monsters produced by the imaginary combination of two normal species, such as sphinxes, mermaids, or centaurs. And this is the invariable resource of the instinctive, imaginative, romantic actor. You will see him weeping bucketsful of tears over Ophelia, and treating the players, the gravedigger, Horatio, Rosencrantz, and Guildenstern as if they were mutes at his own funeral. But go and watch Mr. Forbes Robertson's Hamlet seizing delightedly on every opportunity for a bit of philosophic discussion or artistic recreation to escape from the 'cursed spite' of revenge and love and other common troubles; see how he brightens up when the players come; how he tries to talk philosophy with Rosencrantz and Guildenstern the moment they come into the room; how he stops on his country walk with Horatio to lean over the churchyard wall and draw out the gravedigger whom he sees singing at his trade; how even his fits of excitement find expression in declaiming scraps of poetry; how the shock of Ophelia's death relieves itself in the fiercest intellectual contempt for Laertes's ranting, whilst an hour afterwards, when Laertes stabs him, he bears no malice for that at all, but embraces him gallantly and comradely; and he dies as we forgive everything to Charles II for dying, and makes 'the rest is silence' a touchingly humorous apology for not being able to finish his business. See all that; and you have seen a true classical Hamlet. Nothing half so charming has been seen by this generation. It will bear seeing again and again.

And please observe that this is not a cold Hamlet. He is none of your logicians who reason their way through the world because they cannot feel their way through it: his intellect is the organ of his passion: his eternal self-criticism is as alive and thrilling as it can possibly be. The great soliloquy—no: I do NOT mean 'To be or not to be'; I mean the dramatic one, 'O what a rogue and peasant slave am I!'—is as passionate in its scorn of brute passion as the most bull-necked affirmation or sentimental dilution of it could be. It comes out so without violence: Mr. Forbes Robertson takes the part quite easily and spontaneously. There is none of that strange Lyceum intensity which comes from the perpetual struggle between Sir Henry Irving and Shakespear. The lines help Mr. Forbes Robertson instead of getting in his way at every turn, because he wants to play Hamlet, and not to slip into his inky cloak a changeling of quite another race. We may miss the craft, the skill double-distilled by constant peril, the subtlety, the dark rays of heat generated by intense friction, the relentless parental tenacity and cunning with which Sir Henry nurses his own pet creations on Shakespearean food like a fox rearing its litter in the den of a lioness; but we get light, freedom, naturalness, credibility and Shakespear. It is wonderful how easily everything comes right when you have the right man with the right mind for it—how the story tells itself, how the characters come to life, how even the failures in the cast cannot confuse you, though they may disappoint you. And Mr. Forbes Robertson has certainly not escaped such failures, even in his own family. I strongly urge him to take a hint from Claudius and make a real ghost of Mr. Ian Robertson[6] at once; for there is no sort of use in going through that scene night after night with a Ghost so solidly, comfortably, and dogmatically alive as his brother. The voice is not a bad voice; but it is the voice of a man who does not believe in ghosts. Moreover, it is a hungry voice, not that of one who is past eating. There is an indescribable little complacent drop at the end of every line which no sooner calls up the image of purgatory by its words than by its smug elocution it convinces us that this particular penitent is cosily warming his shins and toasting his muffin at the flames instead of expiating his bad acting in the midst of them. His aspect and bearing are worse than his recitations. He beckons Hamlet away like a beadle summoning a timid candidate for the post of junior footman to the presence of the Lord Mayor. If I were Mr. Forbes Robertson I would not stand that from my brother: I would cleave the general ear with horrid speech at him first. It is a pity; for the Ghost's part is one of the wonders of the play. And yet, until Mr. Courtenay Thorpe[7] divined it the other day, nobody seems to have had a glimpse of the reason why Shakespear would not trust anyone else with it, and played it himself. The weird music of that long speech which should be the spectral wail of a soul's bitter wrong crying from one world to another in the extremity of its torment, is invariably handed over to the most squaretoed member of the company, who makes it sound, not like Rossetti's Sister Helen,[8] or even, to suggest a possible heavy treatment, like Mozart's statue-ghost,[9] but like Chambers's Information for the people.[10]

Still, I can understand Mr. Ian Robertson, by sheer force of a certain quality of sententiousness in him, overbearing the management into casting him for the Ghost. What I cannot understand is why Miss

Granville[11] was cast for the Queen. It is like setting a fashionable modern mandolinist to play Haydn's sonatas. She does her best under the circumstances; but she would have been more fortunate had she been in a position to refuse the part.

On the other hand, several of the impersonations are conspicuously successful. Mrs. Patrick Campbell's[12] Ophelia is a surprise. The part is one which has hitherto seemed incapable of progress. From generation to generation actresses have, in the mad scene, exhausted their musical skill, their ingenuity in devising fantasies in the language of flowers, and their intensest powers of portraying anxiously earnest sanity. Mrs. Patrick Campbell, with that complacent audacity of hers which is so exasperating when she is doing the wrong thing, this time does the right thing by making Ophelia really mad. The resentment of the audience at this outrage is hardly to be described. They long for the strenuous mental grasp and attentive coherence of Miss Lily Hanbury's[13] conception of maiden lunacy; and this wandering, silly, vague Ophelia, who no sooner catches an emotional impulse than it drifts away from her again, emptying her voice of its tone in a way that makes one shiver, makes them horribly uncomfortable. But the effect on the play is conclusive. The shrinking discomfort of the King and Queen, the rankling grief of Laertes, are created by it at once; and the scene, instead of being a pretty interlude coming in just when a little relief from the inky cloak is welcome, touches us with a chill of the blood that gives it its right tragic power and dramatic significance. Play-goers naturally murmur when something that has always been pretty becomes painful; but the pain is good for them, good for the theatre, and good for the play. I doubt whether Mrs. Patrick Campbell fully appreciates the dramatic value of her quite simple and original sketch—it is only a sketch—of the part; but in spite of the occasional triviality of its execution and the petulance with which it has been received, it seems to me to settle finally in her favor the question of her right to the very important place which Mr. Forbes Robertson has assigned to her in his enterprises.

I did not see Mr. Bernard Gould[14] play Laertes: he was indisposed when I returned to town and hastened to the Lyceum; but he was replaced very creditably by Mr. Frank Dyall.[15] Mr. Martin Harvey[16] is the best Osric I have seen: he plays Osric from Osric's own point of view, which is, that Osric is a gallant and distinguished courtier, and not, as usual, from Hamlet's, which is that Osric is 'a waterfly'. Mr. Harrison Hunter[17] hits off the modest, honest Horatio capitally; and Mr. Willes[18] is so good a Gravedigger that I venture to suggest to him that he should carry his work a little further, and not virtually cease to concern himself with the play when he has spoken his last line and handed Hamlet the skull. Mr. Cooper Cliffe[19] is not exactly a subtle Claudius; but he looks as if he had stepped out of a picture by Madox Brown,[20] and plays straightforwardly on his very successful appearance. Mr. Barnes[21] makes Polonius robust and elderly instead of aged and garrulous. He is good in the scenes where Polonius appears as a man of character and experience; but the senile exhibitions of courtierly tact do not match these, and so seem forced and farcical.

Mr. Forbes Robertson's own performance has a continuous charm, interest, and variety which are the result not only of his well-known grace and accomplishment as an actor, but of a genuine delight—the rarest thing on our stage—in Shakespear's art, and a natural familiarity with the plane of his imagination. He does not superstitiously worship William: he enjoys him and understands his methods of expression. Instead of cutting every line that can possibly be spared, he retains every gem, in his own part or anyone else's, that he can make time for in a spiritedly brisk performance lasting three hours and a half with very short intervals. He does not utter half a line; then stop to act; then go on with another half line; and then stop to act again, with the clock running away with Shakespear's chances all the time. He plays as Shakespear should be played, on the line and to the line, with the utterance and acting simultaneous, inseparable and in fact identical. Not for a moment is he solemnly conscious of Shakespear's reputation or of Hamlet's momentousness in literary history: on the contrary, he delivers us from all these boredoms instead of heaping them on us. We forgive him the platitudes, so engagingly are they delivered. His novel and astonishingly effective and touching treatment of the final scene is an inspiration, from the fencing match onward. If only Fortinbras could also be inspired with sufficient force and brilliancy to rise to the warlike splendor of his helmet, and make straight for that throne like a man who intended to keep it against all comers, he would leave nothing to be desired. How many generations of Hamlets, all thirsting to outshine their competitors in effect and originality, have regarded Fortinbras, and the clue he gives to this kingly death for Hamlet, as a wildly unpresentable blunder of the poor foolish old Swan, than whom they all knew so much better! How sweetly they have died in that faith to slow music, like Little Nell in The Old Curiosity Shop![22] And now how completely Mr. Forbes Robertson has bowled them all out by being clever enough to be simple.

By the way, talking of slow music, the sooner Mr. Hamilton Clark's[23] romantic Irving music is stopped, the better. Its effect in this Shakespearean version of the play is absurd. The four Offenbachian[24] young women in tights should also be abolished, and the part of the player-queen given to a man. The courtiers should be taught how flatteringly courtiers listen when a king shews off his wisdom in wise speeches to his nephew. And that nice wooden beach on which the ghost walks would be the better for a seaweedy looking cloth on it, with a handful of shrimps and a pennorth of silver sand.

1. **Cardiff**. Irving played here in 1897 on a tour during which he made a number of speeches.

2. **Alexander**, George (1858–1918), actor-manager, knighted 1911; he had played Orlando in his own production of *As You Like It* at the St James's Theatre in 1896.

3. **Tree**, Beerbohm. See p. 152.

4. **Garrick**, David. See p. 20. His short farce *Catharine and Petruchio*, based on *The Taming of the Shrew*, held the stage until Daly reverted to Shakespeare (abbreviated) in 1887, but Tree put on Garrick's play as an after-piece on 1 November 1897.

5. **Schopenhauer**, Arthur (1788–1860), German pessimist philosopher.

6. **Robertson**, Ian (1858–1936), actor, Forbes-Robertson's brother.

7. **Thorpe**, Courtenay, actor whom Shaw particularly admired in Ibsen. He had played the Ghost in a production at the Olympic in May 1897, and was to play it again for John Barrymore in London.

8. **Sister Helen**, an allusion to the poem of the same name by Dante Gabriel Rossetti (1828–82) which includes the words 'But oh! his voice is sad and weak!' (l. 177).

9. **Mozart's statue-ghost**. In the last scene of the opera *Don Giovanni* the statue of the Commendatore sings in a bass voice to frightening effect.

10. **Chambers's Information for the People**, reference book which went through several editions between 1835 and 1875.

11. **Granville**, Charlotte (1863–?), appeared mainly in modern plays (including, in 1915, Shaw's *Major Barbara*).

12. **Campbell**, Mrs Patrick (1865–1940), flamboyant actress with whom Shaw later had a long and close friendship; their correspondence, edited by Alan Dent, appeared in 1952.

13. **Hanbury**, Lily (1875–1908), had played Ophelia at the Olympic in May 1897.

14. **Gould**, Bernard (1861–1945), stage name of Bernard Partridge, actor and artist, knighted 1925.

15. **Dyall**, Frank (Franklin, 1874–1950), actor who had a long career on the English and American stage.

16. **Harvey**, Martin (1863–1944), actor-manager, knighted 1921, who frequently played with Irving and became a famous Hamlet.

17. **Hunter**, Harrison (d. 1923), actor.

18. **Willes** [not identified].

19. **Cliffe**, Cooper (1862–1939), actor and singer who played with Irving and later worked mainly in America.

20. **Brown**, Ford Madox (1821–93), pre-Raphaelite painter.

21. **Barnes,** J. H. (1850–1925), actor and writer.

22. **The Old Curiosity Shop,** novel (1840–1) by Charles Dickens.

23. **Clark,** Hamilton (1840–1912), organist, conductor, and composer of music for Irving's Lyceum productions.

24. **Offenbachian,** alluding to the operettas of Jacques Offenbach (1819–80).

〰〰〰〰〰〰〰〰〰〰〰〰〰〰〰〰〰〰〰〰〰〰〰〰〰〰〰

1898, William Archer (1856–1924) on *Julius Caesar*, produced by Herbert Beerbohm Tree (1853–1917) at Her Majesty's Theatre, London, from *The World*; reprinted in his *Study and Stage* (1899), pp. 77–82.

ARCHER, translator of Ibsen, reviewed theatre for a number of publications from 1879 until 1910, and published five volumes of collected criticism from *The World* along with several other books on contemporary theatre and drama. His statement that this production was 'a triumphant success', qualified in the course of his review, is disputed by St John Hankin in a letter to *The Academy* reprinted below. Tree's slowness of diction, on which Archer comments, is evident in his recording of one of Antony's speeches (see p. 14). The production is illustrated in Pl. 9.

MR. TREE'S revival of *Julius Caesar* is a triumphant success. The play, as I have said any time the last eighteen years, is one of the greatest acting plays in the world; and it is superbly staged, and more than adequately rendered. Mr. Tree assures me that every one prophesied failure for his venture, and thought him mad to attempt it. 'Every one' is a large word; but there is no doubt that the wiseacres were sceptical and discouraging. Oh, these wiseacres! Oh, these sapient meddlers and muddlers in theatrical affairs, who go about wrangling over snippets of 'exclusive' and generally delusive news, which they serve up in a hotch-potch of comment, compounded, in equal proportions, of servility and stupidity! *Julius Caesar*, they said, had never had a long run; true, for it had never been revived since the long run came in, or under conditions which made a long run possible. *Julius Caesar* was deficient in female interest; *Julius Caesar* had no comic relief; *Julius Caesar* was stately and classical and full of long speeches, and the public did not like long speeches and classical stateliness. Thus they tried to make a law of their own lack of dramatic and literary insight, and almost succeeded in persuading Mr. Tree himself that the tragedy was a dull and stodgy anachronism. Hence, no doubt, his manifesto insisting on the 'humanity' of the characters; as though any one who knew chalk from cheese ever questioned it! All the more honour to him for braving, not only the difficulty of the three equal parts, but the croakings of the theatrical tipsters, and putting all his strength into an entirely worthy, and in some ways magnificent, revival.

Now 'the sad augurs mock their own presage,' and all the world knows that *Julius Caesar* is one of Shakespeare's theatrical masterpieces. This should be apparent enough, to any one with a spark of imagination, on merely reading the play; yet in vaunting its theatrical qualities, I did not rely on imagination alone, but on the very vividest, perhaps, of all my theatrical experiences. I saw the Meiningen[1] performance of *Julius Caesar*, four or five times; it was incomparably the finest, most impressive, most thrilling thing of its kind I ever saw in a theatre. Frankly—for this is a point of history on which I feel bound to be explicit—the English revival is not so good. It is quite as magnificent, and, for aught I know, it may be even more correct in its archaeological detail; but it falls short both in acting and stage-management. We must remember that, when we saw *Julius Caesar* at Drury Lane, it was not a new production, but was the perfected result of years of patient study and labour, carried out under ideal artistic conditions, and guided and informed by enthusiastic and highly cultivated imagination. It was the hobby of a prince, not the daring experiment of an actor-manager. I draw the comparison, not to depreciate Mr. Tree's most praiseworthy enterprise, but rather *pour encourager les autres*. It is my (perhaps ungrateful) function, with regard to Shakespearean acting, to 'hold high the banner of the ideal.'[2] This is the branch of histrionics that I love most, have studied most, and (in my own esteem) know most about. As to other forms of acting, my impressions are apt to be vague, my judgments perfunctory. When Mr. Max Beerbohm[3] did me the honour to parody me, his best hit, if I may venture an opinion, was in his last sentence: 'I shall speak of the acting next week.' But if, when a Shakespearean revival is in question, I 'speak of the acting next week,' it is only in order to have plenty of space, and probably (as in this instance) to see the performance again and study it more closely. I am just old enough to have seen the last of a great school of poetical acting, of what may fairly be called the Shakespearean tradition, since it could be traced back without a break to Burbage and Taylor,[4] whom the poet himself had 'instructed.'[5] I am just young enough to look forward with reasonable hope to seeing, before I make my exit, a revival of this lost art, purged of some of its vices and extravagances. That is the end towards which I work; and *Julius Caesar* at Her Majesty's, whatever its defects of detail, seems to me a step in the right direction. It is far more living, more poetical, more sonorous than the average Lyceum revival. The sonority does not always come in quite at the proper place or in the proper time; but every here and there the English iambic comes to something like its rights, and that is a great deal to be thankful for. It is quite possible for a performance of *Julius Caesar* to be a little less excellent than the Meiningen performance and yet one of the most notable productions of our time.

It cannot be said, unfortunately, that the prevailing slowness of the first night has been corrected. Mr. Tree has cut some scenes (Act ii. scenes 3 and 4, and the Soothsayer episode at the beginning of Act iii. scene 1) and has made other small compressions, instead of reducing the monstrously exaggerated pauses. It was scarcely to be expected that he should do much in this way, since he himself is the most inveterate offender. He seeks his effects, not in Shakespeare's lines, but in the chasms and abysses which he interposes between them. The part of Antony really begins with his entrance into the Senate House after Caesar's death. His first words Mr. Tree speaks admirably—

> O mighty Caesar! dost thou lie so low?
> Are all thy conquests, glories, triumphs, spoils,
> Shrunk to this little measure?

Mr. Tree does nothing better than this; but his whole scene with the murderers, though overloaded with self-conscious ingenuities of byplay, is good. His action when left alone with the body of Caesar, is lacking in dignity, and his speech is far too loud. From 'A curse shall light upon the limbs of men' down to 'Cry "Havoc!" and let slip the dogs of war,' his tone is not one of reflection, however bitter and bodeful, but of frenzied exhortation. He seems to be already moving the stones of Rome to rise and mutiny, or trying to awaken the corpse at his feet. This is sonority exaggerated and misplaced. As for the famous oration, Mr. Tree's rendering of it produces a considerable effect, and is so far justified; but it has nothing in common with the thrilling effect of irresistible eloquence which Shakespeare evidently intended, and Herr Barnay[6] attained. There are speakers, and good speakers in their way, whose method consists in a calculated deliberation. They drop their phrases, like pebbles, into a pool of silence, and wait until the ripples caused by one have subsided, before they let slip the next. Mr. Tree's Mark Antony belongs to this school of orators. Every line of his speech—nay, every phrase, for there are certainly more pauses than lines—is thrown into relief against a background of either mute expectancy or inarticulate emotion on the part of the crowd. It is almost as though he cared less for the immediate effect of his words than for the accuracy of the report in the morning papers, and knew that the stenography of the day could not get beyond some fifty words a minute. There are clever turns and ingenious emphases in his delivery, and, what between the speaker and the populace, we are kept thoroughly interested and entertained. But are we moved, excited, carried away? Not for a moment. How different would our emotion be if Mr. Tree would only take Antony at his word and 'speak right on,' making of the speech a torrent of irony, pathos and invective, an ever-growing tidal wave, instead of a rivulet meandering drop by drop, as it were, through great expanses of silence. Almost the only point where Antony does *not* pause is after the lines—

> Even at the base of Pompey's statua,
> Which all the while ran blood, great Caesar fell—

where a considerable pause, and a total change of key, are surely imperative.

Mr. Lewis Waller's[7] fine voice and good enunciation give beautiful effect to many of Brutus's speeches. Nevertheless, he scarcely fills the large outline of Shakespeare's Brutus, the supremely self-satisfied Stoic, whose inflexible idealism overbears the more politic sagacity of Cassius, and ruins their common enterprise. Mr. Waller is too nervous, too tense; his outward manifestations of the struggle that is going on within him are too obvious and commonplace. For instance, while Cassius is enlarging on Caesar's physical weakness, and asking why he should 'so get the start of the majestic world,' Brutus sits with corrugated brows nodding his head in intent acquiescence, as though these commonplaces were new and luminous thoughts to him. They are nothing of the kind. Shakespeare is here illustrating the different characters of the two men—the diversity, not the identity, of their motives. Antony, at the close, says of Brutus—

> All the conspirators save only he
> Did that they did in envy of great Caesar.

Why, then, should Mr. Waller show Brutus apparently won over by the very speech in which Cassius most clearly unmasks his envy? Brutus should sit lost in reverie, lending only half an ear to the shrewish rhetoric of Cassius, and working towards the same conclusion along his own very different line of thought. In the quarrel-scene, although it is right to contrast the impassivity of Brutus with the vehemence of Cassius, Mr. Waller showed too little feeling at the turning-point—the speech beginning 'Sheath your dagger.' But oh! what an incomparable scene! If I were an actor-manager, I should without hesitation give the florid Antony the go-by, and play Cassius, for the sake of that wonderful passage beginning 'Of your philosophy you make no use' and ending 'O ye immortal gods!' Mr. Franklyn M'Leay's[8] Cassius struck me as a very sound and excellent performance. It was a little stiff, perhaps, and seemed a little stagey, in contrast with the too studious reserve of Mr. Waller's Brutus; but this contrast, I believe, did Mr. M'Leay some injustice. He took firm hold of the character and played it vigorously, crisply, discreetly, bringing out to admiration the fiery energy which is the keynote of the man's nature. And yet—I have a notion that Mr. M'Leay might do better as Brutus and Mr. Waller as Cassius. Such an exchange of parts was common in the old days; might not the experiment be tried in this case, sometime before the end of the run?

1. **Meiningen**. George II, Duke of Saxe-Meiningen (1826–1914), brought his private company of actors to Drury Lane in 1881 with his production of *Julius Caesar* famous especially for its crowd scenes.

2. **'hold high the banner of the ideal'** [not identified].

3. **Beerbohm**, Max. See p. 160. The parody is one of six in a piece called 'Press Notices on "Punch and Judy"' published in *The Saturday Review* on 16 October 1895, and apparently not reprinted, in which Beerbohm parodies the style of theatre critics of the time. The parody of Archer is headed '*From the "W-rld"*' and ends 'Of the acting, I hope to have something to say next week.'

4. **Burbage and Taylor**. Richard Burbage (1568–1619), leading actor of Shakespeare's company; Joseph Taylor (*c*.1585–1652) took over many of his roles, including Hamlet, after he died.

5. **'instructed'**. The reference is to the statement by John Downes (*c*.1662–1710) that Taylor had been 'instructed' by Shakespeare in the role of Hamlet, and himself 'taught Betterton in every particle of it.' But Taylor seems not to have joined the King's Men until after both Shakespeare and Burbage were dead.

6. **Barnay**, Ludwig (1842–1924), played Mark Antony with the Meininger company in London.

7. **Waller**, Lewis (1860–1915), actor-manager, early matinée idol.

8. **M'Leay** (or MacLeay), Frank (died 1900), a Canadian actor; he also played Hubert in *King John*.

Hankin on Tree's Julius Caesar

5 February 1898, St John Hankin (1869–1909) on Beerbohm Tree's *Julius Caesar*, in *The Academy*, no. 1344, pp. 160–1, reprinted in *Shakespearean Criticism*, vol. 17, ed. Sandra Williamson (Detroit, Gale Research, 1992), pp. 308–10.

HANKIN was a playwright; this letter to the editor provoked a reply from Tree (26 February), also reprinted in the Gale volume. For a different view see Archer's review in *The World*, printed above.

MR. TREE'S 'Julius Caesar' is a triumph of actor-management. It is also, in my humble opinion, a grievous insult to Shakespeare. Shakespeare wrote a play of which the central character was an idealised Brutus. It was the story of how a nobleminded Roman, partly from a traditional worship of 'Liberty,' partly through being worked upon by astute plotters like Cassius, took the life of Julius Caesar. How for a few hours it looked as if all were going well with him and his fellow-conspirators, until the fiery Antony, by a successful appeal to the greed of the mob, turned the tables on them so that they fled from Rome, only to fall at Philippi under the avenging swords of Antony and Caesar's nephew Octavius. That is the play as Shakespeare—a considerable dramatist after all—conceived it. Here it is as Mr. Tree conceives it:

There was a Roman named Antony, who was an intimate friend of Caesar, wore a distinctive costume, and always stood in the middle of the stage. When Caesar was killed he came into the Senate-house and made a speech over the body. He was left making facial contortions over it when the curtain fell. After Caesar's death this Antony made a great speech in the Forum and was loyally cheered by a splendidly drilled crowd of supers, as an actor-manager should be. He subsequently hurled defiance at the conspirators on the plains—or hills—of Philippi, and delivered a famous speech over the body of Brutus. And that's all.

It is hardly wonderful after this that the dramatic critic of the *Standard* should have complained pathetically that 'the play really, to all intents and purposes, ended with the winning over of the mob by the pleading of Antony'; and that the quarrel scene in Brutus's tent—one of the most famous scenes in Shakespeare—which is at present retained in the Her Majesty's acting version, is not 'of the very faintest concern' to the audience! Was I not right, then, in saying that the new 'Julius Caesar' is a triumph of actor-management? Mr. Tree has seized his opportunity of focussing the attention of the house upon himself, and the play is left in ruins.

Now the question is, is this what the playgoing public want? Do they go to Her Majesty's to see Shakespeare's 'Julius Caesar' or to see Mr. Tree? If the former, then the present performance is an unqualified failure, for the whole proportions of the play are spoiled by the present arrangement, a relatively minor character is thrust violently into the front place, and the action of the drama becomes incoherent. Any performance of 'Julius Caesar' which impressed a leading dramatic critic with the opinion that the tent scene between Brutus and Cassius was superfluous, and was not of the faintest concern to the audience, stands condemned on the face of it. If Mr. Tree was bent on playing the principal part at his own theatre, he should have played Brutus. But I imagine that he could not make up his mind to let anyone else deliver Antony's oration. If this is so, the only course for him was to become a sort of Shakespearean Prisoner of Zenda,[1] double the *roles* of Brutus and Antony, deliver both orations in the Forum, and after killing himself (as Brutus) in act v., get up and make the last speech (as Antony) over his own body. Perhaps Mr. Tree will try this arrangement at a special *matinée*.

But it is not the purpose of this letter to scoff at Mr. Tree, and I can even admire the ingenuity with which he has arranged the acts in his production, so that at the fall of the curtain he may always be, so to speak, in possession of the house. It is the privilege of the actor-manager, apparently, always to have the last word. My purpose is rather to point out the sorrowful fact that 'Julius Caesar' is unsuited for modern professional representation. It should only be played by amateurs. Almost every line in the play is pure poetry. This is true even of the speeches of the minor characters. The full value of this poetry can only be brought out by actors who think of their lines more than of themselves. How many such are there on the London stage today? Your professional actor will not 'leave his damnable faces and begin' to speak his lines in a straightforward manner. He must gulp and snivel and 'put tears into his voice,' and employ all the other tricks which spoil the rhythm of blank verse. He overloads his production with set scenes, and lengthens it out with tiresome artifices such as the red roses at which poor Mr. Fulton[2] has to grimace at Her Majesty's nightly. And then half a dozen scenes are cut out in order to prevent the play from being unduly long! Every possible effort is made to distract the attention of the audience from the verse to the actor. And the verse of 'Julius Caesar' is too good for this fooling. The result of all this is that Mr. Tree's production, in my opinion, in spite of the money and ingenuity and taste that he has lavished upon it, is nothing like so effective as the performance given by amateurs at Oxford in 1889, with

Mr. Bourchier[3] as Brutus and Mr. Holman Clarke[4] as Cassius. The mounting on that occasion was comparatively simple, though then also Mr. Alma Tadema[5] designed the scenery and costumes, if I remember right. The play was played through as it is printed, with practically no editing and no 'cuts,' and it lasted only some three hours. At Her Majesty's, when I saw it, in spite of numerous 'cuts,' it lasted three hours and a half, while the noise of 'setting' the heavy scenery behind (with a view to reducing the 'waits') spoiled some of the finest scenes, notably that in Brutus' orchard, which was given to the accompaniment of the muffled thunders of scene-shifting.

How, then, should 'Julius Caesar,' be played? The first point is, that *nothing* should be permitted to interfere with the value of the *verse*. The educated amateur who appreciates blank verse and loves the play will speak it better than any professional actor we have. Again, an agreeable voice, a cultivated intonation is absolutely essential for *every* actor in the cast who has to speak blank verse. The high-pitched cockney twang is impossible in 'Julius Caesar.' The play must be given entire, as it is written. Only so will it be intelligible and convincing to the audience. It is not a miracle of construction, but it tells its story clearly enough when actor-managers allow it to do so and do not cut out the other fellow's lines. The time that would be occupied by these discarded scenes and lines would be more than made up if all the unnecessary posturing and grimacing over blood-red roses and Caesar's body were left out. What business has Calpurnia in the Senate-house at the end of Her Majesty's first act? The only actor in the present production who shows any perception whatever of how to play seems to me to be Mr. Waller.[6] His Brutus is at times quite admirable. This emboldens me to urge him to reconsider his rendering of a famous passage. Brutus is a Stoic. It is his creed to repress all outward emotion. In the tent scene his stoicism breaks down, and he calls Cassius names, and Mr. Waller did this excellently. With such a Cassius, indeed, it must have been easy. I did it myself, and I hope sincerely that 'it is impossible that ever Rome shall breed his fellow'. But, after the reconciliation, Brutus must regain his Stoic self-command. Shakespeare realised this, and his Brutus says in a low, repressed tone—

No man bears sorrow better. Portia is dead.

Mr. Waller says—'Portia (sob) is (sob) d-d-d-d-ead,' and, in very deed, 'makes no use of his philosophy.' In the same way it is ridiculous for Brutus to snort and gulp over the details of Portia's end. He tells them (in

Shakespeare) in the baldest, briefest form, and his tone is an even, monotonous level.

> Impatient of my absence,
> And grief that young Octavius with Mark Antony
> Have made themselves so strong; for with her death
> That tidings came; with this she fell distract,
> And, her attendants absent, swallowed fire.

Mr. Waller's elaborate shudder over the announcement spoils an impressive situation. Cassius—and the audience—may be trusted to do the shuddering if the lines are properly delivered.

1. **Prisoner of Zenda**, title-character of a novel by Anthony Hope (1863–1933), who impersonates a king.

2. **Fulton**, Charles J. (1857–1938), successful actor who played Caesar.

3. **Bourchier**, Arthur (1863–1927), a founder of the Oxford University Dramatic Society who became a successful professional actor in Shakespearian and other roles.

4. **Clarke**, Holman (1864–1925); after playing with the Oxford University Dramatic Society he became a successful professional actor and director.

5. **Alma-Tadema**, Lawrence (1836–1912), painter, knighted 1899, known especially for his reconstructions of Imperial Rome, who designed for Irving as well as Tree; he advised on the scenery for the Oxford production.

6. **Waller**, Lewis. See p. 156.

30 September 1899, Max Beerbohm (1872–1956) on Beerbohm Tree's production of *King John* at Her Majesty's Theatre, London, from *The Saturday Review*, reprinted in his *More Theatres* (1969), pp. 191–3.

MAX BEERBOHM succeeded Shaw as theatre critic of *The Saturday Review* in May 1898, and held the post for twelve years in spite of his distaste for the task: this was the only regular work he ever did. His half-brother, Herbert Beerbohm Tree (1853–1917), controlled the Haymarket Theatre from 1887 to 1897, when he moved to Her (later His) Majesty's. His production of *King John* (from which the death scene forms the basis of the first ever Shakespeare film, made in 1899 and lasting two minutes) was characteristically elaborate, including a spectacular interpolated tableau of the granting of Magna Carta, which Shakespeare had failed even to mention. Beerbohm's review is exceptional in its use of 'disjointed sentences' to convey his impression of the production.

Beerbohm on Tree's King John

I n a nobly vaulted chamber of Northampton Castle are set the thrones of the king and the queen mother. The portly chamberlain, wand-bearing, red-robed, stands waiting on one of the topmost steps of the great staircase. An organ sounds, and he stalks majestically down. After him skips a little jester. A long sombre procession of bowed heads and folded arms, the monks come, chanting a Mass. After them walk the courtiers. The monks pass away through the arches. The courtiers range themselves around the throne. A blast of trumpets heralds the king and the queen mother, who presently seat themselves upon the thrones. In the brief parley with Chatillon—'new diplomacy,' with a vengeance!—one feels that not the king, but the sinister and terrible old figure beside him, is the true power, ever watching, prompting, enforcing. Chatillon flings his master's defiance and is escorted from the presence-chamber. The ill-matched brothers are ushered in; the straight-limbed elder, splendidly confident and insolent; the younger, lantern-jawed and cringing, grinning with fear. At the foot of the throne, the younger whines his cause with quick, wretched gestures. The king suppresses a smile. His eyes wander to the bastard, finding in him 'perfect Richard.' 'Man and no-man' are here—an elemental situation. Sped by a blow of the jester's bladder, 'no-man' scurries out of the chamber, happy in the acquisition of his gold. The bastard is left exulting in his manhood and the glory it has brought him ... Under the walls of Angiers, Philip of France parleys with his enemy. The queen mother holds out her arms to little Arthur, and Constance reads in her eyes all that would befall him in England. The citizens open their gates, and on a cushion the keys of the city are presented to the two kings, who, hand in hand, pass in to hold revelry ... Pandulpho, tremendous embodiment of the Pope's authority, comes to the two kings. John, strong in his mother's presence, receives the curse. Philip snatches his hand away from the clasp of his ally. Torn with conflicting fears, he submits himself to Rome ... You see the two armies 'face to face, and bloody point to point.' In a corner of the dark field, fitfully lit by the flames of a distant village, you see the victorious bastard fell his arch foe and snatch from his shoulders the lion skin of King Richard ... In a glade of slim beeches, John communes with the faithful, grim Hubert. The old soldier stands immovable, while his master whispers in his ear. Beyond, stands the queen mother, watching with her eyes of ill omen. Little Arthur is plucking the daisies. The king smiles down at him as he passes, and the child starts away. There are some daisies growing near the spot where the king has been whispering his behest. Lightly, he cuts the heads off them with his sword ... In the crypt there is no light but from the cresset where the irons will be heated. Arthur runs in, carrying a cross-bow on his shoulder. 'Good morrow, Hubert.' 'Good morrow, little prince...' All the vassals have left their king. The jester who watched the scene from a gallery has fled too. The king takes up the orb and the sceptre, sits haggard upon his throne. Hubert comes in, and the sound of this footstep causes the king to shudder and cry out like a child. But Arthur still lives. Nothing but his death-warrant remains against the king. While the king burns this parchment on the cresset, the monks file in to their Mass. Up the stairs they go, chanting. The king smiles, and then, still standing by the cresset, folds his hands in prayer. He walks, with bowed head, up the stairs, abases himself at the altar... It is the dusk of dawn in the orchard of Swinstead Abbey, and through the apple-trees the monks hurry noiselessly to the chapel. The dying king is borne out in a chair. He is murmuring snatches of a song. The chair is set down, and with weak hands he motions away his bearers. 'Ay, marry,' he gasps, 'now my soul hath elbow-room; it would not out at windows nor at doors. There is so hot a summer in my bosom, that all my bowels crumble up to dust... And none of you will bid the winter come, to thrust his icy fingers in my maw.' The bastard comes in hot haste, and the king, to receive his tidings, sits upright, and is crowned for the last time. He makes no answer to the tidings. One of the courtiers touches him, ever so lightly, on the shoulder, and he falls back. The crown is taken from his head and laid on the head of the child who is now king. The bastard rings out those words in which poetry of patriotism finds the noblest expression it can ever find...

I have written down these disjointed sentences, less in order to enable my readers to imagine the production at Her Majesty's Theatre than to preserve my own impressions. Probably, I have omitted many of the important points in the play and in the show; I have merely recorded the things which an errant memory has kept clearliest. Most of the points I have alluded to are, as you will have observed, points of 'business' and stage management. For this I make no apology. I had never seen the play acted before, and I must confess that, reading it, I had found it insufferably tedious. I had found many beautiful pieces of poetry in it, but drama had seemed to me absolutely lacking. That was because I have not much imagination. Lengths of blank verse with a few bald directions—enter A; exeunt B and D; dies; alarums and excursions; are not enough to make me *see* a thing. (And, I take it, this is the case with most of my fellow-creatures.) Therefore, when I go to a theatre and find that what bored me very much in the reading of it is a really fine play, I feel that I owe a great debt of gratitude to the management which has brought out the latent possibilities. I can imagine that a bad production of *King John* would be infinitely worse than a private reading of it. A bad production would make the play's faults the more glaring. But a good production, as at Her Majesty's, makes one forget what is bad in sheer surprise at finding so much that is good. I can say without partiality, and with complete sincerity, that I have never seen a production in which the note of beauty was so surely and incessantly struck as in this production of *King John*. As for the actual performance, there are many interesting points which, unfortunately, I cannot discuss this week. I shall write about the performance as soon as there are not so many other plays clamouring to be noticed.

᚛᚜

13 **November 1899,** anonymous review of *Richard II*, produced by William Poel (1852–1934) in the lecture theatre of the University of London in Burlington Gardens, London, from *The Times*.

POEL, who founded The Elizabethan Stage Society in 1895, was the great pioneer of the revival of Elizabethan-style staging methods; he was, however, often surprisingly free in his arrangement of texts. The last scene of *Richard II* was severely cut, reducing Richard's prison soliloquy to only five lines. There is an interesting account of the production, deriving in part from Granville Barker, in the 'Stage-History' in the New Shakespeare edition, edited by John Dover Wilson (Cambridge, 1939).

M R. WILLIAM POEL had a surprise in store for the large audience which filled the lecture theatre of the University of London on Saturday afternoon. Acting has not hitherto been the strong point of the society's performances. A fair all-round representation of *Richard II.* was all that was expected. Yet the play had scarcely begun before it was clear that there was one player in the company whose talent would make the performance exceptionally interesting. A few months ago that oddly named piece *The Weather-Hen* showed Mr. Granville Barker[1] in the light of a promising dramatist. *Richard II.* proved him to be also a well-graced and intelligent actor, with gifts specially fitting him for romantic drama. It was fortunate that Mr. Poel was able to secure so satisfactory a representative of Richard. The interest of the play centres entirely upon the figure of the hapless King. Shakespeare drew Richard in his evil fortunes with such pathos that all our sympathy goes with him in spite of his vacillation and folly in the earlier scenes. This is, of course, judging the play as a play, and not as history. The King of the drama is always human and nearly always loveable, but his nature is weak and fitful. A Plantagenet in his kingly bearing, he lacks the Plantagenet force of character. Remind him that he is a King, and his breast swells with pride of sovereignty. He is the sun of the realm that shall make all traitors and rebels

> Stand bare and naked, trembling at themselves.

If men fail him, angels will come to aid 'the deputy elected by the Lord.' But he has not the strength of mind to make his high boastings good. News of disaster, instead of nerving him to greater effort, crushes him to the earth.

> My lord, wise men ne'er sit and wail their woes
> But presently prevent the ways to wail,

says the sturdy old Bishop of Carlisle. But Richard sits and wails unheeding, turning his grief into fantastic shapes of words, while the doer, Bolingbroke, says little, but goes steadily forward to the throne on which his steadfast gaze is set.

It is because we see from the first that Richard is too weak to bear the burden of monarchy in unquiet times that our hearts are touched by his misfortunes. The memories that the play stamps upon the mind are of Richard in his friar's habit landing from Ireland only to hear that his kingdom is lost; of the touching figure which he makes, stripped of his finery, with no supporter to cry 'Amen' to his 'God save the King,' in Westminster Hall; of the sad farewell between the deposed King and his pretty, butterfly Queen; of the final scene in the dungeon at Pomfret, where the life that began amid such brave auspices is taken by an assassin's hand. Gay and princely in the first two acts, Mr. Barker played the later scenes with a decided sense of character, and with pathos that seemed to touch every section of his rather difficult audience. Schoolgirls who are studying the play for the Cambridge Local Examination formed a large proportion of it. Their presence probably accounted for a tendency on the part of the house to laugh at any incident or accident that could be laughed at. This does not, of course, lighten the actors' task of making good the absence of scenery. However, the simple arrangement of the stage worked well, and the picturesque grouping stood out effectively against the tapestry which served for background. Unimaginative persons may find it difficult to supply the setting for each scene. But those who love poetry and drama better than spectacle find their minds well attuned to such a play as *Richard II.* by the plain surroundings which the society offers.

An amateur actor, Colonel Everitt,[2] played John of Gaunt's death scene with remarkable truth and passion. Bolingbroke was presented unsympathetically, as the part demands, but the actor took it too slowly and was inclined to mouth his words. Several of his companions shared in the fault of slowness. It was this which protracted the performance until past 7[3]— an awkward hour for dismissing an audience. But, in spite of its awkwardness, nearly all the spectators stayed until the end. It was little wonder they did, for *Richard II.* is a play seldom acted in London, and the performance was really interesting.

1. **Granville Barker**, Harley (1877–1946), actor, playwright, director and critic, famous especially for his pioneering productions at the Savoy Theatre from 1912 to 1914 and for his *Prefaces* to a number of Shakespeare's plays (1927–45). After remarrying in 1918 he hyphenated his name and virtually retired from the stage. He wrote *The Weather Hen* in collaboration with Berte Thomas.

2. **Everitt**, possibly Colonel Sir William Everitt (1844–1908), knighted 1898, a distinguished soldier.

3. **past 7**. According to a review in *The Athenaeum* (18 November) much concerned with the discomfort of the audience, which finds that, perhaps because 'the representation was scarcely in the full sense a performance, it proved effective', it 'took place between four and eight'.

---

4 December 1899, C. E. Montague (1867–1928) on Frank Benson (1858–1939) as Richard II, reprinted in *The Manchester Stage 1880–1900: Criticisms reprinted from 'The Manchester Guardian'* (n.d.), pp. 76–87, and in *Specimens of English Dramatic Criticism*, ed. A. C. Ward (1945), pp. 223–32.

MONTAGUE was a distinguished man of letters who spent most of his career on *The Manchester Guardian*.

Benson was a touring actor-manager, talented and athletic, especially associated with the Stratford Festival. He was knighted in 1916. His company provided a valuable training ground for young actors, who were especially welcome if they displayed talent as sportsmen.

THE chief interest of the day... attached to Mr. Benson's Richard II., a piece of acting which is much less known here, and to whose chief interest we do not think that critical justice has ever been done. An actor faulty in some other ways, but always picturesque, romantic, and inventive, with a fine sensibility to beauty in words and situations and a voice that gives this sensibility its due, Mr. Benson brings out admirably that half of the character which criticism seems almost always to have taken pains to obscure—the capable and faithful artist in the same skin as the incapable and unfaithful King. With a quite choice and pointed infelicity, Professor Dowden[1] has called Shakspere's Richard II. 'an amateur in living, not an artist'; Mr. Boas,[2] generally one of the most suggestive of recent writers on Shakspere, has called his grace of fancy 'puerile' and its products 'pseudo-poetic'. The general judgment on the play reads as if the critics felt they would be 'only encouraging' kings like the Richard of this play if they did not assure him throughout the ages that his poetry was sad stuff at the best. 'It's no excuse', one seems to hear them say, and 'Serve you right, you and your poetry.' It is our critical way to fall thus upon the wicked or weak in books and leave him half-dead, after taking from him even the good side that he hath. Still it is well to see what Shakspere meant us to, and we wonder whether any one who hears Mr. Benson in this part with an open mind can doubt that Shakspere meant to draw in Richard not only a rake and muff on a throne and falling off it but, in the same person, an exquisite poet: to show with one hand how kingdoms are lost and with the other how the creative imagination goes about its work; to fill the same man with the attributes of a feckless wastrel in high place and with the quite distinct but not incompatible attributes of a typical, a consummate artist.

'But', it will be asked by persons justly tired of sloppy talk about art, 'What *is* an artist; what, exactly, is it in a man that makes an artist of him?' Well, first a proneness in his mind to revel and bask in its own sense of fact; not in the use of fact—that is for the men of affairs, the Bolingbrokes; nor in the explanation of fact—that is for the men of science; but simply in his own quick and glowing apprehension of what is about him, of all that is done on the earth or goes on in the sky, of dying and being born, of the sun, clouds, and storms, of great deeds and failures, the changes of the seasons, and the strange events of men's lives. To mix with the day's diet of gifts and sounds the man of this type seems to bring a wine of his own that lights a fire in his blood while he takes the meal. What the finest minds of other types eschew he does, and takes pains to do. To shun the dry light, to drench all he sees with himself, his own temperament, the humours of his own moods—this is not his dread but his wish, as well as his bent. 'The eye sees what the eye brings the means of seeing.'³ 'A fool sees not the same tree that a wise man sees.'⁴ 'You shall see the world in a grain of sand and heaven in a wild flower.'⁵ This heightened and delighted personal sense of fact, a knack of seeing visions at the instance of seen things, is the basis of art.

Only the basis, though. For that art may come a man must add to it a veritable passion for arresting and defining in words or lines and colours or notes of music, not each or any thing that he sees, nor anybody else's sense of that thing, nor yet the greatest common measure of many trained or untrained minds' senses of it, but his own unique sense of it, the precise quality and degree of emotion that the spectacle of it breeds in him and nobody else, the net result of its contact with whatever in his own temperament he has not in common with other men. That is the truth of art, to be true less to facts without you than to yourself as stirred by facts. And truth it must be with a vengeance. To find a glove-fit of words for your sense of 'the glory and the freshness of a dream',⁶ to model the very form and pressure of an inward vision to the millionth of a hair's breadth—the vocabulary of mensuration ludicrously fails to describe those infinitesimal niceties of adjustment between the inward feeling and the means of its presentment. And indeed it is only half true to speak as if feeling and its expression were separable at all. In a sense the former implies the latter. The simplest feeling is itself changed by issuing in a cry. Attaining a kind of completeness, given, as it were, its rights, it is not the same feeling after the cry that it was before. It has become not merely feeling interpreted by something outside it and separable from it, but fuller feeling, a feeling with more in it, feeling pushed one stage further in definiteness and intensity, an arch of feeling crowned at last. So, too, all artistic expression, if one thinks the matter out, is seen to be not merely a transcription of the artist's sense of fact but a perfecting of that sense itself; and the experience which never attains expression, the experience which is loosely said to be unexpressed, is really an unfinished, imperfect experience and one which, in the mind of an artist, passionately craves for its own completion through adequate expression. 'There are no beautiful thoughts', a fastidious artist has said, 'without beautiful forms.'⁷ The perfect expression *is* the completed emotion. So the artist is incessantly preoccupied in leading his sense of fact up to the point at which it achieves not merely expression but its own completion in the one word, phrase, line, stanza that can make it, simply as a feeling of his own, all that it has in it to be. He may be said to write or paint because there is a point beyond which the joy of tasting the world about him cannot go unless he does so; and his life passes in a series of moments at which thought and expression, the sense of fact and the consummate presentation of that sense, rush together like Blake's 'soul and body united',[8] to be indistinguishably fused together in a whole in which, alone, each can attain its own perfection.

We have drawn out this tedious description of the typical artist because the further it goes the more close a description does it become of the Richard whom Mr. Benson shows us in the last three acts. In him every other feeling is mastered, except at a few passing moments, by a passion of interest in the exercise of his gift of exquisite responsiveness to the appeal made to his artistic sensibility by whatever life throws for the moment in his way. Lamb[9] said it was worth while to have been cheated of the legacy so as not to miss 'the idea of' the rogue who did it. That, on a little scale, is the kind of aesthetic disinterestedness which in Shakspere's Richard, rightly presented by Mr. Benson, passes all bounds. The 'idea of' a King's fall, the 'idea of' a wife and husband torn apart, the 'idea of' a very crucifixion of indignities—as each new idea comes he revels in his own warmed and lighted apprehension of it as freely as in his apprehension of the majesty and mystery of the idea of a kingship by divine right. He runs out to meet the thought of a lower fall or a new shame as a man might go to his door to see a sunset or a storm. It has been called the aim of artistic culture to witness things with appropriate emotions. That is this Richard's aim. Good news or bad news, the first thing with him is to put himself in the right vein for getting the fullest and most poignant sense of its contents. Is ruin the word—his mind runs to steep itself in relevant pathos with which in turn to saturate the object put before it; he will 'talk of graves and epitaphs', 'talk of wills', 'tell sad stories of the death of kings'. Once in the vein, he rejoices like a good artist who has caught the spirit of his subject. The very sense of the loss of hope becomes 'that sweet way I was in to despair'. To his wife at their last meeting he bequeaths, as one imaginative writer might bequeath to another some treasure of possibilities of tragic effect, 'the lamentable tale of me'. And to this intoxicating sense of the beauty or poignancy of what is next him he joins the true passion of concern for its perfect expression. At the height of that preoccupation enmities, fears, mortifications, the very presence of onlookers are as if they were not. At the climax of the agony of the abdication scene Shakspere, with a magnificent boldness of truth, makes the artist's mind, in travail with the lovely poetical figure of the mirror, snatch at the possibility of help at the birth of the beautiful thing, even from the bitterest enemy,—

> say that again;
> The shadows of my sorrow; ha, let's see.

And nothing in Mr. Benson's performance was finer than the King's air, during the mirror soliloquy, as of a man going about his mind's engrossing business in a solitude of its own making. He gave their full value, again, to all those passages, so enigmatic, if not ludicrous, to strictly prosaic minds, in which Richard's craving for finished expression issues in a joining of words with figurative action to point and eke them out; as where he gives away the crown in the simile of the well, inviting his enemy, with the same artistic neutrality as in the passage of the mirror, to collaborate manually in an effort to give perfect expression to the situation. With Aumerle Richard is full of these little symbolic inventions, turning them over lovingly as a writer fondles a phrase that tells. 'Would not this ill do well', he says of one of them, like a poet showing a threnody to a friend.

There was just one point—perhaps it was a mere slip—at which Mr. Benson seemed to us to fail. In the beginning of the scene at Pomfret what one may call the artistic heroism of this man, so craven in every thing but art, reaches its climax. Ruined, weary, with death waiting in the next room, he is shown still toiling at the attainment of a perfect, because perfectly expressed, apprehension of such sad dregs as are left him of life, still following passionately on the old quest of the ideal word, the unique image, the one perfect way of saying the one thing.

> I cannot do it; yet I'll hammer it out.

Everybody knows that cry of the artist wrestling with the angel in the dark for the word it will not give, of Balzac[10] 'plying the pick for dear life, like an entombed miner', of our own Stevenson,[11] of Flaubert[12] 'sick, irritated, the prey a thousand times a day of cruel pain' but 'continuing my labour like a true working man, who, with sleeves turned up, in the sweat of his brow, beats away at his anvil, whether it rain or blow, hail or thunder'. That 'yet I'll hammer it out' is the gem of the whole passage, yet on Saturday Mr. Benson, by some strange mischance, left the words clean out. He made amends with a beautiful little piece of insight at the close, where, after the lines

> Mount, mount, my soul! Thy seat is up on high,
> Whilst my gross flesh sinks downward, here to die,

uttered much as any other man might utter them under the first shock of the imminence of death, he half rises from the ground with a brightened face and repeats the two last words with a sudden return of animation and interest, the eager spirit leaping up, with a last flicker before it goes quite out, to seize on this new 'idea of' the death of the body. Greater love of art could no man have than this, and it was a brilliant thought of Mr. Benson's to end on such a note. But indeed the whole performance, but for the slip we have mentioned, was brilliant in its equal grasp of the two sides of the character, the one which everybody sees well enough and the one which nearly everybody seems to shun seeing, and in the value which it rendered to the almost continuous flow of genuine and magnificent poetry from Richard, to the descant on mortality in kings, for instance, and the exquisite greeting to English soil and the gorgeous rhetoric of the speeches on divine right in kings. Of Mr. Benson's achievements as an actor his Richard II. strikes us as decidedly the most memorable.

1. **Dowden**, Professor Edward (1843–1913); the quotation is from his long-popular *Shakspere—His Mind and Art* (1875, etc.), p. 195.

2. **Boas**, F. S. (1862–1957), scholar and critic; the quotation is from his *Shakespere and his Predecessors* (Oxford, 1896), p. 251.

3. 'The eye sees what the eye brings the means of seeing' [unidentified]

4. 'A fool sees not the same tree that a wise man sees', from *Proverbs of Hell* by William Blake (1757–1827).

5. 'You shall see the world in a grain of sand and heaven in a wild flower', from Blake's *Auguries of Innocence* ('To see . . .').

6. 'the glory and the freshness of a dream', from 'Ode. Intimations of Immortality' by William Wordsworth (1770–1850).

7. 'There are no beautiful thoughts without beautiful forms' [unidentified]

8. 'soul and body united', a recurrent theme in Blake's '*The Marriage of Heaven and Hell*'.

9. **Lamb**. The allusion is to 'New Year's Eve', one of the *Essays of Elia* (1823), where Lamb writes 'It was better that our family should have missed that legacy, which old Dorrell cheated us of, than that I should have at this moment two thousand pounds *in banco*, and be without the idea of that specious old rogue.'

10. **Balzac** [quotation not identified].

11. **Stevenson**, Robert Louis (1850–94), like the other writers mentioned here, a passionate stylist.

12. **Flaubert** [quotation not identified]

30 **May 1903**, Max Beerbohm on *Much Ado About Nothing* at the
Imperial Theatre, London, with Ellen Terry as Beatrice and
designs by Gordon Craig, from *The Saturday Review*, reprinted
in his *More Theatres* (1969), pp. 573–6.

BEATRICE was one of Ellen Terry's finest roles; she played it from 1880,
frequently with Irving at the Lyceum, and finally, in 1916, for a charity matinée
at the Middle Temple. The performance reviewed by Beerbohm was given
during a season which she put on at the Imperial Theatre mainly as a showcase
for the talents as a designer of her son, (Edward) Gordon Craig (1872–1968).
Beerbohm was exceptional in his understanding and appreciation of Craig's
avant-garde methods, which have had a profound influence on twentieth-
century theatre. The garden setting is illustrated in Pl. 7.

I N an article on *The Vikings*,[1] I said that Mr Gordon Craig's way with
the proscenium could not harmonise with any play in which our
illusion ought not to be an illusion of sheer fantasy. I said that it could
not, for instance, be well applied to an ordinary Shakespearean comedy.
Of course, in the playhouse there can be no means of absolute realism. It
is fantastic, when we come to think of it, that we should see men and
women behind a rectangular gilt frame. But we don't come to think of it,
if the frame is of the traditional shape. If the frame is suddenly made tall
and narrow, we do come to think of it before all things. In time we might
grow accustomed to it, taking it as a matter of course. But I have my
doubts. The traditional shape has this advantage over the shape as altered
by Mr Craig: it corresponds more nearly with our natural and ordinary
range of vision. Well! in the design of *Much Ado About Nothing*, at the
Imperial Theatre, Mr Craig has skilfully modified his method in such
wise that no objection can be made to it on grounds of drama. (Decorat-
ively, it was beyond reproach—making a much prettier or more impressive picture than we ever got through the old method.) He has not restored
the old 'border'. His scenery still towers up beyond the limit of the
proscenium itself. But the men and women on the stage no longer
symbolise the insignificance of the human race that crawls on our globe's
surface. They have regained that fallacious magnitude which is so real to
us. For the scenery itself is a sort of inner proscenium. True, in the church
scene, the characters are dwarfed in Mr Craig's first manner. But it is
realistically right that they should be so. We see them in exactly that
proportion to which the nave of a real cathedral would, by its narrow
upward stretch into the infinite, so emphatically reduce them. For truth

and beauty combined, this dim scene is incomparably finer than any other attempt that has been made to suggest a cathedral on the stage. Whatever the Philistines might urge against Mr Craig's art, they could not deny that it is, at least, the handmaid of religion. In the other scenes, the human race has all its customary aspects of importance. Behold it in the tapestried hall of Leonato's house. There is a vast expanse of tapestry, but it is hung on a wall descending to that side of the hall's ceiling which is nearest to the foot-lights. The ceiling itself is comparatively low. The wall above it is, as I have said, a kind of inner proscenium. The characters are not conscious of it, and so are not measured in proportion to it, any more than, if there were the old-fashioned 'border', they would be measured in proportion to the whole outer proscenium. In the garden of Leonato a similar effect is made by similar means. The characters are set under and between a gigantic treillage of vine, the front of which corresponds in form with that tapestried wall, and bears exactly the same relation to the men and women beneath it. Thus Mr Craig, without any sacrifice of principle, has brought his new theories into harmony with that kind of drama against which one had thought they must needs strike a discord. Apart from the proscenium, be it said that he proves his method to be not only the most decorative, but also the most dramatic, method of illustrating a play. By the elimination of details which in a real scene would be unnoticed, but which become salient on the stage, he gives to the persons of the play a salience never given to them before. Even when he dwarfed them, they were midgets clearly defined by reason of the simplicity surrounding them. Now that he gives them their full size, they are more definitely men and women (and therefore more dramatic) than they could be under any other system. As for beauty, it stands to reason that figures moving or posed before simple backgrounds must create a more beautiful effect than is created by figures moving amongst a lot of objects as definitely salient as themselves. Perhaps the most beautiful of Mr Craig's effects in *Much Ado*, and the most characteristic of his especial style, is when Balthazar sings to the accompaniment of three long-robed minstrels who are seen by us silhouetted against the sky, in the arches of a long straight viaduct of clipped yew. To a certain extent Mr Craig is hampered by dealing with a definite period and place, wherein the dresses must be more or less correct in archaeology. His wildly exquisite inventiveness in costume is one of his strongest points, and it is a pity that he must not always insist on it. In Leonato's masque, indeed, he can and does let himself go. An enchanting sight are the masquers, in their uniform gowns of silver lozenges, with diadems of mistletoe on their heads, and waving in their hands great hoops of green leaves. Otherwise, Mr Craig curbs himself. I hope that ere long, as a reward, he will have another sheerly fantastic play whereon to lavish the fantasy of his own spirit. There are many such plays that need him. Above all, no play of Maeterlinck² has yet been entrusted to him. That is to say, Maeterlinck has not yet been staged in the right way by the right man—by the one man who could realise for us those children of mystery, all astray in illimitable spaces and dimness.

If Miss Ellen Terry had offered up her son on the altar of some realistic modern dramatist, one would not have cried 'shame', so utterly and so nobly did she immolate herself for his sake in *The Vikings*. If Mr Craig had not been able to make anything of *Much Ado*, he ought still to have undertaken the job, in gratitude, seeing that there never has been, nor ever will be, so perfect a Beatrice as Miss Terry, and that Miss Terry never will be, nor ever has been, more perfect than as Beatrice. Beatrice, in all her sunniness and jollity; a tease, a romp; a woman with something beyond her generous womanhood—some touch of fairydom in her—here is she incarnate and unrivalled. A pity that she has missed a Benedick to match her. Sir Henry Irving, as I remember him, was too sardonic, too spiritual, not human enough. Mr Oscar Asche³ is quite human enough, but he lacks those light and subtle graces of humour, those brilliant surface-tricks, without which Benedick becomes a boor. The 'merry war' of words between the young lord of Padua and the young lady of Messina is not, in itself, very merry, though it is undoubtedly war-like. 'You're another' (and usually 'another' very ugly thing, according to modern canons) is the sum of their dialogue, with much of that industrious twisting of words than which (to us) nothing is more tiresome. Yet the dialogue can be shorn both of dullness and of offence if it is treated in the right way. Half of it is so shorn by Miss Terry. The other half, in Mr Asche's hands, continues to bristle. Mr Asche's deportment persuades us that Benedick is not a high-spirited young bachelor, but a very serious widower, with a very large family. So we attach a literal importance to all the words that drop from his lips. They drop so very weightily. They should fly so very mercurially. There is a tradition that Dogberry should be fat; and thus has been wrecked what might have been a delightful performance by Mr Norman Forbes.⁴ I suppose the tradition sprang from the belief that stoutness entails a slow wit, and slightness a quick wit. Neither entails either, of course. There is, however, a difference in manner between the stupidity of a stout man and the stupidity of a slight man. Not long ago, Mr Norman Forbes, who is clever and slight, gave a memorable rendering of the stupidity of Sir Andrew Aguecheek. But now, padded to the traditional bulk of Dogberry, and being unable, for all his cleverness, to get out of his own skin, he collapses between what he could do and what he would do. He shows us the stupidity of a slight man in the body of a stout man. The effect is unearthly. Don John is played by Mr William Luff,[5] very intelligently, but one misses the personal weight and magnetism without which that 'plain-dealing villain' is bound to seem slightly—more than slightly—ridiculous. Mr Julian L'Estrange,[6] as Don Pedro, has all the grace and distinction which the Shakespearean grandees need and seldom get. Mr Holman Clark[7] handles the part of Leonato with all the ease of his long experience in such parts. It is a pity he does not more often have, as he had in *The Vikings*, something on which he can imaginatively enlarge. Next to Miss Terry's Beatrice, which most impressed me was the Borachio of Mr Hubert Carter.[8] For good, sound, rollicking Shakespeareanism, nothing, except that Beatrice, could have been better. One bad shock was administered to me in the course of the evening. When Balthazar came on to sing 'Sigh no more', I could hardly believe my eyes. Always I had supposed that the sun might fall into the sea and be extinguished, and the mountains be levelled with the earth, and time and space themselves be whelmed into unmeaning, but that never, never would another than Mr Jack Robertson[9] be Balthazar.

1. *The Vikings (of Helgeland)*, play by Ibsen which Beerbohm had reviewed on 25 April 1903.

2. **Maeterlinck**, Maurice (1862–1949), Belgian symbolist poet and dramatist, best known for *Pelléas et Mélisande* (1892).

3. **Asche**, Oscar (1871–1936), actor who had worked with Benson and went on to play many other Shakespearian roles (as well as appearing in his own enormously successful musical *Chu-Chin-Chow*).

4. **Forbes**, Norman (1858–1932), actor, brother of Johnston Forbes-Robertson; he had worked extensively with Irving.

5. **Luff**, William (1872–1960).

6. **L'Estrange**, Julian (1878–1918), actor.

7. **Clark**, Holman. See p. 160.

8. **Carter**, Hubert (died 1934 aged 65).

9. **Robertson**, Jack. A. J. G. Robertson played Balthasar in 1882 and 1891 (with Irving) and again in a 'Dramatic reading' at the Garrick in 1909.

7 **November 1903,** Max Beerbohm on *The Tempest* at the Court
Theatre, London, from *The Saturday Review,* reprinted in his
Around Theatres (1953), pp. 293–7.

OVER certain of the plays of Shakespeare broods darkly the superstition that they don't 'act well.' Whenever a manager dashes in,
undaunted by this shadow, and produces one of these plays, we are
startled to find that the play does act very well indeed. 'Julius Caesar,'
'King John,' 'Richard II,' 'A Midsummer Night's Dream,' were all of
them, within recent years, regarded as forlorn hopes. 'The Tempest' was
in like case. More artistically compact, and therefore more modern, in
form than any other Shakespearean play, it was yet scouted as apt only to
'the study.' True, Mr. Benson[1] had it in his repertory (as, indeed, he had
also two, at least, of those other plays which I have named). But somehow,
admirable though they are in many ways, Mr. Benson's productions do
not make a sharp and durable impression. They are enjoyed, but not
cherished in recollection. Though Mr. Benson proved to London, two or
three years ago, that 'The Tempest' was apt to the stage, the lesson,
conclusive at the moment, has been forgotten. Here comes Mr. J. H.
Leigh,[2] to teach it again. But do not run away with (or rather from) the
idea that Mr. Leigh is a mere educationist. The unfamiliarity of his name,
and the deviousness of his venue (the Court Theatre), and the report that
his cast is recruited from an histrionic academy, might make you—
probably *have* made you—a trifle shy and suspicious. Courage! Hold
not back! Press boldly on to Sloane Square! For Mr. Leigh's production
is quite vivid and pretty, quite untainted by pedantry. Some of my
colleagues have called it a compromise between the spectacular method
and the method of the Elizabethan Stage Society. That fosters a false
impression. To the method of Mr. Poel[3] (quem, I hasten to add, honoris
causa nomino) there is not in Mr. Leigh's method the faintest affinity.
The play is treated here, not as a dead thing, at which in its shroud we
may be permitted to peer, but as a live and kicking organism, as a thing
visible from a modern standpoint, susceptible to a modern method—in
fact, as a classic, in the true and full sense. The method is not the less
spectacular because the spectacle has to be on a small scale. No vast sums
of money could be forthcoming for a venture of this kind; but there has
been no stint of taste and ingenuity. From so small a stage as the Court's
we cannot gain that illusion of airy distance which we need for a full sense
of the mysterious island. But the scene-painter has done his best, and a
very decent best it is. The fairies and nymphs and other spirits cannot

swarm here, as ideally they would; but we behold very respectable samples of them. In one sense, the smallness of the stage is a positive gain for us. Against the advantages of a very big stage must be set always this defect: the characters become less than life-size, and thus shed much of their proper dignity and importance. To atone for their tininess, the mimes proceed to make terrific efforts, talking at a far higher pitch, forcing their feet to take far longer strides, and their hands to make far more comprehensive arabesques, than can be reconciled with the true expression of nature. They cease to be men and women impersonating men and women. They seem rather like a multiplied incarnation of the frog in the fable. Of course, there are mimes in whom the effort is not painfully apparent; but the effort is always there, a drag on the art of acting; and from the purely physical standpoint, there is not a single mime who can make the right effect, for giants find it more lucrative to be exhibited singly in side-shows than to take their chance on the legitimate stage. On a very big stage the fairies at Prospero's command would be of exactly the right size. At the Court they are of the wrong, the human, size. But Prospero himself is of the human, the right, size. And that is the more important point, surely. Sprites are nearer to humanity than is the gravely predominant Prospero to spritedom.

It is mainly from Prospero that 'The Tempest' draws for us its peculiar interest and fascination. Of course, its technical difference, to which I have alluded, is an interesting and fascinating point. Here, one might say, is the least Shakespearean of all Shakespeare's plays. For what is the salient thing about Shakespeare? Surely, the careless exuberance, the headlong impatience, of his art. Like the age in which he wrote, he was essentially young. In the heat of his creative power, he cared not at all—could not pause to bother—how he expressed himself. Everything came out anyhow, shot by blind and irresistible impulse. Consider that debauch of uncontrolled fancy, 'A Midsummer Night's Dream.' With it 'The Tempest' is often bracketed, by reason of the supernatural element in either play. But the two are at opposite poles. The one is a debauch, the other a work of art. True lovers of Shakespeare must needs prefer the debauch. 'The Tempest' seems, by comparison, cold and calculating. One misses the headiness, the mad magic, of the youthful work. The divinely-overdone poetry has been chastened and straightened into something akin with prose. We have been transported from Thebes to Athens. Or say, we have passed from the rose of dawn into the twilight of evening. Yes, 'The Tempest' is essentially the work of an elder. And for that very reason it seems, as I suggested, so modern. Art triumphs only over impoverished vitality. The reason why modern artists are so artistic is that they are not overwhelmed with a surplusage of emotions and ideas. They can practise restraint only because they have little to restrain. So it was with Shakespeare, when, before letting fall the pen from his hand, he wrote 'The Tempest.' Yet of all his plays 'The Tempest' is not only the most artistic, but also the most original. I say 'yet,' for a paradox must be broken gently, that its truth be accepted. 'Therefore' were the right conjunction. Not in the heat of creativeness are artists ever original. Having so much to give forth, and being by that impulse so pressed for time, they snatch at the handiest means. Into ready-made moulds they can pour quicklier their genius. In fact, like other spendthrifts, they will beg, borrow, or steal. But their unscrupulousness comes of wealth, not of poverty. That is the paradox, and the tragedy, at the root of all great literature. In some other planet there may be, but never will be in ours, a great writer expressing the full vigour of his greatness in his own way, and with exquisite care. An artistic conscience, and the desire for originality—a desire bred of self-consciousness and pride—will find entrance only when the breast shall have been eased of its tumultuous and surging contents. I have called 'The Tempest' the least Shakespearean of Shakespeare's plays. It is that because into it Shakespeare put more of himself than into any other. Generation after generation of German and other commentators has been groping dustily, fustily, mustily, for 'the sources' of this play. Every other play has been tracked down to the place it was filched from. 'The Tempest' alone is unproven a theft. Mustily, fustily, dustily, the commentators are groping, everywhere, still, at this moment. But their labour is in vain, I think. I think the reason why this one story has not been tracked down to Italy or elsewhere is that Shakespeare invented this one story. Enchanting though it is, perhaps it is not in itself a great story. But as an allegory it is perfect. Obviously, Shakespeare, at the close of his career, wished to write an epilogue to his work, an autobiography, in allegorical form. That was a very natural wish. And what more natural than that he could not lay hands on any ready-made story whereby to symbolise his meaning? And what more natural than that he should proceed to evolve from his own brain, now at leisure for the task, a story after his own less quickly-pulsing heart? The very difference in form, the neat unity, of 'The Tempest' may be taken as internal evidence that here the poet was working untrammelled from without. Though age had checked his diffuseness in other plays, too, 'The Tempest' is the only one that satisfies the modern standard of art. And age, alone, is not enough to account for the singularity.

To impersonate Prospero is a solemn and difficult task for any actor. He has to impress us, not merely as a rightful Duke, endowed with supernatural powers, and now quitting his enchanted place of exile for his native duchy, but also as Shakespeare, retiring from dramatic authorship into privacy and leisure. By the way, I ought to have qualified my assertion that the allegory is perfect. The island is a perfect symbol for the theatre. Ariel is a perfect symbol for the genius which had served Shakespeare to weave his spells and was now to be hard-worked no more. Caliban (beyond his merely topical symbolism for the Virginian as slave) is a perfect symbol for the 'groundlings' whom Shakespeare, having tried in vain to elevate them, was glad to leave in untroubled possession of the theatre. But one does not see why Shakespeare, a bourgeois, relapsing to obscurity from the sphere in which his genius had shone so lustrously, should sneer so persistently at his own 'rough magic,' and at theatrical art in general, and should imply that he is returning to a nobler and worthier sphere. Had he been, besides a dramatist, a master of scientific philosophy, believing, like Bacon,[4] that 'it is not good to stay long in the theatre,' and had he, as had Bacon...but I am treading on a volcano, and I will not risk that eruption of fury which immediately overwhelms any definite refusal to treat a still open question as settled for ever. Enough that he who impersonates Prospero impersonates also the creator of Prospero, and that so we need of him a double dignity and weight. Mr. Acton Bond[5] acts in a scholarly and charming way, and has enough authority to carry him well through the part of Prospero proper. But he does not quite satisfy our hunger for a realisation of Prospero's creator. Mr. Leigh himself plays Caliban, and is duly 'savage,' but ought surely to be more 'deformed.' Miranda, that extremist among ingénues, loses nothing by Mrs. Leigh's[6] interpretation of her, and Mr. Charles Lander[7] speaks well the lines of Ferdinand. Ariel is less lucky. Better the suggestion of a mere human being, however helpless, than of a pantomime fairy, however capable.

1. **Benson**, Frank. See p. 165.
2. **Leigh**, J. H. (1859–1934), actor, lessee of the Court Theatre.
3. **Poel**, William. See p. 163.
4. **Bacon**, Francis (1561–1626). Not traced, and certainly not from Bacon's *Essays*. At times Beerbohm (like certain Elizabethan writers) ascribed his own words to eminent authorities.
5. **Bond**, Acton (1861–1941).
6. **Leigh**, Mrs (1884–?), also known as Thyrza Norman.
7. **Lander**, Charles (1863–1934).

(*above*). 'Give me the daggers!'
David Garrick and Hannah Prit-
hard in *Macbeth*; oil painting,
1768, by Johann Zoffany. Garrick's
short stature is apparent; costumes
and wigs are of the period. The
Gothic setting may resemble that
used at Drury Lane.

. John Philip Kemble as Coriolanus; engraving after the oil
painting, 1798, by Sir Thomas
Lawrence.

3 (*above*). Thomas Rowlandson's
impression of the Theatre Royal,
Covent Garden, 1809; Falstaff and
Prince Hal in *Henry IV, Part One*, 5.4.
Accompanying verses described the
theatre as a 'vast profound ... Too
large to hear, too long to see, | Full of
unmeaning symmetry.'

4. Charles Kean as Leontes, Ellen
Terry as Mamillius, *The Winter's Tale*,
1858, an early theatrical photograph,
posed in a studio.

(*above*). The Theatre Royal, Drury Lane, 1813. The stage, *c.*80 feet wide and 46 feet deep, had 6 sets of wing grooves. The auditorium held *c.*3,120 persons—twice as many as the Royal Shakespeare Theatre today.

(*below*). Nearly Home. The 'panoramic illusion of the passage of Theseus's barge to Athens' in Augustin Daly's *A Midsummer Night's Dream*, Daly's Theatre, London, 1895.

much ado about nothing. Act. II a IV.

7. Gordon Craig, design for *Much Ado about Nothing*, the Imperial Theatre, London, 1903.

8. John Barrymore as Hamlet in Robert Edmond Jones's setting, New York, 1922, London, 1925. '... the most beautiful thing I have ever seen on any stage. The vast arch at the back served as the battlements, and was hung with curtains for the indoor scenes, played on two platforms intersected by a flight of steps.' (James Agate, *Brief Chronicles*, 1943, p. 249).

(*above*). The Forum Scene (3.2) in Beerbohm Tree's *Julius Caesar*, Her Majesty's Theatre, London, 1898, Tree as Mark Antony. The production, with massive reconstructions of Roman temples, employed some 250 extras in this scene.

(*below*). 'The potent poison quite o'ercrows my spirit.' The final scene, centre-stage, from Barry Jackson's *Hamlet*, Kingsway Theatre, London, 1925; Colin Keith-Johnston as Hamlet.

11 (*above*). 'Welcome to Rome, renownèd Coriolanus!' *Coriolanus*, 2.1, in Peter Hall's production, Stratford-upon-Avon, 1959; Laurence Olivier as Coriolanus faces Mary Ure, Virgilia; bottom right, Edith Evans as Volumnia, Harry Andrews as Menenius; top right, Paul Hardwick as Cominius.

12 (*below*). 'And as she fled, her mantle she did fall'; the last scene of *A Midsummer Night's Dream* directed by Peter Brook, Stratford-upon-Avon, 1970.

3 (above). *Henry IV, Part One*, 2.4:
Prince Harry (Michael Pennington,
centre) and Poins (Charles Lawson,
right) interrogate Falstaff (John
Woodvine, left) in the English
Shakespeare Company production,
1986.

4. 'Give signs, sweet girl . . .', *Titus
Andronicus*, 4.1, in Deborah Warner's
Stratford-upon-Avon, Swan Theatre
production, 1987; Lavinia, Sonia
Ritter; Titus, Brian Cox; Marcus,
Donald Sumpter; Lucius, Jeremy
Gilley.

15 (*above*). '... thank heaven, fasting, for a good man's love': *As You Like It*, 3.5, directed by Declan Donnellan for Cheek by Jowl, 1991 and 1994; Phoebe, Wayne Cater; Rosalind, Adrian Lester; Celia, Simon Coates.

16 (*below*). 'Speak, old Egeon': the final scene of *The Comedy of Errors*, directed by Tim Supple for the RSC, 1996. The Abbess, Ursula Jones; Antipholus of Ephesus, Simon Coates; Antipholus of Syracuse, Robert Berman; Egeon, Christopher Saul.

8 April 1905, Max Beerbohm on H. B. Irving (1870–1928) as Hamlet
at the Adelphi Theatre, London; from *The Saturday Review,*
reprinted in his *Last Theatres* (1970), pp. 147–52.

HENRY Brodribb (always known as H. B.) Irving, elder son of Sir Henry, played
many of his father's roles. Beerbohm's review is notable particularly as an essay on
verse speaking and character portrayal.

'IT is hardly too much to say, in reference to this latest production of
what is perhaps the masterpiece of our great national poet, that the
ghost of Hamlet's father is the most impressive within our recollection.
Heartiest commendation is due to Mr Maskelyne[1] for having contrived in
co-operation (as the programme informs us) with the Committee of the
Society for Psychical Research, an illusion so abundantly convincing. The
vague diaphanous form scarcely palpable to the audience, and the faint
twittering sounds emitted through it by Mr Horne,[2] the well-known
ventriloquist—sounds in which, most rightly, only a word here and
there was distinguishable—combined to make for the first time credible
to us the hitherto somewhat disconcerting scene between the youthful
prince and his much-wronged parent.'... This is a fragment of dramatic
criticism in a morning newspaper which has somehow been wafted to me
from the year 1924. It is interesting, as a document. I am glad to have this
peep into futurity. But I would rather have learned, thus magically, something which I could not have foreseen, in the ordinary way, by deduction
from present tendencies. In the past twenty years or so, the tendency in
performing *Hamlet* has been, ever more and more, to present a sensible,
realistic, modern drama of psychology, and to let the poetry shift for itself.
The Ghost, as being a sort of detached figure, is still allowed to drag
poetry in, speaking his lines sonorously and with rhythm. But the days of
his privilege are surely numbered. Let him make the most of them. He
will soon be brought into line with the definitely corporeal persons of
the play. He will soon have to be as real, prosaic, modern a ghost as they
are real, modern, prosaic ladies and gentlemen. The Player King and the
Player Queen, they too when they appear in *The Mousetrap*, are still
allowed to be poetic. But from them too the permission will soon be
withdrawn. For remember! the audience at Elsinore is a modern audience;
and to a modern audience poetry is a quite ridiculous thing; insomuch
that King Claudius and Queen Gertrude would not really, if *The Mouse-
trap* were declaimed for the music of the words, be quaking with fear
upon their thrones, but would be rolling upon their thrones with laughter;

and this would never do. *The Mousetrap* must, to produce the requisite impression, be acted in precisely the same manner as *Hamlet*. Perhaps the First Player will always be allowed to recite rhythmically and sonorously the turgid lines of 'Aeneas's tale to Dido'—just to show us how foolish a thing poetry is, and what fools the old-time actors were, and how well we are rid of them. And, maybe, one or two benighted souls in the audience will clutch fondly at the one straw not blown away by the tempest of modernity.

This tempest rages more vehemently now at the Adelphi than it has raged yet elsewhere. I cower. A slight shelter is kindly provided for me by Mr Oscar Asche.[3] He, as King Claudius, does remember that Shakespeare wrote the part in blank verse—does speak rhythmically, and with reverence for sound, and does comport himself with a large tragic dignity. But the rest! Really, 'the rest is silence'—for any pleasure afforded by it to the human ear. Miss Maud Milton,[4] as Queen Gertrude, talks in easy conversational style, exactly as though Queen Gertrude were gossiping across a teacup. It is a wonderfully natural performance; but poetry, tragedy, queenliness, are quite out of it. Mr Lyall Swete[5] is wonderfully natural as Polonius. He gives his advice to Laertes exactly as if each axiom occurred to him on the spur of the moment. Throughout the play he is a light and airy old gentleman, such as you might meet any day, without remarking him much, in the smoking-room of any club. Miss Brayton[6] is very pleasant in the sane scenes of Ophelia; but one would hardly be surprised if at any moment she entered springing off a bicycle. In the mad scenes of Ophelia she tries hard not to be so pleasant, and manages to give a realistic representation of lunacy. This seems to me a mistake. Lunacy is a painful thing, and Shakespeare did not mean the mad scenes of Ophelia to be painful: he merely meant them to be beautiful: he turned them, in accordance to his notion of Ophelia's own power, 'to favour and to prettiness.' The only right way for an actress to interpret these mad scenes is through her sense of beauty. They are too irrelevant to be treated tragically. They are dragged in, just for beauty's sake. Even more obviously dragged in for that sake is the Queen's account of Ophelia's death. 'There is,' says lyric Shakespeare, 'a willow grows aslant a brook,' and he proceeds to revel in the landscape, quite forgetting (to our eternal gain) that he speaks through the lips of an agonised lady. What is the agonised lady to do? There is but one thing for her to do. She must forget that she is an agonised lady, and speak the words as beautifully and as simply as she can. Then there will be no absurdity. But what could be more absurd than to hear a lady talking, as Miss Maud Milton talks, about 'crow-flowers, nettles, daisies, and long purples' with tragic gasps and violent gestures of woe, and dwelling with special emphasis on 'long purples' as though they were quite the most harrowing thing of all? Here the passion for natural-ness leads to sheer nonsense. Elsewhere, for the most part, its mischief is merely negative. It merely deprives the play of beauty and of tragic dignity. But beauty and tragic dignity seem to me (who am an old fashioned pedant, if you will) the two first things to be conserved in such a work as *Hamlet*. They are not the only things. But they are the first things. Remembering them I was not able to be enraptured by Mr H. B. Irving, who, as the Prince, remembered them, like his colleagues, so very vaguely—or, rather, gave them the go-by so very sternly.

Of course, I admire his performance very much. He has a strong personality. He has intellect. He has imagination. He has fire. He has force. He has all sorts of things. Judged from the fashionable modern standpoint, his performance is splendid. Judged in relation to what he himself was especially striving for, his success is complete. Hamlet's character is strongly seized at by him, and is interpreted by him with infinite subtlety in detail. He is a life-sized and a living Hamlet. I do not say that he gives us a wholly consistent or wholly intelligible picture. He doesn't. But we must not blame him for that. We must blame Shake-speare. Or, rather, we must praise Shakespeare. None of us is wholly consistent or wholly intelligible—at any rate to himself, who knows most about the matter. To his acquaintances a man may seem to be this or that kind of man, quite definitely. That is only because they know so little about him. To his intimate friends he is rather a problem. To himself he is an insoluble problem. Shakespeare, drawing Hamlet, drew him from within—drew him with a full knowledge of the many conflicting elements in him—drew not, in the usual way, one of his sets of qualities, or one of his sets of moods, but drew him in all his complexity and changefulness. We are all of us as changeful and complex as Hamlet was. There is nothing peculiar about Hamlet. The peculiarity is but in the fulness of his portrayal. Shakespeare made of a puppet a whole human being. Necessarily, since every human being is a mystery at close quarters, Hamlet's character cannot be made clear to anyone—to anyone, I mean, who studies it at all closely. If anyone said to me about an impersonator of Hamlet 'He made me understand Hamlet,' I should deduce that either the actor had omitted nine-tenths of his lines, or that my informant had dozed during nine-tenths of the performance. We must not ask of any actor that he shall explain Hamlet to us. The most we can expect is that he shall give unity to the divergent characteristics and moods—that all these shall seem to be contained in one person, not in many different persons. In a circus somewhere, years ago, I saw a man drive a team of a hundred and fifty horses round the ring. I thought him wonderful. I admire not less the actor who does not let Hamlet get 'out of hand.' I admire Mr Irving's grip immensely.

But—but 'never were Shakespeare's words spoken with so entire an absence of pose and mannerism; never was this melancholy hero, with his rarely beautiful smile, depicted so much as a brilliant and romantic young man whom we could meet round the corner of the next street.' No, reader, this is not another fragment from 1924. I cull it from last Wednesday's *Daily Telegraph*. Hating to cavil frankly, I have recourse to this fragment, which, written with gratulatory intent, does yet define so exactly the grounds on which I myself object to Mr Irving's Hamlet. Just because I, like Mr W. L. Courtney,[7] feel that I might at any corner collide with this Hamlet, and just because of that 'absence of pose and mannerism' (alias, that contempt for the conventions of poetic utterance) for which this Hamlet is remarkable, I cannot acclaim this Hamlet as ideal—cannot even accept it as satisfactory. A thoroughly modern Hamlet, a round-the-corner Hamlet; a Prince (if Prince he be) not of Elsinore, but of Bernstoff; a Hamlet who breaks up his sentences into prose, squeezing the words together, or stretching them interminably out, with no reference at all to their rhythm, and often muttering them inaudibly, on the assumption that they are so familiar to us all that they need not be re-communicated; a Hamlet, in fact, without style—this is not the Hamlet for me. I crave, first of all, the beauty which Mr Irving sacrifices to exact realism. Next to that, I crave the tone of tragedy. Hamlet, of course, is not always in tragic vein. He is often comedic, sometimes farcical. But he is a figure in a tragedy; and in all his moods he should be seen through a veil of tragedy. Mr Irving rends away that veil. In the final scene, for instance, he behaves just like any young man in a fencing-club. We cannot believe that he and all those other persons are going to die. Our aesthetic sense of tragedy is banished; and, consequently, the various deaths, when they occur, seem violently out of place—seem absurd. . . . In 1924, perhaps, these deaths will be omitted, and the whole play trimmed into a comedy. Modern audiences shrink from tragedy. One of the reasons for the great popularity of Mr Forbes Robertson's Hamlet was that he so notably brightened the play up. Mr Irving's Hamlet is as much brighter as it is less beautiful than Mr Forbes Robertson's. I am sure than in 1924 the last vestiges of gloom will have been swept out of Elsinore. A fantastic forecast? Well, twenty years ago you could not have conceived that *Hamlet* would ever be enacted as a play in prose. And from tragedy to comedy it is not a further cry than from poetry to prose.

1. **Maskelyne**, John Nevil (1839–1917), magician who performed many dramatic sketches, especially, from 1873 to 1904, at the Egyptian Hall in Piccadilly, which was known as the 'Home of Mystery'.

2. **Horne**, Mr [not identified; possibly imaginary].

3. **Asche**, Oscar. See p. 174.

4. **Milton**, Maud (1859–1945), acted from 1892 to 1902 with Irving; she had played Gertrude with Martin Harvey in 1904.

5. **Swete**, Lyall (1865–1919), actor and producer.

6. **Brayton**, Lily (?1876–1953), played many leading roles in a long stage career. She married Oscar Asche.

7. **Courtney**, W. L. (1850–1928), writer and critic who reviewed for *The Daily Telegraph*.

ᘓᘓᘓᘓᘓᘓᘓᘓᘓᘓᘓᘓᘓᘓᘓᘓᘓᘓᘓᘓᘓᘓᘓᘓᘓᘓ

28 September 1912, John Palmer (1885–1944) in *The Saturday Review* on *The Winter's Tale* directed by Harley Granville Barker at the Savoy Theatre, London.

THIS was the second of the three epoch-making productions at the Savoy in which Barker carried over into the professional theatre some of Poel's ideas of a return to the basic principles of Elizabethan and Jacobean staging (the others were of *Twelfth Night*, also 1912, and *A Midsummer Night's Dream*, 1914). He was more of a textual purist than Poel—this production used a virtually complete text—but less austere in the visual aspects of his staging. After these productions he virtually retired from the theatre.

John Palmer, author of *Political Characters of Shakespeare* (1945), was theatre critic of *The Saturday Review* from 1910 to 1915 and of the *Evening Standard* from 1916 to 1919.

MR. BARKER's production of 'The Winter's Tale' on Saturday last is probably the first performance in England of a play by Shakespeare that the author would himself have recognised for his own since Burbage[1]—or, at any rate, Davenant[2]—retired from active management. There is yet no evidence of an impression upon those who have visited the Savoy of the extreme importance of this revival. Critics seem for the most part to have spent their time in an unprofitable inspection of Mr. Rothenstein's[3] costumes and Mr. Norman Wilkinson's[4] decoration. I am not proposing to consider Mr. Barker's adventure of last Saturday as an opportunity for exhibiting objets d'art et de vertu. Suffice it to say that Mr. Wilkinson's decoration, so far as it was unobtrusive, was wholly admirable; and that Mr. Rothenstein's costumes, so far as they compelled your attention, were entirely mischievous. Perhaps, in the case of Mr. Rothenstein, this should be qualified; for 'The Winter's Tale', from a producer's point of view, may lawfully be regarded as the exception which proves everything. A little virtuosity of mounting may perhaps be excused in a play which, like 'The Tempest', is essentially a virtuoso play. Mr. Barker, in the introduction to his acting edition (a chapter of literary and dramatic criticism which proves that the business of a producer is not necessarily incompatible with an educated taste for the humanities), seems to be not unaware of the curious delight and the not unnatural awe with which Shakespeare in 'The Winter's Tale' viewed the perfection of his own achievement. I think it must have struck every really devoted and close reader of the plays of Shakespeare how in 'The Winter's Tale' and in 'The Tempest'—surely the two greatest masterpieces of pure style in any literature—much of the charm is in the conscious thankfulness with which Shakespeare enjoys his perfect command of instrument and material. His happiest effects are brought off with an indolent flourish. Surely, then, the costumier and the decorator may be permitted a small liberty to be fantastical—to tune their endeavours in the same wilful and self-conscious mode. Mr. Rothenstein's costumes are pardonable in 'The Winter's Tale'. Their intrusion is in the spirit of the master. In 'Hamlet' or 'Macbeth' to notice the costumes at all would for ever extinguish their perpetrator as a man of art.

The value of Mr. Barker's revival—apart from the acting—rests almost wholly upon his production[5] of the stage into the auditorium; for thereby hangs all that distinguishes Elizabethan plays and playing from Restoration comedy. Mr. Barker's innovation—innovation, of course, in the sense that it is new in West End productions of Shakespeare—is not a merely topographical trick of stage management. There were precious moments in the Savoy Theatre on Saturday when it was possible to be thrillingly conscious of precisely the appeal which Burbage made as he issued from the tiring-house to the vacant platform before Elsinore. Personally, I was the more conscious of this, as I was sitting in the front of the stalls, almost in the position from which the good man[6] of Beaumont and Fletcher interfered so successfully with the progress of 'The Knight of the Burning Pestle'. Like the Elizabethan critic, who was mercifully not required to print his opinion, I was in direct, almost personal, contact with the players. Gone was the centuries-old, needless and silly illusion of a picture stage, with scene and atmosphere ready-made, and mutoscopically viewed. I had no illusion, and could wait receptively for Shakespeare himself to build it. Never before had his splendid rhetoric, his glamour of resistless verse, the true and vivid illusion upon which he alone and so successfully relied, reached me in a London theatre. If we had been all round the stage instead of upon one side only; if Mr. Rothenstein's costumes had not ever and again become really noticeable; if Mr. Barker had discarded the whole sack of intelligent naturalistic artifices of the Court Theatre equally with the whole sack of unintelligent naturalistic artifices of His Majesty's; if Perdita had been enacted—say—by a boy-player in the place of an obviously pretty young woman; if the whole company at the Savoy had been as aware of the beauty of their lines as were Mr. Ainley[7] and Miss McCarthy;[8] if—well, in that case the illusion would have been stronger still. Of course, I am perfectly aware that I am asking Mr. Barker actually to build an Elizabethan theatre, and to raise up a school of Elizabethan players, simply in order that the actual illusion at which Shakespeare aimed as a practical playwright may once more be realised by English people that affect to do him reverence. Instead of asking this I should perhaps praise him with a full heart for a really splendid achievement.

Mr. Barker, in half restoring the Elizabethan style of production, has naturally been driven to a restoration of a few essential points of the Elizabethan or rhetorical style of playing. How gloriously effective, for instance, upon an Elizabethan stage is the aside, vehemently declaimed full at the spectator, or secretively breathed in his ear. A very convincing book might be written, showing that the health of our national drama (as opposed to the naturalised French importation) was inextricably bound up with the stage aside and the soliloquy. No wonder Shakespeare so affected them! Another point in which Mr. Barker has restored Shakespeare to us as a playwright is in his abolition of interpolated acts and scenes, and in his insistence upon speed. The tempo of dialogue and of action was throughout admirable, especially in the first act. It varied dramatically with the play's rhythm—a rhythm not alone of the verse, but of the play's procedure and emotion. Some contrasts of style between the various players were also well arranged. I do not mean, of course, the damnable contrast between the players who could deliver their verses and the players who could not. Mr. Barker cannot raise a school of playing in a single night. But he should very severely deal with the members of his company who slip into the colloquial and conversational tones adopted by actor-managers who seem to think that verse is merely prose which for some obscure reason has been metrically arranged by the author.

As to the acting, first, and I am afraid it must also be last, there was the very beautiful contrast between Leontes as played by Mr. Ainley and Hermione as played by Miss McCarthy. It is difficult to speak critically of Mr. Ainley's Leontes without falling into the language of the practised encomiums usually bestowed by Mr. Puff[9] upon the idols of the commonalty.[10] If the phrase continued to have a meaning to-day, I should say that Mr. Ainley's Leontes is the finest piece of Shakespearian acting I have yet seen. It was absolutely in the spirit of the platform stage; and Shakespeare's seventeenth-century audience would have risen to him in wildest admiration. His delivery was splendid throughout; his gestures were swift, sure, and reserved with strict economy for the rhymic crises of his emotion; his passion was positively infectious. His art was the more striking for its contrast in style with the playing of Miss McCarthy. I am indeed glad to see her in a rôle that is worthily difficult. Miss McCarthy has already revealed her grasp of the classical ideal of still severity in the playing of Iphigenia.[11] But Hermione is perhaps the most difficult part in the whole range of dramatic literature. Shakespeare in the last act of 'The Winter's Tale', enjoying his own sense of mastery, has almost neglected to observe that he is also making a tremendous demand upon the powers of his interpreters. The final scene of 'The Winter's Tale' may so easily be ruined and turned to ridicule; and to fall would be immeasurably disastrous, as the scene is immeasurably great. Miss McCarthy falls neither here, nor, conspicuously, in any scene. It would be mere extravagance to say that Miss McCarthy has at a step sprung to the supreme heights of tragic playing. Continuing to interpret Shakespeare, she will range through his characters, and return one day to Hermione to wonder that she did so well. Like Mr. Barker, she need not, at any rate, be apprehensive of competition. There is to-day no practising and living player that can successfully assume the heroines of Shakespeare.

I hope, if 'The Winter's Tale' continues to run—as run it must—I shall be able to return to Mr. Barker's production later in the season. Meantime let every self-respecting playgoer visit the Savoy, not as the critics would have him do, to wonder at some strange, bedizened monster of Mr. Barker's contrivance, but to recover for the first time on a modern West End stage something of the strength, glamour, and delicacy of Shakespeare himself. Mr. Barker's bedizened monster is purely the invention of his commentators. His simple aim was to recover Shakespeare, or a piece of him, for as many of the London public as cared to seize the opportunity; and Mr. Barker has succeeded, so far as, in all the circumstances, it was possible to succeed. If London playgoers do not support the adventure they will fall into the ridiculous and shameful suspicion of being actively influenced by the critics. Let them forget the critics; frequent the theatre in pure holiday mood; surrender to the obvious zeal of every member of Mr. Barker's company to win their good opinions;

> 'And home returning soothly swear
> Was never scene so sad and fair'.[12]

1. **Burbage**, Richard. See p. 5.

2. **Davenant**, William. See p. 20.

3. **Rothenstein**, William (1872–1934), painter, knighted 1931, best known for portraiture.

4. **Wilkinson**, Norman (1882–1934), stage designer.

5. **production**. Possibly a misprint for 'projection', though it could mean 'prolongation, extension'.

6. **the good man**, the Citizen who appears in the framework device of the play.

7. **Ainley**, Henry (1879–1945), actor who had scored a great success as Malvolio in Barker's previous production.

8. **McCarthy**, Lillah (1875–1960), Barker's first wife, later a theatre manager as well as performer.

9. **Mr Puff**, a character in *The Critic* (1779) by R. B. Sheridan, here used generally of an effusive theatre critic.

10. **idols of the commonalty** [not identified].

11. **Iphigenia**, in *Iphigenia in Tauris*, the tragedy by Euripides (*c.*484–*c.*406 BC), at the Kingsway Theatre in March of 1912.

12. 'And home...' '*The Lay of the Last Minstrel*' by Sir Walter Scott (1771–1832), Canto 2, ll. 17–18.

〜〜〜〜〜〜〜〜〜〜〜〜〜〜〜〜〜〜〜〜〜〜〜〜〜〜

1 January 1922, Harley Granville-Barker (1877–1946) on *Twelfth Night* directed by Jacques Copeau (1879–1949) at the Vieux-Colombier, Paris, from *The Observer*.

Copeau, an influential actor-manager and director, founded the Théâtre du Vieux-Colombier in 1913. For Granville-Barker, see p. 165.

It is very cheering to an Englishman to see a crowded French audience carried away in spontaneous enjoyment of a Shakespeare play. It was as cheering, and even more remarkable, for the Englishman to find his own enjoyment of the performance just, apparently, as spontaneous. The good cause of Anglo-French friendship[1] is (quite seriously) in debt to Jacques Copeau for his production of *Twelfth Night*. It seems to be a sterling success. It was first staged in May, 1914, and now has a firm place in the repertory; there was hardly a vacant seat at this particular performance. I do not suggest that the production makes the Briand–Lloyd George conversations[2] of the moment any easier; I certainly do not wish to imply that an officially-organized theatrical propaganda of friendship would do anything but defeat its own too obvious end. But Shakespeare is a good ambassador. And he has colleagues, dead and living, who could do their country greater service abroad than most politicians contrive to. Truly it is a simpler, in that it can be a more disinterested, service. No use in thrusting such an embassy across the Channel, but all our thanks to the Frenchmen who make a lodging for it and extend a welcome.

The translation of any play is a plaguily difficult matter; of a poetical play one must admit that in any logical completeness the thing can't be done. When I opened *La Nuit des Rois* to discover that—

> If Music be the food of Love—play on;
> Give me excess of it, that, surfeiting,
> The appetite may sicken and so die,

had become—

Si la musique est la nourriture de l'amour, qu'elle reprenne! Donnes-m'en à l'excès, et que ma gourmandise défaille de nausée,

I feared the worst. It was so perfectly right that it could not fail, I thought, to be utterly wrong. But before Monsieur Jean le Goff[3] had spoken ten lines (even though he looked a little too like a blend of le Grand Monarque[4] and Charles II[5]) I had forgotten what I was missing. And the French audience had never any need to know. And for all I can tell, of course, 'le son savoureux qui souffle sur un parterre de violettes, dérobant et rendant un perfum,' may mean as much to them as

> . . . the sweet South
> That breathes upon a bank of violets
> Stealing and giving odour.

This is no criticism of the translation; I am indeed not qualified to make one. And, as I say, Monsieur le Goff resolved my doubts without more ado by the distinction, the passion, the sense of beauty with which he informed his opening scene. One made, in fact, the appalling discovery that French actors can speak Shakespeare better than English actors—let us say—usually do. This is not a paradox. It is demonstrable, I think, that the Elizabethan theatre demanded a fire and rapidity of diction which Elizabethan actors presumably possessed, which Georgian actors have quite undoubtedly lost the habit of, in which, alas, Georgian audiences do not appear to delight. (How should they, one may ask? No audience can demand the supply of such a commodity.) But French audiences do unaffectedly appreciate beautiful speech and French actors are expected to give it them. Swiftness, intensity, precision, variety, clarity, and above all, passion, the passion informing a beauty of thought and feeling that only just does not defy expression—it was with these, the fine sound and poise of these, that the actors of the Vieux Colombier, even at a translated distance from the fount of their inspiration, thrilled their audience again and again. It is no use; English actors must go to school again in the matter of Shakespearean verse; and—this, indeed, is a paradox!—here in France, apparently, is the school. An explicable paradox, perhaps. Shakespeare was a child of the Renascence, of its quiet unquestioning approbation of things, of its ruthlessness, of the readiness to pay Nature the price of her favours. In France the Renascence is not spent. In England our 17th-century Puritans doused its artistic side with cold water, and, though we are at last just about dry, the rheumatic effects remain. We move stiffly still in these matters.

Twelfth Night is not a perfect production; one should not expect such a thing. Jacques Copeau uses the platform stage, with an apron lower by a few steps, but he does not seem to have thought out its full application to the play. He does not see the importance, where mere indications of time and place are given, of their being precise and constant indications; nor how the structural integrity of the play, and therefore the mental comfort of the audience, depend upon obedience to this. He does not clearly define his opening masses—the Court of Orsino, the household of Olivia—nor differentiate sufficiently between the conduct of the main and the conjunctive scenes. This is not pedantry; the right ordering of such things quite naturally makes for the better enjoyment of the play. And in one important matter he has been, I regret to say, shamefully betrayed by his English designer, Mr. Duncan Grant.[6]

Whatever may be M. Copeau's disabilities for the full understanding of Shakespeare's intentions, Mr. Duncan Grant has none. If he does not know that Olivia and all her household are in deep mourning, a cursory reading of the play will inform him. It may be very good fun to dress her up in a harlequinade of colour (a most attractive dress, the lady herself a temptation to any dress-designer!); it may be equally amusing to turn Sir Andrew Aguecheek into the likeness of a rag doll, and Malvolio into a mechanically outrageous figure of fun that even the wildest horse-play cannot animate. But Mr. Duncan Grant, I take it, was not called in to amuse himself, but to interpret Shakespeare. It is worthwhile to speak plainly on this point. We all want to bring artists of distinction to the service of the theatre, but if they cannot recognise that it is a service as strictly conditioned for them as for any other of the play's interpreters, if their one idea is to show off at the expense of the dramatist and actors (it is really very much as if the actor playing Orsino insisted upon rewriting the part and singing a song and dancing a breakdown[7] occasionally), then they had better amuse themselves elsewhere. And it is perhaps worthwhile to speak plainly in this instance, as Mr. Duncan Grant, even in his most inappropriate efforts, shows just such a talent as the theatre needs. His line might be finer and more precise (formless effects are no use upon a platform stage), but his colour is enchanting, gay and reposeful, too, the combinations always a little unexpected, but never disturbing.

One more grumble, and I only hope I may have space left for half the praise I could spend. Will M. Copeau for his next Shakespeare production not only follow the play's text, as he commendably does in this instance (I could not detect a line cut, and the audience, with *les jeunes filles* much in evidence, laughed heartily and naturally even at the few jokes now considered too indelicate for English ears.) The Renascence, as I say, is still alive in France, but will he study it as well, to the exclusion of the pseudo-traditions of the English stage? Had he done so in this instance he would have saved himself from the capital errors of a Maria more like a kitchen-maid than a companion to Olivia, of the village-idiot Sir Andrew, and of a Malvolio incomprehensibly clowning. French audiences, quite naturally, do not take their Shakespeare for granted as we do. So much the better; they are likely to get the more out of him. But the divine William has enough lapses of his own to answer for without being burdened by the accumulation of his interpreters' misdeeds. The one occasion in *Twelfth Night* upon which this audience displayed inappropriate hilarity was when Olivia and Sebastian made their lightning match. Shakespeare, as was his wont in such cases, attempted (though he hardly succeeded) to carry this off with a fine flourish of verse. But, deprived of this, the French actors were helpless; and though the audience did its best to consider their feelings and to be polite to the venerable ecclesiastic who came in off the mat (so to speak) to tie the knot, it was evident that Olivia lost caste a little by the incident.

But for all this—and, indeed, just because of this—I would beg M. Copeau to trust to Shakespeare and to no one else in more important matters. It will not have escaped him that, while the audience delighted in his comedians for the play's first hour, thereafter they had to work ever harder, to strain at effects, to coarsen the comedy in what was still, on the whole, a failing attempt to command attention. It need not have been so. One has only to face the simple fact that Shakespeare's Malvolio, Feste, Maria, Sir Toby, and Andrew will last out the play, whereas the arbitrary funniments of actors will probably not. Shakespeare, for all his faults, M. Copeau, did know his business as a playwright, and as long as he enjoyed writing a character we may be pretty sure that the actor has more to gain by interpreting it than by using it as a peg upon which to hang his own, or anyone else's, ideas.

Albert Savry's[8] Malvolio was, indeed, for half the time quite excellent. He had taken, I should say, Maclise's[9] picture for the figure of the man. The self-sufficiency that can only be sustained upon contempt for one's fellow-creatures, the quick transition from the sarcastic immobility of his attitude of service to the hiss of waspish tyranny when he is released from it, the diseased over-quick apprehension in the letter scene, running like fire among stubble, till it bursts into a blaze of egomania—all legitimately studied and excellently done. Why, then, Monsieur Savry, let one pair of cross-fastened yellow stockings (Shakespeare asked no more, for all that Mr. Duncan Grant so over-obliged him!) lure you into those skipping atrocities? An excellent, if rather sentimental, Antonio (made up, I think, after Charles Kemble[10] as Brutus), a good Sebastian, a first-rate Fabian, Fabian being by no means a third-rate part; Romain Bouquet[11] a richly coloured, totally unexaggerated, really amusing Sir Toby; and for a Viola, the most distinguished actress I have seen, it seems to me, since Duse[12] ceased playing.

As, from personal taste, I can write no higher praise, I look back upon the words with slight hesitation. But my recollection of Madame Susanne Bing's[13] performance confirms the opinion and, in particular, the choice of that epithet. One could dispute several aspects of her reading of Viola. She emphasises the background of tragedy in the girl's life at the expense of the youthful high spirits—the cheerfulness that would come creeping in, and that Shakespeare needed, here and there, for the sustaining of his comedy. As a consequence some important passages—such, notably, as the soliloquy with the ring—slip rather disastrously into a minor key, not only lose their significance, but endanger the contrasting effects around them. This (to my mind) too sustained note of half-pathetic irony is arguably legitimate from a Viola's point of view, but it needs more accommodation to the general purpose of the play. There are times when this failing turns virtue, as when Madame Bing definitely does not accommodate herself to the accustomed clowning of the duel scene, and so preserves the romantic interest of the story at a time when—with the Olivia–Sebastian incident looming—it is about to be severely shaken.

But, granted her reading of the part—which possesses besides the extrinsic virtue that it is both a direct reading of the text and a sympathetic divination of Shakespeare's great tenderness towards women in general at this time of his writing—one can have nothing but praise for the art with which Madame Bing presents it. You may know her in just one minute for a supreme actress, not only by her perfect physical repose, but by the lack of all anxiety to impress the part—far less herself—upon you. An actor's anxiety to impress you is in direct ratio to his generally justified fear that he can't; his hurry to show you that he knows all about the part he is playing is invariably a sign that he knows very little. But there are not many actors or actresses so sure of themselves that by doing nothing at all for two minutes—by doing, that is to say, what they do so simply that it seems nothing, seems, as they wish it to, a simple 'being'—can so raise your interest that you wait anxiously for their reappearance, watch for every rare gesture or movement of feature, try to note the significance of the tone of every sentence they speak, are impatient yourself for the character's development.

It is in the power to arouse and sustain and fulfil such interest that the art of great acting lies. And while almost anyone who is sufficiently attractive can display themselves attractively and earn innocent applause, the infinitely different power to draw you out of your royal self, sitting there in the consciousness of an honestly paid-for seat to be kow-towed to, away from the theatre and into the world of the play, comes not (for the actor) but by the stern suppression of that easily and obviously exhibitive self in favour of that part of him, of his mind, of his emotions, that can effect a communion with the intangible stuff of the play. It will then be surprising—and how one is always surprised and delighted afresh by fine art!—of what comparatively small account the more material things become. Madame Bing, for instance, spoke very beautifully; she moved with grace. But the movements did not exist apart from their meaning, and every sentence (another sure sign of the supreme actor) came out conceived as a whole, as a thought and a feeling, not as a variously valued collection of words. And so complete the assimilation of the personality of the actress to the idea of the part, and so far, by such an example, did she lead her audience into the world of the play and into the inner world of the imagined Viola, that after a while, by watching as we did for the magnetic moment when thought and feeling were, it seemed, ever freshly conceived, the moment before speech gave them form, one could so nearly oneself conceive what they would be, as to partake with her of her sorrow or joy, one's watching and listening becoming as subsidiary a mechanical matter as the mechanism of the acting itself.

Yet a further gain from the sacrifice of the exhibitive self. The imagined Viola, released, so to speak, from the constant demand upon her to do credit to an actress' performance, can passively reflect, by a critical attitude or two, other aspects of her fellow-characters than those they can actively present. In this lies, doubtless, one of the last refinements of the actor's art. But in Viola, 'knowing all, herself unknown,'[4] there are peculiar chances of exemplifying it. And certainly one learnt as much more about Orsino by following the lights and shades of this Viola's love for him as Orsino himself declared. And as much more about Olivia; though here Shakespeare has been verbally downright, and Viola's attitude to Olivia is one of the obvious tests of the part's playing. Madame Bing's was almost impeccable in this. Her main conception of a Viola whose real sorrows, carried so lightly, infinitely outweigh the fantastic griefs of which she is the messenger, much helped her—though just once there was a tolerant smile where, I thought, no smile should be. But, needless to say, she did not make Olivia either a butt or the excuse of working off a few purple passages; on the contrary, her shy humility at the beauty's unveiling set the relations between the two in a key in which she could and did do much more than if she had tried to assume the mastery of the scenes from the beginning. And to that other test passage, the recognition of Sebastian—but, truly, the Viola who cannot make your eyes swim here does not know the beginning of her business—Mme. Bing responded, not with a more emotional effect, but more admirably by rounding the character to its completion. Here again was the Viola who could not glibly tell her love, whom outward life had used so hardly that she must keep her treasures secretly in her heart. Shakespeare indeed rounded off his play pretty cavalierly, but he had completed his Viola nearly enough.

For a final word of most respectful praise to Mme. Bing—her Viola is fine, I think, chiefly because it is fine all through. There are no purple passages, no doubtful ones. She has visualized a Viola, and with certain art, by complete self-abnegation, she makes her vision ours.

As a final word of compliment to Jacques Copeau—but it would take many words of discerning praise to express my appreciation of his work at the Vieux Colombier. And he does not need them. If he wants to sense his achievement (still, let it be granted, in the achieving) he has but to mingle with his audience as it leaves the theatre. It is a very mixed audience—workmen, students, some foreigners, a taste of literary and learned Paris, a sprinkling of fashionable Paris. But they have coalesced in enjoyment of the play and—this is the test, this is why managers should always mingle with a departing audience—they separate again exhilarated, not exhausted, not as having seen a show, but as having helped, they too, even actively, in the consummation of a worthy work of art.

1. **Anglo-French friendship**. After the First World War differences between France and England on the terms of peace strained relations between the countries.

2. **Briand–Lloyd George conversations**. In December 1921 the British Prime Minister, David Lloyd George (1863–1945) engaged in discussion with Aristide Briand (1862–1932), the French Prime Minister, in the hope of stopping hostilities between Greece and Turkey, Poland and Russia, in the aftermath of the War.

3. **le Goff**, Jean (1888–1973), acted at the Vieux-Colombier from 1920 to 1924, and with the Comédie Française from 1929 until he retired in 1951.

4. **le Grand Monarque**, Louis XIV (1638–1715), King of France.

5. **Charles II** (1630–85), King of England who lived in France during the Civil War.

6. **Grant**, Duncan (1885–1978), painter much associated with the Bloomsbury circle.

7. **breakdown**, a riotous dance especially associated with black entertainers.

8. **Savry**, Albert, actor at the Vieux-Colombier from 1920 to 1924.

9. **Maclise**, Daniel (1806–70), painted many Shakespearian subjects; his scene from *Twelfth Night* showing Malvolio in his yellow stockings before Viola and Olivia, now in the Tate Gallery, London, was exhibited at the Royal Academy in 1840.

10. **Kemble**, Charles, see p. 112. The *Actors' Dictionary* lists 117 images of him, but none in the role of Brutus; in *Julius Caesar* he played Mark Antony.

11. **Bouquet**, Romain (1897–1943), a leading actor for Copeau who stayed with him until the closing of the Vieux-Colombier, after which he worked with Louis Jouvet.

12. **Duse**, Eleonora, see p. 144.

13. **Bing**, Susanne (1885–1967), actress and translator who worked closely with Copeau.

14. **'knowing all, herself unknown'** [not identified].

20 **November 1922,** Stark Young (1881–1963) on John Barrymore (1882–1942) as Hamlet, directed by Arthur Hopkins, at the Sam H. Harris Theater, New York, from *The New Republic*, reprinted in his *Immortal Shadows* (New York and London, 1948; repr. New York, Dramabooks series, n.d., pp. 8–14).

JOHN BARRYMORE, stage and screen actor, was a member of a famous American theatrical family; his Hamlet had 101 performances, breaking (deliberately) by one performance the American record set up by Edwin Booth. He was to play the role again in London in 1925. Stark Young was a critic, dramatist, director and translator. Robert Edmond Jones's setting is illustrated in Pl. 8.

MR. JOHN BARRYMORE seemed to gather together in himself all the Hamlets of his generation, to simplify and direct everyone's theory of the part. To me his Hamlet was the most satisfying that I have seen, not yet as a finished creation, but a foundation, a continuous outline. Mounet-Sully's[1] Hamlet was richer and more sonorous; Forbes-Robertson's[2] at times more sublimated; Irving's[3] more sharply devised; and Sothern's,[4] so far as we are concerned strictly with the verse pattern, was more securely read. But there is nothing in Mr. Barrymore's Hamlet to get in the way of these accomplishments also, with time and study. And in what he has done there is no inherent quality that need prevent his achieving the thing most needed to perfect, in its own kind, his Hamlet; I mean a certain dilation and abundance in all his reactions. This Hamlet of Mr. Barrymore's must give us—and already promises—the sense of a larger inner tumult and indeed of a certain cerebral and passionate ecstasy, pressing against the external restraint of him. He needs the suggestion of more vitality, ungovernable and deep, of more complex suffering, of not only intellectual subtlety but intellectual power as well, all this added to the continuity of distinction that he already has, the shy and humorous mystery, the proud irony, the terrible storms of pain. Mr. Barrymore brings to the part what is ultimately as necessary to a fine actor as to a fine singer, the physical gifts that enable him to express his idea. He has a beautiful presence, a profound magnetism. His English, much of which is but recently acquired through the teaching of the remarkable Mrs. Margaret Carrington,[5] is almost wholly reborn from what it once was, and is now almost pure, even and exact, though not yet wholly flexible. His voice, also to a considerable extent Mrs. Carrington's production, is not supreme. It is not a rich and sonorous volume such as Mansfield[6] had, but is capable of high, intelligent training, and is already in the middle tones highly admirable.

With such an artist as Mr. Barrymore has risen to be, one cannot escape the matter of the technical means by which he fills out and develops the kind of truth that he sees in his role, or confuses and prevents its realization. His chief technical triumph, I think, lies in the absence from his work of all essentially theatrical faults. There are no idle tricks of the voice, no empty display of actor vanity and professional virtuosity, no foolish strutting, none of the actor idol's way of feeling his oats. There is no egotistical intrusion on the play, no capricious distortion of the truth in the service of histrionic exhibitionism. Throughout the performance the technical method is invariably derived from the conception of the part and never allowed to run ahead of it.

Mr. Barrymore's important technical limitations at this stage of his achievement seem to me to be two. The first concerns the verse. The 'resistant flexibility,' to use an old phrase, that is the soul of fine reading, he has not yet completely acquired. Much of his reading is excellent; but now and again in his effort to keep the verse true to its inner meaning and to the spiritual naturalness that underlies it—and because, too, of a lack of concentration on his projection at times—Mr. Barrymore seems to be afraid to admit the line for what it is, verse. Sometimes he allows the phrases to fall apart in such a way that the essential musical pattern of the verse—which is a portion of the idea itself—is lost. In the line—to take an example—

Why, she would hang on him,

he put a heavy stress on the word 'hang' and almost let the 'him' disappear; a useless naturalism, for the same effect of sense emphasis can be secured and yet the verse pattern of the lines preserved, by sustaining the nasals in 'on' and 'him' with no more actual stress on them than Mr. Barrymore used.

For one more instance out of a good many, take the line

Must, like a whore, unpack my heart with words.

Mr. Barrymore let the phrase 'like a whore' fall out solid from the verse, which then began anew with 'unpack.' But there is a certain sustained unity to the line; 'must' and 'unpack' have a resistant connection together—to be secured by the tone—which the intervening phrase does not break off. And, as a matter of fact, everywhere in Shakespeare the long, difficult, elaborate and complex passages depend above everything on their musical unity to recreate out of their many details that first profound unity of emotion from which they sprang. Without this unity these details appear to be—as in fact they often are, in the earlier plays especially—mere images and ornaments thrown in, whose artificiality is only embarrassing.

The other technical limitation that I feel in Mr. Barrymore is in his rendering of decreasing emotion. To be able to rise successfully to emotional heights is one measure of an actor's art; but this declining gradation is a no less sure test of it. For an illustration of what I mean, take the passage in the closet scene where the Ghost vanishes.

> HAMLET: Why, look you there! look how it steals away!
> My father in his habit as he lived!
> Look, where he goes, even now, out at the portal!
> QUEEN: This is the very coinage of your brain;
> This bodiless creation ecstasy
> Is very cunning in.
> HAMLET: Ecstasy!
> My pulse as yours doth temperately keep time,—

Mr. Barrymore repeats the word and goes on with the speech in a reasonable and almost even tone. But in such places a part of the effect of preceding emotion appears in the gradual lessening of it in the actor's manner and voice. This speech of Hamlet's is reasonable, yes, but the calm in the thought precedes the calm in the state of emotion; the will and the idea are to rule but only after conflict with the emotion.

I cannot admire too much Mr. Barrymore's tact in the scenes with Polonius. Most actors for the applause they get play up for all it is worth Hamlet's seemingly rude wit at the old man's expense. But Mr. Barrymore gave you only Hamlet's sense of the world grown empty and life turned to rubbish in this old counselor. And, without seeming to do so he made you feel that Polonius stood for the kind of thing in life that had taken Ophelia from him. How finely—even in that last entreaty to Laertes for fair usage—Mr. Barrymore maintained an absence of self-pity in Hamlet, and thus enlarged the tragic pity of the play! What a fine vocal economy he exercised in the scene where Horatio tells him of his father's ghost! And what a stroke of genius it was, when by Ophelia's grave Hamlet had rushed through those mad lines, piling one wild image on another, and comes to the

> Nay, and thou'lt mouth,
> I'll rant as well as thou

to drop on that last, on the 'I'll rant as well as thou,' into an aspirate tone, hoarse, broken with grief and with the consciousness of his words' excess and the excess of irony in all things!

And I must admire the economy of business—not all Mr. Barrymore but partly due to Mr. Arthur Hopkins,[7] Mrs. Carrington and Mr. Jones[8]—all through the part. The nunnery scene with Ophelia was done with a reaching out of the hands almost; the relation of Hamlet to his mother and through her to the ghost was achieved by his moving toward the ghost on his knees and being caught in his mother's arms, weaving together the bodies of those two, who, whatever their sins might be, must belong to each other at such terrible cost. There were no portraits on the wall with a ghost stepping out, as Hackett[9] used to do it in the sixties. There was no crawling forward on the floor to watch the King during the play, as so many actors have done; and none of Ophelia's peacock fan for Hamlet to tap his breast with and fling into the air, as Irving used to do. About all this production there were none of those accessories in invented business; there was for the most part, and always in intention, only that action proceeding from the inner necessity of the moment and leaning on life, not on stage expedients. The inner limitations of Mr. John Barrymore's Hamlet are both less tangible and less amendable perhaps. They are in the direction of the poetic and human. With time, meditation and repetition it will gain in these respects no doubt; but it needs now more warmth, more abundance in all the reactions, more dilation of spirit. It takes too much for granted, makes Hamlet too easy to understand, and so lacks mystery and scope. It needs a larger inner tumult, more of a cerebral and passionate ecstasy pressing against the outward restraint of the whole pattern. It needs more of the sense of an ungovernable vitality, more complex subtlety and power. It needs more tenderness and, above all, more, if you like, generosity.

Miss Fuller's Ophelia could not dominate the longer speeches in her first scenes. But in the mad scenes she sang her ballads with unheard-of poignancy; and the mere slip of her white, flitting body was itself the image of pathos. Miss Fuller sharpened the effect of madness by putting into it a hint of that last betrayal that insanity brings to Ophelia: indecency. Miss Yurka, though she subsided at times out of the part when she had nothing to do, read her lines admirably; and contrived to suggest without overstating it the loose quality in this woman that subjected her to the King. Mr. O'Brien's Polonius was good, simplified rather far, perhaps, but with a certain force of truth that rendered what Polonius, despite his fatuity, has: a kind of grotesque distinction. Mr. Reginald Pole brought to the Ghost's lines a fine ear and an exact method of reading the verse that you gratefully detect before he is three lines under way. The Laertes of Mr. Sidney Mather is the only very bad performance in the company. The role is extra difficult because of its Renaissance approach, through character and reality, to the flowery gallantry and lyric expedition required; though the bases of Laertes' feelings and actions seem to me fresh, accessible and human. The fact remains, nevertheless, that unless the actor gets the manner and flourish of Laertes, the expression of his vivid, poignant and decorative meaning cannot find its due outlet. Mr. Tyrone Power's[10] King—superb in voice and meter—was admirable. He suggested not mere villainy but rather a tragic figure of force and heavy will. Mr. Power's King gave us also the sense of great charm exerted upon those around him that is attributed to the character in the play.

It is in the scene where Hamlet catches the King praying and does not kill him—the climax of the play—that the method of production employed by Mr. Hopkins and Mr. Jones is reduced, it seemed to me, to its most characteristic terms. The King enters through the curtain, already used a number of times, with the saints on it. He kneels, facing the audience. He lifts his hands and speaks to heaven. Hamlet enters through the same curtain. He debates the fitness of the time for the King's murder, decides against it, withdraws. The King says

> My words fly up, my thoughts remain below;
> Words without thoughts never to heaven go.

and rises and goes out. One man is here, one is there. Here are the uplifted hands, there the sword drawn. Here, sick conscience, power, and tormented ambition; there, the torture of conflicting thoughts, the irony, the resolution. Two bodies and their relation to each other, the words, the essential drama, the eternal content of the scene. No tricks, no plausible business, no palace chapel. And no tradition.

Tradition of conception there is now and again, of course; but throughout the entire production there is very little concern about external tradition. And what of it? If we had some kind of Théâtre Français, a conservatory where a classic like *Hamlet* would be seen from time to time as a star returns on its course; or if in our theatre we had a succession of rival Hamlets, as was once the case, the question of tradition would be more important. Under such conditions a certain symbolism of stage business might develop, full of deep significance, familiar and accepted, and not to be abandoned too readily. But in the American theatre today the disregard of Shakespearean tradition is easy and commendable. To pursue it doggedly is to block the way with dead husks of forms once full of meaning. It only thwarts the audience and Shakespeare's living matter with a kind of academic archaism and, even, with a certain fanaticism; which consists, as Santayana[11] says, in redoubling your effort when you have forgotten your aim. Messrs. Hopkins and Jones and Barrymore have, for the most part, let sleeping dogs lie. Nothing could be easier than not to do so; hence their eminence.

Mr. Robert Edmond Jones has created a permanent setting of architectural forms and spaces, bounded across the stage, and down two-thirds to the front line of it, with a play of steps. Within this, easy variations are possible to indicate the changes of scene. The design of the setting cannot be conveyed in words, of course, but it is princely, austere and monumental. It has no clutter of costumes or elaborate variations in apartments, but instead a central rhythm of images, of light and shade innate to the dramatic moment. The shortcoming of this bold and eloquent setting is that it either goes too far or does not go far enough. In this respect the limit was reached when the time came for the scene of Ophelia's burial, where the setting was at least enough like a palace to make the grave toward the front of the stage—and therefore the whole scene—appear to be incongruous if not absurd. A greater vastness of imagination was thus required of the designer. In his defense it should be said, however, that our theatre does not easily allow for repeated experiment, with the discarding and choosing and the expense involved.

This production of *Hamlet* is important and is out of class with Shakespeare production from other sources. This is not through any perfection in the field of the Shakespearean so called; but because it works toward the discovery of the essential and dramatic elements that from the day it was written have underlain this play. The usual Shakespeare production, however eminent, goes in precisely the opposite direction. It does not reveal the essential so much as it dresses up the scene at every conceivable angle, with trappings, research, scenery, business.

Such a production as this of *Hamlet* could not hope to be uniformly successful. But in its best passages, without any affectation of the primitive or archaic, it achieved what primitive art can achieve: a fundamental pattern so simple and so revealing that it appeared to be mystical; and so direct and strong that it restored to the dramatic scene its primary truth and magnificence. For a long time to come this *Hamlet* will be remembered as one of the glories of our theatre.

1. **Mounet-Sully**, Jean (1841–1916), famous French actor, member of the Comédie Française.

2. **Forbes-Robertson**, Johnston. See p. 144.

3. **Irving**, Henry. See especially pp. 106.

4. **Sothern**, Edward Hugh (1859–1933), American actor who played Hamlet in 1900.

5. **Carrington**, Margaret (1877–1942), American voice coach who worked intensively with Barrymore; sister of the actor Walter Huston, she later married the designer Robert Edmond Jones.

6. **Mansfield**, Richard (1857–1907), American romantic actor.

7. **Hopkins**, Arthur (1879–1954), American director.

8. **Jones**, Robert Edmond (1887–1954), innovative American designer, director, and writer.

9. **Hackett**, James Henry (1800–71), American actor-manager especially known as Falstaff.

10. **Power**, (Frederick) Tyrone Edmund (1869–1931), American actor who played many Shakespeare roles on the New York stage.

11. **Santayana**, George (1863–1952), American philosopher and poet.

[1923], Herbert Farjeon (1887–1945) on Nigel Playfair's production of *The Merry Wives of Windsor*, with Edith Evans (1888–1976) as Mistress Page, at the Lyric Theatre, Hammersmith; from his *The Shakespearean Scene* ([1949]), pp. 20–1.

HERBERT FARJEON, actor, playwright, theatre manager and critic, was a versatile writer and man of the theatre who reviewed for many newspapers and magazines. The actor-manager Nigel Playfair (1874–1934, knighted 1928) ran the Lyric Theatre, Hammersmith, from 1919 until he died.

THE revival of *The Merry Wives of Windsor* at the Lyric Theatre, Hammersmith, is a very jolly affair. This was almost inevitable, for the play is essentially so jolly, so blithe, and, withal, so thick-skinned as to be practically producer-proof. The best possible description of the mood in which Shakespeare wrote it is to be found in the terms applied by the Host of the Garter Inn to Master Fenton: 'He capers, he dances, he has eyes of youth: he writes verses, he speaks holiday, he smells April and May, he will carry't, he will carry't, 'tis in his buttons, he will carry't.' Master Fenton does not fulfil the expectations aroused by these exuberant, bouncing words. In the event, he proves himself a weak walking gentleman rather than a triumphant bounding boy. But how the comedy itself capers, dances, has eyes of youth! how it speaks holiday, smells April and May! how Shakespeare carries it, from the pribbles and prabbles of the opening squabble till 'candles and starlight and moonshine be out'! how burstingly it is 'in his buttons'!

When the curtain fell on the first performance last Saturday night, Mr. Nigel Playfair, answering the clamour for an anti-climax, described the piece as a Christmas entertainment. To make it so, there is no need, as Mr. Oscar Asche[1] apparently thought there was some years ago, to contradict the spirit of every line by providing a Christmas-card setting of snow, and so superfluously adding to the agonies of Falstaff's ducking. *The Merry Wives* will do for any holiday. Its production would, indeed, serve as a capital excuse for a holiday, like the visit of a celebrity to his old school; it does not, like so many of the plays rushed on this Christmas, need a holiday as an excuse for its appearance. We are for ever routing out excuses for the presentation of poor plays. When we are busy, we have become, it is urged, so tired by nightfall that we are fit only for frivolous trifles. When we are idle, we are so carefree that to offer anything but frivolous trifles would be out of keeping. It is a relief, then, to find the Hammersmith Lyric staunchly uncontaminated by the vogue for amateurish puerilities dominant at this season of the year. And it is worth recording that the first-night audience was so hearty in its response that a few encores, after the fashion of *The Beggar's Opera*,[2] would no doubt have been rapturously welcomed.

The honours of the performance fell to Miss Edith Evans.[3] She is that rare thing, an actress with both breadth and subtlety. She is that equally rare thing, an actress who can bring out the full literary flavour of every word. To those who know their Shakespeare before they see him on the stage, how maddening it is to find word after word misunderstood, slurred over, debased, diminished, or subjected to the ignominy of substitution by the performers. But Miss Evans quickens every syllable, recognizes in a choice epithet something as three-dimensional as a living being, reveals new wonders unsuspected and never to be forgotten. Miss Ellen Terry's[4] Mistress Page was more electric, more gallivanting, possessed more animal magnetism. But Miss Evans is more in period, more sweepingly domin-ant, and, I verily believe, the better actress. Miss Dorothy Green[5] put up a good bold show as Mistress Ford, but comparatively she never stood a chance. Indeed, it is difficult to remember the other people in the play.

Referring to my programme, I am reminded of Mr. Randle Ayrton,[6] who achieved the uncommon feat of making Ford credible without making him too realistic. I am reminded again of Mr. Playfair's Host, a stout, tough, ample slice of work. And there was Mr. Roy Byford's[7] Falstaff, more nimble of foot, if less nimble of wit, than most Falstaffs, because Mr. Byford is, off the stage as well as on, a man of monstrous bulk, and consequently knows how nimble of foot the corpulent can be in emergency. But Miss Evans would have dwarfed an even larger and better Falstaff than Mr. Byford's.

The production by Mr. Bridges Adams[8] is resolutely reactionary. There is picture scenery of the most undistinguished type; there is incidental music for the various entries of Falstaff and of the Merry Wives, to mark them unmistakably from the minor characters; there are cuts, perversions of the text, misinterpretations of the text, even additions to the text; none of them glaring, but all of them obviously deliberate and indicative of Mr. Adams's views on Shakespearean production. Ford's frenzied search in impossible places, with rag, tag and bobtail at his heels, is infectiously worked up. The duel between the terrestrial Doctor and the celestial Parson is rattling rough-and-tumble. But does not Sir Hugh, counting the stars when he is felled to earth, savour less of Shakespeare than of the less original moments provided by modern musical comedy clowns in cricket caps and Boston garters?[9]

1. **Asche**, Oscar. See p. 174.

2. *The Beggar's Opera*. Playfair's revival of John Gay's work, which had an unprecedented run of 1,463 performances, established the Lyric Theatre's reputation and was instrumental in reviving interest in Restoration and eighteenth-century drama.

3. **Evans**, Edith (Dame of the British Empire, 1946), 'discovered' by William Poel, for whom she played Cressida in 1913, was becoming recognized as a great performer of, especially, high comedy. She was to give her classic performance as Millamant in William Congreve's *The Way of the World* at the Lyric Theatre in the following year.

4. **Terry**, Ellen. See p. 99.

5. **Green**, Dorothy (1886–1961), actress who played many Shakespearian and other roles at Stratford and elsewhere.

6. **Ayrton**, Randle (1869–1940), actor who was to play many leading roles in Shakespeare.

7. **Byford**, Roy (1873–1939), actor who specialised in comic roles.

8. **Bridges-Adams**, William (1889–1965), directed the Stratford Festival from 1919 to 1934. He had trained with William Poel.

9. **Boston garters** [not identified].

30 **August 1925**, Hubert Griffith (1896–1953) on *Hamlet* directed by
   Barry Jackson (1879–1961) at the Kingsway Theatre, London,
   from *The Observer*, reprinted in *Specimens of English Dramatic
   Criticism*, ed. A. C. Ward (1945), pp. 307–11.

BARRY JACKSON, director and theatre manager (knighted 1925), founded (1913)
the Birmingham Repertory Theatre. He produced pioneering modern-dress
productions of Shakespeare there during the 1920s, beginning with *Cymbeline*
in 1923. The final scene of this production is illustrated in Pl. 10.

Do you know what it is when some scheme, thought of its nature to
be beyond attainment, is suddenly, to use a phrase eternally current
in political circles, 'brought within the bounds of practical politics'? It is, I
assure you, a highly exhilarating feeling. There must always have been
among those who feel any curiosity about *Hamlet* at all, a curiosity to be
able to judge *Hamlet* as though, by some inconceivable flight of burning
genius, a modern playwright, say Tchekhov,[1] had written it. All the idea
needed, as it happens, was a few dress suits and a few Court uniforms. But
no one before Sir Barry Jackson happened to think of it, and now Sir
Barry Jackson and his company have done it.

   This production so pleased me and excited me, so amused me and
thrilled me, that I find it difficult to collect my thoughts about it or to
become articulate on the subject. Early in the proceedings I ceased to be
an intelligent spectator with an account to render afterwards. I merely
enjoyed, and lost myself in enjoyment. There was quite enough of the new
and the unexpected to absorb, and to take all one's faculties of absorption.
I can only give a scattered note to explain why the present *Hamlet* at the
Kingsway is the richest and deepest *Hamlet* I have ever seen. It is rarely
that one is profoundly moved in a theatre, and, when one is, the pleasure
is so great that an unreadable notice at the week-end seems a small price
to pay for it.

   To begin with, there is a difference between '*Hamlet* in Modern Dress'
(as the production calls itself), and '*Hamlet* as a modern play', as it actually
is played. The one suggests Daisy Ashford and Mr. Salteena[2]—which is
far from the truth. We are quite simply at a little modern Catholic
court—say of Ruritania, say of any small Baltic Kingdom. The King
and his ladies and gentlemen, his secretaries and officials, wear evening
dress or morning dress. (Hamlet, as befits his status of antagonist and
intellectual, never gets beyond a dinner jacket and a soft shirt.) The
younger men from the 'Varsity, Laertes, Rosencrantz, Hamlet himself,

show a predilection for tweeds. There is a sprinkling of uniforms at the Court. And that is really all that need be said in the matter of costumes. They are easy, natural, appropriate. None of them gets a laugh, and none of them is meant to. They merely transport us to the modern world. But, as Wordsworth said, 'Oh, the difference to me!'[3] The difference in the main is not to Hamlet himself, who at once becomes easier to play because his surroundings become ten times as interesting, but in the others, who surprise one by suddenly leaping to life. (Mr. Colin Keith-Johnston,[4] a really impressive and inspiring young Hamlet, must have tribute returned him. But I may say at once that I felt he was on to such a chance and opportunity as no actor had ever had before him.)

The King is the main beneficiary. Ordinarily, I am never so bored as when the King in *Hamlet* is speaking. He seems indistinguishable from the Player King except for his longer part. I now doubt if I was ever so interested in any modern gentleman as I was in Mr. Frank Vosper[5] (clean-shaven, well dressed, easy in manner, a polished and dignified usurper) speaking the same lines at the Kingsway. Polonius, by the same treatment—the venerable dotard, choked with beard, becomes the dapper little middle-aged Secretary of State—loses nothing, and gains much (and Mr. Bromley-Davenport,[6] much worked up by the general atmosphere of high comedy and excitement that the piece created, has never given a more inspiriting performance). Laertes also. Laertes ordinarily emerges a lay figure ready-made from the property room. Who has ever before violently cared what Laertes does or thinks? And yet, once make him an ordinary decent undergraduate, warped by a rancorous hatred in his heart for the young man who he thinks has seduced his sister—let him once be seen as a young man of to-day, and not as a walking costume—and I know that the Laertes of the trunk-hose, or, alternatively, of the winged-helmet Viking tradition, is a creature I never want to endure again in a modern theatre.

What exactly Sir Barry Jackson and his company have done is to show that *Hamlet* in all its parts is a great deal better play than any company of actors have ever dared to think it before. The breathless, deathless beauty of the language, the language of fire and dew, of boldness, of subtlety, of soaring loveliness, is not lost by being set among a masterpiece of modern drama. It merely puts the dialogue of most modern drama to blush by its magnificence. It is the old supreme virtue to which all the other virtues have now been added.

By doing *Hamlet* in modern clothes, the Birmingham company have shown how the ideas of later centuries were ransacked for its making.

Imagine the play to be by Tchekhov. This is not mere flippancy. I beg you to go to this *Hamlet* and imagine that Tchekhov wrote it. Imagine that he composed that talkative, idiosyncratic, extraordinarily vivid and mercilessly observed crowd of struggling figures. The canvas is larger than he would have attempted. The boldness of its lights and shades is a world different from his quiet monotone. But in the strange harmony by which all art that is great is seen to have an underlying unity with all other art that is great, it is possible to see that Tchekhov, by a heightening of his genius, might have composed such a *Hamlet*. The difference is in degree, not in kind.

It has always been possible to see that *Hamlet* contained in it the germs or fragments of ideas of nearly all other plays that have ever been written, much as *David Copperfield*[7] can be found to contain the germ of many other great novels besides itself, and all musical combinations can be found to occur in Bach. But never till now has it been possible to see that *Hamlet*—played as it should always now be played, as a play of contemporary life—could make one huge bonfire of the lot and soar aloft in the combined radiance of them all.

1. **Tchekhov**, Anton (1860–1904), Russian playwright.

2. **Daisy Ashford and Mr Salteena**, the nine-year-old author of *The Young Visiters* (1919; it is comically preoccupied with matters of dress) and her central character.

3. **Wordsworth**. See p. 54. These are the last word of his 'Lucy' poem beginning 'She dwelt among the untrodden ways'.

4. **Keith-Johnston**, Colin (1896–1980); he went on to have a long career on stage and screen.

5. **Vosper**, Frank (1899–1937), actor and dramatist

6. **Bromley-Davenport**, Arthur (1867–1946), stage and screen actor.

7. *David Copperfield*, novel (1849–50), by Charles Dickens (1812–70).

༺ༀༀༀༀༀༀༀༀༀༀༀༀༀༀༀༀༀༀༀༀༀༀༀༀༀༀༀ༻

30 **September 1933**, Virginia Woolf (1882–1941), on *Twelfth Night* directed by Tyrone Guthrie (1900–71) at the Old Vic Theatre, London, from *The New Statesman*; reprinted in *The Death of the Moth and Other Essays* (1942; Harmondsworth, 1961, pp. 43–7).

THE great novelist wrote this review out of friendship for Geoffrey Maynard Keynes and his wife, Lydia Lopokova, who had won fame as a ballet dancer; she had a strong Russian accent. Woolf referred to it in her diary as 'Lydia's extortion' (10 September 1933, in *Diaries . . .*, vol. 4, 1931–45, Hogarth Press, 1982); and in a letter to Ethel Smyth of 14 September she wrote 'my horror is that I must write an article on it...' (*Letters*, ed. Nigel Nicolson, vol. 5 (1979), p. 225). Her dismay increased when she read a review by W. A. Darlington in *The Daily Telegraph*, which declared that 'Lydia Lopokova makes her bow...as the most humourless female in literature...What possessed anybody to give the part of Olivia to her?' 'My god; what shall I say?', she wrote in a letter to Quentin Bell (19 September); 'I think the only possible line to take is how very exciting it is to see Shakespr mauled...Well. Pity me.' In the event she produced a beautifully written essay on the difference between reading and seeing plays.

SHAKESPEAREANS are divided, it is well known, into three classes; those who prefer to read Shakespeare in the book; those who prefer to see him acted on the stage; and those who run perpetually from book to stage gathering plunder. Certainly there is a good deal to be said for reading *Twelfth Night* in the book if the book can be read in a garden, with no sound but the thud of an apple falling to the earth, or of the wind ruffling the branches of the trees. For one thing there is time—time not only to hear 'the sweet sound that breathes upon a bank of violets' but to unfold the implications of that very subtle speech as the Duke winds into the nature of love. There is time, too, to make a note in the margin; time to wonder at queer jingles like 'that live in her; when liver, brain, and heart'...'and of a foolish knight that you brought in one night' and to ask oneself whether it was from them that was born the lovely, 'And what should I do in Illyria? My brother he is in Elysium.' For Shakespeare is writing, it seems, not with the whole of his mind mobilized and under control but with feelers left flying that sport and play with words so that the trail of a chance word is caught and followed recklessly. From the echo of one word is born another word, for which reason, perhaps, the play seems as we read it to tremble perpetually on the brink of music. They are always calling for songs in *Twelfth Night*, 'O fellow come, the song we had last night.' Yet Shakespeare was not so deeply in love with words but that he could turn and laugh at them. 'They that do dally with words do quickly make them wanton.' There is a roar of laughter and out burst Sir Toby, Sir Andrew, Maria. Words on their lips are things that have meaning; that rush and leap out with a whole character packed in a little phrase. When Sir Andrew says 'I was adored once,' we feel that we hold him in the hollow of our hands; a novelist would have taken three volumes to bring us to that pitch of intimacy. And Viola, Malvolio, Olivia, the Duke—the mind so brims and spills over with all that we know and guess about them as they move in and out among the lights and shadows of the mind's stage that we ask why should we imprison them within the bodies of real men and women? Why exchange this garden for the theatre? The answer is that Shakespeare wrote for the stage and presumably with reason. Since they are acting *Twelfth Night* at the Old Vic, let us compare the two versions.

Many apples might fall without being heard in the Waterloo Road, and as for the shadows, the electric light has consumed them all. The first impression upon entering the Old Vic is overwhelmingly positive and definite. We seem to have issued out from the shadows of the garden upon the bridge of the Parthenon. The metaphor is mixed, but then so is the scenery. The columns of the bridge somehow suggest an Atlantic liner and the austere splendours of a classical temple in combination. But the body is almost as upsetting as the scenery. The actual persons of Malvolio, Sir Toby, Olivia and the rest expand our visionary characters out of all recognition. At first we are inclined to resent it. You are not Malvolio; or Sir Toby either, we want to tell them; but merely impostors. We sit gaping at the ruins of the play, at the travesty of the play. And then by degrees this same body or rather all these bodies together, take our play and remodel it between them. The play gains immensely in robustness, in solidity. The printed word is changed out of all recognition when it is heard by other people. We watch it strike upon this man or woman; we see them laugh or shrug their shoulders, or turn aside to hide their faces. The word is given a body as well as a soul. Then again as the actors pause, or topple over a barrel, or stretch their hands out, the flatness of the print is broken up as by crevasses or precipices; all the proportions are changed. Perhaps the most impressive effect in the play is achieved by the long pause which Sebastian and Viola make as they stand looking at each other in a silent ecstasy of recognition. The reader's eye may have slipped over that moment entirely. Here we are made to pause and think about it; and are reminded that Shakespeare wrote for the body and for the mind simultaneously.

But now that the actors have done their proper work of solidifying and intensifying our impressions, we begin to criticize them more minutely and to compare their version with our own. We make Mr. Quartermaine's[1] Malvolio stand beside our Malvolio. And to tell the truth, wherever the fault may lie, they have very little in common. Mr. Quartermaine's Malvolio is a splendid gentleman, courteous, considerate, well bred; a man of parts and humour who has no quarrel with the world. He has never felt a twinge of vanity or a moment's envy in his life. If Sir Toby and Maria fool him he sees through it, we may be sure, and only suffers it as a fine gentleman puts up with the games of foolish children. Our

Malvolio, on the other hand, was a fantastic complex creature, twitching with vanity, tortured by ambition. There was cruelty in his teasing, and a hint of tragedy in his defeat; his final threat had a momentary terror in it. But when Mr. Quartermaine says 'I'll be revenged on the whole pack of you,' we feel merely that the powers of the law will be soon and effectively invoked. What, then, becomes of Olivia's 'He hath been most notoriously abused'? Then there is Olivia. Madame Lopokova[2] has by nature that rare quality which is neither to be had for the asking nor to be subdued by the will—the genius of personality. She has only to float on to the stage and everything round her suffers, not a sea change, but a change into light, into gaiety; the birds sing, the sheep are garlanded, the air rings with melody and human beings dance towards each other on the tips of their toes possessed of an exquisite friendliness, sympathy and delight. But our Olivia was a stately lady; of sombre complexion, slow moving, and of few sympathies. She could not love the Duke nor change her feeling. Madame Lopokova loves everybody. She is always changing. Her hands, her face, her feet, the whole of her body, are always quivering in sympathy with the moment. She could make the moment, as she proved when she walked down the stairs with Sebastian, one of intense and moving beauty; but she was not our Olivia. Compared with her the comic group, Sir Toby, Sir Andrew, Maria, the fool were more than ordinarily English. Coarse, humorous, robust, they trolled out their words, they rolled over their barrels; they acted magnificently. No reader, one may make bold to say, could outpace Miss Seyler's[3] Maria, with its quickness, its inventiveness, its merriment; nor add anything to the humours of Mr. Livesey's[4] Sir Toby. And Miss Jeans[5] as Viola was satisfactory; and Mr. Hare[6] as Antonio was admirable; and Mr. Morland's[7] clown was a good clown. What, then, was lacking in the play as a whole? Perhaps that it was not a whole. The fault may lie partly with Shakespeare. It is easier to act his comedy than his poetry, one may suppose, for when he wrote as a poet he was apt to write too quick for the human tongue. The prodigality of his metaphors can be flashed over by the eye, but the speaking voice falters in the middle. Hence the comedy was out of proportion to the rest. Then, perhaps, the actors were too highly charged with individuality or too incongruously cast. They broke the play up into separate pieces—now we were in the groves of Arcady, now in some inn at Blackfriars. The mind in reading spins a web from scene to scene, compounds a background from apples falling, and the toll of a church bell, and an owl's fantastic flight which keeps the play together. Here that continuity was sacrificed. We left the theatre possessed of many brilliant fragments but without the sense of all things conspiring and combining together which may be the satisfying culmination of a less brilliant performance. Nevertheless, the play has served its purpose. It has made us compare our Malvolio with Mr. Quartermaine's; our Olivia with Madame Lopokova's; our reading of the whole play with Mr. Guthrie's;[8] and since they all differ, back we must go to Shakespeare. We must read *Twelfth Night* again. Mr. Guthrie has made that necessary and whetted our appetite for the *Cherry Orchard, Measure for Measure,* and *Henry the Eighth* that are still to come.

1. **Quartermaine**, Léon (1876–1967), distinguished actor who often appeared in America as well as England.

2. **Lopokova**, Lydia (1892–1981), Russian-born dancer and actress who danced with Diaghilev's company and performed mainly in England and America.

3. **Seyler**, Athene (1889–1990), English actress with a special talent for high comedy.

4. **Livesey**, Roger (1906–76), versatile stage and screen actor with a special talent for eccentric comedy.

5. **Jeans**, Ursula (1906–73), wife of Roger Livesey; she had a successful career on stage and screen.

6. **Hare**, Ernest Dudley (b. 1900), actor who played many supporting roles at the Old Vic.

7. **Morland** (actually Morland Graham; 1891–1949).

8. **Guthrie**, Tyrone (1900–71), British director who worked in England, the USA, and Canada, where he directed the Stratford, Ontario Festival from 1953 to 1957; knighted 1961.

---

18 November 1934, James Agate (1877–1947) on John Gielgud (born 1904) as Hamlet in his own production at the New Theatre, London, from *The Sunday Times*, reprinted in his *Brief Chronicles: A Survey of the Plays of Shakespeare and the Elizabethans in actual performance* (1943), pp. 264–9.

JAMES AGATE was theatre critic of the *Sunday Times* from 1923 until he died. He published many volumes of theatre criticism, and his voluminous diaries, full of theatre gossip, were published under the title of *Ego* (9 vols., 1932–47).

Gielgud (knighted in 1953) first played Hamlet at the Old Vic in 1930; it became his most famous role.

WHEN a piece of acting is as good as Mr. Gielgud's Hamlet is known to be, it becomes the critic's duty to say not how far it exceeds the lowest standard but by how much it falls short of the highest. He must, when the highest honours are at stake, 'find quarrel in a straw'. Roundly, then, this Hamlet, beginning where most leave off, is fine; yet by a curious perversity it is only half as fine as this perfectly graced actor could make it. Now gather, and surmise.

The soldiers have stopped marvelling, and the curtain has risen on the first Court scene. Their Majesties are already seated, in a setting of such rich, if sombre, magnificence that the house breaks into applause. The King has made his opening speech and is asking Laertes what he wants, and we have still not made up our minds which among the courtiers is Hamlet! Or would not be able to do so if we were strangers to the London theatre and did not know Mr. Gielgud. Can it be that they are going to play Hamlet without the Prince? No; for at last we spot him, as much withdrawn as the width of the stage permits. Is he a trifle too spectacularly in the shade, a thought too determined to be the unobserved of all observers? Is there too petulant a charm in the sweep of chin and throat, like Byron sitting for his portrait? There may be, but these things are immediately forgotten in the exquisite and touching delivery of the 'Seems, madam' speech and the 'Too, too solid flesh' soliloquy. When Mr. Gielgud played the part four years ago[1] I suggested that while knowing when he ought to be pathetic he had not, in fact, much pathos. This has been remedied to a very remarkable degree, and the spectator must have a heart of stone not to be moved by Hamlet's obvious affection for his dead father, made manifest in the little 'Take him for all in all' colloquy with Horatio. Mr. Jack Hawkins[2] plays very well here, being staggered at Hamlet's 'Methinks I see my father', a little disappointed to find that his news is no news, and not sorry to hear that Hamlet is talking only of his mind's eye. The scene on the platform is well done, though Hamlet omits the longish and rather dull speech about the 'mole of nature'. Something, of course, has to be cut, and this is a good bit to be rid of, except that its retention underlines a point which cannot be made too often in connection with this play. This is that Shakespeare is a writer, not of acute psychological treatises to be pored over by obtuse Germans, but of stage plays of which one part can be inconsistent with another, provided each passes muster at the moment of performance. Nobody can be more natural than Shakespeare when being natural is his cue; and nobody can do more violence to nature if unnaturalness is the more paying proposition. (For example, every reader of Shakespeare must have asked why Horatio does not tell Hamlet about Ophelia's death when he meets him at the railway-station, and every Shakespearean playgoer knows that the answer is to permit of the tragi-comic colloquy with the

Grave-diggers and the revelation to Hamlet *in view of the audience*.) As for the 'mole of nature' speech, it is not conceivable that any human being, expecting at any moment to meet his father's ghost, could or would embark upon that long and involved tirade about the power of a single flaw to undermine a character. That Shakespeare violates nature here is due to one of two causes—either the itch for spilling moral beans, or the mere dramatic necessity for prolonging the suspense. Owlish professors blinking at the passage will see in it elucidation of Hamlet's character, whereas Shakespeare probably puts it in to keep Hamlet, Horatio, and Marcellus a little longer in the dark. But that is by the way.

In all that immediately follows the Ghost's speech Mr. Gielgud a little disappoints, as here almost all exponents have a little disappointed. Oddly enough, of all the Hamlets I have seen, Tree[3] fell least short here because, being an actor-manager aesthetically unencumbered, he had a spotlight by which to see him working hysterically up to that astonishing, romantic cry: 'Hillo, ho, ho, boy! come, bird, come.' Mr. Gielgud has to do this in the dark on a staircase, so that the working-up can only be vocal, and the actor's voice despite its range and melodic outline is not quite up to this feat. A spectator who did not know the words: 'Come, bird, come', would not hear them. Nor do I think that this Hamlet makes quite enough—if indeed he says it—of the little speech ending 'for mine own poor part Look you, I'll go pray'. It was here that Forbes-Robertson[4] made Hamlet suddenly perceive that he is a doomed man; in saying: 'For every man hath business and desire, such as it is', his Hamlet realized that whereas business and desire may be sorry things, it is his unhappiness that he must abstain from both. Mr. Gielgud's rendering of the 'fellow in the cellarage' is ineffective, and singularly little is made of the promise to put on an antic disposition. This is perhaps intentional because, except for one subsequent hurried disarrangement of hair and garments, there is never any question, so far as I can detect, of the Dane being either mad or pretending to be. He is not even mad north-north-west; whatever winds blow he remains a model of lucidity.

It is at this point that the spectator becomes aware of a fixed determination on the actor's part to make as little as possible of anything that can be called the orthodox 'acting' of the part, to throw away—in the actor's sense—everything except the highest of its poetry and the most sensitive of its philosophy. The result, strange to say, is not an enhancement but a diminishment of the character. Hamlet, interrupted in his reading by Polonius, should put on a mock solemnity whereby the old man does not know that he is being made fun of. Mr. Gielgud is cheeky here, so that we wonder that the old fellow does not resent the boyish impertinence. But then, in my view, all the play's urbanity is given insufficient value. Mr. Gielgud pulls himself together for the 'Rogue and peasant slave' soliloquy, which he delivers grandly, rendering it like the first movement of some tremendous concerto and so that the 'To be or not to be' speech, which follows almost immediately, has the tenderness of a Mozartian slow movement. The scene with Ophelia must always beat any actor who is not content to take it as music, unless, of course, he is prepared to accept Sir Arthur Quiller-Couch's[5] contention that this is a jumble of Shakespeare's play and that earlier story in which the bait used by the King and Polonius to discover Hamlet's secret was not Ophelia but a courtesan. Nothing else that I know of, except the madness motive, explains Hamlet's: 'I never gave you aught', which occurs at the beginning of the scene before he realizes he is being watched. The confusion of the two texts justifies Hamlet's planting upon Ophelia the vices of the courtesan, always on the supposition that Shakespeare jumped at this chance of invective and wasn't going to discard it because of its inconsistency with Hamlet's knowledge of Ophelia's character. Anyhow, the madness and Sir Arthur's contention between them accomplish the trick of making the scene feasible. But the most fascinating speculations must not lure us out of playhouse logic. Since Mr. Gielgud jettisons all suggestion of madness and since not one playgoer in a thousand has read Sir Arthur's lectures, we come back willy-nilly to the scene played as sheer music. Our present Hamlet, realizing that this is one of the great things in the play, tackles it for all his vocal grace and physical and mental elegance are worth, and his pathos here is again extraordinary. This in the present version brings the first part of the play to an end. After 'throwing away' the Advice to the Players, perhaps on the score that it is hackneyed, Mr. Gielgud again commands the most of our admiration for the rapt beauty of his speech to Horatio: 'Nay, do not think I flatter'. Then follows some more deliberate underplaying, and so rapid and casual is the dialogue here that I cannot remember having heard about either 'hobby-horse' or 'miching mallecho'. And surely Hamlet's lightning 'The Mouse-trap' should be a dagger driven up to the hilt into the King's conscience? Whereas when Claudius asks: 'What do you call the play?' Hamlet makes so little of the reply that the King could conceivably not hear him.

The end of the Play Scene is given effectively and prestissimo, after which there is another lapse, the scene with the recorders being given too slowly and as a dialectical exercise instead of being the ground-swell of a storm which has still to subside. And frankly it is permissible to hold that the scene with the Queen could do with a little less intellectual passion and a little more of the other sort. Here Mr. Gielgud receives insufficient help from Miss Laura Cowie,[6] and what should be an emotional duet becomes a cold lecture on moderation in second marriages. But perhaps the cooling off is again deliberate, since Mr. Gielgud has no intention of giving the magnificent postscript about the 'convocation of politic worms'. How any actor can omit this beats me utterly, since half of Hamlet is portrayed here. The player returns to his best self in the almost mathematical exposition of the 'How all occasions' soliloquy, though the omission of the scene with the King and the resulting joining up of two lots of moralizing make this over-nice debater a colder-blooded fellow than the real Hamlet of the full text. If the concluding scenes do not wholly satisfy it is because we feel the want of something, though it is difficult to say what. The impression we have by this time gathered is of a Hamlet who can fly into the most shattering of pets. He has accesses of grief, but they do not leave him moody, there is no melancholy in him, his mind has not the richness of its words, he is not fey or marked for death, and his talk of ripeness is academic and not the ultimate philosophy of a man who feels that his course is run. To sum up, this Hamlet's specific gravity is akin to Romeo's, and when he dies we are conscious of losing no more than a gay, gallant, romantic companion; we do not feel that part of ourselves has died with him. I hope that the foregoing is not an ungenerous estimate. If it is, it is because the actor so wantonly sacrifices the acting strength of the play to no discoverable purpose. If he would reconsider this and give to the prose passages that loving attention he has given to the poetry, one would modify one's attitude almost without knowing it. One would then say wholeheartedly that this is Mr. Gielgud's intensest fulfilment of himself, and not inquire too closely whether an Irving or a Forbes-Robertson had richer stores of magic upon which to draw. This Hamlet abounds in loveliness, but one feels that the actor's treasury could yield more. It would be wrong not to insist upon the wealth of beauty and accomplishment contained in that half of the character which is fully explored. Elsewhere it is as though Hamlet had taken his own advice to the players too much to heart. And didn't the first dramatic critic say something about considering 'some necessary question of the play'? If Mr. Gielgud will reconsider the many necessary questions of this play he will make his performance the whole which at present it is not. The poetic half, having attained perfection, should be left severely alone.

The ladies who call themselves Motley[7] have provided some enchanting scenery and dresses. Mr. Vosper's[8] King is satisfying, and would be even better if Nature had not made the player's cheeks creaseless; this being so Mr. Vosper has to rely on his voice, which he uses excellently. Mr. George Howe[9] makes Polonius a most engaging old fool; Mr. William Devlin's[10] Ghost is insufficiently ghostly though beautifully spoken; and Mr. Glen Byam Shaw's[11] Laertes looks like one of the naughty children whom Struwwelpeter's[12] tall Agrippa dipped into the inkpot. Laertes and Ophelia are of the company of Shakespeare's golden lads and lasses and should be played as such. The rest is silence, including Ophelia, for whom in my opinion that charming little actress, Miss Jessica Tandy,[13] is quite pathetically miscast.

1. **four years ago**. Gielgud had played Hamlet at the Old Vic in 1930. Agate's review is reprinted in his *Brief Chronicles* (1943), pp. 257–9.

2. **Hawkins**, Jack (1910–73), actor who had a successful career on stage and screen.

3. **Tree**, Beerbohm. See p. 152. He played Hamlet in Manchester (where Agate was educated) in 1891 and at the Haymarket Theatre, London, the following year.

4. **Forbes-Robertson**. See p. 144.

5. **Quiller-Couch**, Sir Arthur (1863–1944), scholar and author. The reference is to lectures printed as *Shakespeare's Workshop* (1918, etc.), pp. 209–10.

6. **Cowie**, Laura (1892–1969). Gielgud writes that she was 'magnificently sensuous in the part, playing with especially fine effect in her scenes with Vosper' (*Early Stages*, 1939, p. 259).

7. **Motley**, a design team (originally Audrey Harris, Margaret Harris, and Elizabeth Montgomery) which worked extensively in English theatre from 1932 to 1964.

8. **Vosper**, Frank. See p. 206.

9. **Howe**, George (1900–86), actor who gave his favourite parts as Polonius and Mr Pickwick.

10. **Devlin**, William (1911–79), actor who made his first professional appearance in 1934, in which year he made a success as Lear at the Westminster Theatre. He went on to play many other roles in Shakespeare and other dramatists.

11. **Shaw**, Glen Byam (1904–86), actor and director; Director of the Shakespeare Memorial Theatre, Stratford-upon-Avon from 1956 to 1959.

12. **Struwwelpeter**, 'Shock-headed Peter', central character of the children's book by Heinrich Hoffmann (1809–74).

13. **Tandy**, Jessica (1909–94), English actress who had married Jack Hawkins in 1932; she emigrated to America in 1940 and continued a successful career on stage and screen.

17 October 1935, James Agate on John Gielgud's production of
Romeo and Juliet at the New Theatre, London, with John
Gielgud, Peggy Ashcroft (1907–91), Laurence Olivier (1907–89)
and Edith Evans (1888–1976), from *The Sunday Times*,
reprinted in his *Brief Chronicles: A Survey of the Plays of
Shakespeare and the Elizabethans in actual performance* (1943),
pp. 208–12.

As Agate recognized, this production had an exceptional cast. Edith Evans
(Dame of the British Empire, 1946), 'discovered' by Poel, was already recognised
as a great performer, especially in high comedy. Olivier, knighted in 1947, Life
Peer, 1970, founder of the National Theatre, was, along with Gielgud, the
greatest classical actor of his time. Peggy Ashcroft (Dame of the British Empire,
1956), cooler and more classical in style than Dame Edith, was nevertheless her
natural successor. She often acted with Gielgud (see p. 210). Valuable information on this production is given by Jill Levenson in '*Romeo and Juliet*', Shakespeare in Performance series (Manchester, 1987).

T HURSDAY evening was all that an evening in the theatre should be—
exciting, moving, provocative. Here in conjunction were the flower
of Shakespeare's young genius and the best of young English acting
talent. The producer was our leading Shakespearean actor, and the scenery and costumes were by the artists who had attained fame through the
productions of *Richard of Bordeaux*[1] and *Hamlet*. In other words, Mr.
Gielgud had once more invested him in his Motley[2] and given these
young ladies leave to speak his mind. Let me begin with a word or two
about the production, normally tucked away at the end. The difficulty of
producing plays written for the Elizabethan and transferred to the picture
stage must always be resolved by compromise, which means that good and
bad must go hand in hand. The good point about this production is that it
enables that fiery-footed steed which is this tragedy to gallop sufficiently
apace. Now, though the acquisition of speed has been a triumph, it has
entailed certain sacrifices. For Mr. Gielgud's, and consequently Motley's,
method is a combination of the Elizabethan and modern stages, with
Juliet's bedroom and balcony a permanent part of the setting; that people
may walk beneath it the thing is supported on posts, so that it looks rather
like a hotel-lift which has got stuck half-way up to the mezzanine floor.
The device also precludes the full use of the stage, so that the action seems
to take place not so much in Verona as in a corner of it. I fault the
lighting, too, in that gone are the sun and warmth of Italy and the whole

thing appears to happen at night, the tomb scene being the cheerfullest of all! The costumes are charming, even if the football jerseys of the rival factions remind us less of Montague and Capulet than of Wanderers and Wolves.[3] Elsewhere Motley have rightly differed from Dickens's Flora,[4] who could not conceive any connection between Mantua and mantua-making. In the theatre there is every connection, and Motley have caught the spirit of the place and time, brilliantly for example in Romeo's case, though in Juliet's oddly reminiscent of the pre-Raphaelite way of looking at Ellen Terry.

Mr. Olivier's Romeo suffered enormously from the fact that the spoken poetry of the part eluded him. In his delivery he brought off a twofold inexpertness which approached virtuosity—that of gabbling all the words in a line and uttering each line as a staccato whole cut off from its fellows. In his early scenes this Romeo appeared to have no apprehension of, let alone joy in, the words he was speaking, though this may have been due to first-night nervousness, since he improved greatly later on. But throughout one wanted over and over again to stop the performance and tell the actor that he couldn't, just couldn't, rush this or that passage. If ecstasy is present in this play it must be at the meeting in the Friar's cell, where Romeo's words hang on the air like grace-notes:

> Ah, Juliet, if the measure of thy joy
> Be heap'd like mine, and that thy skill be more
> To blazon it, then sweeten with thy breath
> This neighbour air, and let rich music's tongue
> Unfold the imagined happiness that both
> Receive in either by this dear encounter.

This is music and must be spoken as music. Again, what is the use of Shakespeare writing such an image as: 'The white wonder of dear Juliet's hand' if Romeo is not himself blasted with the beauty of it? Never mind Shakespeare's precepts; his verse must be recited line upon line, here a little hurry and there a little dwell. Apart from the speaking there was poetry and to spare. This Romeo looked every inch a lover, and a lover fey and foredoomed. The actor's facial expression was varied and mobile, his bearing noble, his play of arm imaginative, while his smaller gestures were infinitely touching. Note, for example, how lovingly he fingered first the props of Juliet's balcony and at the last her bier. For once in a way the tide of this young man's passion was presented at the flood, and his grief was agonizingly done. 'Is it e'en so? Then I defy you, stars!' is a line which has defied many actors. Mr. Olivier's way with this was to say it tonelessly, and it is a very moving way. Taking the performance by and large, I have no hesitation in saying that this is the most moving Romeo I have seen. It also explains that something displeasing which I have hitherto found in Mr. Olivier's acting—the discrepancy between the romantic manner and such ridiculous things as cuff-links and moustaches. Now that these trivia have been shorn away and the natural player stands forth, lo and behold he is very good!

Mercutio is always a problem, for the reason that the Queen Mab speech, obviously inserted to satisfy an actor's demand, is not in keeping with that arch-materialist. In my opinion the way to play the part is to go all out for the sensualist, treat the speech as a cadenza,—in the way a fiddler will plonk one of his own into the middle of somebody else's concerto—bow, decline an encore, and then get back into the character! Mr. Gielgud reverses the process and builds his Mercutio out of the Queen Mab speech which, of course, he delivers exquisitely. This means a new death scene and saying 'A plague o' both your houses!' with a smile which is all a benison. Not good Shakespeare, perhaps, but very beautiful Gielgud. In these circumstances Mercutio is not our old friend but a Frenchified version, say Théodore de Banville's:

> Jeune homme sans mélancolie,
> Blond comme un soleil d'Italie.[5]

Miss Peggy Ashcroft's Juliet has been greatly praised. Certainly the eager and touching childishness of the early part could not be bettered, so that we prepared to be greatly moved. Personally, I found the performance heartrending until it came to the part where the heart should be rent. And then nothing happened, though all the appurtenances of grief, the burying of the head in the Nurse's bosom and so forth were present. When Juliet lifted her head, her face was seen to be duly ravaged, but she continued to the end with the same quality of ravagement, which as a piece of acting spells monotony. In my view Miss Ashcroft implied Juliet without playing her. That is to say, she did not move me nearly so much as any of the children who have played in *Mädchen in Uniform*.[6] But then it is very difficult indeed, perhaps impossible, for any Mädchen to put on Shakespeare's uniform. Mr. Granville-Barker[7] dismisses as 'parroted nonsense' the saying that no actress can play Juliet till she is too old to look her. Let this acute observer produce an actress past or present to support him! According to a great critic of the 'eighties,[8] Ellen Terry herself failed not only to conjure up the horrors of the charnel house but to make the scene impressive. In my judgment Miss Ashcroft succeeded in the first half, only to fade away later. On the other hand, the success so far as it went was complete.

I have not space to enumerate the admirable supporting cast, and can only congratulate Mr. Gielgud upon a production triumphant everywhere despite the fact that Romeo cannot speak his part, Juliet cannot act more than half of hers, and Mercutio is topsy-turvy. To crown all, remains Miss Evans's[9] Nurse, knocking the balance of the play into a cocked hat, just as would happen if the Porter were the centre of *Macbeth*. She ruled the entire roost. Obviously of the German-Flemish school, this was Hugh Walpole's Agatha Payne[10] metamorphosed into good instead of bad angel. It was a grand performance, and the pathos of it should have taught young playgoers what pathos was in younger days. One felt that whenever such grief is heard in the theatre, Mrs. Stirling's[11] heart will hear it and beat, though it should have lain for a century dead.[12]

1. *Richard of Bordeaux*, play by Gordon Daviot, pen-name of Elizabeth Mackintosh (1896–1952), who also wrote as Josephine Tey, in which Gielgud appeared with great success in 1932.

2. **Motley**. See p. 215.

3. **Wanderers and Wolves**, alluding to football teams, (probably) Bolton and Wolverhampton Wanderers.

4. **Flora**, Flora Finching in *Little Dorrit* (1857) by Charles Dickens; the allusion is to Chapter 9 of Book the Second.

5. **de Banville**, Théodore (1823–91), French poet; these are the opening lines of one of his Odelettes, 'A Adolphe Gaïffe'.

6. *Mädchen in Uniform*, a play adapted as *Children in Uniform* by Barbara Burnham from the script of a 1931 German film by Christa Winsloe. It was acted in London in 1932 and 1934, and Agate described it as 'The most moving play of recent times' (*More First Nights* (1937), pp. 282–3).

7. **Granville-Barker**, Harley. See p. 165. The allusion is to the section on Juliet in his *Preface* (1930, etc.).

8. **a great critic of the 'eighties** [not identified].

9. **Evans**, Edith. See p. 216.

10. **Agatha Payne**, a character in *The Old Ladies*, adapted by Rodney Ackland from the novel by Hugh Walpole (1884–1941), acted in 1935 with Edith Evans in the role. Agate's review is in his *More First Nights* (1937), pp. 133–9.

11. **Stirling**, Mary Ann (Fanny; 1815–95); she triumphed as the Nurse with Irving and Terry at the Lyceum in 1882.

12. **heart...dead**. A reminiscence of Tennyson's *Maud*, Part One, XXII. xi.

12 **November 1937**, John Mason Brown (1900–69) on Orson Welles's production of *Julius Caesar* at the Mercury Theatre, New York, from *The New York Post*, reprinted in his *Two on the Aisle: Ten Years of American Theatre in Performance* (New York, 1938), pp. 38–43, and in *Shakespearean Criticism*, vol. 17, ed. Sandra Williamson (Detroit, Gale Research, 1992), pp. 319–21.

JOHN MASON BROWN was theatre critic of *Theatre Arts Monthly* from 1924 to 1928, and of *The New York Evening Post* from 1929; in 1944 he became theatre critic for the *Saturday Review*. There is a chapter on this production in *Orson Welles: The Road to Xanadu* by Simon Callow (1995).

THIS is no funeral oration such as Miss Bankhead[1] and Mr. Tearle[2] forced me to deliver yesterday when they interred *Antony and Cleopatra*. I come to praise *Caesar* at the Mercury, not to bury it. Of all the many new plays and productions the season has so far revealed, this modern-dress version of the mob mischief and demagoguery which can follow the assassination of a dictator is by all odds the most exciting, the most imaginative, the most topical, the most awesome, and the most absorbing. The touch of genius is upon it. It liberates Shakespeare from the strait-jacket of tradition. Gone are the togas and all the schoolroom recollections of a plaster Julius. Blown away is the dust of antiquity. Banished are the costumed Equity members, so ill at ease in a painted forum, spouting speeches which have tortured the memory of each member of the audience.

Because of Orson Welles's inspiration and the sheer brilliance of his staging, Shakespeare ceases at the Mercury to be the darling of the College Board Examiners. Unfettered and with all the vigor that was his when he spoke to the groundlings of his own day, he becomes the contemporary of us who are Undergroundlings. What he wrote with Plutarch in his mind, we sit before with today's headlines screaming in our eyes.

New York has already enjoyed its successful Shakespearean revivals in modern dress. There was *Hamlet*. There was *The Taming of the Shrew*.[3] Then, under this same Mr. Welles's direction, Harlem flirted with a tantalizing, if unrealized, idea in its Voodoo *Macbeth*.[4] But these productions, vivifying as they have proven, have at their best been no more than quickening experiences in the theatre. The astonishing, all-impressive virtue of Mr. Welles's *Julius Caesar* is that, magnificent as it is as theatre, it is far larger than its medium. Something deathless and dangerous in the world sweeps past you down the darkened aisles at the Mercury and takes possession of the proud, gaunt stage. It is something fearful and turbulent which distends the drama to include the life of nations as well as of men. It is an ageless warning made in such arresting terms that it not only gives a new vitality to an ancient story but unrolls in your mind's eye a map of the modern world splotched increasingly, as we know it to be, with sickening colors.

Mr. Welles does not dress his conspirators and his Storm Troopers in Black Shirts or in Brown. He does not have to. The antique Rome, which we had thought was securely Roman in Shakespeare's tragedy, he shows us to be a dateless state of mind. Of all of the conspirators at work in the text, Mr. Welles is the most artful. He is not content to leave Shakespeare a great dramatist. He also turns him into a great anticipator. At his disposal Mr. Welles places a Time-Machine[5] which carries him away from the past at which he had aimed and down through the centuries to the present. To an extent no other director in our day and country has equaled, Mr. Welles proves in his production that Shakespeare was indeed not of an age but for all time. After this surly modern Caesar, dressed in a green uniform and scowling behind the mask-like face of a contemporary dictator, has fallen at the Mercury and new mischief is afoot, we cannot but shudder before the prophet's wisdom of those lines which read:

> How many ages hence
> Shall this our lofty scene be acted over
> In states unborn and accents yet unknown!

To fit the play into modern dress and give it its fullest implication, Mr. Welles has not hesitated to take his liberties with the script. Unlike Professor Strunk,[6] however, who attempted to improve upon *Antony and Cleopatra*, he has not stabbed it through the heart. He has only chopped away at its body. You may miss a few fingers, even an arm and leg in the *Julius Caesar* you thought you knew. But the heart of the drama beats more vigorously in this production than it has in years. If the play ceases to be Shakespeare's tragedy, it does manage to become ours. That is the whole point and glory of Mr. Welles's unorthodox, but welcome, restatement of it.

He places it upon a bare stage, the brick walls of which are crimson and naked. A few steps and a platform and an abyss beyond, from which the actors can emerge, are the setting. A few steps—and the miracle of spotlights which stab the darkness with as sinister an effect as the daggers of the assassins which penetrate Caesar's body. That is all. And it is all that is needed. In its streamline simplicity this setting achieves the glorious, unimpeded freedom of an Elizabethan stage. Yet no backgrounds of the winter have been as eloquent or contributive as is this frankly presentational set. It is a setting spacious enough for both the winds and victims of demagoguery to sweep across it like a hurricane. And sweep across they do, in precisely this fashion.

Mr. Welles's direction is as heightening as is his use of an almost empty stage. His groupings are of that fluid, stressful, virtuoso sort one usually has to journey to Russia to see. He proves himself a brilliant innovator in his deployment of his principals and his movement of his crowds. His direction, which is constantly creative, is never more so than in its first revelation of Caesar hearing the warning of the soothsayer, or in the fine scene in which Cinna, the poet, is engulfed by a sinister crowd of ruffians. Even when one misses Shakespeare's lines, Mr. Welles keeps drumming the meaning of his play into our minds by the scuffling of his mobs when they prowl in the shadows, or the herd-like thunder of their feet when they run as one threatening body. It is a memorable device. Like the setting in which it is used, it is pure theatre; vibrant, unashamed, and enormously effective.

The theatrical virtues of this modern dress *Julius Caesar* do not stop with its excitements as a stunt in showmanship. They extend to the performances. As Brutus Mr. Welles shows once again how uncommon is his gift for speaking great words simply. His tones are conversational. His manner is quiet; far too quiet to meet the traditional needs of the part. But it is a quiet with a reason. The deliberation of Mr. Welles's speech is the mark of the honesty which flames within him. His reticent Brutus is at once a foil to the staginess of the production as a whole and to the oratory of Caesar and Antony. He is a perplexed liberal, this Brutus; an idealist who is swept by bad events into actions which have no less dangerous consequences for the state. Like many another contemporary liberal he is a Caspar Milquetoast,[7] so filled with the virtues of Sir Roger de Coverley[8] that he can do nothing.

George Coulouris[9] is an admirable Antony. So fresh is his characterization, so intelligent his performance, that even 'Friends, Romans, Countrymen' sounds on his tongue as if it were a rabble-rousing harangue he is uttering for the first time. If only he began it with '*My* friends, Romans, countrymen,' you could swear last night's radio had brought it to you freshly heated from a famous fireside.[10] Joseph Holland's Caesar is an imperious dictator who could be found frowning at you in this week's news-reels. He is excellently conceived and excellently projected. Some mention, however inadequate, must also be made of Martin Gabel's[11] capable Cassius, of John Hoystradt's Decius Brutus, of the conspirators whose black hats are pluck'd about their ears, and Norman Lloyd's[12] humorous yet deeply affecting Cinna.

It would be easy to find faults here and there; to wonder about the wisdom of some of the textual changes even in terms of the present production's aims; to complain that the whole tragedy does not fit with equal ease into its modern treatment; and to wish this or that scene had been played a little differently. But such fault-findings strike me in the case of this *Julius Caesar* as being as picayune as they are ungrateful. What Mr. Welles and his associates at the Mercury have achieved is a triumph that is exceptional from almost every point of view.

1. **Bankhead**, Tallulah (1902–68), a flamboyant performer on stage and screen who had appeared in an extravagant and disastrous production of *Antony and Cleopatra* which opened and rapidly closed a few days before Welles's *Julius Caesar*.

2. **Tearle**, Conway (1878–1938), half-brother of the more famous actor Godfrey Tearle (see p. 266).

3. *Hamlet . . . Taming of the Shrew*. Modern-dress versions of both plays starring Mary Ellis (born 1900) and her husband Basil Sydney (1894–1968) had been seen in New York in 1925 and 1927 respectively.

4. **Voodoo** *Macbeth*, a controversial production directed by Welles in 1936 for the Negro Theatre Project.

5. *Time-Machine*, The, a novel (1895) by H. G. Wells (1866–1946).

6. **Strunk**, William, Jr., of Cornell University; he assisted in the production of George Cukor's film of *Romeo and Juliet* (1936), and was presumably the textual adviser for the production of *Antony and Cleopatra* mentioned above.

7. **Caspar Milquetoast**, 'a cartoon character created by H. T. Webster in 1924', used for 'a timid or unforthcoming person' (*OED*).

8. **Sir Roger de Coverley**, a simple country squire portrayed by Richard Steele (1672–1729) in *The Spectator* and developed by Joseph Addison (1672–1719); also the name of a country dance.

9. **Coulouris**, George (1903–89), British-born actor who pursued a successful stage and screen career in Britain and the United States.

10. **a famous fireside**, alluding to broadcasts by Franklin Delano Roosevelt (1882–1945), President of the USA from 1933 to 1945.

11. **Gabel**, Martin (born 1912).

12. **Lloyd**, Norman (born 1914), actor and director who has had a long and distinguished career.

[1944], Ronald Harwood (born 1934) on Donald Wolfit (1902–68) as
  Lear, in his *Sir Donald Wolfit: His life and work in the
  unfashionable theatre* (1971), pp. 160–4.

THE playwright Ronald Harwood, born in South Africa, worked with Wolfit as
an actor. His play *The Dresser* (1980) is based on this experience. Wolfit played
many Shakespearian roles, including Hamlet at Stratford-upon-Avon in 1936.
In 1937 he formed his own company with which he toured extensively in the
English provinces and overseas, occasionally also playing in London. His roles
included Hamlet, Macbeth, Falstaff, Richard III, Othello, Iago, Bottom,
Iachimo, and Lear, the role in which he was most admired. James Agate hailed
his performance as 'the greatest piece of Shakespearean acting since I have been
privileged to write for the *Sunday Times*'. Harwood's is a composite account of a
performance given when he was ten years old. Wolfit gave his last Shakespeare
performances in 1953, except for recital programmes.

THE night of Wednesday 12 April 1944 was misty and damp and chill.
London was again under attack, but the weather was shortly to
improve and the raids slackened.

Wolfit had taken the Scala Theatre for a thirteen-week season which
had begun in February; after nine weeks, he decided to try *King Lear* once
more.

He arrived at the theatre with Rosalind¹ at five, dressed in a voluminous
brown teddy-bear coat acquired in Canada while touring with Barry
Jackson.² Black homburg on head, shoulders stooped, the actor advanced
towards the stage-door, paused and glanced at nearby bomb damage,
appeared to nod gravely as if he understood some symbolic message
contained in the ruins, and marched into the theatre.

Being the first performance of the play that season, he went on to the
stage, lit by the naked bulbs of working lights, to make sure all was in
order. He surveyed the grey set, something like Stonehenge, gazed up at
the position of the spotlights, nodded once more, and retired to his
dressing room; it was noticed that he was unusually preoccupied.

He undressed and, wrapped in a pink towelling dressing gown, began
to make up, painting in the heavy lines on his forehead and about the
eyes, whitening his thick bushy eyebrows, high-lighting his nose with a
broad line. Next came the white beard, then the wig, stuck down with
white-hard varnish. As the make-up took form, as wig and beard were
fixed in place, and the joins disappeared under the thick grease-paint, so
his hands began to tremble, his eyes to narrow and appear rheumy, his
head to shake. At last he powdered—Brown and Polson's cornflour—and

brushed it off, once more to reveal the aged face of the King. Last, he lined his hands, to age them, too.

With forty-five minutes to go to curtain-up, he called for his dresser. In silence, the clothes were handed to him until at last the heavy cloak sat upon the bent shoulders; the triple coronet was offered and he fixed it securely on his head, nodding and shaking as if with palsy.

When the assistant stage-manager called five minutes to the rise of the curtain, Wolfit slowly descended to the stage, his dresser in attendance, carrying a silver salver upon which stood a moist chamois leather, a glass of Guinness and—rare in war-time—some peeled grapes. Actors who happened to be waiting in the corridors stood aside to allow the little procession to pass; Wolfit nodded to them with an expression of infinite weariness. The silence backstage was oppressive.

He waited in the wings, doing his best not to concern himself with the bustle of activity that precedes the performance; this, in itself, was un-usual, for in other plays, no matter how large or wearying the part, he would be hissing last-minute instructions to the stage management, electricians and actors. But not this night; he stood perfectly still, with Rosalind, ready as Cordelia, beside him, occasionally glancing at her with a look that seemed to want to make sure that she understood the weight of all the world was upon his shoulders. He talked to no one; members of the company gave him a wide berth if they had to pass. He did not even enquire about the size of the audience; he might be expected to gaze through the peep-hole, but he did not; the house, in fact, was painfully thin, less than half-full.

His stage-director ordered the actors to stand by. The house lights dimmed. Rosabel Watson[3] received her cue, and the trumpet sounded. The curtain rose slowly.

Kent and Gloucester begin. In the wings, Wolfit fidgets with his cloak, sceptre and crown, pulling at his beard, relaxing his neck muscles. Now comes his cue: Eric Maxon,[4] as Gloucester, says, 'He hath been out nine years, and away he shall again.' The trumpet sounds once more. 'The King is coming'.

Lear enters from the extreme down-stage position, and crossing to centre, orders 'Attend the lords of France and Burgundy, Gloucester.' It is a sombre voice, accustomed to command. The King reaches centre and turns his back on the audience, pauses, his head shaking almost imperceptibly, and then advances towards his throne; once seated, he commences the division of his kingdom, which the actor believes to be the first step in the betrayal of Kingship upon which the tragedy is built.

How gentle but firm he is with Goneril, as if making himself more affectionate than is his wont; and so with Regan, more indulgent perhaps, yet no less certain of his authority. To Cordelia, he invites her honesty by a slight descent into sentimentality. Her reply halts him. 'Nothing will come of nothing' is uttered with a contempt for her sincerity. Her banishment is delivered as if Lear pronounces on behalf of some primeval, barbaric power. The King is set on his path, obstinate, angry, unreasonable.

It is a gentle Lear who toys with the disguised Kent, an indulgent King who is amused by the Fool, played by Richard Goolden[5] almost as old as his master. At the first insult delivered by Oswald, Lear is incredulous.

LEAR: My lady's father? my lord's knave, you whoreson dog, you slave, you cur!
OSWALD: I am none of this, my lord, I beseech you pardon me.
LEAR: Do you bandy looks with me, you rascal?

And with sudden savagery, the King reveals his whip—Ayrton's whip[6]—and flays the insolent steward, punishing him out of a savage, determined impulse. But in the scene that follows with the Fool, Lear's mood reflects his concern for his own frail position, preoccupied with the unexpected hardening of his eldest daughter's affections. His temper is unpredictable; the whip dangles by his side, twitching dangerously from time to time. His tongue lashes round 'No lad, teach me'; 'Dost call me fool, boy?' is puzzled, but not without venom; the relationship between King and Fool is founded on love and compassion, which deepens as the scene proceeds, as if the King, sensing his alienation, admits the wise clown to Cordelia's place in his heart.

The King's fury with Goneril is at first a show of paternal wrath, but as the scene gains momentum, so the actor's reshaping of the text begins to work to his advantage, for he has built slowly and carefully to the hideous curse upon Goneril:

> Into her womb convey sterility,
> Dry up in her the organs of increase,
> And from her derogate body never spring
> A babe to honour her! If she must teem,
> Create her child of spleen, that it may live
> And be a thwart disfeatur'd torment to her,
> Let it stamp wrinkles in her brow of youth,
> With cadent tears fret channels in her cheeks,
> Turn all her mother's pains and benefits
> To laughter and contempt, that she may feel

> How sharper than a serpent's tooth it is
> To have a thankless child!

And from the air, arms upstretched, Lear clutches the physical parcel, as it were, of his savage imprecation, pulls it down and then, to be rid of it, hurls it at his ingrate daughter.

When the King next appears it is with the Fool and Kent, and he cannot keep from his voice a growing, agonising hurt, the pain of rejection. 'O let me not be mad, not mad, sweet heaven! Keep me in temper. I would not be mad!' It is spoken like the first distant echo of the wind; it is a vocal intimation of the storm; the thunder breaks from him on seeing Kent in the stocks. 'By Jupiter, I swear no,' is not idly spoken; it rumbles. Now the passion, the fury, the pain increase. In the scene with Regan, the old man is consumed with emotion, bordering on self-pity. 'I can scarce speak to thee,' he utters crying; tears are on the actor's cheeks. But the mood changes. Regan begins to advise her father on how he should behave; his response, 'Say, how is that?' contains danger, which quickly turns to incredulity at his daughter's persistence, then to irony, from irony once more to fury. It is an incredible display of shifting mood and emotion. 'How came my man i' the stocks?' he demands in a pathetic attempt to regain authority. The actor has laid the seeds of the King's madness in the instability of the old man's passions. The appeal to the gods, 'If you do love old men', is an appeal for sanity.

But Lear is more than a father spurned by ungrateful and ambitious children, more than a man whose reason is endangered. 'I gave you all,' he cries, and the actor speaks the line as though aware for the first time of the enormity of his own self-betrayal: it is the King, stripped bare of power and authority. His strength is drained in the argument concerning the number of his retinue, and again he is no more than man, aged, helpless. He turns his back on the audience, crouching low, sobbing into his hands. Regan asks, 'What need one?' Now cries the wind: 'O reason not the need' it pleads, and the actor's voice is burdened with piercing, whining overtones, then is entrapped in despair, '...let not women's weapons, water-drops, Stain my man's cheeks!' The vocal thunder cracks. 'No, you unnatural hags' is accompanied by an electrifying effect: Lear's cloak, a wide full circle, swirls in a petrified arc as the King turns upon his daughters, and the actor embarks on the major climax of Lear's mounting crisis.

> I will have such revenges on you both
> That all the world shall—I will do such things,—

What they are, yet I know not, but they shall be
The terrors of the earth. You think I'll weep;
No, I'll not weep: I have full cause of weeping.
But this heart shall break into a hundred thousand flaws,
Or ere I'll weep. O fool, I shall go mad!

The 'terrors of the earth', delivered in the nasal register, harsh and grating, is echoed by a thunderclap which seems to arrest the King's anger, for it is the gentle, pitiful frailty of 'O fool, I shall go mad' that finally takes him out onto the heath.

The storm that night was not, nor on any subsequent night would ever be, loud enough to drown the actor's voice which soars above wind and thunder and rain. 'Blow, winds, and crack your cheeks! rage! blow!' he commands, daring the elements, taunting them to overwhelm him. The actor has ascended into the cosmos. He obeys Granville-Barker's[7] injunction, 'Lear *is* the storm'. With Kent and Fool crouching at his feet, he stands against a tall obelisk, bathed in white light, the tempest in his mind communing with the outraged elements:

Let the great gods,
That keep this dreadful pother o'er our heads,
Find out their enemies now.

cracks like a mighty lightning flash and the power is spent; tones of child-like simplicity enter the actor's voice, so bereft of reason and majesty; all that remains is naked man, a tormented soul, sheltering in the hovel. 'Wilt break my heart?' asks Lear, before entering; it is not a king's question in the actor's reading, but man's, base and brought low, humiliated, humbled. For the actor is playing, too, for the scene that is to come with blind Gloucester. 'Ay, every inch a king,' jogs Lear's ancient memory of some glorious past. 'I am a king, my masters, you know that,' has a forlorn, hollow dignity, as the actor pulls the two knights with whom he plays the scene, to their knees, demanding of them meaningless obeisance. The more pitiful still the exit: 'Nay, if you get it, you shall get it with running. Sa, sa, sa, sa,' comes like an infantile game, devoid of reason, begging compassion.

The actor achieves sublime peace in his waking after the storm; an untroubled calm pervades his person. For one terrible moment he leads all to believe he may have regained his sanity as he recognises his Cordelia, but the hope passes.

The physical test of the actor is still to come and, incredibly, he has voice to rend the air. 'Howl! Howl! Howl!' catches yet again the wind, but it is the final terror. He carries Cordelia, the rope hanging from her neck; he places her on the ground, touches her face with infinite gentleness, distractedly tugs at the rope, and strokes her hair.

> And my poor fool is hang'd! No, no life!
> Why should a dog, a horse, a rat, have life,
> And thou no breath at all? O thou wilt come
> No more; never, never, never, never, never.

The actor treats the finality as if seeing a dark, awesome vision of eternity. The tragedy of King Lear has come almost to its end:

> The oldest hath borne most; we that are young
> Shall never see so much, nor live so long.

The solemn chords of the dead march are heard; the curtain falls.

The atmosphere back-stage had, all through the performance, been infected with auspicious excitement. Wolfit, when not on stage, behaved with strange, unaccustomed remoteness. Even during his change of cloak, which was always performed by Rosalind, he said nothing to her, but she could feel an unfamiliar tension in every muscle of his back.

The few in the audience that night bellowed their acclaim loud enough for twice their number. The shouts of 'bravo', the cheers, were an acknowledgement of a momentous performance. As Wolfit stood waiting for his turn to bow, he dabbed at his face with the moist chamois leather, downed the last drop of Guinness—he had drunk and sweated out eight bottles that evening. At last, his turn came: as was his custom, he pounded the curtain with his fist ('let 'em know you're coming' he used to say) and stepped out through the opening, into the light, clutching the curtain for support. The volume of acclaim washed over him; the actor who had not surrendered to the storm, surrendered now to his public. Wearily, he raised a hand for silence—it came at once. In a spent voice he offered his thanks for the way they had received 'the greatest tragedy in our language'. Exhausted, he withdrew, the sound of renewed cheering still ringing in his ears.

In the privacy of his dressing room, he undressed, unstuck beard and wig and, holding on to the back of a chair, instructed his dresser to sprinkle surgical spirit over his back and to rub hard with a towel.

That night the actor slept well.

1. **Rosalind** Iden (1911–90), Wolfit's wife from 1948.
2. **Jackson**, Barry, see p. 204. Wolfit led a company from the Birmingham Repertory Theatre on a tour of Canada in 1931.

3. **Watson**, Rosabel, theatre musician who died in 1959 aged 94.
4. **Maxon**, Eric, actor and costume designer.
5. **Goolden**, Richard (1895–1981), actor with a special talent for gentle pathos.
6. **Ayrton**, Randle, a famous Lear; Wolfit played Kent with him in 1936, and Ayrton gave Wolfit his 'Lear whip' (with which he threatened the Fool on 'Take heed, sirrah—the whip', 1.4.109) on hearing that he was going into management. See p. 203.
7. **Granville-Barker**. See p. 165. In the early pages of his *Preface* to the play (1927, etc.) he writes of Lear 'in the midst of... almost a part of' the storm.

[1944–5], Kenneth Tynan (1927–80) on Laurence Olivier (1907–89) at the New Theatre, London, as Richard III, in his *He that Plays the King* (1950), pp. 32–6.

KENNETH TYNAN was a witty and unorthodox theatre critic who worked for a number of periodicals, including, from 1954 to 1958, and then 1960 to 1963, *The Observer*. His book *He that Plays the King* and his highly allusive and determinedly brilliant reviews show the influence of his recent Oxford education as well as of the reviewing style of James Agate. Laurence Olivier invited him to become Literary Adviser to the National Theatre, a post he occupied from 1963 to 1969. Olivier's stage performance as Richard III formed the basis of his film (1955) of the play.

FROM a sombre and uninventive production this brooding, withdrawn player leapt into life, using the circumambient gloom[1] as his springboard. Olivier's Richard eats into the memory like acid into metal, but the total impression is one of lightness and deftness. The whole thing is taken at a speed baffling when one recalls how perfectly, even finically, it is articulated: it is Olivier's trick to treat each speech as a kind of plastic vocal mass, and not as a series of sentences whose import must be precisely communicated to the audience: the method is impressionist. He will seize on one or two phrases in each paragraph which, properly inserted, will unlock its whole meaning: the rest he discards, with exquisite idleness. To do this successfully he needs other people on the stage with him: to be ignored, stared past, or pushed aside during the lower reaches, and gripped and buttonholed when the wave rises to its crested climax. For this reason Olivier tends to fail in soliloquy—except when, as in the opening speech of *Richard*, it is directed straight at the audience, who then become his temporary foils. I thought, for example, that the night-piece before the battle sagged badly, in much the same way as the soliloquies in the *Hamlet* film[2] sagged. Olivier the actor needs reactors: just as electricity, *in vacuo*, is unseen, unfelt, and powerless.

I see that I have used the word 'trick' to describe this characteristic; I want to make it clear thus early that it is used in this book with connotations of applause and admiration. A 'trick', when we set about defining it and stop using it in the vaguely pejorative sense in which an unsuccessful actor will always describe a successful one as 'a bundle of tricks', is nothing more despicable than a unique piece of technique, a special catch of the voice, tilt of the head, or manual gesture. It becomes offensive only when it is used in a part irrelevant to the aspect or aspects of the actor's personality which it represents: for instance, if Olivier were to use his famous 'traffic-policeman' pose while playing Morell in *Candida*,[3] it would almost certainly jar, and would thus become a 'mannerism'. But tricks can quite legitimately be used to eke out dull parts or heighten good ones. It is surprising how many of the most exciting and exhilarating performances one has ever seen are written off by the profession as 'naughty—terrible naughty'. By this is meant that the actor has outstripped the classic norm of part-interpretation, and imported ingenuities and subtleties of his own; he is naughty as a schoolboy is who asks unanswerable questions. (For the standard exemplar of naughtiness, look at Charles Laughton.[4]) Tricks are to acting what phrase-making is to poetry; within a good formal contour they are luminous gems. The opposite of a 'tricky' or 'naughty' actor is a 'lovely' or 'charming' one, by which the profession means that in him it recognizes a player severely enough type-cast and self-effacing enough not to be counted as a possible rival.

Craggy and beetlebrowed, Olivier's face is not especially mobile: he acts chiefly with his voice. In Richard it is slick, taunting, and curiously casual; nearly impersonal, 'smooth as sleekstone',[5] patting and pushing each line into shape. Occasionally he tips his animal head back and lets out a gurgling avuncular cackle, a good-humoured snarl: and then we see the over-riding mephitic good humour of the man, the vulgar joy he takes in being a clever upstart. Ingrowing relish at his complotting kindles him, making him smoulder with laughter. We laugh, too; and some attempt has been made to prove that we laugh too sympathetically. T. C. Worsley[6] in the *New Statesman* very ably took up this cudgel, and said that Richard's humour should arouse the chuckle that is born of nervous fear, not the belly-laugh. Now in ideal terms this argument is not refutable: it would be impossible to *demonstrate* that though no single detail or trick in the whole performance is in itself macabre in the correct manner, the total gesture is one of unpleasant and vulgar nastiness: in the same way an obscene statue can be made of pure gold. The kind of laugh Worsley is objecting to and I am supporting is that which Olivier gets when the head of Hastings is brought on in a bag: he peeps in with wistful intentness, looking almost elegiac—then, after a pause, hurriedly turns the bag as he realizes he has been looking at the head upside down. That gets its laugh, and it is, I agree, not unsympathetic to Richard. Only afterwards are we struck with the afterthought that we have just laughed at a very foul piece of casual dissembling: and we are rather ashamed. What, in fact, would Mr. Worsley have us substitute? a crazy peal of laughter? or that oldest of film-Gestapo tricks, a slow, meditative, malevolent smile? The point about evil is surely that one does not notice until afterwards that it is evil at all: it is a door through which, unwitting, we pass, and which we observe only as it slams behind us. To me cats, sunflowers, white tiles in suburban kitchens, urinating horses, silk-scarved youths on Sunday, marionettes and glades of fir trees, all innocent in themselves, are unaccountably among the harbingers of evil. I say all this to indicate that an evil thing need not be horrid or repellent in itself: it must deceive us into thinking it good. To tempt at all, Satan must charm us. I do not think it would be true to say that Olivier's Richard ever makes us warm to him; we never feel delight or admiration; we simply laugh, and that implies neither encouragement nor hostility, but mere acceptance of an act performed. I think of Sidney: '...though laughter may come *with* delight, yet cometh it not *of* delight'.[7] The two things are different: and Olivier rightly taps only the former.

In this Richard was enshrined Blake's[8] conception of active, energetic evil, in all its wicked richness. A lithe performance, black at heart and most astutely mellow in appearance, it is full of baffling, irrational subtleties which will please while they puzzle me as long as I go to theatres. I remember the deep concern, as of a bustling spinster, with which Olivier grips his brother George and says, with sardonic, effeminate intentness: 'We are not safe, Clarence; we are *not* safe'; while, even as he speaks, the plot is laid which will kill the man. The persistent *bonhomie* of middle age shines in his face as he jests with his chosen victims: how often he skirts the footlights, his eyes tipped skyward, on some especially ironic aside: with what icy disregard he slights his too ambitious minion Buckingham! 'I am not in the giving vein to-day:' the words fall like drops of frozen dew. The rejection of Buckingham is beautifully prepared, too, in the moment at the end of Shakespeare's Act III after Gloster has been coaxed into accepting the crown. From the window in Baynard's castle where he stands, Richard leaps down, tossing his prayer book over his shoulder, to embrace Buckingham and exult over their triumph. In mid-career he stops, mindful of his new majesty; and instead of a joyful hug, Buckingham sees the iron-clad hand of his friend extended to him to be kissed, and behind it, erect in horrid disdain, the top-heavy figure of the King of England.

Vulgar pride is an important point of departure for many of this Richard's major effects. The monstrous, inquisitive nose (aquiline in elephantiasis), boorishly intruded where least welcomed, emphasizes it, and the doglike sniff and cock of eye when he points a comic line. In movements he is gawkily impulsive, with a lurching limp reminiscent of the stage gait of Mr. Jimmy James:[9] only the arms, wonderfully free and relaxed, are beautiful. He flings them out and they come to rest in grace. The secret of the passion Olivier generates is that intuition and impulse, not premeditation, control Richard's actions. The vulgar heart beats through it all: with a marvellous tact he suggests its presence in the contemptuous emphasis he gives to: '. . . you, *Lord* Rivers and *Lord* Grey'. Secure in triumph, conscious of his failings, he revels in exposing them, since none may gainsay him. And when the end approaches, his hoarse, strangled roar for a horse sums up all the impotent fury of a Machiavellian who must yield up his life and the fruits of his precise conspiring because of an accident of battle. To be vanquished by the ill luck of being unseated is a final ignominy to this enormous swindler. His broken sword clutched by the blade in both hands, he whirls, dreadfully constricted, and thrashes about with animal ferocity, writhing for absolute hate; he dies, arms and legs thrusting and kicking in savage, incommunicable agony, stabbing at air.

When Olivier revived this production in 1949 with a vastly inferior supporting company, the part of Lady Anne was given to Vivien Leigh,[10] who quavered through the lines in a sort of rapt oriental chant. It was a bad performance, coldly kittenish, but it made the wooing credible, since this silly woman would probably have believed anything. And Olivier managed even to draw pathos from the grisly courtship, and put me in mind of Sidney's elegiacs:

> Unto a caitiff wretch, whom long affliction holdeth,
> And now fully believes hope to be quite vanished,
> Grant, grant yet a look to the last moment of his anguish.[11]

For a moment the hunchback *histrio* joined the stricken ranks of repulsed Renaissance lovers, and one could have wept for him.

Has anyone, I wonder, discovered this neat summary of the general significance of the history plays? It comes in Gorki's *Lower Depths*:[12]

LUKA: Everybody is trying to be boss, and is threatening everybody else with all kinds of punishment—and still there's no order in life ... and no cleanliness—
BUBNOV: All the world likes order, but some people's brains aren't fit for it. All the same—the room should be swept. ...

1. **circumambient gloom**, from the poem 'Mycerinus' by Matthew Arnold (1822–88).
2. *Hamlet* **film**. Olivier's film was first shown in 1948.
3. *Candida*, the play (1897) by G. B. Shaw (see p. 132).
4. **Laughton**, Charles (1899–1962), British-born actor who became an American citizen and famous film star.
5. **'smooth as sleekstone'** [not identified].
6. **Worsley**, T. C. See p. 244.
7. **Sidney**, Sir Philip (1554–86); the quotation comes from towards the end of his *An Apology for Poetry*, published posthumously in 1595.
8. **Blake**, William (1757–1827): 'Evil is the active springing from Energy', *The Marriage of Heaven and Hell (c.*1793).
9. **James**, Jimmy (died 1965 aged 71), comedian.
10. **Leigh**, Vivien (1913–67), distinguished stage and screen actress married to Olivier.
11. **Sidney's elegiacs**. These are the opening lines of the first poem in Book Three of *Arcadia* (published posthumously in 1595).
12. *Lower Depths*, a play by Maxim Gorki (1868–1936) first acted in 1902; the quotation comes towards the end of Act One.

[1945–6], Kenneth Tynan on Laurence Olivier and Ralph Richardson (1902–83, knighted 1947), in *Henry IV, Part One* and *Part Two*, directed by John Burrell for the Old Vic Company at the New Theatre, London, from his *He that Plays the King* (1950), pp. 48–53.

FROM a production so unobtrusive that at times it looked positively mousy, three very great pieces of acting emerged. The Old Vic was now at its height: the watershed had been reached, and one of those rare moments in the theatre had arrived when drama paused, took stock of all that it had learnt since Irving, and then produced a monument in celebration. It is surprising, when one considers it, that English acting should have reached up and seized a laurel crown in the middle of a war, and that the plays in which the prize was won should have been plays of battle, tumult, conspiracy and death, as the histories are. There was a bad atmosphere then amongst the acting clubs of London—an atmosphere such as one finds in the senior common-rooms of the women's colleges at Oxford: an air of pugnacious assurance and self-sufficiency mixed with acrid misogyny. There were roughly two groups of actors: the elder, who seemed to be suffering from thyroid deficiency, a condition which induces a blunt and passive sedentariness in the sufferer: and the very young ones, afflicted by the opposite sickness, thyroid excess, whose symptoms are emaciation and nervous constriction. The good, mature players were silent: the state of society had tied their hands, and they tied their own tongues. It was left to Richardson and Olivier to sum up English acting in themselves; and this was what, in *Henry IV*, they achieved.

Richardson's Falstaff was not a *comic* performance: it was too rich and many-sided to be crammed into a single word. The humour of it, as in Max Beerbohm's prose, was in the texture: there were no deliberate farcical effects. This was the down-at-heel dignity of W. C. Fields[1] translated into a nobler language: here was a Falstaff whose principal attribute was not his fatness but his knighthood. He was Sir John first, and Falstaff second, and let every cock-a-hoop young dog beware. The spirit behind all the rotund nobility was spry and elastic: that, almost, of what Skelton in a fine phrase called 'friskajolly younkerkins';[2] there was also, working with great slyness but great energy, a sharp business sense: and, when the situation called for it, great wisdom and melancholy ('Peace, good Doll! do not speak like a death's-head: do not bid me remember my end' was done with most moving authority). Each word emerged with immensely careful articulation, the lips forming it lovingly and then spitting it forth: in moments of passion, the wild white halo of hair stood angrily up and the eyes rolled majestically: and in rage one noticed a slow meditative relish taking command: 'Marry, there is another indictment upon thee, for suffering flesh to be eaten in thy house, contrary to the law; for the which I think—thou—wilt—howl': the last four words with separate thrice-chewed pungency. Richardson never rollicked or slobbered or staggered: it was not a sweaty fat man, but a dry and dignified one. As the great belly moved, step following step with great finesse lest it overtopple, the arms flapped fussily at the sides as if to paddle the body's bulk along. It was deliciously and subtly funny, not riotously so: from his height of pomp Falstaff was chuckling at himself: it was not we alone, laughing at him. He had good manners and also that respect for human dignity which prevented him from openly showing his boredom at the inanities of Shallow and Silence: he had only recently sunk from the company of kings to the company of heirs-apparent. None of the usual epithets for Falstaff applied to Richardson: he was not often jovial, laughed seldom, belched never. In disgrace, he affected the mask of a sulky schoolboy, in the manner of Charles Laughton:[3] in command, he would punch his wit at the luckless heads of his comrades, and their admiration would forbid response. The rejection scene at the end of Part 2 came off heartrendingly well: with his back to the audience Richardson thumped forward to welcome the new king, his whilom jackanapes: and after the key-cold rebuke which is his answer, the old man turned, his face red and working in furious *tics* to hide his tears. The immense pathos of his reassuring words to Shallow even now wets my eyes: 'I shall be sent for soon at night.' He hurried, whispered through the line very energetically, as if the whole matter were of no consequence: the emptiness of complete collapse stood awfully behind it. It was pride, not feasting and foining, that laid this Falstaff low: the youthful, hubristic heart inside the corporeal barrel had flown too high, and must be crushed. Cyril Connolly[4] might have been speaking of this performance when he said: 'Imprisoned in every fat man a thin one is wildly signalling to be let out'—let out, and slaughtered. Beside this Falstaff, Nicholas Breton's[5] picture of a drunkard seems almost blasphemous: 'a tub of swill, a spirit of sleep, a picture of a beast and a monster of a man'.

Enough has already been written of Olivier's Hotspur, that ferocious darling of war. With the roughness and heedlessness of the warrior chieftain, he mixed the heavyhanded tenderness of the very virile husband: and knotted the performance into a unity by a trick, the stammer which prefaced every word beginning with the letter 'w'. This clever device fitted perfectly with the over-anxiousness, the bound-burstingness, the impotent eagerness of the character. The long speech of explanation to the king about the unransomed prisoners, beginning 'My liege, I did deny no prisoners', is essentially an apology: for this Hotspur it was an aggressive explosion of outraged innocence:

> ...for it made me *mad*   [almost a shriek]
> To see him shine so brisk and smell so sweet
> And talk so like a waiting-gentlewoman
> Of guns and drums and w—w—

(Here the face almost burst for frenzy: the actor stamped the ground to loosen the word from his mouth. Finally, in a convulsion of contempt, it sprang out)

> w-*wounds*—God save the mark!

This impediment dovetailed so well with Hotspur's death that one could not escape concluding that Olivier had begun his interpretation of the part at the end and worked backwards: the dying speech ends thus:

> ...no, Percy, thou art dust,
> And food for—
> HENRY: For worms, brave Percy.

I need not add that Olivier died in the throes of uttering that maddening, elusive consonant.

The most treasurable scenes in these two productions were those in Shallow's orchard: if I had only half an hour more to spend in theatres, and could choose at large, no hesitation but I would have these. Richardson's performance, coupled with that of Miles Malleson[6] as Silence, beak-nosed, pop-eyed, many-chinned and mumbling, and Olivier as Shallow, threw across the stage a golden autumnal veil, and made the idle sporadic chatter of the lines glow with the same kind of delight as Gray's *Elegy*.[7] There was a sharp scent of plucked crab-apples, and of pork in the larder: one got the sense of life-going-on-in-the-background, of rustling twigs underfoot and the large accusing eyes of cows, staring through the twilight. Shakespeare never surpassed these scenes in the vein of pure naturalism: the subtly criss-crossed counterpoint of the opening dialogue between the two didderers, which skips between the price of livestock at market and the philosophic fact of death ('Death, saith the Psalmist, is certain; all must die'), is worked out with fugal delicacy: the talk ends with Shallow's unanswered rhetorical question: 'And is old Double dead?' No reply is necessary: the stage is well and truly set, and any syllable more would be superfluous. The flavour of sharp masculine kindness Olivier is adept in: for me the best moment in his 'Hamlet' film was the pat on the head for the players' performing dog which accompanied the line: 'I am glad to see thee well.' And it was in the very earth of this Gloucestershire orchard. Olivier was the Old Satyr in this Muses' Elizium;[8] 'Through his lean chops a chattering he doth make, which stirs his staring, beastly-drivell'd beard.' This Shallow (pricked with yet another nose, a loony apotheosis of the hook-snout he wore as Richard) is a crapulous, paltering scarecrow of a man, withered up like the slough of a snake; but he has quick, commiserating eyes and the kind of delight in dispensing food and drink that one associates with a favourite aunt. He pecks at the lines, nibbles at them like a parrot biting on a nut; for all his age, he darts here and there nimbly enough, even skittishly; forgetting nothing, not even the pleasure of Falstaff's page, that 'little tiny thief'. The keynote of the performance is old-maidishness, agitated and pathetically anxious to make things go with a swing: a crone-like pantomime dame, you might have thought, were it not for the beady delectation that steals into his eyes at the mention of sex. (Shallow was, as Falstaff later points out, 'as lecherous as a monkey'.) His fatuous repetitions are those of importunate female decrepitude: he nags rather than bores. Sometimes, of course, he loses the use of one or more of his senses: protesting, over the table, that Falstaff must not leave, he insists, emphasizing the words by walking his fingers over the board: 'I will not excuse you, sir; you shall not be excused; excuses shall not be admitted; there is no excuse shall serve; you shall not be excused'—and after his breathless panic of hospitality, he looks hopefully up: but Falstaff has long since gone. Shallow had merely forgotten to observe his departure: and the consequent confusion of the man, as he searches with his eyes for his vanished guest, is equalled only by his giggling embarrassment at finding him standing behind him.

Of all the wonderful work Olivier did in this and the previous Old Vic season, I liked nothing more than this. A part of this actor's uniqueness lies in the restricted demands he makes on his audience's rational and sensual capacities. Most actors invite the spectator either to pass a *moral* judgment on the characters they are representing; or to pass a *physical* judgment on their own appearance. A normal actor playing a moderately sympathetic part will go all out to convince the audience that he is a thoroughly good man, morally impeccable; playing a villain, he will force them to see the enormity of the man's sins. He will translate the character into the terms of a bad nineteenth-century novel. An attractive actor playing the part of a *jeune premier* will try primarily to arouse the admiration of the women and the envy of the men; a player of farce will rely chiefly on grotesque make-up to establish the character for him. But most actors do insist on a judgment of one kind or another: and they are better or worse actors according to the degree to which it is obvious that they are *insisting*. Olivier makes no such attempts to insist, and invites no moral response: simply the thing he is shall make him live. It is a rare discretion, an ascetic tact which none but he dares risk.

1. **Fields**, W. C. (1880–1946), American comedian and film actor.

2. **Skelton**, John (?1460–1529), poet and satirist. The allusion is to his 'A Replication Against Certain Young Scholars Abjured of Late', which Tynan may have read in *The Complete Poems*, ed. Philip Henderson (1931, 2nd edn 1948), p. 415.

3. **Laughton**, Charles. See p. 234.

4. **Connolly**, Cyril (1903–74), literary critic and journalist; the quotation is from *The Unquiet Grave* (by 'Palinurus', first published in *Horizon*, 1944; revised 1945; 1973 edn, p. 58).

5. **Breton,** Nicholas (?1545–?1626), poet and prose writer. The allusion is to 'A Drunkard', No. 42 in Breton's *The Good and the Badde* (1616). Tynan might have read it in *A Book of Characters* ed. Richard Aldington (n.d.).

6. **Malleson,** Miles (1888–1969), actor and dramatist who specialized in eccentric comedy roles.

7. **Gray,** Thomas (1716–71); the allusion is to his 'Elegy in a Country Churchyard', completed in 1750.

8. **Muses' Elizium,** a poem by Michael Drayton (1563–1631); the quotation is from 'The Tenth Nimphall'.

⫷℘⫸℘⫷℘⫸℘⫷℘⫸℘⫷℘⫸℘⫷℘⫸℘⫷℘⫸℘⫷℘⫸℘⫷℘⫸℘⫷℘⫸℘⫷℘⫸℘⫷℘⫸℘⫷℘⫸℘⫷℘⫸℘⫷℘⫸℘⫷℘⫸℘

[1947], Kenneth Tynan on Donald Wolfit and Frederick Valk (1895–1956) in *Othello* at the Savoy Theatre, London, in his *He that Plays the King* (1950), pp. 84–8.

FOR Wolfit, see p. 224. Valk, German-born, worked with the German Theatre in Prague from 1933 to 1939 when he left for Britain. He learned to play in English, though with a strong accent.

To be present, to assist at the spinning out of events which will surely plume up and refurbish the tapestry of Western culture— is not this a pleasant thing? Had it not been fine to have snapped up and savoured the first copy of *The Rape of the Lock*[1] as it came, cool and acid and fair, from the press? To have seen and shaken at the face of Swift[2] as he penned the last cruel, grimy pages of *Gulliver*? To have sat by and quivered at the embarrassed wriggles of some poor questioner, swallowed up in the terrific finality of a Johnsonian[3] 'No, sir'? My point, when at last it comes wheeling round to us, is that I have seen a public event of constellated magnitude and radiance. I have watched a transfusion of bubbling hot blood into the invalid frame of our drama. Some, I am told, boast of having seen the Chicago fire;[4] others of having escaped the Quetta[5] earthquake by the merest pebble's breadth; and I have known men swell as they recalled the tremendous and bloody exploits at Hiroshima.[6] My vaunt is this: I have lived for three hours on the red brink of a volcano, and the crust of lava crumbles still from my feet. I have witnessed a performance of *Othello* in which Donald Wolfit played Iago, and Frederick Valk Othello. How hushed I was! How young and how chastened: so much so that for days afterwards, long after I had sent my final, particular roar of 'Bravo' coursing and resounding about the theatre, I could speak of little but these twin giants, and the authentic ring of their titles to greatness. In the mind's middle distance, I think I perceive that other players flickered intermittently across that bare stage—that flat scene of astounding war; I can, if I screw up my memory, hear them now, grunting and twittering and shrilling. Who they were, I have not the slightest notion. They lie *perdu*: an irrelevant flurry of colour and dim noise in the midst of which gigantic things were going forward. They it was, as I think, who buzzed and rattled when the big gladiators fell fatigued. I should prefer to ignore them, thus dismissively.

Othello is, of course, a moral play: rigidly and cruelly so; though I confess I had inclined to skirt glibly round this central part of its structure and fortification. I should not have neglected Johnson, who said: 'We learn from Othello this very useful moral, not to make an unequal match.... I think Othello has almost more moral than any other play.'[7] What paroxysms of fright and foreboding must have consumed Shakespeare's Jacobean audiences! Here, proudly booming before them, was a monstrous blackamoor, a black gargoyle, concealing within him racks on which to stretch himself and those about him until the excruciated lyric cry was released; and bearing in his baggage explosive coils of taut, dangerous springs. Anything might happen while this nigger devil yet lived. Horrors and Domdaniel[8] excess crowded the horizon. I had never fully shared this expectancy of terror until Mr. Valk pressed me, at pistol point, to accept it.

Shakespeare, perhaps for fear of too much alarming his spectators, has dealt very unfairly with Othello. Up to the crucial temptation scene (III, iii) he utters only 240 lines of verse to Iago's 574. And Mr. Wolfit took full advantage of this early ascendancy. What a muscular actor he is! Yet his ponderous gait contrasts oddly with his rasping whine of a voice. I need not celebrate again the virtues of his Iago: its stout craft, its unhurried certainty and precision. I would append only a tiny animadversion, upon his treatment of poetry. To listen to Mr. Wolfit speaking good verse is an experience analogous to watching a rebellious rogue elephant walking a tight-rope. It is enjoyable because it is very, very strange. Like a prize-fighter nursing a young flower, like John Steinbeck's Lenny[9] petting a puppy, so is Mr. Wolfit when a line of poetry is delivered into his hands. He has doubtless cultivated a love for the stuff, but I trace hints of an unwilling courtship that went badly against a rather uneven grain. This quibble apart, I salute a performance which laid quite bare that 'diseased intellectual activity' of which Hazlitt[10] spoke: a performance worth seeing if only to hear Mr. Wolfit giving the hapless word 'Nature' its full eight or nine syllables.

But this was Mr. Valk's private adventure, no other near, and we were soon made to realize it. In appearance he was quintessential teddy-bear; 'not' (I hear Coleridge[11] grumbling) 'thoroughbred gentleman enough to play Othello'. No aristocracy of bearing; no regularity of profile; in short, no flair. Yet temperamentally (and this is the unseekable key) there is no other such tragic player on our stages. This was (to borrow another phrase from Coleridge) Shakespeare by flashes of lightning, with a pall of heavy thunder over all, and a sullen Southern sky. I cannot believe there is blood in the man's veins: it must be some vile compound of corrosive venoms, arcane and nameless; some crazy river having its dayspring in spleen, and adulterated with black bile. Why, he was to be touched into mad, lambent flame in an instant; he broke every law of our stage-craft, this berserk Colossus. Following the imperious rules of his agony, his voice would crack and pause, minute-long, in mid-line: and there would be speechless signallings the while, and rushes as of a wild bull. Then the voice would rise and swoop again into unknown pastures of word-meaning, scooping up huge, vasty syllables of grief as though carving an ancient bed of clay. He seemed, at times, almost to sing, so unlike our custom was his elocution; a bully's song, a bludgeoner's song, yet its strains moved to pity, as great verse should. I shall see him always in a dim dusk-light singing impious lullabies to soothe his own congenital disquiet. You could almost hear thin skins splitting and half-shut minds banging and locking themselves around you: the theatre was perturbed, but pin-still.

Usually I go to Shakespeare for the poetry, worn though it now is: there seems to be little else, in an averagely good performance, to enrapture the mind. Under Valk, I discover, verse collapses. I have heard it plausibly objected to him that, with his Czech emphases, he loses all the music in words. Now I believe that words are neither harmonious nor discordant in themselves: the verse is either smooth and end-stopped or it is not. It is very hard to write an unmelodious heroic couplet. But this kind of minuteness is blankly impertinent when Valk is acting, piercing to the core of elemental and therefore wordless things, willing to tear a heart from sheer granite. There was no time for R.A.D.A. modulations and exquisiteness: a man was hacking a horrid path for himself, and it was not pretty, or fanciful: it was inviolable rage, and there were gulfs awash with tears opening all round him. He stood, petrifact, bellowing in their dreadful midst. Cadence, and that careful forethought by which English actors contrive to ignore the existence of consonants, went quite by the board. The highest praise I can summon up for Valk is that he gave what could by no standards be described as 'a beautiful performance': for beauty is regular and predictable, and this was neither. The fury of sound had overcome him: yet with grave *naïveté* he seemed to be listening to himself as he spoke. And when the time came, and Chaos returned, this three-hours' sojourner in Olympian charnels lifted his great lion's head and sent his poor voice piping into the vaulted roof above him: 'Oh the pity of it, Yaggo—the pee-ee-eety of ee-eet!' You could hear the terrible, derisive echo.

The play, the words, all plays, all words were too small for this passion. It transcended the prescribed limits of acted drama, and strode boldly through Hell-lake and bade the white-clad recording imps take notice of foul disorders and evil conceits; of the climax of a great anguish; of the dilapidation of a sturdy tower; of the molten intoxication of a warrior and demi-god. We who saw these things passing were caught up with Valk to his own pinnacles, and when the curtain fell, it was as if an end had been put to the tales of mortal suffering; after this death, there could come no more refinement of woe. The sense of relief preceded the permanent sense of awe: the full tragic action was communicated like the hot breath of the ferocious antique gods.

I cannot tell whether this was a good Othello. I do not even know whether it was a good stage performance. Indeed, at this distance of time I would not care to say that it was a stage performance at all. Except, of course, that I know it chose to be made known in a public theatre, and that might have been accident: lightning may strike anywhere, and even the Savoy 'scapes not the thunderbolt.[12] With every line he uttered and motion he compassed, Mr. Valk left behind him a heap of rules triumphantly smashed and discarded; he trampled on them, and took glory from it. ('There is no such thing', I have heard him insist, 'as an ungainly position.') He battered Othello to dust, and I wish him long life to pursue his angry stampede across other plains: let us see his Lear, with Mr. Wolfit's Edmund at his elbow. And here, I am sure, is at last an adequate Timon. The thick reverberations of that great voice, the killing sureness of its every tremor towards the avalanche; the athletic pathos of that giant frame in motion, stuttering, lurching, toppling; the rhetorical clawings of those hands—gifts like these must not set their bounds in one performance. They must expand, and then Mr. Valk may do still more to strike us free of the old formal bonds of dramatic decency.

But I am hoarse with protest. To pray that there may be no quick cessation of his energies were, as Johnson might have built the phrase, a superfluous genuflexion. Such power is lawless, and bears kinship with the elements. As Chesterton said of Mr. Belloc's[13] voice:

> Nor does it cease. Nor will it cease.

There is nothing perishable in this great Czech.

('After a long succession of noises; as the fall of waters, or the beating of forge-hammers, the hammers beat and the water roars in the imagination long after the first sounds have ceased to affect it: and they die away at last by gradations which are scarcely perceptible.' Thus Burke.[14] I am yet conscious of no such slipping away. But Burke is, I suppose, right: those hammerstrokes and topless cascades will cease, in long time, to roar in my ears and bewitch me.)

1. *The Rape of the Lock*, satirical poem by Alexander Pope (1688–1744), first published in 1711.

2. **Swift**, Jonathan (1667–1745); *Gulliver's Travels* appeared in 1726.

3. **Johnsonian**, alluding to the forceful utterances of Samuel Johnson (1709–84).

4. **the Chicago fire**, a disastrous fire in 1871.

5. **Quetta**, a city in Pakistan almost destroyed by an earthquake in June 1935.

6. **Hiroshima**, Japanese city largely destroyed as the result of the first atomic bomb on 6 August 1945.

7. **Johnson.** The quotation is from James Boswell's *Life of Samuel Johnson Ll.D.* (1791), Everyman edition, 2 vols. (1906, etc.), ii. 28; the last phrase should read 'has more moral than almost any play'.

8. **Domdaniel**, the hall or house of Daniel, 'used by Carlyle in the sense of "infernal cave", "den of iniquity"' (*OED*).

9. **Lenny**, a character in the novel *Of Mice and Men* (1937) by John Steinbeck (1902–68).

10. **Hazlitt.** See pp. 9–10, 38. The quotation is from his essay on *Othello* in his *Characters of Shakespere's Plays* (1817, etc.).

11. **Coleridge**, Samuel Taylor. See p. 9. The first reference is to Coleridge's reported description of Othello as 'noble, generous, open-hearted' (ed. Raysor, ii. 227); the second is to his description of Edmund Kean's acting, recorded in *Table Talk*, 27 April 1823.

12. **'scapes not the thunderbolt** 'Some innocents 'scape not the thunderbolt', *Antony and Cleopatra*, 2.5.77.

13. **Chesterton**, Gilbert Keith (1874–1936); **Belloc**, Hilaire (1870–1953). I have not been able to find a reference for this.

14. **Burke**, Edmund (1729–97). The quotation is from the section on 'Infinity' in Part 2 of his 'An Essay on the Sublime and Beautiful' (1756); I have corrected minor errors.

23 July 1949, T. C. Worsley (1907–77) on Tyrone Guthrie's
production of *Henry VIII*, at the Memorial Theatre, Stratford-
upon-Avon, from *The New Statesman*, reprinted in his *The
Fugitive Art: Dramatic Commentaries 1947–1951* (1952), pp. 87–91.

A LONG, detailed, and eulogistic review of this production by Muriel St Clare
Byrne appears in *Shakespeare Survey 3* (Cambridge, 1950), pp. 120–9. T. C.
Worsley wrote mainly for the *New Statesman* and the *Financial Times*.

THERE are two Tyrone Guthries, as there are at least two of most of us.
There is Mr. Tyrone Guthrie, one of our leading producers, an
original artist with a most imaginative mind, a great feeling for the visual,
a highly developed sense of theatre. Then there is his *alter ego*, Master
Tony Guthrie, let us call him, an inky urchin, with a fourth-form sense of
humour and a violent self-destructive streak: the kind of urchin who,
having completed a lovely neat fair copy, can never resist the fleeting
impulse to spatter it with blobs of ink. These two Guthries fight it out
in the new production of *Henry VIII*, the last play to be added to the
Stratford Repertory this season. It begins as a close race. Or rather—more
exactly—those who have put their money on 'producer's theatre,' and on
Mr. Guthrie the artist, are able for quite a long time to remain hopeful.
The urchin keeps putting himself in front, it is true; but the artist is also
running magnificently. Style, they used to tell us, will always win in the
end. And Mr. Guthrie gives a great display of style. But, as so often, they
told us wrong: style doesn't win in the end. By the three-quarters mark it is
no use even hoping: it is clear that the urchin will win in an easy canter.

By tradition *Henry VIII* is a producer's play. Its pageants, masques and
pomps invite a rich use of crowd movement and display: Mr. Guthrie is a
master of this. Miss Tanya Moiseiwitsch[1] has provided dresses both
appropriate and enchanting, rich velvety blacks, greys and yellows for
the Court in contrast to the scarlets and purples of the Church. The eye,
as is common with this school of production, is amply indulged. Then
again, though the main characters in the play are rather sketchily drawn,
and though the dramatic interest is in danger of running down towards
the end unless it is carefully managed, there are five or six excellent
dramatic scenes; three of them at least are handled by Mr. Guthrie with
a sure touch so as to bring out the maximum of tension. There are here, in
short, the elements of a really fine production.

But that is to forget little Master Guthrie, who is also a producer. He is
the leader of what we may call the 'Wouldn't-it-be-fun (just for a change)'

school. Master Guthrie is continuously being visited by bright, clever, silly notions. And Mr. Guthrie senior, like an over-indulgent parent, never seems able to deny this tiresome child anything. Wouldn't it be fun if, when Cranmer is making the great prophecy speech on one side of the stage, the nurse carrying the infant Princess Elizabeth on the other side, should have a fit of sneezing? Oh wouldn't it be fun! And in this silly gag goes. Wouldn't it be fun if, in the Court scene, our attention should be distracted from the speeches by the noise of the scriveners driving their quills over the parchment? And then couldn't Henry come ponderously down from his throne and push a clerk off his stool? And couldn't some-one else imitate him and do it again? 'But aren't the speeches rather hard to follow meanwhile?' Never mind. Anyhow they're very boring. We must try to *make* something of this scene.

It is really the most perverse production. For every felicity, an ink-blob. For every build-up, a clever silly let-down. I tried hard to explain it all to myself as some sort of attempt to catch an Elizabethan lack of sophistica-tion in the middle of their pomp. I tried hard not to be distracted by the fidgetings, the bum-scratchings, the gossipings, the restless human inter-est business that keeps filling every corner of the stage—choir-masters tumbling over backwards, old men being chased like frightened hens, first gentleman's comic teeth, and so on, and so on. I strained my ears while important speeches were mumbled by characters turned deliberately up-stage. And I even extracted for a time a great deal of pleasure from the performance by a most determined Will to Enjoy and a firm belief in Mr. Guthrie the artist.

But finally I had to give in. The first bitter blow came with the brilliantly handled climax to the court scene where Henry perceives that the cardinals are playing some deep ecclesiastical game of their own: and the shadow at last falls on Wolsey. For the King suddenly summons over to his side from among the indiscriminate crowd at the back, Wolsey's successor-to-be, Cranmer. Excellently done, but for one revealing detail: the Cranmer is made a funny character with a facial twitch. And then it looked as if the producer were simply chucking in his hand, and not even trying to tackle the problem of play as a whole. He is just having fun, and will treat the closing scenes as mere burlesque. And so he did—the King degenerating into a sort of Charles Laughton[2] clown, and the vital scene of his overlooking the Council's treatment of Cranmer wantonly cut. For with a weak Cranmer, it wouldn't make sense.

That brings us to the interval, after which there is another brilliant patch which revives our hopes, that magnificent scene where King and nobles begin the baiting of Wolsey. We are left free for almost ten whole minutes to admire Mr. Quayle's[3] ponderous but cunning King, Mr. Andrews'[4] purse-lipped Wolsey and to feel the drama mounting, mounting, mounting. But is it allowed to be crowned with the fine ranting rhetoric of the 'Farewell to Greatness' passage? Oh no. We must have something different. So they decide to whisper this speech into what used to be the orchestra pit (which is now occupied by halberdiers and comic choirmen, waiting to dash on).

On my way home, with this piece of clever/silly production very much in my mind, I decided to start a new school of 'Wouldn't-it-be-fun (just for a change)' dramatic criticism which would just pop down any clever/silly idea that came into its head. For instance I began imagining the dialogue at the rehearsal of this scene as it might be invented by a 'Wouldn't-it-be-fun (just for a change)' dramatic critic.

Mr. Andrews, an experienced Shakespearian actor, advances towards the footlights and delivers a speech in the fine musical voice with which nature has endowed him.

Mr. Andrews: Farewell, a long farewell to all my greatness!
This is the state of man; today he puts forth
The tender leaves of hope, tomorrow blossoms,
And bears his blushing honours....

Mr. Guthrie: No! No! Sorry, old boy, we can't have *that*.

Mr. A.: No?

Mr. G.: No! Léon Quartermaine[5] speaks a whole speech straight in the first act as Buckingham.

Mr. A.: Sorry, old boy. I thought this was the big speech.

Mr. G.: So it is, old boy. That's the trouble. Everyone will know it. We must do something *different*.

Mr. A.: What do you suggest?

Mr. G.: Let's think now. Something *new*.... You couldn't be drunk, I suppose?

Mr. A.: Well....

Mr. G.: No, I've got it. A stroke.

Mr. A.: A stroke?

Mr. G.: Yes, you die quite soon after, remember? Have a stroke at...let me see, 'Cromwell, I charge thee, fling away ambition....'

Mr. A.: That comes at the very end, old boy. There are about a hundred lines to get through first.

Mr. G.: So there are.... Tell you what. Just sit down where you are and throw 'em away.

Mr. A.: All of them?

Mr. G.: Why not? Wouldn't it be fun! Just sit down. There. That's right. Tap with your ring on the floor...to show stress, old boy. That's it. Now— throw it away.

Mr. A.: (*Mumbles three lines before the producer interrupts*).

Mr. G.: Sorry to keep stopping you, old boy.

Mr. A.: That's all right.

Mr. G.: There's just one thing. You're keeping in the rhythm. All those bloody feminine endings, you know.

Mr. A.: Sorry, old boy. They seem to come quite naturally.

Mr. G.: I dare say they do. But don't let 'em, break 'em up. Smash 'em. Throw it away *in bits*, old boy. Throw it away *in bits*. Take it again.

Mr. A.: (*Mumbles three more lines before the producer interrupts*).

Mr. G.: Sorry, old boy. Can you bear one more interruption?

Mr. A.: Of course, old boy.

Mr. G.: That's much better, much better. Hardly recognisable. But just one more thing.

Mr. A.: Yes, old boy?

Mr. G.: Look! I'm sitting way back in the third row of the stalls and I can still *hear* quite a lot.

Mr. A.: God! Sorry, old boy. I'll keep it down.

Mr. G.: If you would, old boy.

Mr. A.: Fair...great...state...puts...hopes...blushing...him. The...a...

Mr. G.: Splendid, old boy! Hold that. Perfect. Just enough to tantalise 'em without giving 'em a clue. Miss Wynyard![6]

Stage Manager: Calling Miss Wynyard!!

Mr. G.: Ah, Miss Wynyard. Would you mind coming and listening to this, darling. This is more or less how I want your death scene to go....

And go, more or less like that, the death scene did. If I were a real 'Wouldn't-it-be-fun (just for a change)' man, I should now relate my dream. For in this school we are never content with just one clever/silly notion. We put them all in. As it is, I will only tell, because it is very relevant, the part where the dream became a nightmare. I was in a 'producer's theatre,' charged with an important message from the whole audience to the Director. I fought my way to his office through Romeos with false noses, Hamlets carrying Gladstone bags and Macbeths with stutters. The Director was charming. What could he do for me? No, he didn't in the least mind my being a dramatic critic. He always read them, and tried to profit by their advice. I delivered my message. He cupped his hand round his ear and said 'What?' I repeated it. He still couldn't hear. I shouted and still he couldn't. That was the nightmare. This theatre had on it the curse of inaudibility. I woke up before he ever did hear what I had come to say. But I remembered it in the morning, this heartfelt cry from the whole audience I had been charged to deliver; and I write it down now in case these words should catch someone's eye at Stratford: PLEASE MAY WE BE ALLOWED TO HEAR THE WORDS?

1. **Moiseiwitsch**, Tanya (born 1914), designer who frequently worked with Guthrie.
2. **Laughton**, Charles. See p. 234.
3. **Quayle**, Anthony (1913–89), stage and screen actor, Director of the Shakespeare Memorial Theatre, Stratford-upon-Avon, 1948–1956; knighted 1985.
4. **Andrews**, Harry (1911–89), actor who frequently appeared in classical roles.
5. **Quartermaine**, Léon. See p. 210.
6. **Wynyard**, Diana (1906–64), actress who worked at Stratford from 1948.

[1950], Richard David (1912–93) on *Measure for Measure* directed by Peter Brook (born 1925) at the Shakespeare Memorial Theatre, Stratford-upon-Avon, with John Gielgud and Barbara Jefford, from *Shakespeare Survey 4* (1951), pp. 135–8.

RICHARD DAVID was a scholar, editor, and publisher who as a young man acted with the Marlowe Society, Cambridge, and later lectured on Stratford productions; his publications include the Arden edition of *Love's Labour's Lost* (1951) and *Shakespeare in the Theatre* (Cambridge, 1982). The young Brook, who was to become one of the most original and influential directors of the twentieth century, had already directed *Love's Labour's Lost* and *Romeo and Juliet* at Stratford. The review printed here is from an article, 'Shakespeare's Comedies and the Modern Stage', and follows discussion of a production of *Love's Labour's Lost*.

THE simplicity of the text of *Measure for Measure*, as compared with that of *Love's Labour's Lost*, is a function of its more serious mood. It is a play of ideas rather than of impressions and is concerned more with lines of conduct followed out to their logical conclusions than with the confusions and compromises of real life. There is still controversy as to how far these ideas form a coherent argument, and *Shakespeare Survey*[1] has already given space to notable pleadings on either side. The one maintains that *Measure for Measure* is Shakespeare's considered opinion on the apparent conflict in Renaissance theory between the Christian duty of the Ruler to secure Justice, and that of the individual to be merciful. The other finds in the purpose and character of Isabella and the Duke as many dislocations as in the time-scheme, and holds that Shakespeare, here more even than usual, was concerned only to contrive a series of fine dramatic moments, heightening the effect of each as best might be, without regard to the philosophic or psychological coherence of the whole. A modern producer is apparently faced with the alternative of abandoning any totality of effect for the sake of the incidental beauties, or of clouding these by the imposition of a 'programme' that will be bewildering to his audience.

Peter Brook's solution of the conundrum was symbolized in the setting that he himself devised for the play. This was a double range of lofty arches, receding from the centre of the stage on either side to the wings upstage. These arches might remain open to the sky in those scenes where some air and freshness is required—the convent at night where Isabella hears from Lucio of her brother's plight, Mariana's moated grange, and the street scene in which all odds are finally made even; or, in a moment, their spaces could be blanked out, with grey flats for the shabby decorum of the courtroom, with grilles for the prison cells. Downstage, at either side, stood a heavy postern gate, also permanently set, serving as focus for the subsidiary scenes to which the full stage would have given undue emphasis, or those, such as the visiting of the imprisoned Claudio, which gain by a cramped setting. The single permanent set gave coherence to the whole; its continuous shadowy presence held together the brilliant series of closet-scenes played on a smaller section of the stage, that glorious succession of duets, Lucio–Isabella, Isabella–Angelo, Claudio–Duke, Isabella–Claudio, in which Shakespeare conceived the action. These were given all the more definition, and urgency, by the apparently confined space in which they were played, although their scope was restricted more by lighting than by any material barrier, and at any moment the whole span of the stage might spring to life and remind us of our bearings in the play. The occasions for such a broadening of effect are not many, but the producer made the most of them. To the progress of Claudio and Juliet to prison, with all corrupt Vienna surging and clamouring about them, and to the final marshalling of all the characters for judgement, he added a third full-stage scene, in which the prisoners, processing through the central hall of the prison, brought its holes and corners for a moment into relation with each other. Shakespeare's text gives only the slimmest pretext for this, in Pompey's enumeration of the old customers whom he has met again in his new employment; but the expansion—in both senses—came happily as a central point of relief in a chain of scenes each requiring a confined attention.

The great duets largely play themselves. It is they that make the play memorable, and such tense and moving writing is found elsewhere in Shakespeare only in the great tragedies. There is of course the notorious danger that to a modern audience Isabella may appear unbearably self-centred and priggish. Isabella knows, and a Jacobean audience took for granted, that there can be no compromise with evil, that, though the only road to right may appear to lie through wrong, the taking of it can do no one any good. Claudio acknowledges it, when not blinded by his panic, for he finally begs his sister's pardon for suggesting otherwise; and we know it, too. But we are shy of being dogmatic about it in the manner of the Jacobeans; though we may admit Isabella's reasons we find it hard to swallow her matter-of-fact schematization of them—'More than our brother is our chastity.'

The producer and Barbara Jefford[2] together saved our faces. Miss Jefford's was a young Isabella, a novice indeed, with no mature *savoir-faire* with which to meet her predicament, but only the burning conviction that two blacks cannot make a white. When she came to the perilous words she turned, from speaking full to the audience, to hide her face passionately against the wall behind her, as if herself ashamed that her intellect could find no more adequate expression of her heart's certainty. In the same way her tirade against her brother, when he begs her to save his life at any cost, was made to appear as much anger with her own failure as a witness to truth, her own inability to communicate it to others. It was indeed skilful, and a good illustration of one kind of 'translation', to substitute the pathos of the inarticulate for an affronting insensitivity, and convert what is often an offence to modern playgoers into the very engine to enforce their sympathy. Altogether it was a moving performance, that found its perfect foil in the suppressed and twisted nobility of John Gielgud's[3] Angelo. With such interpreters the producer could risk the boldest effects. The climax of the play was breathtaking. Mariana has passionately implored Isabella to kneel to the Duke for Angelo's pardon; the Duke has warned her that to do so would be 'against all sense'—'He dies for Claudio.' The pause that followed must have been among the longest in theatre history. Then hesitantly, still silent, Isabella moved across the stage and knelt before the Duke. Her words came quiet and level, and as their full import of mercy reached Angelo, a sob broke from him. It was perfectly calculated and perfectly timed; and the whole perilous manoeuvre had been triumphantly brought off.

Yet it is not Isabella, still less Angelo, that is the crux of the producer's problem, but the Duke. If the play is to mean anything, if it is to be more than a series of disjointed magnificences, we must accept the Duke's machinations as all to good purpose, and himself as entirely wise and just. Peter Brook presented Vincentio rather as Friar turned Duke than as Duke turned Friar, and maintained throughout the impressiveness of his appearance at the cost of rendering his disguise completely unconvincing. He had found in Harry Andrews[4] a Duke whose commanding presence could dominate the play, as the half-seen arches the stage, and whose charm of manner could convince us of his integrity and wisdom. If his speaking could have been more measured, more confident, more natural ease and less careful manipulation, we might have had the Vincentio of a generation.

It remains (since *Measure for Measure* is still a comedy) to say something about the comics. In refreshing defiance of tradition, Pompey, Elbow, and Abhorson were left to make their proper effect as natural English 'characters', instead of being reduced, as in most productions of the play, to circus clowns and fantastics. Peter Brook has not always escaped censure for that over-emphasis on 'business' which I have already denounced as the fatal Siren of modern producers. Here, where so much depended on control, the supporting elements in the play were not allowed to get much out of hand. The Viennese mob was extremely loud and energetic, but then the outrageousness of its manners (a motif echoed in the Brueghelesque[5] grotesquery of Brook's costumes) is an essential contrast to the nobility of the play's main themes. Pompey was assiduous in distributing advertisements of Mistress Overdone's establishment to all with whom he came in contact, a 'turn' for which the cue can only be wrung from the text with difficulty; but it is in character, and was carefully confined to those moments when no 'necessary question of the play was then to be considered'.[6] It was permissible, too, having provided a pit from which an admirable Barnardine emerged with his true effect, to use it for a tumultuous 'exeunt omnes' at the end of the scene. The only real excrescence was some buffoonery with Pompey's fetters that for a moment put the Duke's dignity in jeopardy. This must be forgiven a producer of such restraint elsewhere that he could keep the crowd in the background of his prison scenes silent and motionless through almost an entire act; could dispense with music, save a tolling bell and the herald's trumpet; and at the close could allow his couples merely to walk, 'hand in hand, with wandering steps and slow',[7] in silence from the stage—and to what great effects!

1. *Shakespeare Survey*. The articles intended are 'The Renaissance Background of *Measure for Measure*' by Elizabeth Pope and 'The "Meaning" of *Measure for Measure*' by Clifford Leech in *Shakespeare Survey 2* and *3* (1949, 1950) respectively.
2. **Jefford**, Barbara (born 1930). Isabella was the first of the many major Shakespeare roles she has played.
3. **Gielgud**, John. See p. 210.
4. **Andrews**, Harry. See p. 248.
5. **Brueghelesque**, alluding to the highly detailed style of the Flemish painter of peasant life Pieter Brueghel (*c.*1520–69).
6. **'necessary...considered'**, *Hamlet* 3.2.42–3 ('be then').
7. **'hand...slow'**, from the last lines of *Paradise Lost*, by John Milton (1608–74), describing the departure of Adam and Eve from the Garden of Eden.

---

2 September 1955, Evelyn Waugh (1902–66) on *Titus Andronicus* directed by Peter Brook at the Shakespeare Memorial Theatre, Stratford-upon-Avon, with Laurence Olivier as Titus; from *The Spectator*.

THE satirical novelist Evelyn Waugh wrote rarely on theatre; he appears to have seen *Titus*, in which Olivier had one of the greatest triumphs of his career, early in its run but not on the first night.

FROM the extremity of the circle, which at Stratford-on-Avon is politely misnamed a 'box,' every face in the audience can be plainly seen. Dense, devout, heterogeneous, Americans, negroes and orientals, little girls and grandfathers, they extended without a gap from wall to wall and from roof to floor. The English were dressed, it seemed, for the beach at Broadstairs, the exotics more respectably. How many, I wondered, were there by habit? How many, like myself, had been brought into Warwickshire that day by other business, had booked their tickets blind and had learned with something like chagrin that the play to be presented was *Titus Andronicus?* How many had planned their visit in expectation of a great treat?

Curiosity was the emotion proper to the evening. Producer and players were engaged on the creation of an original work out of what had been for centuries absolute void. There is no tradition of *Titus Andronicus;* only the established faith that it is unactable. Reread on the eve of the performance the unfamiliar text seemed to hold no potentiality save of burlesque. Its notorious horrors, repellent to gentler generations, seemed drab today, consisting as they do of plain butchery devoid of evil or pity. There is no plausible character, still less a likeable one. There is no line of poetry, hardly a dozen lines of memorable rhetoric. There are three scenes of gross absurdity: where Lavinia reveals the identity of her ravishers, where the distracted Titus looses flights of arrows to the Gods, and where Tamora disguises herself as the Spirit of Revenge. How could even the masterly Mr. Peter Brook and all his eminent company make anything of this preposterous composition? One brief great scene there was, waiting to catch the discerning eye—where Aaron receives his blackamoor child and defends it against the Gothic princes—but it needed an expert to spot it, and an unusually zealous actor to convey it to the layman.

So we assembled and waited with no very high expectations until the lights came up on the stage and we rather suddenly realised that we were in for something of rare quality.

The revelation was not immediate. The author's opening is, I suppose irredeemable—a trite wrangle before a background of solid but unident-ified classical architecture. Dire foreboding seemed to be confirmed. But it was brief. The actors got through it somehow and very soon we had Sir Laurence Olivier[1] on the stage, full of experience and authority and with him Miss Maxine Audley[2] as a flashy Tamora, more Ptolemy than Goth. The first corpses came too with their attendant mutes. What seemed the plinth of a column opened ponderously to disgorge glowing priests of Babylonish aspect. It was a very pretty spectacle but still the words dragged until Sir Laurence reached the abysmal line: 'O sacred receptacle of my joys'. He boldly gave us 'rĕcĕp/tāclĕ.' Here was panache. Here, or so I took it, was the first hint, a broad wink, telling us: 'This is not a hallowed text. We have a great lump of almost intractable raw material on our hands. Just wait and see what we make of it.' All that in a freak of prosody.

Mr. Brook's problem was to avoid the ludicrous. The one sure armour against ridicule is humour. If he had treated the whole work as sublime, making Titus a minor Lear; if he had treated it as simple melodrama, a thing of plot and passion—do Stratford audiences, I wonder, ever laugh in the wrong places? My 'box' offered none of the conventional privacies. If Mr. Brook had handled the play in any other way than he did, I fear that I at least must have disgraced myself. But he resolved his problems by treating them, as literary dons say, at various levels. Each scene was played for all it was worth and no more. There was a consistent unifying dignity of spectacle. The supers were superb. The costumes audaciously various, with no attempt at historical propriety. Fourteenth-century justices and fourth-century legionaries mingled felicitously with visions from Bakst[3] ballet. The stage carpentry was just adequate. The doors and aperture in the plinth had to work overtime—opulent changes of scene are least of the casualties in the war of attrition waged everywhere by the artisan against the artist. But the full burden of holding the piece together fell on Sir Laurence himself and was triumphantly borne.

Titus is an arduous part. He is on the stage almost continuously as heroic veteran, stoic parent, implacable devotee of barbarous pieties, crazy victim, adroit avenger. Sir Laurence is a *great* impersonator. He is the one actor who, on the stage, is never himself. He has a vitality which never flags and a keen intelligence. It is this intelligence I think which comes between him and poetry. That and the age he lives in. Elderly persons have long suspected that the idiosyncrasies of many writers now acclaimed as poets spring quite simply from defective ear, and lately a youngish critic,[4] more shameless than his fellows, has proclaimed as 'moribund' the belief that 'the vowel and consonantal sounds' of a poem have any part in its power. Sir Laurence can be trusted to get the deepest meaning out of all he has to say. In Shakespeare he excels in the prose passages. His film of *Hamlet*[5] touched greatness once—in the words never, I think, previously illumined; 'Father and mother is man and wife, man and wife is one flesh, and so, my mother'. For the full organ-notes and delicate melody of Shakespeare's poetry we look to him in vain; but, as I said above, there is no poetry in *Titus Andronicus*, so here for the first time in Shakespearean drama we could see all his talents fully extended and applaud them without reservation.

What is more, this absence of poetry helped the play by maintaining the momentum which is its prime virtue. In the great works we sit, as it were, crunching the nuts and waiting for the decanter to come round bringing the vintage of the famous speeches.... 'Not quite up to the Gielgud '38.' 'Ah, but you're too young to remember the Forbes-Robinson[6] '08.' *Titus Andronicus* was all novelty and there are fewer superfluities in it than in any play of the period. It comes as though straight from the cutting room. Mr. Brook had to make few adjustments of the text. To compensate little Lucius for missing the cannibal feast, he was given a fly to squash. One critic, I notice, complained of the omission of 'Baked in that pie'.[7] I thought I heard it spoken. It should have been there, certainly. The only complaint that could be made against Mr. Brook was of squeamishness. He did well, I think, to have the Gothic princes executed off-stage and to strangle the midwife rather than stab her, but I should have liked to see the severed hands—gloves full of plasticine perhaps—properly displayed. And why moble[8] the heads of Martius and Quintus? Livid masks would have looked well in the cages. The corpses that accumulated about the stage were very elegant, particularly the ladies. I don't suppose the stalls could see them well. They played to the gallery, lying gracefully disposed, all unlike the real debris of carnage.

Mr. Quayle[9] has been fully and justly praised for his performance of Aaron. It is a rich part and he exploited it splendidly. Praise is also due to the Gothic villains. They maintained a revolting rubbery exuberance, nimble as PT instructors, amoral and sub-human.

Miss Vivien Leigh,[10] as Lavinia, celebrated a private rite of enchantment. It is an empty part; she filled it with humour and made it a delicious little work of art. (I am not in her confidence in this matter. Heaven forfend a gaffe!) When she left us to collect a basin full of blood she mimed a demure Victorian bride. When she mewed over the bookshelves, when she raised her paws to enumerate her ravishers, she just hinted an affinity with Dick Whittington's cat. She wrote in the sand with endearing nonchalance. When she was dragged off to her horrible fate she ventured a tiny impudent, barely perceptible, roll of the eyes, as who should say: 'My word! What next?' She established complete confidence between the audience and the production. 'We aren't trying to take you in,' she seemed to say. 'You're too clever, and we are too clever. Just enjoy yourselves.' It was the grain of salt which gave savour to the whole rich stew.

1. **Olivier,** Laurence. See p. 216.

2. **Audley,** Maxine (1923–92), played many classical roles at Stratford, the Old Vic, and elsewhere; she listed Tamora among her three favourite roles.

3. **Bakst,** Léon (1866–1924), Russian painter and designer who worked with Serge Diaghilev for the Ballets Russes from 1909 onwards.

4. **a youngish critic** [unidentified].

5. **film of** *Hamlet.* Olivier's film was first shown in 1948.

6. **Forbes-Robinson,** probably simply an error for Forbes-Robertson (see p. 144).

7. **'Baked in that pie'** The words (actually '... this pie') spoken as Titus reveals the heads of Tamora's sons in the pie 'Whereof their mother daintily hath fed' (5.3.59–60) are marked for omission in the prompt-book.

8. **moble** muffle (obsolete except as an echo of *Hamlet* 2.2.505, 'mobbled queen').

9. **Quayle,** Anthony. See p. 248.

10. **Leigh,** Vivien (1913–67), stage and screen star, married to Olivier at this time.

[1959], John Russell Brown (born 1923) on *All's Well that Ends Well*
directed by Tyrone Guthrie at the Shakespeare Memorial
Theatre, Stratford-upon-Avon, from his review article 'Three
Adaptations' in *Shakespeare Survey 13* (1960), pp. 137–45; 140–2.

JOHN RUSSELL BROWN has done more than most to span the worlds of the
theatre and the academy. Editor of the Arden edition of *The Merchant of Venice*
and of the Revels editions of plays by John Webster, he also founded the Drama
Department of the University of Birmingham and worked with Peter Hall at the
National Theatre.

TYRONE GUTHRIE, directing *All's Well that Ends Well* at Stratford in
1959, made some additions to the dialogue to fill out those scenes
which had particularly attracted him: so a major-domo instructs lesser
servants about 'hastening the musicians' and moving a platform 'more to
the left', a courtier inquires about the 'good old king' and there are many
'Quite so's', 'Hear, hear's', petty oaths, orders and exclamations; more
ambitiously, the Duke of Florence enquires 'Is this the machine?' But
Guthrie's invention—in keeping with the present reluctance to accept
rewriting—was more plainly shown in numerous dumb-shows, excisions,
actions in contradiction to what is said, and deliberate and effective mis-
speaking of Shakespeare's lines.

Yet after he had taken all this trouble, it was hard to see his leading
purpose in adapting the play. During the first half, the scenes in which the
Countess appears were set in and around an elegant Chekhovian man-
sion: in a tender, brownish light, a grove of bare and slender trees bend
gracefully, from both sides of the stage, towards a summer-house, and,
while its inhabitants are voguish and precise in dress, from classical urns
dead leaves and tendrils hang untended. At the end of the play the same
house becomes, surprisingly, a vast hall, sketchily furnished in trivial blue,
white and gilt. The King's Court at Paris is a dark ballroom, glittering
occasionally with lights and dancing figures but, more often, empty and
comfortless, so that its inhabitants protect themselves with tall leather
screens. All these scenes were presented as if the action took place just
before the First World War, but in later scenes among the soldiers in
Florence the stage was set as for the Second World War: there is a
microphone and a megaphone of the latest design, and the men are
dressed in khaki shorts, the officers in tunics, black ties and berets. The
widow's household was presented in a mixture of the two periods: for,
gaping and giggling at the soldiers, the girls are dressed in housecoats and

headscarves, and one sucks a fruit lolly; but for travelling, Diana appears in an Edwardian coat and hat, to match Helena's, who has come, unchanged in her style of dress, from the other part of the play.

The treatment of the text was as various as that of the setting. At one extreme, Lavache, the old clown, is cut completely, and at the other, the Countess is played by Edith Evans[1] with assured dignity, feeling and intelligence, in keeping with the sense and music of Shakespeare's lines. The King, both when dying and when restored to health, is a tetchy princeling: in Robert Hardy's[2] performance, he has nothing of the Countess' assurance, but strives continually to exert himself; he toys with Helena and pats his courtiers; his lines are ingeniously spoken so that 'I fill a place, I know't' is a petulant rebuke, 'My son's no dearer' an affected self-advertisement, and 'the inaudible and noiseless foot of Time' a jest that amuses its speaker. Diana, who is called a 'young gentlewoman... of most chaste renown' and claims to be descended from 'the ancient Capilet', is played by Priscilla Morgan for restless comedy: on her first entrance she looks as if she passed her days reading cheap magazines and staring at men, and this appearance is half-reconciled with her lines about virginity, virtue and pity in that she speaks them with a pert and knowing avidity. Angela Baddeley,[3] as her widowed mother, keeps the audience laughing by little tricks which emphasize her decrepit old-age and prudence to the exclusion of everything else. The bizarre effect of mingling these interpretations may be exemplified from the final scenes: here Parolles takes his proper place as Lafeu's fool without the encounter with Lavache to establish his new status; the king does not sit in judgement, but moves continually among his courtiers, so that he often steps up to a character before addressing him; only the Countess is unmoving and dignified and so, in the continual bustle, draws all eyes to herself—but there seems to be little purpose in this, for Shakespeare has written few words for her in this scene. In this disorder, some expectancy is awakened for Helena's final entry by sweet and soothing music played off-stage.

Guthrie's liveliest invention was reserved for an interpolated dumb-show in Act III, sc. iii. In Shakespeare's play this is a brief moment when the audience is shown the Duke of Florence welcoming the boy Bertram as a man and soldier of worth, and without any of the references to his father's virtues which he has always heard before. As such it is a step forward in the presentation of Bertram, but Guthrie has used it for introducing an entertaining episode in which a comic duke (a grotesque caricature of General Smuts,[4] short-sighted and falsetto) inspects a comic army (a pair of trousers threaten to fall down, someone catches a sword between his legs, a flag slips from its staff as the general salutes, and most of the words are inaudible); this farce lasts six or seven minutes, in which time less than a dozen of Shakespeare's lines are heard, or partly heard. Similar comic invention was utilized every time the soldiers appeared after this, so that the braggart Parolles is shown up as a coward and liar among soldiers that could never fight a battle, and the audience has to suppose that Bertram achieves 'the good livery of honour' in a crazy-gang army. Of course the whole economy of Shakespeare's play has been altered, its proportions, tempo, tensions, emphases, and its comic spirit.

Shakespeare's progressive presentation of the relationship between Helena and Bertram is particularly subtle, yet Guthrie has freely changed this in accordance with his own conception. In the original, Helena hesitantly approaches each of the King's other wards before she confronts Bertram, and then, realizing the presumption of demanding him as husband, she only gives herself to him:

> I dare not say I take you; but I give
> Me and my service, ever whilst I live,
> Into your guiding power.

In Guthrie's version, Helena's choice is made while she engages in a series of lively and sentimental dances: Bertram offers himself, unprompted, as her partner for the last dance and Helena of course is delighted, and, when the dance concludes, addresses him in modest joy, not in fearful resolution; Bertram relinquishes her hand later, only when the King insists that he must call her wife. Here Guthrie has lessened the nervous embarrassment of Helena, and directed the audience's attention away from her and her feelings; he has also introduced some entertaining *divertissements* and heightened the sense of surprise. When the King demands their marriage, overriding everyone's wishes, Guthrie has directed Bertram to walk right across the stage in a general silence and, after a pause, to say the line Shakespeare has given him, very deliberately: 'I cannot love her, nor will strive to do't.' Again this heightens the dramatic excitement through suspense, but it alters Shakespeare's portrayal of Bertram, making him appear so deliberate that it is no longer credible that, in his inexperience, his action is 'but the boldness of his hand ... which his heart was not consenting to'. Next, Guthrie played confidently for pathos: numerous courtiers take silent leave of Bertram, as if sympathizing with him, and then Bertram and Helena walk together across the empty hall towards the marriage ceremony, and are followed by the far brisker steps of Longaville who has been ordered to conduct them.

Shortly afterwards an entirely new scene has been added, the re-entry of Helena and Bertram as from their marriage, holding ceremonial candles and attended by a priest. In all these mute actions, Bertram treats Helena with a quiet, dazed tenderness which is in direct contrast with the brusque, reiterative words Shakespeare has given to him: 'I take her hand.... Although before the solemn priest I have sworn, I will not bed her.... O my Parolles, they have married me! I'll to the Tuscan wars, and never bed her.' For immediate dramatic gains of suspense or pathos, or in order to introduce dance and movement, the director has altered the presentation of Helena and Bertram.

Whether he was following Shakespeare's text, or deliberately misconstruing it, or introducing some new incident, Guthrie was continually in command of the whole stage; and if his adaptation fails (like Davenant and Dryden's *Enchanted Island*[5]) to sustain any comprehensive dramatic interest, it is always (again like the earlier adaptation) diverting, varied and spirited. If this was the full scope of Guthrie's intentions, he has been brilliantly successful—with the proviso that his version is seen once only. The third or fourth time it is seen, the additions and alterations cease to hold the playgoer's attention, and those parts where he has followed Shakespeare most closely tend to dominate everything else: Zoe Caldwell's[6] tense and emotional Helena in the earliest scenes and Anthony Nicholls's[7] unvariedly elegant Lafeu both gain in stature and interest when they are seen without the new distractions, and Edith Evans's Countess still more realizes the human understanding and poetic utterance which have always been the hall-marks of Shakespeare's original plays.

1. **Evans**, Edith. See p. 216.

2. **Hardy**, Robert (born 1925), stage and screen actor who has played many classical roles.

3. **Baddeley**, Angela (1904–76), married to Glen Byam Shaw (see p. 215).

4. **Smuts**, Jan Christian (1870–1950), South African statesman well known in Britain.

5. *Enchanted Island*, adaptation (1667) by John Dryden (1631–1700) and William Davenant (1606–68) of *The Tempest*, revived at the Old Vic in 1959 and discussed in the earlier part of this review.

6. **Caldwell**, Zoë (born 1934), Australian-born actress who went on to work mainly in England and America.

7. **Nicholls**, Anthony (1907–77), actor who played many classical roles at Stratford and elsewhere.

[1959], Laurence Kitchin (born 1913) on Laurence Olivier as Coriolanus, directed by Peter Hall (born 1930) at the Shakespeare Memorial Theatre, Stratford-upon-Avon, from his *Mid-Century Drama* (1960), pp. 143–9.

LAURENCE KITCHIN, writer and translator, was a theatre critic for *The Times* from 1956 to 1962, but his essays reprinted in this volume were written for the books in which they appear. Peter Hall succeeded Glen Byam Shaw as Director of the Shakespeare Memorial Theatre in 1960. Under his regime it became the Royal Shakespeare Theatre and greatly expanded its activities. He was Director of the National Theatre from 1973 to 1988 and has directed distinguished productions of Shakespeare plays. The production in illustrated in Pl. II.

OLIVIER as Coriolanus again, twenty-one years after he played it at the Old Vic. Casson,[1] the director on that occasion, was now eighty-three years old and the Memorial Theatre production of 1959 was in the hands of Hall, aged twenty-eight. On the afternoon of September 10th I arrived at Stratford-on-Avon to find the riverside lawns flanking the theatre a sapless brown, beaten by the sun and the feet of tourists to the same consistency and colour as the grass of London parks in the most torrid summer within living memory. People sagged in deckchairs, launches and rowboats moved lazily past the swans; the theatre with its retinue of empty, parked cars had the hushed, barricaded look it wears during a matinée.

Inside it that night Aronson's[2] uncurtained set laid down the rules of the game. This was going to be a vertical production, with coigns of vantage on steps, landings and an isolated projection resembling the Tarpeian rock. The biggest uninterrupted plane, no bigger than a cramped provincial repertory stage, was bounded by the prompt corner, archaic subtarpeian doors and steps leading up to a city gate. There could be no ceremonial entrances between ranked guards of honour, of the kind Groucho Marx discredited in *Duck Soup*[3] by awaiting his own entrance at the extreme end of a file, neither could a dense mob assemble nor a marching column gather impetus. An immediate effect of the arrangement was that Olivier's first appearance, on top of the rock, did none of the usual things to invite applause. There, like the apparition of an eagle, he suddenly was.

His preliminary scorn of the plebeians, which is written in such a way as to accommodate very strong playing, this Marcius flicked casually, like a man so much in the habit of it that no effort is required. 'Go, get you home,' it ended, 'you...', and Olivier paused, searching for a fresh term of abuse, before he came out with: 'fragments'. The passage had drawn on his unrivalled flair for projecting impatience; the next, in which the news of Volscian aggression is given, brought out a grander impatience: to fight and, above all, to fight Aufidius. He seemed to expand with spontaneous joy at the very mention of this man, thus telling us a lot about his own character while accentuating a major issue of the play, which revolves finally on the relationship between Coriolanus and his rival, not on the conflicts with plebeians, senators and his mother. One tragic weakness in Marcius is the chivalrous admiration he has for Aufidius. We are dealing with a Roman seen through Elizabethan eyes, remember, and the conflict is between embodiments of flawed chivalry and ruthless expediency. The Castiglione[4] ideal, which rejects the despotic arrogance of Marcius as excessive, and so ultimately vulgar, would applaud the magnanimity of his attitude to a worthy rival. According to tragic irony, then, it is his redeeming feature which destroys Marcius. He yields to a chivalrous impulse in the age of Machiavelli:[5] '...our virtues', says Aufidius, 'lie in the interpretation of the time', and later: '...a man by his own alms empoison'd and with his charity slain.' It might almost be Iago we are listening to.

The point of this digression from an account of performance is to dispose of the criticism which seeks to convey Olivier's art in terms of his virility, humour and emotional power. Great as these are, they are controlled, as our observations on his Macbeth may have indicated, by interpretative intelligence of a very high order. It operates equally well under the direction of Guthrie,[6] Casson, Saint-Denis,[7] Brook[8] or Hall; and in the Stratford performance it could be seen at work in the immediate glow induced by the mention of Aufidius. A separate style of luminous brushwork, so to speak, identified this relationship throughout. There was no doubt at all where the play's climax comes. It is on the sealing of their pact, or so I shall always believe after Olivier's extraordinary handshake. He had been very quiet during the scene. There was a deathly, premonitory misgiving in the way he eventually shook hands; and his eyes were glazed. Whatever integration the character of Marcius had possessed fell apart at that moment. The rest was crumble, detonation and collapse, with part of him fatalistically detached. Incidentally the transition was as subtle and unmistakable as the one Ben Gazzara[9] brought off under essentially melodramatic conditions in *End as a Man*. In neither case would an emphasis on animal vitality go any distance in conveying the effect.

Another strand firmly interwoven was the relationship of Marcius with Volumnia, his mother. When the action first brings them together, on his triumphant return from the exploits at Corioli, Olivier gave her a long smile with the spoilt son's immodest complacency. Although he greeted his wife with a tender break in his voice, the scene was aligned on Volumnia in a way to prepare us for the capitulation later on. Nobody, I think, lacking knowledge of English public-school *mores* could have hit exactly this note of sulky pride, a result of the man of action's narcissism held back by the necessity to belittle success in the presence of social equals. The modesty of Marcius is false modesty, as had already been obvious when Olivier writhed in discomfort at the praises heaped on him by his fellow generals, only to release a cold smile, unabashed, at the sound of his new title, Coriolanus. But this is no wilful modernizing of a text which asks him to claim in the midst of battle that he has not yet been warmed by his work and to joke about blushing. The play itself draws generously on a rhetoric of understatement which Olivier carried over into the scenes with his family, where it stood revealed, particularly in the nasty reference to widows in Corioli, as a cover for vanity.

Apart from its value in outlining emotional immaturity as a source of weakness, the spoilt-son approach paid off memorably on two occasions. The first was during the rebellion of the plebeians, when Olivier's face registered a few seconds of bewilderment; not fear, but a marked surprise that arrogant statements habitual in the family circle and among patricians could have such an inflammatory effect. Disorientated for a time before drawing his sword, he was briefly in need of reassurance, presumably from his mother. We were not to see him at a loss again until the pact with Aufidius, but something more than the dismay of a cornered animal had been expressed. Then came a playing of the admonition scene, which opens with him unrepentant and ends with a promise to mollify, chiefly for laughs.

Tastes differ about his kind of liberty. At such an extreme it ought to be, though too often it is not, Olivier's exclusive privilege. He listened to his mother's reproofs with infantile sullenness and the tone adopted reduced the whole issue to the scale of some breach of etiquette. An habitual battle of wills, fought out not so long ago about apologizing for rough words or the breaking of a companion's toy, was being reopened. 'Let go,' he interjects to Volumnia, 'Let them hang', and to Menenius, 'What must I do?' Having made the most of lines which well bear a petulant interpretation, Olivier next gave the entire scene a turn on a single one, where Coriolanus is told he must go back to the tribunes and replies: 'Well, what then? what then?' He lent the first 'What then?' his celebrated full brass on a rising inflection, caught Volumnia's eye, paused, deflated and repeated 'what then?' quietly and deferentially. Now he was prepared to listen, as comic, contemptuous *obbligato* to Evans's[10] advice. An unforgettable effect had been reserved, however, for the last word of the last line of the scene. For the third time he is supposed to repeat the word 'mildly', which sums up the advice he has been given as to his conduct in face of the plebeians. On this most reluctant of exits Olivier neither spoke the word nor cut it. Instead, at the moment of shaping it with lips and facial muscles, he convulsively retched.

How far was all this justified? In terms of his performance, all the way. We had been given Coriolanus as a spoilt son and were not invited to sympathize with that aspect of him. If he is not at such moments to be contemptible, he might as well be funny, for little else can be made of him in relation to his mother. Volumnia, the stoical Roman matron, is too interesting a character to function merely as a symbol of antique virtue and yet not be defined as anything else. To adapt Perelman's[11] quip, it is evident that before Shakespeare fashioned her he broke the mould. She is the worst kind of aggressive matriarch, ready to put twentieth-century audiences in mind of ageing Edwardians dispensing white feathers to civilians in 1914; and on her knees she inherits Victorian sentimentality, a wife of Calais posing for some bewhiskered President of the Royal Academy. Dryden would have managed her better. If Paxinou[12] undertook Volumnia she would no doubt find hypnotic splendour in the old harridan, but that could only be at the expense of the title part. The alternative is to give her straight, dignified playing, as Evans did at Stratford, and let the unsympathetic elements take effect, so that she doesn't encroach on the play's main theme. Not being able to take this Volumnia seriously, and not invited to, I found no offence in Olivier's comic approach to the scene. It came as a welcome breather after the fury of the rebellion; it threw light on the immaturity, of which the choleric and impatient tendencies mentioned by Plutarch are symptoms, and it echoed the theatrical imagery. What Coriolanus is asked for by his advisers is, he considers, a performance, but in reality a display of the Machiavellian dissimulation without which he is unfitted to be a statesman:

> *You have put me now to such a part, which never*
> *I shall discharge to th' life.*

Later he says: 'I'll mountebank their loves.' By mountebanking the whole scene, Olivier delighted the Stratford audience, at the same time revealing a fatal frivolity in Coriolanus himself. Although we often see actors unable to compass heroic verse fall back on colloquial humour, his was deliberate and not unjustified by the text. The scene begins in hyperbole not far from comic exaggeration, including the notion of ten hills piled on the Tarpeian rock, and ends in sarcasm. Even the nauseated exit could be justified in so far as the conflict between Marcius and his mother is summed up in the one word 'mildly'. By intuition or an act of selection the crucial word had been picked out, an attitude revealed by vulgar facial spasm. If we add the psychological overtone of a child's rejection of food forced on him and the literary overtone of association with Macbeth's 'Amen stuck in my throat', any lingering suspicion that Olivier was indulging in gimmick can be set aside. This was great acting, to hold a day-tripper from Birmingham as tightly as it held American lecturers homesick for the printed page and a bout of close analysis.

All this took place in the tense silence, punctually broken by uninhibited laughter, of an audience piled high to the awkward Memorial Theatre's roof. Any child could have enjoyed it without knowing who Shakespeare was. Olivier, fifty-two years old and already with the afternoon's matinée in the heat-wave behind him, not to mention a day's filming on *The Entertainer*[13] to follow, cleared his throat once or twice between speeches but otherwise exuded the beetle-browed energy further than which so many of his observers fail to see. Subtract him from what was going on, and there would have been much readjustment necessary, no less than a totally different approach to the play. Meanwhile the Apollonian and the Dionysian were at work under the same roof, vested in one person. You could scarcely blame those who were content with the emotive externals and knew nothing of the textual authority for the screamed or vomited word. I only mention it to rebut the fallacy that Olivier is a privileged *id*. The man had brought his intellect to bear on this role; he was not intelligent only in action, from point to point. When he chose to draw a loud laugh from a reference to Hercules in parting with his mother, I did not flinch. Let him enjoy himself; he had earned the right.

Aside from the disintegration before Aufidius and such jewels as the discomfiture of a servant while in disguise, Olivier had three major effects in reserve. Like the others described, they should be read in the familiar context of his martial presence, which had enabled him to beg for his consulate with the tetchy humour of a five-star general trying to unbend in the canteen on Christmas Day. First, the reaction to banishment. Two decades had scarcely dimmed my memory of his 'You common cry of curs!' in Casson's production. Now the delivery was changed. Just before this speech Olivier leaned against the masonry high up on Aronson's set, head rolling from side to side, eyes mad as those of a Sistine Chapel prophetess while he listened to the tribunes. The head movement, I was amused to notice, was one recommended by Elsie Fogerty[14] to her students for relaxing tension in the neck; Olivier was preparing himself. Advancing to the Tarpeian projection on which we had first seen him, he made the speech with less volume than in Casson's production, but with a terrifying concentration of contempt. People who think him a prose actor, because he so often breaks up lines, overlook his sustained power in a passage of invective like this. Only the lyrical escapes him. Here, cursing the plebeians, he gave the phrases such a charge of emotion that he gathered them into a single rhetorical missile, so that the speech had an impact like jagged stones parcelled together and hurled in somebody's face. There was a bizarre impression of one man lynching a crowd.

We had been given the splendours of the verse assigned to this char-acter, the cut-and-thrust of his Elizabethan wit, an appearance fit for some ruggedly aggressive Roman statue, a very few gestures, apt and decisive as Tearle's,[15] to point a climactic phrase like 'mutinous error'. Passages of clowning had all served to emphasize the sometimes inspiring but finally crippling dependence on Volumnia, itself an acted lesson in implied psychology. The boyish eagerness in the chivalrous admiration for Aufidius had its counterpart in an immature spite, equally clearly defined as a motive for his entry into the fatal pact. One of the attractions of such great acting is the confidence you have that the current of expression could be switched off at any moment and the effect just made survive a searching scrutiny. Now, with his subjugation to Aufidius equated with their pact, Olivier's Coriolanus had been fully demonstrated in his extremes of weakness and strength, a tragic figure, doomed long before the alienation effect at the end of the play which turns Aufidius so abruptly from Machiavellian killer to playwright's mouthpiece. Twice before the close, once athletically and once with his voice, Olivier arrested the withering away. He had emphasized the boy in Coriolanus and now must react to Anthony Nicholls,[16] as Aufidius, calling him 'thou boy of tears'. The *fortissimo* he gave to 'Alone I did it, Boy' left one in no state to speculate about the accuracy of the taunt which aroused it. Olivier may have been subjecting Marcius to one of the shocks of recognition he likes to inflict on an audience. But one cannot experience one shock and assess another at the same time. The audience quivered at the sound of Olivier's voice like Avon swans at a sudden crack of thunder. A few seconds later he chose to make the death-fall head downwards from the twelve-foot-high Tarpeian platform, dangling for a time while soldiers, who had caught his ankles, held on. After that, the tragic farewell spoken by Aufidius acted on us like a well-earned tranquillizing drug.

1. **Casson,** Lewis (1875–1969), actor and director, knighted 1945. His wife, Sybil Thorndike, played Volumnia to Olivier's Coriolanus in Casson's 1938 production at the Old Vic.

2. **Aronson,** Boris (1900–80), Russian–American designer.

3. *Duck Soup,* film (1933) starring the Marx Brothers.

4. **Castiglione,** Baldassare (1478–1529), courtier, author of *Il Cortegiano* (1528).

5. **Machiavelli,** Niccolò (1469–1527), political philosopher, author of *Il Principe* (pub. 1532).

6. **Guthrie,** Tyrone. See p. 210. He directed Olivier at the Old Vic in *Hamlet* and *Henry V* (1937), and *Oedipus Rex* (1945).

7. **Saint-Denis,** Michel (1897–1971), French director whose work with Olivier included *Macbeth* at the Old Vic in 1937.

8. **Brook,** Peter, director; Olivier appeared in his Stratford production of *Titus Andronicus*; see pp. 252–5.

9. **Gazzara,** Ben (born 1930), American actor and playwright who scored a hit in the play *End as a Man*, adapted from a novel by Calder Willingham, in New York in 1953. Kitchin had reviewed the film version of 1957, also known as *The Strange One*, advertised as 'the first picture filmed entirely by a cast and technicians from The Actors' Studio, New York', in which Gazzara gave an Iago-like performance.

10. **Evans,** Edith. See p. 216.

11. **Perelman,** S. J. (1904–79), American humorist. I have not traced the allusion, which Laurence Kitchin thinks may be from the script of a Marx Brothers film.

12. **Paxinou,** Katina (1900–73), Greek tragedienne.

13. *The Entertainer,* play (1957) by John Osborne (1929–94); Olivier appeared in the first production as well as the film.

14. **Fogerty,** Elsie (1865–1945), voice trainer who taught Olivier at the Central School of Speech and Drama.

15. **Tearle,** Godfrey (1884–1953), romantic and tragic actor, knighted in 1951.

16. **Nicholls,** Anthony, see p. 259.

[1962], Laurence Kitchin on Peter Brook's production of *King Lear*, with Paul Scofield (born 1922) as Lear, at the Royal Shakespeare Theatre, Stratford-upon-Avon, from his *Drama in the Sixties* (1966), pp. 174–7.

PAUL SCOFIELD worked with Sir Barry Jackson at the Birmingham Repertory Theatre from 1942, and then at Stratford-upon-Avon from 1946, playing a number of leading roles. This production formed the basis of Brook's 1970 film, also starring Scofield.

F OR opposite reasons, Lear is as difficult to cast as Juliet. The actress young enough to look right for her earlier scenes can rarely project the suffering met with later. Lear, on the contrary, must seem old and still have the strength to carry Cordelia on at the finish, preferably in one arm, so as to leave the other free for gesture. By that time he is near the end of the most exacting role in English drama, one with a rhetorical climax written into the very first scene, where Cordelia is disinherited in an outburst like something out of *Tamburlaine*.[1] No wonder we remember the play in terms of monolithic actors: Gielgud,[2] Redgrave[3] and Wolfit.[4] This is frivolous of us, perhaps, though not more than going to hear the pianist in Beethoven's 'Emperor'[5] rather than the orchestra. I like a touch of baroque excess in my Lears, on the lines of Michelangelo's Moses.[6] The verse of the part does invite something of the kind, along with self-indulgent acting of a self-indulgent old man. Better still, I would like to see the mad scenes done with actors of equal authority playing Lear, the Fool and Edgar. These scenes are very modern and demand no less. They are expressionist, but the expressionist side of Peter Brook's production is not mainstream. Too much of it has been filtered through Artaud[7] and Kott.[8] One of the highlights shows Lear overturning a big dining table. But we already know that Mr Brook has a wonderful eye for theatrical effect. What else does it prove? Nothing new about the tragedy.

As always when *King Lear* is acted, his first scene gives many clues to the flavour of the production. It encapsulates the structure of Scofield's performance. The austere, clinical set and drab, leathery costumes admit no display of regality, so that Lear's later references to the court do not link with any ritual we have seen him take part in. But if Scofield is not allowed to be kingly, he still has immediate authority. The voice he adopts reminds me of the conversations in *Citizen Kane*[9] between ruthless old tycoons. You hear it also in elderly generals, rasping and guttural; and in them it sometimes goes with a nimble physique, only to be recognized as senile because the movements are so abrupt. The physical apparatus of the despot is still in working order, but it has torpid rest periods and asserts itself intermittently. At the root of his trouble there appear erratic failures of judgment, such as Lear reveals in this scene. Where other actors have been content with formality leading to surprise and anger, Scofield charts the decay of a personality. The kingdom is being divided, 'that future strife may be...prevented...now'. He is not searching for the word 'prevented' in this most ironic line of all. The fractional pause before and after the word conveys effort, the insecurity of an old man's voice, however loud and penetrative.

When Cordelia opts out of the competitive flattery we are at the turning point. The usual course is for Lear to echo her 'Nothing' more or less incredulously, then to threaten her that nothing will come of this. Scofield does neither. He repeats the first 'nothing' tonelessly, like a reader testing for a misprint. Then he placidly invites her to speak again. He is now the patient teacher whose best pupil has made a slip of the tongue. The time lag in his comprehension enriches this episode and could be the prelude to his outburst. This never comes. Kent's intervention on behalf of Cordelia does not interrupt a dragon's wrath but an old man's impotent anger, which never rises with the resonance of open vowels in the verse. 'Call France!' is ordered in falsetto. Perhaps it's not anger so much as annoyance caused by surprise, old age's disarray at any disturbance of habit. The complaints are growled out with even more of a pumping effect after the shock has disturbed his breathing: 'Better thou hadst not been...born...than not to have pleased me...*bettuh*.' We are gripped by a family quarrel; there is the threat of apoplexy in a boardroom or over the port. Kent's banishment, a terrifying ritual in the feudal world and written with formal deliberation, comes across like the dismissal of a mutinous domestic servant. Curiously, and in spite of its avant-garde trappings, the production domesticates the play. Without properly rising to the trio and quartet of the mad scenes, it points up the Regan and Goneril plot. Never has the paring down of the ex-king's retinue been so brilliantly exploited, or the lines which define him as a hunting squire. Scofield's private residence is in Sussex, and outdoors his Lear's irritable growl put one in mind of the local rustic intonation. Is it Lear who overturns that table, or Squire Western,[10] complete with riding boots and whip? Either way, if anything is to be made of his kingly office, it seems best not to see him too much from Regan and Goneril's point of view. Julian Hall's[11] comparison of this performance to the Mayor of Casterbridge[12] is unflatteringly near to the mark.

As Scofield is a great actor, with all the equipment for a heroic protagonist of tragedy, including the virile declamation he let loose in *Venice Preserv'd*,[13] I find it frustrating that the shape of this performance compels him to play down Lear's curses and to lack all conviction in the early appeals to his pagan gods. Wolfit was closer to the barbaric splendours of the part all through and Gielgud infinitely superior in the later stages, where the defeated are withdrawing into a remote, impregnable wisdom. Scofield does not, like the verse at times, aim to rival the storm. He greets it ecstatically as a refuge. His best moments are downbeat, when the old man's moods subside for a while and he comes to rest on a truth. Thus he builds a vocal climax on the last word of 'here's three on's are sophisticated' and holds a pause before adding, very low, 'Thou art the thing itself'. He reinforces this by the most intense scrutiny of Poor Tom, going as far as to kneel down beside him for a closer look. Another unforgettable thing is the musing, considered way he says of Cordelia, 'I did her wrong'. When he awakes in her care, Scofield's tone is level, subdued, and for the first time patrician. There is a glimpse of the royal, tragic hero who gets elbowed out of this rendering far too often, from fear of skirting Victorian portentousness, no doubt. As far back as Holinshed,[14] Lear was described as 'a prince of right noble demeanor'.

1. *Tamburlaine*, the two-part play (*c*.1587) by Christopher Marlowe (1564–93).

2. **Gielgud**, John. See p. 210. He played Lear at the Old Vic in 1940, in Stratford in 1950, and in London in 1955.

3. **Redgrave**, Michael (1908–85), actor, knighted 1959. He played Lear in Stratford in 1953.

4. **Wolfit**, Donald. See p. 224.

5. 'Emperor' Piano Concerto No. 5 by Ludwig van Beethoven (1770–1827).

6. **Moses**, the sculpture by Michelangelo Buonarotti (1475–1564) in the church of San Pietro in Vincoli, Rome.

7. **Artaud**, Antonin (1896–1948), influential French director and theoretician, author of *The Theatre and its Double* (1938).

8. **Kott**, Jan (born 1914), Polish critic, author of *Shakespeare our Contemporary* (English translation 1964); his ideas influenced Brook.

9. *Citizen Kane*, film (1941) directed by, and starring, Orson Welles.

10. **Squire Western**, character in the novel *Tom Jones* by Henry Fielding (1707–54).

11. **Hall**, Sir Julian (born 1907), had reviewed Scofield's Lear for *The Times*.

12. **Mayor of Casterbridge**, central character of the novel of the same name by Thomas Hardy (1840–1928).

13. *Venice Preserv'd*, tragedy by Thomas Otway (1652–85) in which Scofield acted in 1953.

14. **Holinshed**. The phrase is from one of Shakespeare's sources for the play, the *Chronicles* (1577, etc.) of Raphael Holinshed (died ?1580).

1 **May 1964,** Ronald Bryden (born 1927) on Laurence Olivier as
Othello at the Old Vic Theatre, London, from the *New
Statesman,* in his *The Unfinished Hero and Other Essays* (1969),
pp. 21–3.

BRYDEN, director and writer, appointed assistant director of the National
Theatre in 1975, later taught at the University of Toronto. The title of his volume
refers to the production of *Hamlet* discussed in the next review. A film closely
based on this production and directed by Stuart Burge appeared in 1965.

ALL posterity will want to know is how he played. John Dexter's[1]
National Theatre *Othello* is efficient and clear, if slow, and contains
some intelligent minor novelties. But in the long run all that matters is
that it left the stage as bare as possible for its athlete. What requires
record is how he, tackling Burbage's[2] role for the first time at 57, created
the Moor.

He came on smelling a rose, laughing softly with a private delight;
barefooted, ankleted, black. He had chosen to play a Negro. The story fits
a true Moor better: one of those striding hawks, fierce in a narrow range
of medieval passions, whose women still veil themselves like Henry
Moore[3] sleepers against the blowing sand of Nouakchott's[4] surrealistically
modern streets. But Shakespeare muddled, giving him the excuse to turn
himself into a coastal African from below the Senegal: dark, thick-lipped,
open, laughing.

He sauntered downstage, with a loose, bare-heeled roll of the buttocks;
came to rest feet splayed apart, hip lounging outward. For him, the great
Richard III of his day, the part was too simple. He had made it difficult
and interesting for himself by studying, as scrupulously as he studied the
flat vowels, dead grin and hunched time-steps of Archie Rice,[5] how an
African looks, moves, sounds. The make-up, exact in pigment, covered
his body almost wholly: an hour's job at least. The hands hung big and
graceful. The whole voice was characterised, the o's and a's deepened, the
consonants thickened with faint, guttural deliberation. 'Put up your bright
swords, or de dew will rus' dem': not quite so crude, but in that direction.

It could have been caricature, an embarrassment. Instead, after the
second performance, a well-known Negro actor rose in the stalls bravoing.
For obviously it was done with love; with the main purpose of substituting
for the dead grandeur of the Moorish empire one modern audiences could
respond to: the grandeur of Africa. He was the continent, like a figure of
Rubens[6] allegory. In Cyprus, he strode ashore in a cloak and spiked

helmet which brought to mind the medieval emirates of Ethiopia and Niger. Facing Doge and senators, he hooded his eyes in a pouting ebony mask: an old chief listening watchfully in tribal conclave. When he named them 'my masters' it was proudly edged: he had been a slave, their inquisition recalled his slavery, he reminded them in turn of his service and generalship.

He described Desdemona's encouragement smiling down at them, easy with sexual confidence. This was the other key to the choice of a Negro: Finlay's[7] Iago, bony, crop-haired, staring with the fanatic mule-grin of a Mississippi redneck, was to be goaded by a small white man's sexual jealousy of the black, a jealousy sliding into ambiguous fascination. Like Yeats's crowd[8] staring, sweating, at Don Juan's mighty thigh, this Iago gazed licking dry lips, on a black one. All he had to do was teach his own disease.

Mannerisms established, they were lifted into the older, broader imagery of the part. Leading Desdemona to bed, he pretended to snap at her with playful teeth. At Iago's first hints, he made a chuckling mock of twisting truth out of him by the ear. Then, during the temptation, he began to pace, turning his head sharply like a lion listening. The climax was his farewell to his occupation: bellowing the words as pure, wounded outcry, he hurled back his head until the ululating tongue showed pink against the roof of his mouth like a trumpeting elephant's. As he grew into a great beast, Finlay shrank beside him, clinging to his shoulder like an ape, hugging his heels like a jackal.

He used every clue in the part, its most strenuous difficulties. Reassured by Desdemona's innocence, he bent to kiss her—and paused looking, sickened, at her lips. Long before his raging return, you knew he had found Cassio's kisses there. Faced with the lung-torturing hurdle of 'Like to the Pontic sea', he found a brilliant device for breaking the period: at 'Shall ne'er look back', he let the memories he was forswearing rush in and stop him, gasping with pain, until he caught breath. Then, at 'By yond marble heaven', he tore the crucifix from his neck (Iago, you recall, says casually Othello'd renounce his baptism for Desdemona) and, crouching forehead to ground, made his 'sacred vow' in the religion which caked Benin's altars with blood.

Possibly it was too early a climax, built to make a curtain of Iago's 'I am your own for ever.' In Act Four he could only repeat himself with increased volume, adding a humming animal moan as he fell into his fit, a strangler's look to the dangling hands, a sharper danger to the turns of his head as he questioned Emilia. But it gave him time to wind down to a superb returned dignity and tenderness for the murder. This became an act of love—at 'I would not have thee linger in thy pain' he threw aside the pillow and, stopping her lips with a kiss, strangled her. The last speech was spoken kneeling on the bed, her body clutched upright to him as a shield for the dagger he turns on himself.

As he slumped beside her in the sheets, the current stopped. A couple of wigged actors stood awkwardly about. You could only pity them: we had seen history, and it was over. Perhaps it's as well to have seen the performance while still unripe, constructed in fragments, still knitting itself. Now you can see how it's done; later, it will be a torrent. But before it exhausts him, a film should be made. It couldn't tell the whole truth, but it might save something the unborn should know.

1. **Dexter**, John (1925–90), director especially associated with the Royal Court Theatre and the National Theatre.
2. **Burbage**, Richard. See p. 5.
3. **Moore**, Henry (1898–1986), sculptor.
4. **Nouakchott**, capital of Mauretania.
5. **Archie Rice**, central character of *The Entertainer*, by John Osborne; see p. 266.
6. **Rubens**, Peter Paul (1577–1640), the Flemish painter.
7. **Finlay**, Frank (born 1926), actor who worked extensively with Olivier at the National Theatre.
8. **Yeats's crowd**, apparently an imperfect recollection of 'On Those that Hated "The Playboy of the Western World"' by W. B. Yeats (1868–1939):

> Once, when midnight smote the air,
> Eunuchs ran through Hell and met
> On every crowded street to stare
> Upon great Juan riding by:
> Even like these to rail and sweat
> Staring upon his sinewy thigh.

27 August 1965, Ronald Bryden on Peter Hall's production of *Hamlet* at the Royal Shakespeare Theatre, Stratford-upon-Avon, in his *The Unfinished Hero and Other Essays* (1969), pp. 63–6.

THE four captains kneel on either side of the body. Awkwardly they hoist it on their shoulders, its arms outflung as if in horizontal crucifixion. As they pick their way upstage through heaped bodies, pale courtiers and dumbfounded soldiery, its head lolls behind them, staring back sightlessly at the audience. The lights dim, the stage darkens, a faint spotlight clings with a halo of luminosity to the receding arched throat and hanging head.

The boldest stroke in Peter Hall's *Hamlet* is its last. In a production whose determined novelty has been trumpeted for months, he deliberately ends with the image which has closed every *Hamlet* you remember, formally conventional as a Byzantine icon. Hamlet has become Hamlet, statue, legend, the starry Prince. Death, as Malraux said, transforms life into destiny;[1] life has become art. It's an audacious effect to dice with, for it can work only if all that's gone before *has* been life: fresh, unpredictable, reclaimed from a thousand previous revivals, a thousand commentaries and Bartlett's Familiar Quotations.[2] It worked here.

In other words, against all expectation and professional habit, I have to say that the new Stratford *Hamlet* seems to me a great and historic production. This isn't to denounce every other critic who found it less than satisfactory last Thursday as an insensitive clod. It's raggedly cast round the edges, and further in. In the general dearth of young actresses, it uses the wrong Ophelia and finds only one or two right reasons for doing so. In its quest for freshness, some of its innovations are arbitrary and perverse. Above all, it's slow, badly lacking the headlong impetus the plays needs to reveal its shape: the Old Vic's otherwise unremarkable revival with John Neville[3] in 1957, by handling the scenes from the play-within-the-play to the end as a chase against time, achieved far more suspense and clarity than you'll find here. But I don't see how this could be otherwise. Thursday's was a first performance. Offering a radical and complex new reading of the play, Hall has taken apart and reassembled each line so that the audience can see how it's done. Pace can come when actors and public have had time to get used to the idea. What matters is that the reading really is new, and stands up. It finds something genuinely original to say about the play, not by scissoring about the text but by exploring and illumining dead corners of it.

It succeeds against my expectation, for all Hall's emphasis in his published statements of intent has been on contemporaneity. His talk to the cast, reprinted in the programme, bears the unsubtle thumb-print of Jan Kott[4]—the quotation from Malraux comes from Kott's essay on the play, along with suggestions that the Hamlet for our time should look like James Dean,[5] wear black sweater and jeans and carry a volume of Camus.[6] In fact, the only Kott-marks on the production are the general, not specially revolutionary notion of a young existentialist trapped by politics into a bloody, uncongenial role, and an ambiguous burst of laughter (it can be taken more specifically, and make more sense) by the dying prince at the Absurdity of it all.

The more important debt, it seems to me, is to Eliot's[7] suggestion that the play is unsatisfactory because its plot offered Shakespeare an inadequate 'objective correlative' for the emotions he wished to vent. Hall redeems the play by turning the unsatisfactoriness back into character. He has imagined a Hamlet himself in search of an objective correlative, a cloud of immature and unfocused emotions in search of means to express them. His revenge is inadequate to his disgust because he is not yet adequate for his revenge. Hamlet's buffoonery, said Eliot, is the outlet for an emotion which can find no relief in action. In this Hamlet, it is the buffoonery of adolescent self-disgust: he is like T. H. White's[8] Lancelot, the ill-made knight who forced himself to excel out of hatred for the face he saw in the mirror. This is a prince who must goad himself to princeliness, to a mature magnificence and ruthlessness for which he is not yet fitted. He is Macbeth's obverse: his failure to become king speaks a dual failure in kingliness—he is both too slight for the role and insufficiently narrow. He is an incomplete Machiavel because an incomplete prince. In Hall's production, *Hamlet* is no longer the imperfect tragedy Eliot saw. It's the perfected tragedy of an unfinished hero.

For the revenge he really wishes, and achieves, is on himself for not being the great Hamlet his father was. The key to every *Hamlet* is its ghost. A solid ghost demands an active, believing hero, thwarted by events; an insubstantial one, all light-effects and echoes, a brainsick prince, nerveless and Oedipal. The apparition which swims above the walls of John Bury's[9] Elsinore (a superb inferno of bitumen ramparts and lakes of black marble, whose throne-room swarms with faded frescoes of sad grey Rubens flesh like a wax museum of elderly lasciviousness) is something new: a giant, helmeted shadow ten feet tall which dwarfs his shuddering child in a dark, commanding embrace. 'This was a man,' Hamlet tells Horatio enviously: for once we are shown the other side of the Oedipus complex. This Hamlet is less jealous of his mother's bedfellow than of his father's stature. As the hollow voice beneath the stage cries 'Swear!', his son lovingly measures his length on the ground, as if on a grave; but the voice moves, he cannot cover it. Clutching violently at his mother on her bed, he looks up to find the huge presence of his father towering between them. Every recollection of his mission is a reminder of his sonship, his immaturity.

His pretence of madness is half an admission of this. He shelters in childishness, seeking to appear not merely too insane to be responsible for his actions, but too young. His disguise is not just dishevelment but the wilful untidiness of an undergraduate, the half-baked impertinence of the adolescent who would test his parents' love to the limit of tolerance. He slops ostentatiously through the castle in a greenish, moth-eaten student's gown, peering owlishly over his spectacles to cheek his elders. He knows his position as heir to the throne protects him, and abuses it as far as he can. The easiest disguise for an adolescent with a problem too big for him is that of a problem adolescent.

It's a conception which requires a special kind of actor, young enough to play both buffoon and tragedian. The image may have been Hall's, but clearly it shaped itself around the peculiar talents of David Warner.[10] His Hamlet grows out of his Henry VI and Valentine Brose in *Eh?*:[11] an angelically gawky Danish stork, recognizable compatriot to Kierkegaard[12] and Hans Andersen,[13] who tries on ideas and emotions for size as he tries on the Player King's crown—it slips down over his nose. As he denounces the firmament to Rosencrantz and Guildenstern for a foul and pestilent congregation of vapours, he watches to see if they find his pessimism as impressive as it sounds. Do they believe it? Does he? Or are his emotions as false as theirs? They laugh, swinging teasingly on his long student's scarf, and he turns chastened to the arriving players, to test his rage and grief against those of Pyrrhus and Hecuba.

Warner is the first Hamlet, surely, young enough to play the prince as a real student, learning as he goes along. It's this that gives the production its marvellous new life: he feels each line back to freshness, lives each scene as if for the first time. He simply does not know what to do about Ophelia when he meets her. In his trouble, he has forgotten that she is a separate person, with her own emotions. He falls back shocked and fumbling at her reproaches—this, and her mad scene, are the points at which Glenda Jackson's[14] sharp, self-possessed personality are put to good account.

It's hard to convey the excitement of seeing him make each discovery, seeing the play's machinery dismantled and fitted together before your eyes. As Warner, sickened, fondles Yorick's skull (the earth is visible in its teeth), he tries to steel himself to realization of death. But as he says, 'Now, get you to my lady's chamber,' a lightening in his voice tells you he has not taught himself enough to face the shock, just a minute away, of Ophelia's burial. This is a Hamlet desperately in need of counsel, help, experience, and he actually seeks it from the audience in his soliloquies. That is probably the greatest triumph of the production: using the Elizabethan convention with total literalness, Hamlet communes not with himself but with you. For the first time in my experience, the rhetoric, spoken as it was intended to be, comes brilliantly to life.

The other innovations scarcely matter. Tony Church's[15] Polonius is a consciously pompous old politician, but no fool. Osric and the grave-diggers are less funny than usual; Fortinbras is the empty young con-queror Kott suggests; Brewster Mason's[16] Claudius is beery but briskly efficient, with more perfunctory pangs of conscience than usual. On the whole, the rest of the characters are simplifications, pushed aside to make room for the new, complex Hamlet.

That is the central vitality Hall has reinfused in the old tragedy. Ultimately, I'd say, its inspiration is Brechtian. For Hamlet and Ophelia, things might have gone otherwise. They might have grown differently, taken other roles. Life need not have turned them into legends. The most familiar masterpiece in English becomes new and unforeseeable again. So for the first time in years there can be a Hamlet who voluntarily embraces his destiny, achieving it with a sense both of triumph and of loss. His dying burst of laughter can be interpreted, if you like, as an existentialist's discovery, *à la* Kott, that the universe is absurd and history a trap. It makes more consistent sense in Warner's performance as the ironic con-vulsion of a boy who has finally achieved the princeliness he aspired to by dying, and can find that funny. There will no doubt be other, more traditionally tragic Hamlets carried out after him, head hanging behind the captains, into the dark. I cannot imagine any which, played as if this *Hamlet* had not happened, will be able to renew the same sense of loss.

1. **Malraux,** André (1901–76), French writer: 'Mais, que la... tragédie de la mort est en ceci qu'elle transforme la vie en destin', *L'Espoir* (1937), Part 2, Chapter 9; repr. 1948, p. 182.

2. **Bartlett's Familiar Quotations,** a popular reference book first issued in 1855.

3. **Neville,** John (born 1925), actor who has played many Shakespeare roles at the Old Vic and elsewhere.

4. **Kott,** Jan. See p. 269.

5. **Dean,** James (1931–55), American film actor who became a cult figure.

6. **Camus,** Albert (1913–60), French existentialist philosopher and novelist.

7. **Eliot,** T. S. (1888–1965), poet, playwright and critic. The allusion is to his essay 'Hamlet', first printed in 1919.

8. **White,** T. H. (1906–64), writer of fantasies. The allusion is to his Arthurian epics published together as *The Once and Future King* (1958).

9. **Bury,** John (born 1925), chief designer at the Royal Shakespeare Theatre from 1963 to 1973, head of design at the National Theatre from 1973 to 1985.

10. **Warner,** David (born 1941), joined the RSC in 1963 when he played Henry VI in *The Wars of the Roses.*

11. *Eh?* play (1964) by Henry Livings (born 1929) in which Warner appeared.

12. **Kierkegaard**, Søren (1813–55), Danish philosopher.

13. **Andersen**, Hans (1805–75), Danish writer of fairy tales.

14. **Jackson**, Glenda (born 1936), actress, elected MP for Hampstead in 1992.

15. **Church**, Tony (born 1930), actor with a special talent for Shakespeare and other classical drama.

16. **Mason**, Brewster (1922–87), actor who played many supporting, and some leading, roles with the RSC.

1970, Robert Speaight (1904–76) on Peter Brook's production of *A Midsummer Night's Dream* at the Royal Shakespeare Theatre, Stratford-upon-Avon, from *Shakespeare Quarterly*, 21 (1970), pp. 448–9.

ROBERT SPEAIGHT was distinguished as actor, verse speaker, and critic. Among his books is *Shakespeare on the Stage* (1973). For all its originality, this production played an almost unaltered text. It is illustrated in Pl. 12.

IT was eight years since Mr. Brook had directed a play at Stratford, and one assumed that he would not have directed the *Dream* unless he had something very particular to say about it. In fact, he forced one to forget—not, let me emphasize, the play itself—but anything one had seen done with it, or imagined being done with it, in the theatre. He swept the mind of the spectator as clear as he had swept his stage, allowing the text of the play, beautifully and deliberately spoken, to play upon you with the freshness of words seen for the first time upon the printed page. He persuaded you to forget a century of theatrical tradition, with its conventions and its clichés; and commanded you into a frame of mind where the very notion of magic, of supernatural agency, had to be created afresh. You could, if you chose, harbour a reminiscence of *Alice in Wonderland*,[1] but of nothing else. The French have a phrase which communicates the peculiar, the explosively original, quality of this production. They speak of a *mystère en pleine lumière*, and this suggests the brilliant white light that Mr. Brook threw upon his staring white stage, with only Titania's bright red feather bed to relieve it.

One saw nothing remotely resembling a tree—only coils of wire played out from a fishing rod over the iron railings which encircled the décor from above. One saw nothing remotely resembling a fairy—but then we were not supposed to have been brought up on fairies. Puck, who was also

Philostrate, might have reminded you a little of Pierrot; Theseus dreamt himself into Oberon, and Titania dreamt herself into Hippolyta. There was much play with steel ladders and spinning tops; and if you asked yourself how Mr. Brook was getting away with it all, you might have answered: 'Marry, how, *trapsically*'[2]—because Oberon and Puck descended from the skies on swings with an acrobatic agility. Indeed the virtuosities of the circus gave one a clue to Mr. Brook's translation of midsummer magic into surrealism. Yes, one might object, but how can a play spun out of cobwebs and gossamer, and drenched in the morning dew, stand up to a treatment so metallic and so apparently defiant of mystery? The answer is that the mystery was all the deeper because it was seen so clearly—as clearly, no doubt, as it was once seen on the bare platform of the Globe. Because the words had no visual counterpart, they seized the imagination the more surely. The play was recognized as timeless, because it was neither brought up, nor brought back, to date. Mr. Brook's audacious originality compelled respect, because he himself, in his recreation of a play about which everything had seemed to be said, had allowed it, in the last analysis, to stand gravely and lyrically, and also very amusingly, on its own feet. Utterly novel, it was still endearingly familiar. The laughs came in the right place, and when the poetry soared you caught your breath. This production was no brilliant exercise in cerebration; the pit of the stomach responded to it. Of course it would have been intolerable if the text had not been treated like the Ark of the Covenant, but here I can imagine Mr. Brook saying—'"Night's swift dragons cut the clouds asunder", don't ask me to assist a line like *that* with stage lighting.'

The humours of the play were safe—and indeed traditionally secure—with Mr. Waller [3] as Bottom principally in charge of them. No one I have seen since Ralph Richardson[4] has played the part as well—and that was nearly forty years ago. Mr. Locke's Quince was exquisitely muted to a kind of saintly (and no doubt celibate) simplicity, although why he should have doubled the part with Aegeus I could not quite understand. Miss Kestelman's[5] Titania was as easy to look at as to listen to. But the production was ruled, as it should be, by its Oberon and its Puck. Mr. Kane[6] salted his mischief with a Gallic wit, which I found a welcome relief from the conventional caperings, and spoke his verse as well as I have ever heard it spoken. Mr. Alan Howard[7] combined a patrician charm with an effortless authority, and justified his doubling of the part with Theseus, for alone in this play Theseus and Oberon are rulers. Each untangles the knot which others have tied. Mr. Howard's luminously clear handling of the verse was never so labored that it disturbed the melodic line. At a time when black magic is the only magic that most people any longer believe in, there was much excuse for a production of the *Dream* where the magic was as white as the Arctic snows or the swan's down on the Avon; and there was never a moment's doubt after the opening performance that this one had taken its place in history.

1 *Alice in Wonderland*, fantasy by Lewis Carroll (1832–98).
2 'Marry, how, *trapsically*', playing on Hamlet's 'Marry, how? Tropically' (3.2.226).
3 **Waller**, David (1920–97), actor who worked extensively with the RSC.
4 **Richardson**, Ralph. See p. 234. His roles included Bottom.
5 **Locke**, Philip (born 1928); Kestelman, Sara (born 1944), actors who have worked with the RSC and at the National Theatre.
6 **Kane**, John (born 1945).
7 **Howard**, Alan (born 1937), actor who played many leading roles with the RSC from 1966 to 1982.

[1973], Peter Thomson (born 1938) on *Richard II* directed by John Barton (born 1928) at the Royal Shakespeare Theatre, Stratford-upon-Avon, from *Shakespeare Survey 27* (1974), pp. 151–4.

PETER THOMSON, Professor of Drama at the University of Exeter, has written extensively on the theatres of Shakespeare's time. John Barton has directed many plays for the RSC. As in many of his productions, the text underwent adaptation.

I T would be easy to make John Barton's production of *Richard II* sound gimmicky and gratuitously theatrical, merely by listing some of its ingredients. The designers, Timothy O'Brien[1] and Tazeena Firth,[2] had flanked the central acting area with two escalators joined by a bridge which could ride noiselessly up and down them—a piece of refined visible mechanism that would have made Piscator[3] jealous, and could carry Richard down to the base court like glistering Phaethon on the Victoria Line. For their fight, Mowbray and Bolingbroke had been provided with elaborate hobby-horses similar to those used for *The Chances*[4] during Chichester's opening season. The Percys, 'riding' bigger, ominous-black horses, had to walk on short stilts to carry them. Richard, returned from Ireland, sat *astride* a white horse, erected in the middle of the stage, like the centre-piece of a *tableau-vivant*. Gloucester's widow was played as a ghost, emerging from the downstage grave-trap with a skull in her hand,

and speaking with the aid of echo-effects. v, ii began as a winter scene, with York and his Duchess wrapped against the cold, and a snowman ('a mockery king of snow') quirkily featured in a dominant central position. When York had completed his account of the entry into London of Bolingbroke and Richard, winter cloaks were doffed, the snowman melted, and spring colours greeted the lines:

> To Bolingbroke are we sworn subjects now,
> Whose state and honour I for aye allow.

(v, ii, 39–40)

The Queen's ladies-in-waiting wore decorative masks in their first two scenes, and their movements were stylised throughout. I have no idea why they were required to slither around the stage during Richard's farewell to his wife. In the garden scene, their formality was matched by the gardeners, dressed, again for no clear reason, as monks. It was also as a monk, walking beside Northumberland's horse and chanting *Kyrie Eleison*, that Bolingbroke made his return to England in ii, iii: and the cowl was again a disguise in the sensational substitution of Bolingbroke for Richard's groom in v, v. There is no doubt of the meretricious effectiveness of that theatrical moment when Bolingbroke lowered the hood to reassure Richard, 'What my tongue dares not, that my heart shall say'; but there is nothing else to say in defence of this invention (despite the coincidental use of a groom's disguise by Robert de Vere,[5] Richard's historical favourite). It related to the production's ruling decision—to play Richard and Bolingbroke as twin starring roles, along the lines indicated in Anne Barton's[6] programme note: 'Richard's journey from king to man is balanced by Bolingbroke's progress from a single to a twin-natured being. Both movements involve a gain and a loss. Each, in its own way, is tragic.' Within the terms of what, despite the claims made there, was a wholly theatrical decision, John Barton's production was *not* gimmicky. On the contrary, it was the passionately sensed and consistently argued presentation of a vision.

It has been generally my impression of John Barton's work that ideas encountered in the study are, with some effort, translated into the theatre. This was not so with *Richard II*. The informing idea of this production was the alternation of Richard Pasco[7] and Ian Richardson[8] as Richard and Bolingbroke—in itself a fascinating contrast between an actor naturally warm and 'romantic' and one cooler and more 'classical'. It began with the two actors meeting downstage of the sun-king's draped golden cloak, consulting the prompt-book (which shall play the king tonight?), turning upstage to hold the crown together—and freezing for a moment until the Bolingbroke of the night dropped his hand, and the Richard smiled, laughed, and was ready to lead the play into action. The performance was often in touch with the make-believe of children's games. The horses were an aspect of this. At the end, the 'groom' gave the imprisoned Richard a toy 'roan Barbary', and the coffin carrying Richard's body was a child's. It was, perhaps, this awareness of the child's vision that gave new weight to the concern for kinship of cousin, uncle, aunt. Certainly the opening was as jaunty as a family charade until the sudden hardening of Richard's face at Bolingbroke's first mention of Gloucester's death (i, i, 100), and there was a nursery petulance in the expression of 'We were not born to sue, but to command.' The by-play between Bolingbroke and Aumerle in i, iii preserved the sense of uncertain innocence, as did the chuckle with which Richard preceded his announcement of the banishments. It was during Mowbray's final denial of his guilt that Bolingbroke began the conscious calculation that was to be reinforced when Gaunt's gesture of grace over his head turned into the mimed holding of a crown. Both Richard and Bolingbroke signalled their role-playing to the audience. The kind of part they were playing varied with the play's crises, but not the awareness of themselves as actors. Bored with his pretence as righteous accuser, Bolingbroke broke off before completing his charges against Bushy and Green (iii, i), and the message to Richard in Flint Castle was turned into sportive deception when Northumberland, still on horseback, took it down in note form at Bolingbroke's dictation. When Northumberland assured Richard that Bolingbroke 'doth humbly kiss thy hand' (iii, iii, 104), the usurping actor was, in fact, standing casually downstage right. After a splendidly mobile staging of the often painful gage-throwing scene, iv, i continued to enforce the *double* role-playing. There was a conscious reminiscence of the opening mime in Richard's insistence that he and Bolingbroke hold the crown together, and a comically histrionic use by Richard of the kerchief given to him by Northumberland. Most notably, the circular property mirror was given a prominence which it retained until Richard's death. When Richard had punched out the glass, Bolingbroke lifted the empty ring-frame and placed it over Richard's head deliberately enough for us to see it pass from halo to crown, and from crown to noose to the enormously stressed accompaniment of:

> The shadow of your sorrow hath destroy'd
> The shadow of your face.

(iv, i, 292–3)

The stress on these lines, reinforced by repetition and echo-effects, was to be picked up in the final confrontation when Bolingbroke as Groom held the empty ring of the mirror between his face and Richard's, the mutual reflection of two shadows strutting and fretting their hour upon the stage. The death was a theatrical set-piece, with Richard hoisted by his chains some twelve feet above the stage and shot in the back by an arrow fired from upstage by Exton.

The use of so much that is conventionally associated with the stage's 'magic'—mechanical transformations, melting snowman, pantomime horses, stilt-walking, the tricky curtain-call—was consistent with the perception of the play's conscious theatricality. I am not so happy about the presentation of the narrative. By placing two detailed performances among so many generalised ones—varying from the domestic knockabout of Beatrix Lehmann's[9] Duchess of York (the authority for this is Boling-broke's comment on her entrance in v, iii, 'Our scene is alter'd from a serious thing'), through the sinister, black-clad Percys, to the emptily formal, emotionless Queen—Barton risked some obscuring of the action. The situation was not improved by the ill-advised doubling of Richard's sycophant Bagot and his murderer Exton (a grand piece of work in a small part by Anthony Pedley,[10] who had a workmanlike season throughout). The production laid no stress on the misdemeanours of Richard's favour-ites, and thus gave no serious hint of his homosexuality. The latter was no loss, but audiences unfamiliar with the text might have benefited from a clearer notion of the background to the usurpation. The best director I ever worked with as a student used to shout 'Plot!' whenever he thought we were mishandling crucially informative lines.

This was certainly not a 'straight' production as Professor Muir[11] would intend it. As the programme was at pains to point out, about 500 lines had been cut and twenty others imported from 2 *Henry IV* to give extra body to the role of Bolingbroke. It was, however, an intelligent and outstand-ingly bold attempt to give the text a life not merely *in* but *of* the theatre.

1. **O'Brien**, Timothy (born 1929), designer who became an Associate Artist of the RSC.

2. **Firth**, Tazeena (born 1935), designer who has worked extensively with O'Brien.

3. **Piscator**, Erwin (1893–1966), German designer who used complex, multi-level sets.

4. *The Chances*, play (1682) by George Villiers, 2nd Duke of Buckingham (1628–87) based on the comedy of the same name by John Fletcher (1579–1625) and performed in the opening season of the Chichester Festival, 1962.

5. **de Vere**, Robert (1362–92), 9th Earl of Oxford, close friend and favourite of Richard II.

6. **Barton**, Anne (born 1933), Shakespeare scholar, married to John Barton.

7. **Pasco**, Richard (born 1926), has acted many classical and modern roles with leading companies.

8. **Richardson**, Ian (born 1934), played many leading roles with the RSC from 1960 to 1976.

9. **Lehmann**, Beatrix (1903–79), actress, sister of the novelist Rosamond.

10. **Pedley**, Anthony (a young actor at this time).

11. **Muir**, Kenneth (1907–96), Shakespeare scholar; the earlier part of this review refers to his 'call for "straight" Shakespeare'.

[1976], Roger Warren (born 1943) on *Macbeth*, directed by Trevor Nunn at The Other Place, Stratford-upon-Avon, with Ian McKellen and Judi Dench, from *Shakespeare Survey 30* (1977), pp. 177–8.

ROGER WARREN teaches at the University of Leicester; his writings include *Staging Shakespeare's Late Plays* (Oxford, 1990). Trevor Nunn (born 1940) was appointed Artistic Director of the RSC in 1968 and of the National Theatre in 1996.

TREVOR Nunn's *Macbeth* at the Other Place (the RSC's studio theatre) was the best example of the company's developing work on a single play. Mr Nunn's elaborate version at Stratford in 1974 . . . was drastically simplified for the Aldwych in 1975; it had been further refined for the small confines of the Other Place, where it was played within a black magic circle painted on the floor, outside which the cast sat on boxes until needed; and, as at the Aldwych, there was no interval, which helped prevent the second half from winding down.

Much of the approach and detail was carried over, particularly the clash between religious purity and black magic. Purity was embodied by Duncan, very infirm (in 1974 he was blind), dressed in white and accompanied by church organ music, set against the black magic of the witches, who even chanted 'Double, double' to the *Dies irae*. The 1974 version used black masses, church services, and the coronations of, in turn, Duncan, Macbeth, and Malcolm. Here a gold robe and crown simply passed from one to the other, with the additional point that, by the end, ceremony had become meaningless because Macbeth had so desecrated the office: a stunned weariness overcame Malcolm and the surviving lords, and instead of a coronation, robe and crown were simply carried away after his weary exit, leaving the stage to the weapons and shattered trappings of Macbeth's regime.

Other striking effects reappeared: Lady Macbeth sat on the stool to emphasize that Banquo's ghost was an illusion; the witches were practical and down-to-earth, the first carrying a handbag and mixing her brew in an old kettle, and only the second having any obvious link with the supernatural; Macbeth was compelled to *drink* their brew and was blindfolded to 'see' the inheritance of Banquo and his heirs as an appalling insight of his own. The sharpest development was in the presentation of the besieged Macbeth. When in 1974 he sat on top of a precarious pile of chairs to look for Birnham Wood, it seemed merely a quirky trick. This time, he sat surrounded by the boxes that had served as seats earlier and by the ceremonial robe and crown, completely the focus of attention; the besieging lords played their brief scenes outside the circle while he still sat there; he looked for Birnham Wood by putting just one box on top of another so that he could reach an overhead spotlight which he directed first towards Birnham and then all round the theatre; it then began to sway wildly of its own accord, the estate of the world all undone.

The vital development, though, was that these ideas, interesting in themselves, were forged into a convincing whole because, this time, Mr Nunn had two players able to rise to all the challenges of Macbeth and Lady Macbeth. Ian McKellen, with greased-back hair, black-shirted and coldly efficient, recalled the fascist image of the 1930s. Judi Dench,[1] slight and dressed in sober (drab?) black with a headscarf, was simple and direct, her invoking of the spirits uncluttered by the 1974 trappings of black magic; from this simplicity it was an easy step to the welcome of Duncan, so deceptively open that Duncan dismissed Macduff, who was supporting him ('By your leave') and took *her* arm ('Hostess!') so that she could smilingly lead him to his death. As they left the circle, Macbeth rapidly entered it from the other side and began 'If it were done... then 'twere well it were done *quickly*' very fast, neatly underlining their *combined* handling of the situation.

They certainly seemed husband and wife, not merely in passion but in the quiet, natural, almost colloquial handling of their conversations. She brought out Lady Macbeth's essentially practical qualities: 'It *must* seem / their / guilt' was a slow, emphatic explanation; 'there are two lodged together' was an attempt to calm his fears of the supernatural by stressing the ordinary and the reasonable; her 'Come on!' meant 'snap out of it' in response to 'after life's fitful fever he sleeps well'. All this made the cracking of their relationship especially successful: Macbeth ordered her out of the room ('God be with you') before plotting Banquo's murder; 'Come, seeling night' was addressed directly to her, and at 'scarf up the tender eye' he covered her face, thereby adding to her bewilderment in the text. After the banquet, her hysterical 'go at once!' instantly gave way to an attempt at graciousness ('a kind good night'); there they sat, she bleakly smiling and he waving goodbye in the aftermath of a foaming fit, both total wrecks, a marvellous image of the hollow kingship they risked so much to gain. But then she collapsed; he dragged her up at 'young in deed' and pulled her away, firmly replacing her as the more resolute of the two.

Fine as these scenes were, best of all was the scene with the murderers. Macbeth was at his most briskly administrative, busy with papers, as he blackened Banquo; then he suddenly turned a cold, beady eye upon them to make the distinctions about dogs and men; once the business of the meeting was over, a dismissive jerk of the head to Seyton to get rid of them contrasted with the affable 'abide within' to them. At the end, his vision was one of total nihilism, with no touch of conventional sentimentality at 'troops of friends'.

Mr Nunn, for all his emphasis on black magic versus white purity, also avoided sentimental over-emphasis of those images or passages which are said to embody the 'poetry of the commonweal': John Woodvine's[2] 'temple-haunting martlet' was a genially paternal lesson for Fleance, and the 'positive' value of the image lost nothing by being expressed lightly. If Malcolm was dressed in symbolic white sweater and jodhpurs, as opposed to everyone else's black, there was no forcing in the English scene: Roger Rees[3] was encouraged to play his deception of Macduff and the description of the King's Evil easily and naturally.

On the other hand, Macduff was variable, dour, devoid of personality (as in the text?) and Duncan was so mannered and so infuriatingly holy that he simply cried out for assassination, at total variance with Mr Nunn's setting-up of the character. It is also hard to see how Mr Nunn can encourage (or permit) the presentation of the Porter as a stand-up comedian, hopelessly wrecking his ironic commentary on the main action ('porter of hell-gate', 'devil-porter it no further'), quite apart from the inadequacy of the performance.

1. **McKellen**, Ian (born 1939; knighted 1991), and **Dench**, Judi (born 1934; Dame of the British Empire, 1988) have played many leading roles with the RSC and the National Theatre.

2. **Woodvine**, John (born 1929), played Banquo.

3. **Rees**, Roger (born 1944), played Malcolm.

[1978], Roger Warren on *Love's Labour's Lost* directed by John
  Barton at the Royal Shakespeare Theatre, Stratford-upon-Avon;
  from *Shakespeare Survey 32* (1979), pp. 208–9.

JOHN BARTON had previously directed the play for the RSC in 1965.

IN his 1965 production of *Love's Labour's Lost*, John Barton sought
to 'explore the relationships of the characters beneath the highly-
jewelled surface': the 1978 version took this process further, and paid
even less attention to surface glitter. True, Ralph Koltai's[1] set was exquisitely beautiful and appropriate, enormous boughs of cascading autumnal
leaves entirely enclosing a raked wooden forestage, behind which seats
and a leaf-strewn floor suggested distant parkland. But there was no
external glamour about the two courts, which seemed humbler, less
formal, than usual: the lords took their oaths with little ceremony on a
rustic seat; Rosaline cleaned the Princess's travelling boots and the travel-
stained hem of her skirt in their first scene, and swept up autumn leaves
with a broom in the last; the King and the Princess, especially, were very
unelaborate, untidy even, in appearance, ordinary human beings rather
than heads of state, especially when they first met, a rather endearingly
unimpressive, bespectacled pair: a long silence indicated sudden (to them
embarrassing) mutual attraction.

To cast Richard Griffiths,[2] the company's superbly apt Bottom, Trinculo, and Pompey, as the King of Navarre was clearly a deliberate attempt
to avoid the stereotype of elegant aristocracy. With his quietly conversational style, this was not a Navarre to sound the splendour of the opening
speech or the lyricism of his sonnet. On the other hand, this King could
switch quickly from the chop-logic about Aquitaine to a considerate 'Your
fair self should make/A yielding *'gainst some reason* in my breast', and
could attempt to soften the inhospitable blow with his 'here without you
shall be so receiv'd/As you shall deem yourself lodg'd in my heart', while at
the same time embarrassedly admitting the contradictory situation his
oath has landed him in—'Though so denied fair harbour in my house'.
This King and Princess seemed to be, as Mr Barton said of the Princess in
his 1965 programme note, 'none too sure about how to cope with any
situation'.

Michael Pennington[3] understudied Berowne in the earlier version, and
played it occasionally: a good performance in 1965 became a brilliant one
in 1978. To an easy, relaxed manner for the opening he added a powerful
desire for 'I forsooth in love' and an intense, almost erotic lyricism for the

great defence of Love, which rightly became the climax of the first half. This scene typified the production's quality, building superbly from one humorous peak to another, without loss of humanity: the lords' poems were not guyed, but rather became the rapid, passionate release of pent-up desire, Dumaine bringing us back to earth with his resolve to send 'something else *more plain*' as well. Berowne's mockery gained particular impact from this particular interpretation of the King, Mr Griffiths physically crumpling in plump, blushing confusion.

But after this explosion of gaiety, the lords fell into the sobered realisation that they were 'all forsworn'. Mr Barton emphasised throughout the serious consequences of the oath-breaking to which the characters constantly refer, and for an important reason. As he put it in the 1965 programme,

ridiculous and impracticable, . . . it is an oath all the same, and a serious one. So when the King and the rest break it at the first sight of a woman's eyes, the girls are justified in questioning their oaths of love.

So after the second great outburst of gaiety, the Masque of Russians, the text was slightly re-arranged so that the King's earnest 'Despise me when I break this oath of mine', and the Princess's answering rage against 'perjur'd men', furiously sweeping up leaves with Rosaline's broom, became the 'fair fray' which Costard interrupted; a little later the Princess used her request to see the play ('let me o'errule you now') as an overture of conciliation.

Such relationships were sustained during the play scene, with no sacrifice of humour or invention. The Worthies used a variety of hobbyhorses, and Nathaniel's confused repetition of 'When in the world I liv'd, I was the world's commander' was caused by his gradual overbalancing under the weight of his horse and by the awkwardness of his enormously long lance: Alexander was literally 'overthrown'. But this hilarious sequence was also used in the interests of character, for the Princess and the King, working together, helped him up again and returned his lance.

The long dying fall was more effective, more astonishing than ever. As in 1965, it began with Armado's entry as Hector, accompanied by fading light and an especially haunting old Flemish melody offstage. This elegiac sequence ('The sweet war-man is dead and rotten') modulated into Marcade's entry without in any way diminishing its power or its theatrical and human magic, as the affairs of state took over and all knelt to the new Queen; Armado, still mounted on his lifts as Hector, saluted her with his rapier. Carmen du Sautoy's Princess took off her spectacles as she took on authority: 'Prepare, I say!' had an imperious command as bespectacled uncertainty gave way to new-found domination of the stage, matching the new confident fluency of her verse at this point. And because the oaths had been so stressed earlier, her stern conditions seemed a genuine necessity. As before, Mr Barton retained part of what looks like an uncancelled first draft of the final Berowne/Rosaline exchange at v, ii, 805–7,

> *Berowne.*
> And what to me, my love? and what to me?
> *Rosaline.*
> You must be purged too, your sins are rack'd;
> You are attaint with faults and perjury,

so that Rosaline could sit downstage thinking during the next exchanges, thus prompting Berowne's '*studies* my lady?'; Jane Lapotaire[4] deflated his jaunty cocksureness easily—though the final 'A twelvemonth?' had the wryness of a negotiated peace, Berowne the individualist to the end.

Mr Barton repeated his earlier innovation of having the final songs spoken, thereby throwing greater emphasis onto their vivid images of country life; but he extended the idea so that all the villagers echoed the 'Cuckoo' and 'Tu-whit, tu-who', and, even more important, the court, led by the King and Princess, joined in too, so that the stage became filled with harmonious echoes of country sounds—exquisitely capped by the hooting of a *real* owl above their heads, magically reinforcing Shakespeare's own final emphasis upon the ordinary realities of country life. Such an extraordinarily complex scene, which takes the breath away with its combination of gaiety and sadness, its blending of affairs of state, of the heart, of the countryside, is Mr Barton's special territory as a director. He clearly delights in probing the implications of imagery and characterisation, and is rightly unafraid of fleshing out his discoveries in terms of concrete theatrical effects and sustained, detailed characterisation which, far from over-loading the text, have the supreme advantage of increasing admiration for it, emphasising the sheer confident mastery of Shakespeare's writing in this scene.

Penelope Gilliatt[5] wrote of Mr Barton's earlier version:

When it is done this way, the play can become a marvellous testament of a great writer finding himself; ... and the soaring generosity of the play as it climbs to its sombre ending ... has the grasp of a genius who has suddenly found his life work under his hands.

This magnificently realised scene fittingly concluded a season in which old and new interpretations of Shakespeare's comedies had been most profitably and satisfyingly blended.

1. **Koltai**, Ralph (born 1924), has designed many productions for the RSC and other companies.
2. **Griffiths**, Richard (born 1947), also played Bottom, Trinculo and Pompey during the season.
3. **Pennington**, Michael (born 1943), has played many Shakespeare roles with, especially, the RSC and the English Shakespeare Company (see p. 297).
4. **Lapotaire**, Jane (born 1944), has played many leading roles in classical and other plays.
5. **Gilliatt**, Penelope (1932–93), fiction writer and critic; the quotation is from *The Observer*, 11 April 1965.

29 June 1984, Stanley Wells (born 1930) on Antony Sher (born 1949) as Richard III, directed at the Royal Shakespeare Theatre, Stratford-upon-Avon, by Bill Alexander (born 1948); from the *Times Literary Supplement*, p. 729.

B ILL ALEXANDER'S[1] big, bold production of *Richard III* is distinguished by its respect for the text, its confident but sensitive response to verbal style, and its willingness to draw on the traditions of spectacular theatre to flesh out Shakespeare's rhetorically sophisticated and self-conscious dialogue. William Dudley's[2] set fills the proscenium arch with a two-storey, elaborately sculpted and windowed screen; its style is continued in the benches and doors on each side of the forestage. The screen can rise to reveal a cathedral interior with four massive tombs, two to each side of the main stage. This is a society dominated by at least the forms of religion; Richard's evil is measured by his revolt against it. The thematic deliberateness is stressed by the reprinting in the programme of Browning's[3] 'The Bishop Orders his Tomb at Saint Praxed's Church'.

The set can suggest ironic contrasts. Hastings emerges from the screen, naked to the waist, with a maid and a wordless Jane Shore who help him to wash and dress; while Tyrrel tells Richard of the murders in the Tower they kneel among the tombs and an offstage choirboy sings. But the screen lets us see too little of Richard and the clergymen at Baynard's Castle, and we have to forget the tombs for Bosworth Field, when the forestage comes into its own: there is ample space for Richard's and Richmond's tents at each side. The entire playing area is thrillingly used for the episode of Richard's and Anne's coronation, in which all the actors, richly costumed, fill the stage to sing a resplendent *Gloria* (by Guy Woolfenden[4]) with brass accompaniment from an onstage band. Incense perfumes the air; the sinister, scarlet-clad Richard forms a grotesque centrepiece. We might almost be at Covent Garden in the era of John Philip Kemble.[5] It makes a magnificent climax to the first act.

Alexander has encouraged his actors to match the play's rhetoric with a boldness of declamation corresponding to the visual splendours. Patricia Routledge,[6] as Queen Margaret, unkempt of hair and draped in banners, awes the audience as well as the onstage characters with the vocal range and the fearless intensity of her curses, and Harold Innocent[7] is equally powerful as the dying Edward IV. Not all the actors succeed so well in matching vocal delivery to verbal style, or in encompassing some of the longer verse paragraphs, but shifts of lighting and grouping respond to the play's fluctuations from the particular to the general, and Roger Allam[8] does well by Clarence's introspection.

Interpretation of the play of *Richard III* depends heavily on the performance of the central role. It is a strength of Alexander's direction that it gives full scope to Antony Sher's[9] Richard, a performance which aims at, and achieves, brilliance. The opening lines are spoken quietly, almost didactically; but with 'But I, that am not framed for sportive tricks', Sher advances menacingly on the audience, his body swinging like a missile on the adeptly manipulated callipers that support it, his hump displayed with a kind of inverted pride. Dressed almost throughout in black, a short, curly-headed figure, he looks rather like a spindle-legged, knock-kneed caricature of Henry Irving.[10]

The voice is capable of mellifluousness as well as malice; rapid, jerky movements and a vocal delivery that occasionally sacrifices nuance to speed suggest hyperactive mental activity, a capacity to charm and fascinate as well as to repel. There is an achieved (but not exaggerated) eroticism in his encounters with both Lady Anne and Queen Elizabeth, but essentially he is a cerebral character, a satirist who delights in analysing Lady Anne's weakness—'Was ever woman in this humour wooed?' is delivered to the audience with aggressive, contemptuous insolence.

Though small, he is capable of frightening physical violence, crashing his crutch devastatingly on the table in the council scene, but his mind and purpose control his emotions. Taunted by the little Duke of York— 'Because that I am little, like an ape, / He thinks that you should bear me on your shoulders'—he responds with playful mimicry of an ape; only after York departs does he show resentment.

The second act begins with the crowned Richard in a court apparently suffering an acute hangover after the splendours of the coronation. Only Richard is beginning to recover; a disconsolate Anne hears him tell Catesby to rumour that she 'is sick and like to die'. Other Richards have suggested greater depths with 'I am in / So far in blood that sin will pluck on sin', but the grim self-knowledge with which Sher invests it points to a strength of his performance and of Alexander's interpretation. The play is treated as an ironic tragedy, not as a first sketch for *Macbeth*. 'I am not in the giving vein' is lightly handled, and comedy verges on farce as Richard, carried on a portable throne, has himself rapidly turned from one direction to the other in response to his mother's rebukes; but he is severely shaken by her curse, his tongue flicking like a serpent's as he strives to regain his equilibrium.

In the closing scenes, he is at first ebullient in the face of bad news. 'Is the chair empty?' is not a cry of despair but defiantly, confidently ironical. His soliloquy is an intellectual self-exploration, not an emotional revelation; what shakes him is his subsequent astonished discovery that he is capable of fear: 'Ratcliffe, I fear, I fear.' The oration to the army, delivered from a large black hobby-horse (Richmond has a golden one) betrays this; he is at first hesitant, then rhetorically hectoring. There is pathos in his final, deformed, dismounted, blood-stained helplessness.

He kneels facing us. Richmond, glittering in golden armour and holding aloft a prominently cruciform sword, advances from behind to stab him through the neck of his corslet. We need to have believed Richmond's claim to be one of God's 'ministers of chastisement' not to find a destructive irony in this. The body rocks from side to side as the crown is removed and handed to Richmond. The dead Richard topples sideways, a choirboy's voice is raised, and Richmond's triumph is signalled by another *Gloria*.

1. **Alexander**, Bill, was an Associate Director of the RSC.
2. **Dudley**, William, theatre and opera designer.
3. **Browning**, Robert (1812–89), poet.
4. **Woolfenden**, Guy (born 1937), has composed scores for all Shakespeare's plays for the RSC.
5. **Kemble**, J. P. See p. 33.
6. **Routledge**, Patricia (born 1929).
7. **Innocent**, Harold (1935–93).
8. **Allam**, Roger (born 1953).
9. **Sher**, Antony. Richard III was his first great success.
10. **Irving**, Henry. See p. 106.

[March 1985], Nicholas Shrimpton (born 1948) on a production of
the First Quarto version of *Hamlet* at the Orange Tree Theatre,
Richmond, Surrey, in *Shakespeare Survey 39* (1987), pp. 193–7.

THE first version of *Hamlet* to be printed is the quarto of 1603, known as
the 'bad' quarto because it appears to derive from an unauthorized text,
perhaps compiled from memory by actors who had taken part in performances
by Shakespeare's company. In literary quality it is far inferior to the 'good'
quarto of 1604 and to the version printed in the Folio of 1623; nevertheless, it
has interesting differences, especially in structure, from those texts; it may
incorporate revisions made for performances by Shakespeare's company, and
it provides information about early performances of the play, whether authorized
or not. For these reasons it has occasionally been performed, initially in
modern times by William Poel in 1881, usually by amateurs, but in the production reviewed here by a professional company. Nicholas Shrimpton is a Fellow
of Lady Margaret Hall, Oxford. (The production previously discussed in this
article was Peter Hall's of *Coriolanus*, with Ian McKellen, at the National
Theatre.)

HUMBLER circumstances of every kind attended Sam Walter's[1] production of the 1603 First Quarto of *Hamlet* at the Orange Tree
Theatre, Richmond in March 1985. The text, the setting (a small bare
room above a pub), and the limited cast (nine actors performed nineteen
parts, then re-doubled themselves as the Players) all promised to present
insuperable difficulties. Scholarly curiosity might be satisfied by such an
enterprise, but could anything else be said for it? These fears were wholly
unjustified. The tragic experience proved to be more vividly available
here, in the modern equivalent of an inn-yard, than it had been on the
stage of the National Theatre.

In part this was simply confirmation of the growing sense that *Hamlet*,
in whatever text, is today most effective in studio performance. The
cheek-by-jowl intimacy of the Orange Tree's tiny auditorium suited
both the private processes of Hamlet's introspection and the conspirator-
ial closeness of public life at Elsinore. Sending Hamlet to England
('Lords Rossencraft and Gilderstone shall goe along with you'), Claudius
received a whispered answer, full of soft and deadly irony: 'O with *all* my
heart: farewel mother'. At the same time the spectacular aspects of the
play, which might seem to be at risk in such circumstances, were very little
harmed. Peter Wyatt's[2] rapid and passionate ghost, for example, was
played without smoke, gauzes, or even much of a lighting plot. It seemed
all the better for it.

The text itself, for all its imperfections, contributed something to the freshness of the playing. Walters had, reasonably enough, made absolute fidelity subordinate to the needs of performance and tidied up a few of the more ludicrous or confusing variants. King Hamlet's sepulchre, accordingly, 'op'd' rather than 'burst' his ponderous and marble jaws, Hamlet spoke of 'country' rather than 'contrary' matters to Ophelia, and The Mousetrap took place in familiar Vienna rather than surprising 'Guyana'. This meant that the production was not a perfect test of the quality and status of the First Quarto. In larger matters, however, the actors were true to their distinctive script and the consequences were striking. The brevity of this text (2,154 lines against the 3,723 of the Second Quarto) proved ideally suited to the kind of small-scale performance for which it was, very probably, originally intended. Regional repertory companies who shrink from the cost of a conventional *Hamlet* might well consider this alternative.

Even the oddity had its advantages. Listening to the First Quarto in performance proved to be an experience not unlike hearing the New English Bible read in church. It is commonplace but clear ('*Hamlet*. I never loved you. *Ofelia*. You made me believe you did'), prompting perpetual ghostly memories of the more familiar text but keeping the essential issues always in view. This can, of course, induce its own kind of confusion. But the benefits are also very real. Actors as well as audiences are stimulated by the newness of the lines. Peter Guinness's delivery of 'To be, or not to be, I there's the point' commanded an intense attention which I have rarely seen the uncorrupted text achieve in the theatre. After the second line ('To Die, to sleepe, is that all? I all') he took off his coat and began to exit. Then, suddenly, moved by a fresh thought, he stepped back and continued. Death was vividly in every mind long before he reached 'he may his full Quietus make, / With a bare bodkin', delivered with his dagger in position to cut his wrist.

This is, of course, at least as much a tribute to Guinness's playing as it is to the fortuitous oddity of his material. He was a gaunt and dangerous Hamlet, a pock-marked malcontent who refrained from action only because he chose to. This text is the only one to authorize a teenaged Hamlet. Walters and Guinness ignored such prompting and gave us a mature man whose extensive knowledge of the world only deepened his distress. The affected madness was powerfully handled (one of the incidental benefits of First Quarto proved to be that the court's worry on this score is so strongly indicated), and the early placing of the nunnery scene, whatever the arguments against its authenticity, served to establish the sense of a man who is from the first disgusted with life. First Quarto is a lesser text than its alternatives. But this production gave clarity, energy, and tension to the ideas which it does contain and offered the most entirely satisfactory piece of tragic acting of the year.

1. **Walters**, Sam (born 1939).
2. **Wyatt**, Peter (born 1928).

[1985], Roger Warren on Howard Davies's production of *Troilus and Cressida* at the Royal Shakespeare Theatre, Stratford-upon-Avon, from *Shakespeare Quarterly,* 37 (1986), pp. 116–18.

THOUGH it was presumably acted in Shakespeare's time, and though Dryden's radical adaptation, *Troilus and Cressida, or Truth Found Too Late,* held the stage between 1679 and 1734, we have no certain record of performances of Shakespeare's play until the twentieth century, and even then some of the more influential performances have been given by amateur companies. Since the 1930s it has gained in significance because of its concern with the interaction of war with personal values. Although one of the finest productions, directed by Peter Hall and John Barton for the Royal Shakespeare Company in 1960, was given in classical costumes, many modern directors, including Howard Davies, have updated the action as a way of illuminating its topical significances.

HOWARD DAVIES'S[1] production of *Troilus and Cressida* took place during the Crimean War. A war-shattered nineteenth-century interior was the setting throughout, with heavy Victorian furniture added to suggest the different locations. The Greek council became a war cabinet meeting around a long table. The Myrmidons' mess was a smoky, seedy saloon bar. The Trojan council took place amid the silver and cut glass of a family dining room; Cassandra was a family embarrassment, the mad sister whose remarks were tolerated but could be safely disregarded. This was quite a persuasive nineteenth-century equivalent for the prophetess who was fated never to be believed. The episode represented the gains and losses of the approach. Cassandra's scene did not degenerate into rant, as it often does; but like much of the precise period detail, the solution was almost too neat: there was a loss of scale, of the sense of a society wilfully ignoring plain warnings of imminent disaster.

At first David Burke's[2] greying, humourless Hector seemed merely loud and tedious, grinding out his rebuke to Troilus and Paris for arguing 'superficially'; but gradually the strategy became clear. Placed at the front of the stage, head on to the audience, Hector slowly and coolly established that it was wrong to keep Helen, and then equally coolly announced his intention of doing just that, in the name of the superficial honour he had just discredited. I have never known this celebrated *volte-face* so uncompromisingly presented: the man crumbled before our eyes. In the duel with Ajax, fought with cavalry sabres on the tables in the officers' mess, Hector followed the nineteenth-century code of 'officers and gentlemen,' especially when those officers were related by family ties ('the obligation of our blood'): he called a halt to the fight because Ajax was his 'father's sister's son.' Achilles scandalized everyone because he outraged this officers' code by threatening to kill Hector. After initial hesitations, Hector finally went to the fatal battlefield because he had promised a brother officer to do so: 'I must not *break* my *faith*.' In this nineteenth-century setting, Hector's 'fair play' seemed like an adherence to what are often nostalgically called 'Victorian values,' and its weaknesses were mercilessly revealed.

The very specifically nineteenth-century setting both helped and hindered Peter Jeffrey's[3] Ulysses. He was given commanding positions behind tables that helped him to deliver the Degree and Time speeches with maximum clarity; but coming from a Victorian statesman in a frock coat his wisdom sounded like a series of sententious platitudes. Alan Rickman's[4] Achilles was effective in silent reaction to Ulysses's sharply edged suggestion that he was no longer 'heroical,' but disastrous in speech, ranting and gabbling incomprehensibly. In general the period detail was applied too thickly and slowed down the play, notably in the Helen scene. Helen herself was finely played by Lindsay Duncan[5] as a soft-voiced but hard-centred tease who was obviously very tired both of Paris and of endless talk about love; but to underline the point that a decadent society had degraded her to a mere love-object, Paris and his officers were reduced to loutish public-school boors who drunkenly debagged the civilian Pandarus. Such business was both irrelevant and tedious, and there was so much of it that Thersites's commentaries seemed almost redundant: Alun Armstrong's[6] vivid performance of a soldier from the ranks who despised the officers' code became a vilely funny but extraneous comic turn.

The scenes between Troilus, Cressida, and Pandarus fared best. Since playing Troilus in the BBC television production, Anton Lesser seemed to have acquired a new verbal flexibility that gave individual phrases—'Less valiant than the virgin in the night'—a new immediacy. Juliet Stevenson's[7] mercurial Cressida was an extremely varied performance, mocking and teasing Pandarus about Troilus, yawning and collapsing from boredom at the mere mention of Paris. But the brazen manner was a cover to protect herself from becoming a love-object like Helen. 'You are a bawd,' she told Pandarus accusingly, suddenly serious after their banter: he shrugged, as if to say 'that's life.' Both lovers swore their oaths lightly, increasing rather than diminishing their impact. Mr. Lesser made 'as true as Troilus' the humorous climax of a speech in which he had run out of 'similes'; Miss Stevenson likewise thought her way through the following speech, searching for the appropriate phrases and in the process bringing new life to 'When time is old and hath forgot itself, / When waterdrops have worn the stones of Troy'; a speech of Cleopatra-like variety ended with a tensely whispered 'as false as Cressid.'

When she arrived at the Greek camp, the generals subjected her to brutally violent kisses that amounted to assault. At first appalled, she soon began to play their game, a point brilliantly made when Ulysses asked for his kiss: 'Why, beg then,' she replied tartly, snapping her fingers to indicate that he should kneel. She had become a love-object after all, and Ulysses made the parallel with Helen specific: he would claim his kiss 'when Helen is a maid again, and his.' Miss Stevenson maintained Cressida's volatility and vitality to the end in a very complete performance; but Mr. Lesser unfortunately fell back on his old mannerisms, stabbing at lines like 'This is, and is not, Cressid.' Clive Merrison's Pandarus, younger than usual, lived vicariously through his niece and his friend; after their parting he broke down, and ended up a wreck in dark glasses, obsessively playing the piano throughout the final battle sequences while the set collapsed around him: his world literally disintegrated amid the chaos of war. This image suggested both the crippled hero of *Endgame*[8] and the film *Casablanca*,[9] another story of lovers parted by war. It seemed that the production had to look beyond the nineteenth century for an image to match the bleakness of the ending.

1. **Davies**, Howard (born 1945), joined the RSC as a director in 1975 and became a National Theatre associate director in 1988.
2. **Burke**, David (born 1934).
3. **Jeffrey**, Peter (born 1929).
4. **Rickman**, Alan (born 1946).
5. **Duncan**, Lindsay (born 1950).

6. **Armstrong**, Alun (born 1946).
7. **Stevenson**, Juliet (born 1956).
8. *Endgame*, play (1957) by Samuel Beckett (1906–89).
9. *Casablanca*, film (1943) starring Humphrey Bogart and Ingrid Bergman.

[1986], Stanley Wells on *Henry IV*, Parts One and Two, and *Henry V* directed by Michael Bogdanov (born 1938) and performed on tour by the English Shakespeare Company, from *Shakespeare Survey 41* (1989), pp. 159–62.

THE English Shakespeare Company was founded in 1986 and directed jointly by Michael Bogdanov and Michael Pennington. They later added versions of *Richard II*, the Henry VI plays, and *Richard III* to form a cycle which they toured as *The Wars of the Roses*. The story is told in their book *The English Shakespeare Company: The Story of 'The Wars of the Roses'* (1990). The production is illustrated in Pl. 13.

THE new company's first production presented Parts One and Two of *Henry IV* along with *Henry V* as a cycle, and I saw all three plays at the Old Vic during a single day. Such theatrical endurance tests, though popular, are of doubtful validity. Of course, this one provided an opportunity to enjoy within a short space of time an extraordinary diversity of dramatic writing linked by a narrative thread. It also brought audiences together in a curious sort of bonding with their fellow theatregoers and the performers, with both of whom they experienced an unnaturally close relationship for a concentrated period of time. There is a self-gratulatory air about such audiences, speaking of their experience as a marathon while they queue for lavatories and sit on staircases to eat improvised meals during the relatively short breaks between performances. In the auditorium, heads droop on to neighbouring shoulders as the day wears on, and at the end of it all is a sense of celebration of the successful survival of a self-inflicted ordeal.

Michael Bogdanov's production revealed the artificiality of regarding these three plays as a cycle even by the means it used to weld them together. Absence of *Richard II* both left a gap in the historical narrative and encouraged an emphasis on the development of Prince Hal into Henry V; but the two Parts of *Henry IV* notoriously fail to provide the materials for a clearly developing study.

Bogdanov opened genially with a song in which the whole company joined, sketching a context for the story of 'a king who was mighty, but wild as a boy' and inviting us to 'list to the ballad of Harry Leroy'. Both the popular mode of the ballad and the simplistic reduction of the narrative reflected Bogdanov's missionary zeal as one who would mediate Shakespeare to his notions of what constitutes a popular audience. Costumes (designed by Stephanie Howard) were eclectic and mainly of the twentieth century. Simple settings (by Chris Dyer) suggested locations by the use of minimal properties, hangings, scaffolding, and a movable bridge which provided an upper acting area. Action was steadily paced, speech consistently clear, the meaning well digested and forcefully conveyed. Production devices identified groupings among the characters and set one group against another. The English court was characterized by formality—symmetrical groupings, frock coats and scarlet uniforms, standard English pronunciation. Snatches of classical music—a Bach organ toccata, a Handel coronation anthem—and sometimes the striking of Big Ben introduced their scenes. The rebels generally wore khaki and denims, spoke in an assortment of local accents (not consistently well sustained), swigged from bottles with their feet on tables, and displayed a tendency to take their shirts off—Douglas even on the battlefield. Their scenes were introduced by urgent, strident, modern music.

Shakespeare's set pieces were given their full value. In Part One, the big tavern scene was admirably built up, with on-stage spectators directing the responses of their counterparts in the auditorium, reacting with delight to Hal's and Falstaff's fecundity in the coining of epithets. Welsh speeches were amply written in for the benefit of Lady Mortimer, and a visible group of instrumentalists provided the music that Glyndwr speaks of conjuring up. It was all part of a very proper realization and enjoyment of the text's theatrical values, extending at points to the invention of episodes: Bardolph entered playing 'Silver threads among the gold'[1] on his trombone, followed by John Woodvine's[2] purple-suited Falstaff. Meditatively, Falstaff slowly cracked six eggs, one after the other, into a tankard, filled it to the brim from a vodka bottle, swirled the tankard around, and drank, all to Bardolph's continuous, maudlin accompaniment. The audience applauded. (Presumably it was after this that Falstaff developed his distaste for 'pullet sperm' in his 'brewage'.[3]) In Part Two, Pistol especially provided the opportunity for another series of tableaux; at times I was reminded of children's-paper versions of Shakespeare that print the full text alongside garish, comic-strip illustrations of the action.

The element of simplification in the production style carried over into Michael Pennington's[4] characterization of the Prince. Pennington is a well graced actor, easy of movement, finely built, honey-tongued. In the earlier scenes of Part One he subdued his princeliness to Hal's wilder side. He was affectionate with Falstaff, rather drunk in the first tavern scene, fraternal with Charles Lawson's aggressively Irish Poins, derisively rude (against the implications of the text) to the Sheriff and the Carrier (portrayed, characteristically, as modern policemen) who come to complain of the robbery. Called before the King his father, he was at first detached and sullenly rebellious, gabbling his first expressions of penitence as an empty formality. Only when the King spoke of Hotspur was Hal stung to a sense of responsibility; then he rapidly took on the characteristics of the court party. The closing scenes were rearranged, presumably in order to make more plausible Hal's return to the tavern in Part Two. The King was present to hear Sir John's claim to have killed Percy, and silently showed that he believed it, to Hal's evident distress. The play ended with Sir John's resolution to 'live cleanly, as a nobleman should do'; and when we first saw him in Part Two he wore medals.

A simplified pattern was thus imposed on an already schematic play, and if Pennington's performance lacked subtlety, this may have been through acquiescence in his director's concept. Part Two is more resistant to schematization, but the contrast between court and rebels continues, and though Patrick O'Connell played the King sympathetically, the rebel cause was implicitly endorsed. In Bogdanov's semiotics the swigging of beer from bottles contrasts favourably with the serving of short drinks in glasses. So, in Gaultree Forest, a uniformed Prince John offered wine to the tweedy, cardiganned rebel lords; after he had betrayed them they were shot on stage to the jubilant strains of 'The King shall rejoice'.[5] Hal, entering to the dying King, looked ready for a game of tennis; but the subsequent reconciliation became the play's emotional centre, marked by a closeness of physical contact as well as emotional rapport that made Falstaff's rejection inevitable; when it came, the sense of pain was confined to Falstaff; police brutality in both the carting of Doll Tearsheet and the committal of Sir John to the Fleet suggested that Hal had become head of a police state.

Bogdanov's wooing of the audience sometimes seems at odds with his overall anti-establishmentism. There was condescension in his over-jokey portrayal of the Gloucestershire recruits, and an element of audience flattery in his presentation of the English attitude to war in *Henry V*: the playing of 'Jerusalem'[6] during the embarkation for France might be regarded as satire, but the simultaneous display of a banner inscribed 'Fuck the Frogs' drew delighted applause in which it was difficult not to detect an element of jingoistic self-satisfaction. Later, when Exeter deliberately walked over a cloth on which ladies of the French court were picnicking (drinking champagne from glasses, of course), his rudeness seemed implicitly endorsed as a proper way of treating foreigners.

Pennington's King was not strongly characterized except by the actor's natural grace. His performance was consistently intelligent, but a lack of inwardness, of emotional penetration, made it difficult to discern any strong interpretative bent. He wore battledress like his soldiers, and was comradely but always the officer, whether standing on a tank for 'Once more unto the breach', delivered to soldiers crouched behind piles of sandbags, or wooing the Princess. His men might behave brutally—as Pistol did with Le Fer, cutting his throat on hearing of Henry's order to kill the prisoners—but Henry himself remained aloof. There were original, inventive touches: on 'There's for thy labour', dispatching Mountjoy with a defiant message to the Dauphin, he presented him with a tennis ball. And it was ingenious to treat Grandpré's lines beginning 'The horsemen sit like fixèd candlesticks' as a poem that he was composing on a typewriter, taking the paper out on 'Description cannot suit itself in words'.

As one who prefers classical to popular music, and wine in glasses to beer in bottles (let alone cans), I tend to feel got at by Bogdanov's productions; and I acknowledge, of course, that I may be the kind of person at whom he wishes to get. While I admire his concentration on theatrical values, his determination to illuminate all areas of the text, and his company's intelligent understanding and projection of Shakespeare's language, I am sometimes repelled by reductive over-simplifications and vulgarities. There was much theatrical life in *The Henrys*, but I was left with a feeling that I had been talked down to.

1. 'Silver threads among the gold', a popular sentimental ballad by Eben Rexford (1848–1916).

2. Woodvine, John, see p. 285.

3. 'pullet sperm...brewage' abjured by Falstaff at *The Merry Wives of Windsor*, 3.5.29–30.

4. Pennington, Michael. See p. 289.

5. 'The King shall rejoice', a coronation anthem by George Frederick Handel (1685–1759).

6. 'Jerusalem', the choral song by Sir Hubert Parry (1848–1918) regularly sung with patriotic fervour at the last night of the London Promenade Concerts and on other special occasions.

11 **April 1987**, Michael Billington (born 1939) on *Antony and Cleopatra*, directed by Peter Hall at the National Theatre, from *The Guardian*, reprinted in his *One Night Stands: A Critic's View of British Theatre from 1971–1991* (1993), pp. 278–80.

MICHAEL BILLINGTON has been drama critic of *The Guardian* since 1971.

I ASKED yesterday if we are facing a Shakespearean-acting crisis owing to dearth of opportunity and growing disregard for language. Time alone will tell. But I can say, with ringing certainty, that there is no hint of crisis in Peter Hall's new production of *Antony And Cleopatra* at the Olivier. It is not only the most intelligently spoken Shakespeare I have heard in years but it also contains two performances from Judi Dench and Anthony Hopkins that, in their comprehensive humanity, rank with Ashcroft and Redgrave[1] at Stratford many moons ago.

Like all great Shakespearean productions, Peter Hall uncovers meanings in the text that may seem obvious but that have never hit one so penetratingly before. For me this production is rooted in prophecy and dream. From the Soothsayer's first predictions to Enobarbus's tart comment that the new-found amity between Antony and Octavius cannot hold, everything that happens is foreseeable and foreseen. It is all there in Shakespeare. But I have never before been so aware that this is not a tragedy (like *Hamlet*) of constant narrative surprise but one in which a pattern is fulfilled.

But Peter Hall also deliberately heightens the extent to which the characters exist in a state of intoxicated fantasy. When Michael Bryant's[2] admirable Enobarbus begins his famous speech about Cleopatra's barge, it is in the casual tone of an old sweat reporting what he has seen: as he continues, he gets carried into an imaginative trance from which he has to be roused.

Similarly when Judi Dench's[3] Cleopatra describes her Antony ('His legs bestrid the ocean'), she does so with the intensity of someone recounting a dream. 'Nature,' she says, 'wants stuff to vie strange forms with fancy.' I was reminded, strangely, of *A Midsummer Night's Dream* in which Shakespeare also deals with the transubstantiating power of love.

What this means in practice is that the production—played in Jacobean costume against Alison Chitty's[4] circular, blood-red surround with broken columns and fragmented porticoes—is about two chunkily real people living out some epic fantasy.

And no one could be more real than Judi Dench's breathtaking Cleopatra. She is capricious, volatile, the mistress of all moods who in the course of a single scene can switch easily from breathy languor ('O happy horse to bear the weight of Antony') to cutting humour ('How much unlike art thou Mark Antony' to an effeminate messenger) to a pensive melancholy ('My salad days when I was green in judgement') at the frank acknowledgment of the passing years.

Ms Dench ensures that Cleopatra's sexual magnetism lies not in any Centrefold[5] posturing but in emotional extremism: she can be highly funny, as when she rushes for the door in affronted dignity at being told Octavia is thirty, and highly dangerous as when she fells a messenger with a right hook. Ms Dench even gets over the notorious hurdle of the last Act (how often has one waited impatiently for Cleopatra to die?) by looking for the precise meaning of each speech and by achieving a kind of fulfilment on 'Now the fleeting moon no planet is of mine.' After the boggling inconstancy of her life, Ms Dench goes to her death with single-minded certainty.

She in no way, however, o'ertops Anthony Hopkins's[6] magnificent Antony: a real old campaigner (you can believe that he ate 'strange flesh' in the Alps) for whom Alexandria represents escape and fantasy. Mr Hopkins, who like many heavyweights, is extraordinarily light on his feet, externalises the conflict in Antony between the soldier and the lover: when recalled to Rome he prowls the stage hungrily like a lion waiting to get back in the arena.

But what I shall remember most is Mr Hopkins's false gaiety—and overpowering inward grief—in the short scene where he bids farewell to his servants. From that point on, the knowledge of death sits on Antony; and when Mr Hopkins says he will contend even with his pestilent scythe, it is with a swashbuckling bravura that moves one to tears.

But the strength of this production lies in the way every role has been reconsidered. Tim Pigott-Smith[7] does not play Octavius as the usual cold prig but as a man who combines calculation with passion: it is a superb study of a power-lover who delights in spotting and playing on other men's flaws.

Michael Bryant's Enobarbus is also played, fascinatingly, not as a contrast to Antony but as someone who delights in aping his master's drinking and womanising and who even, as I have indicated, shares in the erotic dream to which he has fallen prey.

I have always, to be honest, had my doubts about this play, feeling that the later stages camouflage in poetic glory what they lack in emotional dynamism. But Hall's production, cinematically dissolving one scene into another and then playing it with due deliberation, banishes my qualms. It is about two middle-aged people—carnal, deceitful, often sad—seeking in love a reality greater than themselves.

1. **Ashcroft and Redgrave.** Peggy Ashcroft (see p. 216) and Michael Redgrave (see p. 269) played in *Antony and Cleopatra* at Stratford in 1953.

2. **Bryant,** Michael (born 1928), has worked extensively for the National Theatre.

3. **Dench,** Judi, see p. 285.

4. **Chitty,** Alison (born 1948), theatre and opera designer.

5. **Centrefold,** presumably referring to the glamorous photographs of female models printed on fold-pages in glossy magazines.

6. **Hopkins,** Anthony (born 1937), stage and screen actor, knighted 1993.

7. **Pigott-Smith,** Tim (born 1946), has worked extensively in classical theatre.

[1987], Stanley Wells on *Titus Andronicus*, directed by Deborah Warner (born 1959) at the Swan Theatre, Stratford-upon-Avon, from *Shakespeare Survey 41* (1989), pp. 178–81.

DEBORAH WARNER'S production of *Titus Andronicus* furthered the critical re-assessment of the play initiated by Peter Brook's production (see pp. 252–5). Unlike all previous modern directors, she used a complete text. The production is illustrated in Pl. 14.

DEBORAH WARNER'S[1] *Titus Andronicus*, in the Swan Theatre at Stratford-upon-Avon, offered no theatrical glamour, none of the allurements of pageantry or of sumptuous costumes with which directors have sometimes sugared what they have obviously regarded as a bitter pill of a play. Her staging, which seemed based on the most austere inter-pretation of Elizabethan methods, could have been transferred with little difficulty into a reconstruction of the Globe, which too could have offered an upper level, a stage pit, and such basic properties as coffins, ropes, a ladder, and a dinner table. Yet the production resembled Peter Hall's of *Antony*[2] in that it seemed exceptionally 'straight', one in which the director did not appear—like Bogdanov[3]—to be inviting us to see modern parallels to the action, or—like Alexander[4] and Noble[5]—to be probing a subtext for psychological resonances. The text was given, exceptionally, with no cuts—even Peter Brook's[6] 1955 production that restored the play to theatrical respectability cut some 650 lines. The violence was not shirked; there was none of the escape into burlesque that has appealed to both critics and directors as an evasion of the play's grimmer aspects. Only the fact that Titus' chopped-off hand and his sons' severed heads were represented by stuffed cloth bags lessened the physical representation of horror; Peter Brook had the sons killed off-stage, but here we saw their murder, and the blood flowed. The director had worked on the premise that everything in the text was there for a purpose, that the dramatist knew what he was about. There was even a degree of pedantry in her determination to test the text at every point with relentless rigour; yet the result was overwhelmingly impressive.

Of course, the production's apparent simplicity was not uncalculated. The play presents a twin problem. How do you stage its horrors—murder, rape, mutilation, cannibalism—without driving the audience over the bounds of credulity into giggling hysteria? And how, on the other hand, do you cope with its self-conscious literariness—the Latin quotations, the extended similes, the long, rhetorical speeches uttered by characters who according to any normal standards of behaviour should be capable of nothing but shocked speechlessness or hysterical incoherence? Deborah Warner's approach to these problems revealed the hand of an immensely skilful, even cunning, director. The rhetoric was plumbed for its deep sources, which were then brought to the surface so that even the most artificial verbal structures became expressive of emotion. Marcus' description of Lavinia immediately after her rape may read like a heartless verbal exercise by a bright boy from the local grammar school; spoken in Donald Sumpter's hushed tones it became a deeply moving attempt to master the facts, and thus to overcome the emotional shock, of a previously unimagined horror. We had the sense of a suspension of time, as if the speech represented an articulation, necessarily extended in expression, of a sequence of thoughts and emotions that might have taken no more than a second or two to flash through the character's mind, like a bad dream.

Inappropriate laughter was avoided by the exploitation of all the genuine comedy latent in the text—along with a little that Shakespeare had not thought of. Brian Cox[7] established Titus as a credible, human character by making him a bit of a card—an odd, shambling hero, very much a law unto himself. In the opening scene he started to paw Tamora, then slapped his cheek as if to remind himself of his unburied sons. He defensively isolated the second line of:

> Romans, of five and twenty valiant sons—
> Half of the number that King Priam had

as if to counter accusations of excessive breeding. And he stuffed his fingers into his ears, pretending not to hear his brother and sons pleading for Mutius' burial. Estelle Kohler,[8] as Tamora, and her two sons played her bombastic accusation of Bassianus as if it were a burlesque playlet put on for their victims' entertainment; Demetrius' sudden stabbing of Bassianus seemed all the more horrific as a result. Acknowledgement of the comedy in the situation when Titus, Lucius, and Marcus squabble over who shall have the honour of losing a hand in the hope of saving Titus' sons intensified the pain of the moment when Titus outwits the others by getting Aaron to mutilate him while they have gone to fetch an axe.

This method reached a climax in the extraordinary, emblematic 'fly' scene when Titus, driven to madness, berates his brother for having killed 'a poor, harmless fly'. Marcus, seeking an excuse, claims that he did so only because 'it was a black ill-favoured fly, / Like to the Empress' Moor'; Brian Cox made a marvellous moment of the transition, represented in the text only by 'O, O, O', from the tragicomic absurdity of his initial reaction, through dawning acceptance of the validity of Marcus' excuse, to the ferocity of frustrated despair with which he cast himself on the table, repeatedly stabbing at his enemy's surrogate. This was masterly acting.

In the last scene, the director permitted herself a wordless interpolation: servants whistled a merry tune as they carried on the furniture for the Thyestean[9] banquet. It was what Romeo calls a 'lightning before death', a sudden shift of perspective of an authentically Shakespearian kind, like the introduction of the Clown in the closing episodes of *Antony and Cleopatra* (and, indeed, of *Titus*). I should never have imagined that the subsequent stretch of action, in which Titus kills his own daughter (sickeningly) to rescue her from her shame, and then, within the space of three lines, kills Tamora and is himself killed by her husband, who is then killed by Titus' son, could have been so chilling in its effect. The chorus of servants played its part, squatting in ranks to each side of the stage before the pie was served ('Welcome, all', said Titus to the inhabitants of the pie, with a last touch of macabre humour), stretching forward in horror at the death of Lavinia, bending as Titus stabbed Tamora, gasping as Saturninus killed Titus, and finally rushing off through the audience as Lucius killed the Emperor. This choric action both directed and channelled off the audience's reactions.

The Swan Theatre seems to concentrate the attention of players in minor as well as major roles. Saturninus might profitably have been more colourfully played, and it seemed perverse to give the role of Aaron to an actor who looks Greek instead of the raven-black Moor of the text, but Richard McCabe[10] was a giggling, psychotic Chiron, Sonia Ritter a quiveringly traumatized Lavinia, Estelle Kohler a stingingly waspish Tamora. Brian Cox searchingly explored the role of Titus in a performance of unremitting concentration and impassioned integrity. He found the shape of the role in a manner that defined the movement of the play, achieving ever-increasing intensity of suffering up to the mirthless laughter with which he preceded the line 'Why, I have not another tear to shed', and playing the rest of the role on an upward curve as Titus found release in the action needed to effect his revenge, marvellously gleeful with his comrades in the scene with the arrows, desperately cunning in his assumed madness.

Like any strong production, this one impelled its audience to revalue the play. *Titus Andronicus* stood in greater need of revaluation than most of its author's works, and this production gave it what it needed at this point in its history. It emerged as a far more deeply serious play than its popular reputation would suggest, a play that is profoundly concerned with both the personal and the social consequences of violence rather than one that cheaply exploits their theatrical effectiveness. I was impressed as never before by the art of its structuring: its twin climaxes of violence, one directed at Titus, the other directed by him; by the force of the counter-action, led by Lucius; and by the part played within the whole by details of language, such as the recurrent, increasingly horrific emphasis on 'hand' and 'hands' (between them, the words occur some seventy times). This production increased my respect, too, for the play's first audiences; groundlings who made this play popular, if they experienced it in full, were not merely seeking cheap thrills. It did not emerge as an unflawed masterpiece in this revelatory production, but subsequent directors will have far less excuse than before for evading its problems by textual adaptation or by evasive theatricalism.

1. **Warner**, Deborah, had founded and worked with the Kick Theatre Company from 1980.

2. *Antony*, Peter Hall's 1987 production at the National Theatre, with Judi Dench and Anthony Hopkins, discussed earlier in this review.

3. **Bogdanov**, Michael, director whose productions for the English Shakespeare Company of *Henry IV*, Parts One and Two, and of *Henry V* (see pp. 297–300) are discussed earlier in this review.

4. **Alexander**, Bill. His RSC productions of *The Merchant of Venice* and of *Twelfth Night* are discussed earlier in this review.

5. **Noble**, Adrian (born 1950), was appointed Artistic Director of the RSC in 1990. His 1986 *Macbeth* is discussed earlier in this review.

6. **Brook**, Peter. See p. 248.

7. **Cox**, Brian (born 1946).

8. **Kohler**, Estelle (born 1940).

9. **Thyestean**. In Greek legend Thyestes made his brother, Atreus, eat the flesh of his two sons at a banquet.

10. **McCabe**, Richard (born 1960).

[1989], Robert Smallwood (born 1941) on *Othello*, directed by Trevor Nunn at The Other Place, Stratford-upon-Avon, from *Shakespeare Quarterly*, 41 (1990), pp. 110–14.

ROBERT SMALLWOOD is Deputy Director and Head of Education of the Shakespeare Birthplace Trust.

THE most remarkable event of this first half of the Stratford season was certainly the production of *Othello* at the Other Place. Officially closed last January before demolition and rebuilding, the tin-shed studio theatre reopened for six weeks in August and September for Trevor Nunn's first Shakespeare production in seven years. The company was a specially recruited one, not drawn from the Swan and main-house Stratford group, and the casting was strong even in the minor roles. The aim, clearly, was to rediscover the power and energy generated by this director's *Macbeth*[1] in the same space in 1976 and Ian McKellen (Macbeth then) returned now as Iago. The production offered a virtually uncut text and played for nearly four hours. The claustrophobic intimacy of the Other Place is an excellent space in which to explore the intensity of the private, family relationships of *Othello*.

Bob Crowley, the designer, provided a basic set of slatted, sun-bleached boards screening an upper level (from which Othello looked down on Iago and Cassio's conversation about Bianca) and a sandy floor over which a carpet was spread for the Venetian scenes. The simplicity of this basic space was overlaid with a large array of furniture and props to create a remarkably detailed sense of environment within a vague period setting: certainly nineteenth-century, but reviewers' surmises varied from mid to late, and guesses at the military ambience from the Franco-Prussian War[2] to the American Civil War[3] to the Crimean.[4] If the where and the precisely when were elusive, however, the space we shared with the actors was one of precise, tangible, almost oppressive immediacy. Iago's shouts to awaken Brabantio set a dog barking in the distance as Brabantio's muffled reply, as if from the depths of the house, was heard; sounds from beyond the auditorium had thus, in the play's first moments, placed the audience in the middle of the action. The old men of the Venetian council met at night in a haze of cigar smoke around a table on which the maps jostled with the brandy decanter and glasses under a green-shaded lamp—a gentlemen's-club atmosphere reminiscent of this same director's court of France in *All's Well that Ends Well*[5] a few years ago. A storm interlude, with thunder and strobe lightning, gave way to the quayside at Cyprus with its splendid brass telescope, soldiers on watch in oilskins, and baggage-bearing seafarers staggering ashore. The sound of cicadas accompanied much of the daylit, sun-drenched action in Cyprus, a colonial outpost with Desdemona and Emilia elegant in long white dresses, making lemonade through a tiny wooden sieve for their administrator-husbands. Above all, though, it was the military world that was most vividly created: bugle calls punctuated the action, stage hands dressed as soldiers moved the furniture with military efficiency, camp beds and kit bags and mobile washstands created a sense of the barrack-room world. Nearly all the men were in uniform throughout, so that the cashiered Cassio looked pathetically conspicuous and a little effete in a white suit and straw hat—the garb of Roderigo before he enlisted as a private to pursue Desdemona. There was much saluting and a constant sense of military discipline and hierarchy in which the presence of Desdemona seemed a potentially volatile aberration: 'Our General's wife is now the General.'

This attention to detail in the setting and costume was reflected in the performances, from the smallest roles to the largest. Clive Swift[6] made Brabantio dignified yet a little pathetic, the poise suggested by a dry, upper-class accent somewhat undercut (whether through grief or confusion) by his tendency to blink as he spoke. He is hurt and embarrassed by the frankness of his daughter's speech to the council, bewildered to find his public world invaded by his private one, refusing Desdemona's eagerness to embrace him in reconciliation, and finally isolated by his conciliar colleagues who clearly feel he is losing his grip to be making such an emotional fuss in public. To watch this performance is to realize that the play gives us one small tragedy before the end of Act I. Michael Grandage's Roderigo, genuinely, even rather movingly, in love with Desdemona, was young, handsome, and aristocratic, desperately vulnerable to the destructive contempt that Iago feels for his class and for his emotional commitment. The suavely dressed civilian gave way to the unkempt, unshaven soldier in Cyprus as Roderigo's desperation grew. In 4.2 he bursts in upon Iago (who has just been comforting Desdemona in her room, following Othello's verbal tirade), so that his claim that he can 'find none' of 'the jewels you had from me to deliver to Desdemona' is based on a direct search of her dressing table: one more example of the production's precise (perhaps in this case excessive) care for detail. There was an excellent Cassio, too, from Sean Baker, slim and elegant, a public-school-boy freshly graduated from military academy, conspicuously different from the officers of the Cyprus regiment, so that his agreement to carouse with them carried more than a hint of patronage. His slumming goes only so far, however: when the messroom high jinks get too boisterous and he seems about to follow one of the Cyprus officers in having his trousers removed, the Scottish puritan snobbism in him bites back and he pulls rank and class to end the fun: 'I hold him to be unworthy of his place that does these things.' 'The lieutenant is to be saved before the ancient,' he goes on, with enough edge and sneer to remind Iago of his original grievance and to elicit the contempt of the real professionals in the Cyprus regiment. (The production drew a subtle distinction between the Cyprus soldiers under Montano's command and the Venetian force under Othello's: it is a distinction as potent, one feels, as that under the British Raj between the Indian Army and the British Army in India.) Left alone with Iago, Cassio is mawkish and self-pitying (a mood exacerbated by his being sick in the washstand), almost deservedly wide open to Iago's ruthlessness. Off he goes to beg Desdemona's aid the next morning, looking rather natty in his white suit and straw hat, with a little box of sweets as an offering, an elegant, plausible, but distinctly shallow young man with a lot to learn.

Two marriages, one new, one old, are at the centre of *Othello*; this production explored them, and their contrasts, in four deeply thoughtful and impressive performances. Never has the part of Emilia seemed to me so significant as in Zoë Wanamaker's splendid presentation. Sad, pale, and watchful, she moves through the play observing its events, suspicious but bewildered until the truth finally dawns on her: 'My *husband*'—and she stops in her tracks on her way to raise the alarm. 'O gull, O dolt,' she says, as much to herself as to Othello, and from her earlier watchful stillness she finds in these last moments, an old black overcoat over her nightdress, a frantic energy that exposes the truth in ending her own life. What has her existence with Iago been like, one wondered; why does she still yearn for attention and affection from him? On her first appearance she had watched the extravagant affection of the greeting between Desdemona and Othello with pained wonder, surprised to find her attention to their embrace interrupted by a rough, affectionless kiss from her husband. For the first scene after the intermission (the break is taken in the middle of 3.3, after the exit of Desdemona and Othello), she came on with a tobacco pipe which she lit apparently in preparation for her husband's arrival, for he took it from her with every appearance of custom when he arrived a few lines later. Again there was an embrace and kiss between them as she gave him the handkerchief, he breaking away to leave her unsatisfied, humiliated: 'I nothing, but to please his fantasy.' The relationship between her and Imogen Stubbs's Desdemona was very moving, the compassionate affection of the disillusioned Emilia support-ing the bewildered naïveté of the grief-stricken girl. The willow-song scene, with the wind soughing outside, reached a poignant climax as Desdemona unlocked the drawer of her dressing table, and both women indulged in the wickedness of a sweet from the box presented earlier by Cassio. Thus we discovered the secret of that drawer so firmly locked earlier against Othello's frantic searches during his questioning of Emilia at the beginning of the brothel scene. Once again the attention to detail was impressive: the guilty secret was just a box of candy, with the little extra irony that it was also the gift of Cassio.

Imogen Stubbs presented a young, beautiful, and very vulnerable Des-demona, an excitable, forthright, utterly committed girl, naive but by no means foolish. The scene in the Venetian council with her father demon-strated her instinctive quality: she tried to touch his arm on her arrival, and even after her speech of commitment to Othello and the decision for Cyprus, she was, even as he sought to evade her, still following him round the council table, first one way, then the other, trying, poignantly, to settle their quarrel with an embrace. On the quayside in Cyprus, after her genuine amusement at Iago's jokes, her tears of anxiety at Othello's continuing absence came flooding back, prompting Cassio to 'take her by the palm' in an attempt to allay her grief. In the brothel scene there was a similar moment of emotional vulnerability: she clearly missed the irony in Othello's responses to her answers—'What, not a whore?' ... 'No, as I shall be saved.' ... 'Is't possible?'—and her face lit up with joy at the prospect that all is to be well again between them, only to crease once more with anguish as the terrible truth came flooding back with his return to brutal abuse. Such moments of openness and emotional intensity gave the performance great power and pathos. At the end of the temptation scene, Desdemona came out to Othello with a large watch to which she pointed in mock anger: 'Your dinner, and the generous islanders / By you invited, do attend your patience.' After failing to tie her handkerchief around his brows, she led him off only to return again a second or two later to collect what she had forgotten—the watch; and there her handkerchief lay unheeded on the floor as the houselights went up for the intermission.

In his casting of Willard White[7] as Othello, Trevor Nunn took, it must be supposed, something of a risk. Mr. White is an opera singer without experience of playing Shakespeare. He is also (remarkably enough) the first black actor to play Othello at Stratford since Paul Robeson[8] thirty years ago. He brought to the part a thrillingly resonant voice, a magnificent stature, and the sort of grandeur that has a touch of the old-fashioned about it. There was something identifiably careful about his speaking of the verse, a slight sense of awe towards the language that distanced him a little from it, while the rest of the cast, experienced Shakespearean professionals all, part of the RSC club, were taking it in their stride. In a curious, almost disturbing way, this seemed to fit the role rather aptly, the alien among the Venetians, the black opera singer among the white Shakespeareans. And as Othello's control of the language disintegrated, so too did his attempt to belong: in military uniform throughout, he appeared for the last wordless phase of his relationship with Desdemona in a defiantly exotic kaftan that made him seem alien and then rather vulnerable in the last pathetic attempt to struggle back to articulacy. Two related moments caught the essence of his relationship with Desdemona: huge and magnificent, he arrives from the storm to the quayside to swing her in his arms like a piece of flotsam, and then (to the apparent embarrassment of his watching soldiers) he stands her on a luggage box as he declares, 'My soul hath her content so absolute...'; in the brothel scene he places her on a pedestal again, this time a bedroom stool, as he berates her as a whore. The murder scene was a violent struggle, Desdemona and Othello shouting at each other across the bed, she making frantic attempts to run away, crashing into the locked door, then a chase, her scramble across the bed before he seizes her, flinging her onto the bed and clambering on top of her; then the convulsive, rhythmic tightenings of the strangulation: it grows and grows as she resists, and then it stops as she goes limp and he rolls off her. And so their love is finished. 'What you know, you know' says Iago to Othello—with chilling intensity in Ian McKellen's[9] performance. What does he know, one wonders: that this consummation in death was the only time Othello ever managed to complete a love encounter on Desdemona's bed without an interruption of Iago's manufacture? Or the more general lesson, that for a black man to imagine he might ever belong in Venetian society was always a foolish dream? (The only other black face on the stage was that of Marsha Hunt's Bianca, the plaything Cassio laughs and sneers at, arrested with such relished violence by Iago.)

One comes, finally, to Ian McKellen's Iago. Every moment, every gesture of this performance seemed precisely calculated to the realization of an extraordinary, psychotic personality. This was a military man through and through, a hard-bitten NCO who, one felt, had always been in the army. His polished boots, spruce uniform always done up tight to the neck (alone among the play's characters he never unbuttons), ramrod back, close-clipped moustache came straight from the parade ground. A constant gesture before an exit was to straighten up, shoulders back, arms down, thumbs straight, chin in, the obedient, uncomplaining, efficient cog in the military machine. The flat, clipped, unsurprisable, take-it-or-leave-it northern accent lost its equilibrium only once: at the moment of the joint oath with Othello, Iago is visibly thrilled and the voice wavers a little in awe on 'I am your own forever.' He is massively efficient and obsessively tidy: he rolls his own cigarettes with a crisp deftness from tobacco kept in a neat little box in his breast pocket; he picks up Roderigo, collapsed in a heap of pettish frustration on the floor, brushes him down and rubs his temples while advising him against drowning, then picks up his hat and cane; he tidies the messroom and empties Cassio's sick-bowl while mocking his concern for reputation, then puts him to bed, tucking in his blanket while advising him to seek Desdemona's assistance, before launching into the soliloquy (over a sleeping Cassio) 'And what's he then that says I play the villain,' yawning halfway through it, as though he's dreaming the whole thing up. To everyone he is so very dependable, so very genial, wholly trusted by the astute and battle-hardened Cyprus soldiers, excellent at the little entertainment to amuse people as they await Othello's arrival from the storm, the life and soul of the barrack-room party, making the punch and leading the singing, and, after the fray, binding Roderigo's head and whimsically arranging his tufts of hair around the bandage. Obviously he is the man to go to when you need cheering up, as Desdemona reveals on her arrival in Cyprus and again after the brothel scene. And on both occasions the comfort he offers is the merest trifle more physical than is entirely necessary. She is too innocent to notice, but the arm around the waist, the comforting cuddle, are a little too heavy, giving an extra edge to his admission 'I do love her too.' But it would be reductive to find in this, or in the fury he evinces at the idea of Othello with his 'nightcap,' the explanation for his behaviour. This is a personality warped and eaten up by jealousy, by a contemptuous sense of his own inability to wield power, a gnawing longing to do so—and to stop others from doing so. There is a cool precision in the way he presides over Othello's destruction in the temptation scene, his comings and goings executed with the usual military exactness, saluting just as the drill-book requires. At the end his bearing remains unchanged, the order to 'Look on the tragic loading of this bed' obeyed with the usual straight-backed step forward and then a stare of cold, detached, emotionless curiosity, the last thing we see as the lights go out.

1. *Macbeth*. See pp. 283–5.
2. **Franco-Prussian War** (1870–1).
3. **American Civil War** (1861–5).
4. **Crimean** (War, 1854–6).
5. *All's Well that Ends Well*. Trevor Nunn had directed the play at Stratford in an Edwardian setting in 1981.
6. **Swift**, Clive (born 1936).
7. **White**, Willard (born 1946), bass singer and actor.
8. **Robeson**, Paul (1898–1976). The African-born singer and actor played Othello in London (1930), New York (1943) and Stratford (1959).
9. **McKellen**, Ian. See p. 285.

༺༻

3 October 1990, Paul Taylor (born 1955) on *The Tempest*, directed by Peter Brook; from *The Independent*.

PETER BROOK first directed the play at Stratford in 1957, with Gielgud as Prospero, returning to it in Stratford again in 1963 (with Clifford Williams as co-director), in Paris and London in 1968, then in the production reviewed here which opened in Zürich on 14 September 1990 before presentation in Paris at the Théâtre des Bouffes du Nord, followed by a tour. The play was given in a French translation. Paul Taylor, who has been theatre critic for *The Independent* since 1988, saw it in Glasgow.

THE bleeping of digital watches is a common enough curse in theatres, but during the press night for Peter Brook's production of *La Tempête*, the competition came from an actual alarm clock. It was the kind that climbs into a peevish apoplexy unless instantly humoured and, as its owner scrabbled desperately in his/her bag, one's annoyance slowly turned to sweating compassion.

This unscheduled alienation effect had its instructive side. In temporarily breaking the production's spell, it brought home just how potently absorbing that is. It also turned out to be the evening's most vivid expression of temporal urgency, which might be thought odd when you consider that Prospero's plot is very much a now-or-never race against the clock. Possessed of a lovely, light gracefulness, Brook's production plays down the drama's anxiety and inner turbulence. The pace is even and deliberate; the underlying mood is one of calm good-nature.

With a rock as its single fixture, the island is a tennis court-shaped stretch of sand set amidst red shale borders and the exposed brickwork of the Tramway. Charming in both senses, Prospero's Spirits tease the newly arrived Ferdinand (Ken Higelin) by shifting around comically token bits of greenery, some of it sprouting between their toes. Brook extracts some delightful comedy from such pranks, as when he has the large, black Ariel (Bakary Sangaré) dress up in the same ridiculous finery as the small, Balinese Trinculo (Tapa Sudana) who, convinced he is gazing into a mirror, delightedly copies all the Spirit's irreverent gestures. But what is striking about these tricks is their lack of any real vindictiveness or malice.

Resembling a tall, black El Greco[1] saint, their master Prospero (Sotigui Kouyaté) never looks in any grave danger of choosing vengeance over virtue. That curious scene in Act II where Antonio and Sebastian decide to take the life of the sleeping Alonso is, for example, given a very unambiguous interpretation. It's an important episode because it provides Prospero with renewed confirmation of his brother's evil and fresh cause for revenge. The question a director has to decide is how far the magician has rigged the experiment. Totally, is Brook's suggestion. Instead of Ariel's music giving all the courtiers an equal chance to fall asleep, the Spirits enter and manually sedate the virtuous characters. (Alonso even manages to mutter 'Merci' as Ariel lowers him to the floor.) Having thus furnished the villains with the perfect opportunity for evil, the Spirits watch the inevitable outcome with droll amusement, perched on sword-sticks. At the (almost) kill, these weapons are helpfully offered to the would-be assassins.

You might have thought that such overt manipulation would cast Prospero in an unflattering light. But the scene, as it is played here, has a faintly rum, larky feel: the antics of the non-human participants distract attention from the human vileness on display. It's arguable that Brook's hero has set his enemies up partly so as to leave the charitable possibility dangling that they would not have acted in that way, necessarily, if left alone. It constitutes an aid to clemency, not vengeance. Certainly in the reconciliations at the end, Mr Kouyaté evinces no great distaste for his brother, while Mamadou Dioume as Antonio is not the usual cynical outsider, but seems honestly impressed and baffled by the happy ending.

This paradox, whereby Prospero is at liberty to forgive his brother only by the trick of having constrained his freedom of action, fits in too with the production's exploration of the contradictory nature of freedom. A bit bashful throughout about bringing up the subject of his manumission, Mr Sangaré's likeable, emotionally dependent Ariel turns hesitantly back, on being released at the end, as though half-hopeful that Prospero will reinstate him. No brutish hulk, David Bennent's Caliban is a furious, stunted-looking urchin, much given, in the first half, to bashing turnips to death with a wooden log. A roiling[2] bundle of frustration, he learns that there are worse masters than Prospero when he becomes enslaved to the buffoons and their drink. His experiences with this pair seem to teach this Caliban, whose flashes of sensitivity the actor expertly conveys, an unfamiliar self-respect, and it's a sobered-up, responsible-seeming creature who is dismissed at the end to look after and control himself. With Brook's Prospero, what impresses most is not the rejection of revenge, but the intense, still sadness with which Mr Kouyaté, sitting amidst a magic ring of pebbles, renounces the illusory and illicit liberty afforded him by his art.

As always with this director, the effects are achieved with a wonderfully charged simplicity. To loud drumming, bamboo poles evoke the tiltings of the storm-tossed masts or, held upright by spirits, suggest a protective grove where Miranda (Shantala Malhar-Shivalingappa) and Ferdinand converse. For the condensed masque and the revelations at the end, blue and gold silks are unfurled over the surface of the sand—their disparate textures a sensuous shorthand for the incongruous overlap of the wild and the civilised. Above all, the impression is one of harmony. It is characteristic that Sebastian's cry 'A most high miracle' ('une immense miracle' in Jean-Claude Carrière's adaption) is not the usual side-of-the-mouth sceptical mutter but an exclamation of unmistrustful wonder.

1. **El Greco** (1541–1614), Spanish painter who characteristically elongated the human form.

2. **roiling**, moving 'in a confused or turbulent manner' (*OED*).

6 December 1991, Paul Taylor on *As You Like It*, directed by Declan
Donnellan (born 1953) for the touring company Cheek by Jowl;
from *The Independent*.

CHEEK BY JOWL, founded in 1981 by Donnellan and the designer Nick
Ormerod, tours productions of classical plays at home and overseas. This production is illustrated in Pl. 15.

THE odds against a strapping 6ft black male actor being able to create
not just a convincing but a captivating Rosalind are, you might have
thought, fairly formidable. Adrian Lester[1] makes short work of this
assumption, however, in Cheek By Jowl's delightful all-male production
of *As You Like It* now to be seen at the Lyric, Hammersmith.

The company's director, Declan Donnellan, has always been mischie-
vously alert to the sexual politics that are in play in the disguise-conven-
tions of Shakespearean comedy. At the end of his version of *Twelfth
Night*,[2] for example, Viola wisely forced Orsino to feel her breasts, as if
to remind him that this person he has fallen in love with (but oddly
enough never seen except in male costume), is no boy.

Here, the homosexual element in the hero's attraction was not suddenly
swept aside in the statutory fifth-act pairing-off of straights. Donnellan is
no stranger to bold, gender-swap casting either. His *Tempest*[3] gave us not
the King, but the Queen of Naples, a Thatcher-clone who, flanked by her
cabinet, stalks round the island as though in search of somebody new to
handbag.

If, in the past, some of these touches have seemed *outré* and heavyhanded, this *As You Like It* is remarkable for the comic tact and restraint
with which it readopts the Elizabethan practice of males playing females.
Given that in her mock-wooing scenes with Orlando, Rosalind is a
woman pretending to be Ganymede pretending to be Rosalind, to cast a
male actor in the role presents the audience with the spectacle of a man
playing a woman playing a man playing a woman. You might think that
this would cause chronic mental squinting. In fact, the result is funny,
touching, and at times *frisson*-inducing. Lester, who bears a spooky
resemblance to Josette Simon,[4] somehow manages to evoke femininity
without resorting to any of the cheap mannerisms of female impersonation, and he is nicely contrasted with Tom Hollander's dumpy, cherubic
Celia, a picture of pouting, curl-chewing disapproval into which faint
elements of a drag act have beguilingly crept.

The scenes between Ganymede and Patrick Toomey's excellent

Orlando have a beautifully comic erotic tension and a sexual ambiguity that's heightened because both players are men. Toomey tries to hide his obscure embarrassment behind playful, manly cuffs and rabbit punches that Lester feels obliged, dutifully if unconvincingly, to return.

Donnellan has inserted a realistic momentary glitch in the happy ending that awaits this couple. When Orlando lifts Rosalind's bridal veil in the final scene, he looks appalled and stalks away as though massively offended at the benign trick she has played on him, only relenting when she subsides in tears on her father's shoulder. This brief outbreak of injured masculine pride (crossed perhaps with a little pang for the displaced 'Ganymede') is swiftly followed, however, by moving proof of how much he has learned, under Rosalind's tuition, to respect women. When his new father-in-law insists on ceding a dukedom to him, Orlando gracefully hangs the medal round the heroine's neck.

The play is communicated with admirable directness and a cunning simplicity of means. The court scenes are delivered on a bare stage: later, toilet-roll strips of green descend to evoke Arden which is eventually dappled with verdant light. A strong cast manages to break out all the foolishness of the forest's range of bumpkins, without patronising them. I enjoyed Mike Afford's Corin whose thoughts come so slowly it's like listening to a partially blind person reading out an optician's chart, and Richard Cant's hilarious Audrey, all vacantly benign leers.

In this *As You Like It*, Joe Dixon's lachrymose Jaques is (rather unconvincingly) prevailed on to return to the festive gathering at the end. It's fitting, though, that this production should end in a joyous group tango with no one excluded, for it celebrates the tenth birthday of this provocative (sometimes provoking), but always intriguing company.

1. **Lester**, Adrian (born 1969).
2. *Twelfth Night*, produced by the company in 1986.
3. *Tempest*, produced by the company in 1988.
4. **Simon**, Josette, black actress whose roles include Isabella in *Measure for Measure* at Stratford in 1987.

[1992], Peter Holland (born 1951) on *Richard III* produced by Barrie Rutter for Northern Broadsides on tour, from *Shakespeare Survey* *47* (1994), pp. 185–7.

BARRIE RUTTER has played many classical roles, preferring, as the reviewer explains, to retain his northern accent. Peter Holland is Professor of Shakespeare Studies and Director of the Shakespeare Institute of the University of Birmingham.

No one could accuse Barrie Rutter's production of *Richard III* of taking its time. Spoken at high speed, the text whistled by, concentrating attention on the thrill of the unfolding narrative, the vitality of the characters' relationships and the verve of the actors, much more than on the possible virtues of individual line-readings. Only rarely so fast as to be breathless, the lines had an easiness and immediacy, almost a contemporaneity, by the way they seemed to fit the actors' tongues so naturally.

Rutter's company, Northern Broadsides, had toured the production widely and triumphantly across the north of England before a season at the Riverside Studios in London. The actors, mostly from Yorkshire, were allowed, usually for the first time in their professional careers, to use their natural voices in a classical play. The company was mocked by some critics for doing Shakespeare in Yorkshire accents, most noticeably by John Peter[1] in a swingeing attack on 'a piece of karaoke theatre in which Shakespeare provides the orchestra, and the actors have fun providing the voices', which he found condescending. But the actors were not choosing accents but instead allowing their voices to relax from conventions of Received Pronunciation and official Shakespeare diction so that the text's fluency and excitement was not mediated by an imposed accent, the convention of classical theatre that all speech has the accent of London. If the result was that 'Naught to do with Mrs Shore?' (1.1.99) sounded more like 'Nowt to do wi' Mistress Shawah? or 'Something we will determine' (3.1.190) was adapted into 'Summat we will do', it seemed a small price to pay for the infectious energy of the production.

Defiantly played as cheap theatre, with a shoulder-pad borrowed from Bradford Northern Rugby League club for Richard's hump and an old fur coat as the queen's robe passed from Elizabeth to Anne and then offered by Richard to Elizabeth again for her daughter, Rutter's production enjoyed its theatricality. The rival armies of Act 5, for instance, slowly donned boiler-suits and clogs during the build-up to Bosworth where the generals were wheeled around mounted on porters' trolleys and the armies stamped thunderous rhythms in their clogs. Richard died at the hands of the ghosts whose sticks and clogs enacted a folk-ritual of exorcism of the devil. His corpse was placed inside the wire enclosure that had been a permanent presence on audience right and on whose perimeter fence articles symbolizing Richard's victims had accumulated in the course of the performance. The drumming of the clogs slowed and quietened and eventually stopped as Richmond spoke of 'this fair land's peace' (5.8.39). The soldiers, copying Richmond, took off their clogs and dungarees, dumping the paraphernalia of war on the body of the cause of bloodshed, closing the enclosure fence on him and leaving on the opposite side of the stage towards a strong light streaming through open doors. I have never before found the end so complete, the sense of purification of the demonic so absolute, the calm of the new order so effective. If the result is simplifying, it is also fine theatre, powerful and thoughtful and, above all, clear in its communication of what Bosworth has accomplished.

The battle sequence was, by some way, the largest of the production's effects. More often, the energy of narrative came through with the rapidity of naturalism. The disputes of the rival factions took on overtones of a family squabble in a gritty northern realist drama of the 1950s, with Ishia Bennison's splendid Queen Elizabeth someone who the others clearly thought had got above herself in her gold dress and mink coat. In 1.3 Polly Hemingway's Margaret, a bag-lady who has wandered into the court, could be calmed by Dave Hill's authoritative but benignly soothing Buckingham, making sure there was no fuss, but alone with the other women in 4.4 she could kick Elizabeth to the ground, pull the hair of the Duchess of York, and leave the stage with clenched fist raised triumphantly aloft like a street-fighter who has beaten up rivals. But none of these moments diminished the text; the implications of the struggles of dynastic factions or the threat of Margaret's prophetic curses were no less powerful for the recognizability of the characters. Rutter's Richard was no less dangerous for appearing an engaging and impish comedian with a prancing walk (wearing one shoe and one clog) and one hand permanently thrust in his trouser pocket. The worried conversations of the citizens (2.3) came over all the more concerned since the fate of the nation was in hands insufficiently different from their own.

Rutter's production was more than happy to find comedy outside Richard himself in, for example, Clarence's diminutive murderers, a good six inches shorter than their victim, or the Duke of York in 2.4, an adult in school-cap playing games on the benches, a school-boy bored by adult conversation. But on the immense width of the Riverside stage, moves of anger were frighteningly large as Richard, furious at Hastings's 'If' (3.4.73), pursued him at high speed across the whole stage-width. The transitions of mood were startlingly fast as comedy or gentleness modulated into evil: Richard planted a sweet kiss on Anne's forehead before pushing her at Catesby to be taken off to murder. The audience could not help but admire Richard's brassneck, that northern word for arrogant nerve, even as his actions disgusted.

Rutter's production proclaimed its regionalism but it also trumpeted its sheer, unabashed pleasure in the play with a directness that more conventional work is embarrassed by. Where some productions seem almost to be apologizing for doing Shakespeare at all, Northern Broadsides shows why he was the English Renaissance's most popular dramatist and why he should continue to be the centre of vitality in our theatre culture. If that is 'condescending' it is a condescension more companies should copy.

    1. **Peter,** John, theatre critic of *The Sunday Times*. The quotation is from a review dated 13 December 1992.

[1996], Robert Smallwood on *The Comedy of Errors*, directed by Tim Supple for the Royal Shakespeare Company at The Other Place and on tour; from *Shakespeare Survey 50* (1997), pp. 215–19.

EXCEPTIONALLY, this production neither padded out the play with extraneous material nor over-played its farcical elements. Tim Supple is Director of the Young Vic Theatre, London. Pl. 16 illustrates the staging of the final scene.

TIM Supple's version of *The Comedy of Errors*, which opened (prior to a national and international tour) at The Other Place in Stratford in June, came from a world of Shakespeare production altogether different from Ian Judge's.[1] Curious, therefore, that this was the first time the RSC had offered the play since Judge's own main stage production in 1990, when one actor played both Antipholuses and one both Dromios, creating an evening of slick and brilliant theatrical razzmatazz in which the romance of the play's ending was entirely destroyed by the need to resolve (through the use of doppelgängers) the technical problems created by the doubling. Supple's reading of the piece was infinitely simpler. It presented the play in an unchanging set (designed by Robert Innes Hopkins) of a brick floor backed by a wall with central double doors, a window with a grille, and a bell in a niche above—the simplest of suggestions of a sunlit square in Greece or Turkey. As one entered the theatre one encountered an elderly man dressed in a dirty, ragged cloak and chained to a grid in the centre of the floor, alternately slumped in despair or pacing in anguish and frustration to the limit of his chain. The sound of breaking waves could be heard in the distance, and as 7.30 approached the music that would accompany the production began faintly, hauntingly on that Turkish equivalent of the lute, the *'ud*; then the bell rang sharply, the old man stood up, and, accompanied by a gaoler carrying a great sword and a blindfold, in strode Leo Wringer's crisply dapper Solinus, a black man in a white, high-buttoned military suit, a whiff of Caribbean dictatorship about him, to order, not without a touch of contempt, 'Merchant of Syracuse, plead no more'.

The opening dialogue made clear the principles upon which the rest of the production would be based. It was straightforward, sharply focused, and attentive to the language, and it neither sought, nor needed, to extract from Aegeon's narrative any cheap laughter at the succession of unhappy coincidences that had befallen him. The power of the story was conveyed to us partly by the simplicity with which Christopher Saul's Aegeon told it, but more by the intensity of the listening from Solinus, who was transfixed by what he heard, his attitude changing from the terse and official to the personal and committed as the account progressed. There was no padding, no pantomime pauses and double-takes, just a grief-worn old man telling of his journeyings to despair, punctuated by sad and sympathetic sounds from the little collection of middle eastern instruments—*'ud, zarb, balafan, sitar*, with a violin and female singer—that brought a quality of eeriness, of strangeness and mystery, to the play. The use of music to underscore Shakespearian dialogue so often has the depressing effect of putting a generalized emotional wash over everything that the success of the accompaniment here is worth remark. It derived partly from its spareness, and from the unfamiliar quality of instrumental sounds, but chiefly from the fact that musicians and actors had rehearsed together from the start, language and sound growing into organic unity. Only once, at the end, did the music intrude. The intensity of the play's conclusion was so fully conveyed to the audience that we needed to make our contribution to the event, to make the play and the space ours, through applause, long before the singer had concluded her valedictory vocalizing. It was an odd failure of judgement on the part of a director who otherwise conveyed his respect and affection for the play with unstinted tact.

He costumed the production in modern dress, the Antipholuses in pale linen suits and suede shoes, their similarity carried most tellingly in identical curly brown hair-styles and jutting little beards. Their Dromios both wore baggy black shorts and T-shirts, but it was Duke Vincentio's[2] formula for blurring identity, shaven heads, that most effectively persuaded us into believing in the confusions. Adriana, in an elegant modern suit with a boldly slit skirt, contrasted sharply with her sister Luciana, modest to the point of austerity (if not dowdiness) in long-skirted grey. And for once the Courtesan (Maeve Larkin) and Dr Pinch (Leo Wringer) remained within the realms of credibility, her red high-heeled shoes being the principal, rather innocently transparent, signal of her professional status, while he, in shiny black, tight-fitting suit and black hat, and brandishing a Bible (or book of spells), combined a sense of the evangelical preacher from the southern United States with a hint of the voodoo magician in a way that was both witty and disturbing.

There have, no doubt, been productions of *The Comedy of Errors* in which the central scenes of mistaken identity were more boisterously farcical. Not that the big set pieces—the visiting Antipholus's bewildered response to Adriana's recriminatory tirade, his Dromio's fear of sexual possession by the kitchen maid, the increasing pace and panic of the final arrest and asylum sequence—were not splendidly funny. But they were played against a strong sense of the deeper issues being explored in the play. The complaints of Sarah Cameron's brittle, ill-at-ease Adriana derived from genuine and painful bewilderment and hurt at the loss of her husband's love. Thusitha Jayasundera brought to Luciana a quiet, self-contained intelligence, an apparently knowing caution about emotional commitment and the 'troubles of the marriage-bed' (II.1.27), that gave the role a stillness and depth that contrasted tellingly with the rawness of her sister's anxieties and vulnerabilities. To her brother-in-law's ardent wooing she responded with a firm and dignified, though wistful, rejection. His hopeful eagerness for a kiss, which she seemed about to allow but at the last moment rejected, left her with tears in her eyes—for her sister, but also for herself and for him. Even at the end, the impediments gone, she remained cautious and thoughtful, the feminist conscience of the play, uncertain about commitment. Robert Bowman's Antipholus of Syracuse responded to the blandishments of Ephesus with a beautifully poised mixture of innocent delight and wary bafflement. His distrust (aided by the plaintive, otherworldly music, reinforcing his suspicions of magic and witchcraft) could be seen gradually developing into frightened uncertainty about the stability of his own identity ('If everyone knows us and we know none...' (III.2.160)), forcing him into closer alliance with his Dromio (Dan Milne) in a relationship that was always, and quite rightly, more trusting, and fonder, than that of their twins. His voice, lighter than his Ephesian brother's and with a faint crack to it, gave him a gentle, hesitant, slightly fey quality, very different from his twin's solid, four-square bass. Simon Coates's Antipholus of Ephesus found all the harshness of the part, his resentments fierce, his anger towards his wife bitter and self-righteous, his rage with his Dromio (Eric Mallett) hard and unamused, the beatings he gave him undisguisable as slapstick comedy, the attempts of funny noises in the musical percussion so to present them ceasing precisely when the audience stopped believing them.

The production, then, treated the play with deep respect and with a thoughtful, affectionate delight in the story it had to tell. The effect of all this was most marked, and most welcome, at the play's ending. Aemilia—who last time at Stratford, in a hat like a double lampshade, had been the last in a succession of absurd caricatures—was here, in Ursula Jones's performance, a figure of quiet dignity and gentle authority, costumed simply in a nun's habit. The revelations that accompanied her arrival had a feeling of the miraculous about them, giving to the reunions something of a sacred quality. From here, it was clear, the route to the restoration of Sebastian to Viola, of Marina to Pericles, of Hermione to Leontes, was straight and direct. The ending was not, however, all unalloyed joy—any more than it is in those later plays. The wonder and delight had a touch of muted uncertainty, of hesitation about daring to believe, that gave them a profound seriousness. Much was still to be understood, much to be forgiven. Precisely what had happened between brother and sister-in-law at Adriana's dinner? He had certainly appeared after it in a state of bemused exhaustion and now, at the end, its memory cast its little shadow over the long-yearned-for reunion with his brother. And how much did Adriana deserve the Abbess's energetic telling off that left her publicly humiliated, the Courtesan sniggering in the background? Precisely how culpable was the Ephesian Antipholus's friendship with the Courtesan? Adriana winced and glared at him as he thanked her rival for his 'good cheer'; he registered his wife's pain and revealed his own embarrassment and shame. Theirs had been the first embrace in the reunion sequence, the long stare of uncertain wonder between the brothers broken by Antipholus of Ephesus's energetic 'No, I say nay to that' (V. 1.372) as Adriana was about to repeat her dinnertime confusion between them. He held her in his arms tentatively, awkwardly; these two, one knew, had a lot of bridges to mend. The two pairs of brothers finally achieved their embraces after Aegeon's unfastened chains had clattered to the floor, an event that followed hard upon the Goldsmith's last little moment of fuss about *his* chain. Then, and most movingly, those two elegantly dressed young men in turn took their ragged, exhausted father, just rescued from death's door, in their arms and Aemilia began her final speech of blessing, receiving the embraces of her sons as she declared her heavy burden finally delivered. The verbal benedictions done, she blessed everyone as they knelt in front of her before making their exits to the gossips' feast: the Duke, benevolent and eager; Aegeon returning her long, hesitant gaze before going in, without an embrace—thirty-three years of separation, and a nun's habit, clearly requiring a great deal more thought on both sides; Adriana compelled, in spite of protest, to accompany the Courtesan; Luciana, silent through the scene, once moving close to Antipholus of Syracuse but forced away again by the pressure of the scene's events and now departing alone; an unwilling Balthazar, his financial obsessions and sartorial vulgarity strongly suggesting that abbeys are unfamiliar territory; and Aegeon's erstwhile guard, respectfully removing his cap and leaving his sword at the door—an exquisitely detailed and thoughtful sequence of exits. The two pairs of twins were thus left to face the future, Antipholus of Ephesus much less certain that he regarded it with enthusiasm than his brother—for he'd not been searching for anyone, anywhere, and life for him had been just fine until this appalling day. He watched his brother kiss his servant Dromio on the lips, a kiss that rendered thanks for loyalty and patience and friendship through years of wandering, but also marked the end of all that; for, now that it was no longer to be just the two of them, things would never be quite the same again. The Ephesian Dromio watched that kiss too and seemed to will his master to perceive the need for symmetry. His Antipholus did, indeed, think about the possibility for a moment or two; but there was no way that he could change so quickly—or that this director would be tempted along so sentimental a road. Perceiving the unkissed Dromio's disappointment, Antipholus of Syracuse rescued the situation by instructing his servant to 'Embrace thy brother there', a piece of sensitivity to the text that was typical of so much in the production. And so the two shaven-headed, bare-kneed sufferers of the play's blows and buffets, real and metaphorical, were left alone to discover from each other, with poignant hopefulness, that after all they were sweet-faced youths, and to scurry off, hand in hand, after the rest.

And it was all done in precisely two hours, without fuss and without self-indulgence, by constant alertness and sensitivity to the play's language and delight in the wonders of the story it has to tell. A pity we weren't allowed to applaud it quite as soon as we wanted to.

1. **Judge**, Ian, is a director of operas and plays, including *The Comedy of Errors* for the RSC in 1990.
2. In *Measure for Measure*.

FURTHER READING

THIS is a highly selective list. Place of publication is London unless otherwise stated. Many of the books listed are out of print and so obtainable only through libraries or in second-hand bookshops.

Works of General Reference

Avery, Emmett L., Charles Beecher Hogan, and others (eds.), *The London Stage: A Calendar of Plays, Entertainments and Afterpieces, 1660–1800*, 11 vols. (Carbondale, Ill., 1960–5)

Bate, Jonathan, and Russell Jackson, eds., *Shakespeare: an Illustrated Stage History* (Oxford, 1996)

Burnim, Kalman A., Philip H. Highfill, and Edward A. Langhans (eds.), *A Biographical Dictionary of Actors, Actresses, Musicians, Dancers, Managers, and Other Stage Personnel in London, 1660–1800*, 16 vols. (Carbondale, 1973–93) (known as *The Actors' Dictionary*)

Hogan, Charles Beecher, *Shakespeare in the Theatre: A Record of Performances in London, 1701–1800*, 2 vols. (Oxford, 1952–7): partly superseded by *The London Stage*

Merchant, W. Moelwyn, *Shakespeare and the Artist* (Oxford, 1959): includes much material on theatre history

Odell, G. C. D., *Shakespeare, from Betterton to Irving*, 2 vols. (New York, 1920; repr. New York, 1963): a lively, opinionated history, dated but still a standard work

Shattuck, Charles, *Shakespeare on the American Stage. From the Hallams to Edwin Booth* (Washington, DC, 1976)

——, *Shakespeare on the American Stage: from Booth and Barrett to Sothern and Marlowe* (Washington, DC, 1987)

Speaight, Robert, *Shakespeare on the Stage* (1973): a lively account with many interesting illustrations

Primary Works

This section lists collections of criticism devoted entirely or substantially to performances of Shakespeare.

Agate, James, ed., *The English Dramatic Critics 1660–1932* (n.d. [1932]): a useful anthology

Agate, James, *Brief Chronicles: A Survey of the Plays of Shakespeare and the Elizabethans in actual performance, 1923–42* (1943)

Archer, William, *The Theatrical World for 1893* [n.d.], and... *of 1894* (1895),... *of 1895* (1896),... *of 1896* (1897),... *of 1897* (1898)

——, *Study and Stage* (1899)

Baxter, Beverley, *First Nights and Noises Off* (1949)

——, *First Nights and Footlights* (1955)

Beerbohm, Max, *Around Theatres* (1953)

——, *More Theatres* (1969)

——, *Last Theatres* (1970)

Billington, Michael, *One Night Stands: A Critic's View of British Theatre from 1971–1991* (1993)

Brown, Ivor, *Theatre 1954–55* (1955)

——, *Theatre 1955–56* (1956)

Brown, John Mason, *Two on the Aisle: Ten Years of American Theatre in Performance* (New York, 1938)

Bryden, Ronald, *The Unfinished Hero and Other Essays* (1969)

Clapp, Henry Austin, *Reminiscences of a Dramatic Critic* (Boston and New York, 1902)

Cook, Edward Dutton, *Nights at the Play* (1883)

Crosse, Gordon, *Shakespearean Playgoing 1890–1952* (1953)

David, Richard, *Shakespeare in the Theatre* (Cambridge, 1982)

Dent, Alan, *Nocturnes and Rhapsodies* (1950)

Farjeon, Herbert, *The Shakespearean Scene: Dramatic Criticism, 1913–44* [1949]

Fenton, James, *You Were Marvellous. Theatre Reviews from 'The Sunday Times'* (1983)

Forster, John, *Dramatic Essays by John Forster, George Henry Lewes*, ed. William Archer and Robert W. Lowe (1896)

Gentleman, Francis, *The Dramatic Censor; or, Critical Companion*, 2 vols. (1770, repr. 1969): essays on plays with comments on contemporary performance, especially by Garrick

Grein, J. T., *Dramatic Criticism* (1899)

——, *Premières of the Year* (1900)

——, *Dramatic Criticism, Vol. 3, 1900–1901* (1902), *Vol. 4, 1902–1903* (1904), *Vol. 5, 1903* (1905)

Hazlitt, William, *Hazlitt on Theatre*, ed. William Archer and Robert Lowe (London, 1895, repr. New York, Dramabooks [1957])

Hobson, Harold, *Theatre* (1948)

——, *Theatre 2* (1950)

——, *The Theatre Now* (1954)

Hunt, Leigh, *Leigh Hunt's Dramatic Criticism 1808–1831*, ed. L. H. and C. W. Houtchens (New York, 1949)

James, Henry, *The Scenic Art*, ed. Allan Wade (1949)

Kitchin, Laurence, *Mid-Century Drama* (1960)

——, *Drama in the Sixties* (1966)

Knight, Joseph, *Theatrical Notes* (1875)

Lewes, George Henry, *Actors and Acting* (1875); and see Forster, John

Lichtenberg, G. C., *Lichtenberg's Visits to England*, edited by M. L. Mare and W. H. Quarrell (Oxford, 1938)

MacCarthy, Desmond, *Drama* (1940)

——, *Theatre* (1954)

Marston, Westland, *Our Recent Actors*, 2 vols. (1888)

Montague, C. E., and others, *The Manchester Stage 1880–1900: Criticisms reprinted from 'The Manchester Guardian'* (n.d.)

Further Reading

Morley, Henry, *The Journal of a London Playgoer* (1866; repr. 1891)

Rowell, George, ed., *Victorian Dramatic Criticism* (1971) (includes reprints of a number of reviews of Shakespeare performances)

Salgādo, Gāmini, ed., *Eyewitnesses of Shakespeare: First Hand Accounts of Performances 1590–1890* (Hassocks, 1975): a useful anthology

Scott, Clement, *Thirty Years at the Play and Dramatic Table Talk* [1891]

——, *From 'The Bells' to King Arthur'. A Critical Record of the First-night Productions at the Lyceum Theatre from 1871 to 1895* (1896)

Shakespeare Quarterly (Washington, DC), reviews of performances (1950–)

Shakespeare Survey (Cambridge), reviews of performances (1948–)

Shaw, George Bernard, ed. Edwin Wilson, *Shaw on Shakespeare* (New York, 1961; Harmondsworth, 1969)

Stone, Mary Isabella, *Edwin Booth's Performances: The Mary Isabella Stone Commentaries*, edited and annotated by Daniel J. Watermeier (Ann Arbor, Mich., and London, 1996): moment-by-moment descriptions of Booth's Hamlet, Iago, and Othello, with notes on his Lear

Trewin, J. C., *Shakespeare on the English Stage, 1900–1964* (1964)

Tynan, Kenneth, *He that Plays the King* (1950)

——, *Curtains. Selections from the Drama Criticism and Related Writings* (1961; revised edn., Harmondsworth, 1964)

——, *Tynan Right and Left* (1967)

Ward, A. C., ed., *Specimens of English Dramatic Criticism XVII–XX Centuries* (Oxford, 1945) (an invaluable, helpfully annotated, anthology)

Winter, William, *Shakespeare on the Stage* (1912)

Worsley, T. C., *The Fugitive Art: Dramatic Commentaries 1947–1951* (1952)

Young, B. A., *The Mirror up to Nature: A Review of the Theatre 1964–1982* (1982)

Young, Stark, *Immortal Shadows* (1947; repr. New York, Dramabooks series, n.d)

Other writings

This section includes selected writings relevant to the extracts included in this volume. It does not aim to list all the works cited in headnotes, or, for example, biographies of all the theatre personnel mentioned, but rather to include studies especially relevant to the student of Shakespeare in performance.

Allen, Shirley S., *Samuel Phelps and Sadler's Wells Theatre*, Middletown, Wesleyan University Press (1971)

Bartholomeusz, Dennis, *Macbeth and the Players* (Cambridge, 1969)

——, *'The Winter's Tale' in Performance in England and America 1611–1976* (Cambridge, 1982)

Bedford, Kristina, *Coriolanus at the National: "Th'Interpretation of the Time"'* (Selinsgrove, London and Toronto, 1992) (on Peter Hall's 1985 production, with Ian McKellen)

Bogdanov, Michael, and Michael Pennington, *The English Shakespeare Company: The Story of 'The Wars of the Roses' 1986–1989* (1990)

Carlson, Marvin, *The Italian Shakespearians: Performances by Ristori, Salvini, and Rossi in England and America* (Washington, DC, 1985)

Cochrane, Claire, *Shakespeare and the Birmingham Repertory Theatre, 1913–1929* (1993)

Davies, Thomas, *Dramatic Micellanies [sic]*, 3 vols. (1784)

Downer, Alan S., *The Eminent Tragedian: William Charles Macready* (Cambridge, Mass., 1965) (includes a chapter on Macready's *Macbeth*)

Felheim, Marvin, *The Theater of Augustin Daly* (Cambridge, Mass., 1956)

Gilder, Rosamund, *John Gielgud's 'Hamlet': A Record of Performance* with 'The Hamlet Tradition' by John Gielgud (1937)

Greenwald, Michael L., *Directions by Indirections: John Barton of the Royal Shakespeare Theatre* (Newark, NJ, and London, 1985)

Gross, John, *Shylock* (1992)

Hakola, Liisa, *In One Person Many People: The Image of the King in Three RSC Productions of William Shakespeare's 'King Richard II'* (Helsinki, 1988): on productions by John Barton (1973), Terry Hands (1980) and Barry Kyle (1986)

Haring-Smith, Tori, *From Farce to Metadrama: A Stage History of 'The Taming of the Shrew', 1593–1983* (1985)

Hazlitt, William, *Hazlitt on Theatre*, ed. William Archer and Robert Lowe (1895; repr. New York, [1957])

Hildy, Franklin J., *Shakespeare at the Maddermarket: Nugent Monck and the Norwich Players* (Ann Arbor, Mich., 1986)

Hughes, Alan, *Henry Irving, Shakespearean* (Cambridge, 1981)

Jackson, Russell, 'Shakespeare in the Theatrical Criticism of Henry Morley', *Shakespeare Survey 38* (1985), pp. 187–200

Kennedy, Dennis, *Harley Granville-Barker and the Dream of Theatre* (Cambridge, 1985)

——, *Looking at Shakespeare: a Visual History of Twentieth Century Performance* (Cambridge, 1993)

Lamb, Margaret, *'Antony and Cleopatra' on the English Stage* (Cranbury, NJ, 1980)

Lelyveld, Toby, *Shylock on the Stage* (1961)

Lowen, Tirzah, *Peter Hall Directs 'Antony and Cleopatra'* (1990)

Lundstrom, Rinda F., *William Poel's Hamlets: the Director as Critic* (Ann Arbor, Mich., 1984)

Maher, Mary Z., *Modern Hamlets and their Soliloquies* (Iowa City, 1992)

Mander, Raymond, and Joe Mitchenson, *Hamlet through the Ages: A Pictorial Record from 1709* (2nd edn., 1955)

Matteo, Gino J., *Shakespeare's Othello: the Study and the Stage 1694–1904* (Salzburg, 1974)

Miller, Tice L., *Bohemians and Critics: American Theatre Criticism in the Nineteenth Century* (Metuchen, NJ, and London, 1981)

Mills, John A., *Hamlet on Stage: the Great Tradition* (Westport and London, 1985)

Ripley, John, *Julius Caesar on Stage in England and America, 1599–1973* (Cambridge, 1980)

Rosenberg, Marvin, *The Masks of Othello: The Search for the Identity of Othello, Iago and Desdemona by Three Centuries of Actors and Critics* (Berkeley, Calif., 1961)

——, *The Masks of King Lear* (Berkeley, Calif., 1971)

——, *The Masks of Macbeth* (Berkeley, Calif., 1978)

Scott, Clement, *Some Notable Hamlets of the Present Time* (1900)

Selbourne, David, *The Making of 'A Midsummer Night's Dream': An Eye-Witness Account of Peter Brook's Production from First Rehearsal to First Night* (1982)

Senelick, Laurence, *Gordon Craig's Moscow 'Hamlet': A Reconstruction* (Westport and London, 1982)

Shattuck, Charles H., *The Hamlet of Edwin Booth* (Urbana, Ill., 1969)

——, ed., *Mr Macready Produces 'As You Like it': A Prompt-Book Study* (Urbana, Ill., 1962)

——, ed., *William Charles Macready's 'King John': a facsimile prompt-book* (Urbana, Ill., 1962)

Shaughnessy, Robert, *Representing Shakespeare: England, History and the RSC* (Hemel Hempstead, 1993)

Sher, Antony, *Year of the King, an Actor's Diary and Sketchbook* (1985)

Speaight, Robert, *William Poel and the Elizabethan Revival* (1954)

Sprague, Arthur Colby, *Shakespeare's Histories: Plays for the Stage* (1964)

——, *Shakespearian Players and Performances* (1954): studies of individual performances

Trewin, J. C., *Benson and the Bensonians* (1960)

Tynan, Kenneth, ed., *'Othello': The National Theatre Production* (1966)

Warren, Roger, *Staging Shakespeare's Late Plays* (Oxford, 1990)

Wells, Stanley, *Royal Shakespeare: Four Major Productions at the Royal Shakespeare Theatre* (Manchester, 1977)

——, 'Shakespeare in Max Beerbohm's Theatre Criticism', *Shakespeare Survey 29* (1976), pp. 132–44

——, 'Shakespeare in Hazlitt's Theatre Criticism', *Shakespeare Survey 35* (1982), pp. 43–55

——, 'Shakespeare in Leigh Hunt's Theatre Criticism', *Essays and Studies 1980*, pp. 119–38

Wood, Alice I. Perry, *The Stage History of 'King Richard the Third'* (Columbia, 1909; repr. New York, 1965)

Three useful, ongoing series of volumes on individual plays are 'Shakespeare in Performance' published by Manchester University Press under the General Editorship of J. R. Mulryne and James C. Bulman, 'Text and Performance' published by Macmillan under the General Editorship of Michael Scott, and 'Plays in Performance' (Cambridge University Press), various editors. Selected reviews are printed in certain volumes of the ongoing series 'Shakespearean Criticism' published by Gale Research Inc. (Detroit, 1984, etc.).

INDEX

Index

Index

Index

Index

ACKNOWLEDGEMENTS

Aitken & Stone Ltd for **Ronald Harwood**: extract from *Sir Donald Wolfit: His life and work in the unfashionable theatre* (Secker & Warburg, 1971), © 1971 Ronald Harwood

Cambridge University Press and the authors for extracts from **John Russell Brown**: 'Three Adaptations' in *Shakespeare Survey* 13 (1966); **Richard David**: on *Measure for Measure* in *Shakespeare Survey* 4 (1951); **Peter Holland**: on *Richard III* in *Shakespeare Survey* 45 (1994); **Nicholas Shrimpton**: on *Hamlet* in the first quarto version in *Shakespeare Survey* 39 (1987); **Robert Smallwood**: on *The Comedy of Errors* in *Shakespeare Survey* 50 (1997); **Peter Thomson**: on *Richard III* in *Shakespeare Survey* 27 (1974); **Roger Warren**: on *Macbeth* in *Shakespeare Survey* 30 (1977) and on *Love's Labour's Lost* in *Shakespeare Survey* 32 (1979); and **Stanley Wells**: on *Henry IV*, Parts I and II, and *Henry V*, and on *Titus Andronicus* both in *Shakespeare Survey* 41 (1989)

Faber & Faber Ltd for **Ronald Bryden**: 'Laurence Olivier as Othello' and 'Peter Hall's Production of *Hamlet*', both from *Unfinished Hero and Other Essays* (Faber, 1969)

Gervase Farjeon for review of *The Merry Wives of Windsor* extracted from **Herbert Farjeon**: *The Shakespearean Scene* (Hutchinson 1949), Copyright © Gervase Farjeon for the Herbert Farjeon Estate

Nick Hern Books for **Michael Billington**: 'Antony and Cleopatra' in *One Night Stands: A Critic's View of British Theatre from 1971–1991* (Nick Hern Books, 1993)

The Independent Newspaper Publishing plc for reviews by **Paul Taylor** from *The Independent* 3.10.90 and 6.12.91, both Copyright © The Independent

Professor **Laurence Kitchin** for his review of Olivier as Coriolanus from *Mid-Century Drama* (Faber, 1960) and on Peter Brook's *King Lear* from *Drama in the Sixties* (Faber, 1966)

Guardian News Service for **T. C. Worsley** on Tyrone Guthrie's production of *Henry VIII* from

The New Statesman, 1949, Copyright © New Statesman and Society

The Peters Fraser & Dunlop Group Ltd on behalf of the author's Estate for **Evelyn Waugh**: review of *Titus Andronicus* directed by Peter Brook in *The Spectator*, 1955

Sir Rupert Hart-Davis on behalf of Mrs Eva Reichman for **Max Beerbohm**: reviews of *King John* and *Much Ado About Nothing* from *More Theatres* (1969); and reviews of *Hamlet* and *The Tempest* from *Last Theatres* (1970)

Shakespeare Quarterly: for reviews by **Robert Smallwood** from 'Shakespeare at Stratford-upon-Avon, 1989 (Part 1)' in *Shakespeare Quarterly* 41 [1990]; **Robert Speaight** from 'Shakespeare in Britain' in *Shakespeare Quarterly* 21 [1970]; and **Roger Warren** from 'Shakespeare in Britain, 1985' in *Shakespeare Quarterly* 37 [1986]

The Society of Authors on behalf of the Bernard Shaw Estate for **Bernard Shaw** essays originally published in *The Saturday Review* reprinted in *Shaw on Shakespeare* (Cassell); and as the literary representative of the Estate of Virginia Woolf for **Virginia Woolf**: essay originally published in *The New Statesman*, reprinted in *The Death of a Moth and Other Essays* (1942)

The Times Literary Supplement and the author for **Stanley Wells** on *Richard III* directed by Bill Alexander from the *Times Literary Supplement*, 29.6.84

Times Newspapers Limited: for **James Agate**: 'Mr Gielgud's Noble Attempt' from *The Sunday Times*, 18 Nov. 1934, © Times Newspapers Limited, 1934; and 'Mr Olivier and Mr Gielgud' from *The Sunday Times*, 17 Oct. 1935, © Times Newspapers Limited, 1935

Although every effort has been made to trace and contact copyright holders before publication, this has not always been possible. If notified, the publisher will be pleased to rectify any errors or omissions at the earliest opportunity.